Legalization of Human Rights in Africa

Most countries on the African continent have ratified or acceded to several human rights treaties, including the Torture Convention and the African Charter on Human and People's Rights. This book assesses the progress African countries have made in institutionalizing human rights laws prohibiting torture, extrajudicial killings, and disappearances domestically.

States ratify human rights treaties for a variety of reasons. Some commentators defend an honest sincerity of purpose, whereas others might point to material incentives. The contributors to this volume go beyond the ratification puzzle to instead reframe legalization according to Lon Fuller's conceptualization of congruence. Congruence is an interactive variable that measures the continuous efforts of government and the public to shape the law and its implementation. By reframing legalization as an ongoing process, the model created by the authors is used to test several hypotheses about what impacts legalization in Africa more broadly, and in countries such as Mali, Cameroon, Botswana, Zimbabwe, and Tunisia, more specifically. The contributors to this volume demonstrate that the legalization of human rights is never a finished product, but is a moving target influenced by exogenous and endogenous phenomena.

This volume is useful for researchers of genocide, human rights, and atrocity prevention, as well as for those interested in legalization and democratization both within Africa and other regions of the world.

Stacey M. Mitchell is Associate Professor at Georgia State University's Perimeter College, USA.

Veraline Nchotu is a Research Fellow at Northeastern Illinois University's Genocide and Human Rights Research in Africa and the Diaspora Center, USA.

Lem Lilian Atanga is Associate Professor and Research Fellow, Centre for Gender and African Studies, University of Free State, Bloemfontein, South Africa.

Routledge Contemporary Africa

African Women and Intellectual Leadership
Life Stories from Western Kenya
Edited by Dannica Fleuss, Maurice N. Amutabi, Emily Achieng' Akuno and Humphrey J. Ojwang

Monuments and Memory in Africa
Reflections on Coloniality and Decoloniality
Edited by John Sodiq Sanni and Madalitso Phiri

Higher Education Transformation in Africa
A Quest for Epistemological Rupture
Edited by Emnet Tadesse Woldegiorgis, Logan Govender and Dennis Zami Atibuni

African Media and Communication
Foundational Conversations
Edited by viola c. milton and Winston Mano

Marriage in Contemporary Zimbabwe
Identity, Community, and Change
Edited by Manase Kudzai Chiweshe

African Fans of European Football
Cultural Globalisation in Kenya and Zimbabwe
Edited by Manase Kudzai Chiweshe and Solomon Waliaula

Legalization of Human Rights in Africa
The Institutionalization of Laws Prohibiting State-Sanctioned Violence and Torture
Edited by Stacey Mitchell, Veraline Nchotu, and Lem Lilian Atanga

For more information about this series, please visit: https://www.routledge.com/Routledge-Contemporary-Africa/book-series/RCAFR

Legalization of Human Rights in Africa

The Institutionalization of Laws Prohibiting State-Sanctioned Violence and Torture

Edited by Stacey M. Mitchell, Veraline Nchotu, and Lem Lilian Atanga

Routledge
Taylor & Francis Group
LONDON AND NEW YORK

First published 2025
by Routledge
4 Park Square, Milton Park, Abingdon, Oxon OX14 4RN

and by Routledge
605 Third Avenue, New York, NY 10158

Routledge is an imprint of the Taylor & Francis Group, an informa business

British Library Cataloguing-in-Publication Data
A catalogue record for this book is available from the British Library

ISBN: 978-1-032-74949-5 (hbk)
ISBN: 978-1-032-74951-8 (pbk)
ISBN: 978-1-003-47167-7 (ebk)

DOI: 10.4324/9781003471677

Typeset in Sabon
by SPi Technologies India Pvt Ltd (Straive)

Contents

Figures

Tables

Author Biographies

Lilian Atanga is Associate Professor of Gender, Discourse, and Politics, formerly at the University of Dschang Cameroon and currently a visiting Senior Research Fellow at the University of the Free State, Bloemfontein, South Africa. She obtained her PhD from Lancaster University, UK, in the areas of gender, discourse, and politics focusing on gender and power in parliamentary settings. Lilian has published extensively in the areas of gender, discourse, and politics with books including *Gender Discourse and Power in the Cameroonian Parliament* (Langaa Publishers 2009); *Gendered Discourses in African Contexts: Tradition, Struggle and Change* (John Benjamins 2013); and recently a poetry collection titled *When the Sun Turns Red* (Spears Books 2022). She has several articles in peer-reviewed journals and encyclopedias.

Khedija Arfaoui has a BA and PhD from the University of Tunis and an MPhil from George Washington University. She majored in American Studies and Women's Studies. Retired from Higher education, she is a free-lance feminist peace activist, researcher, author, and lecturer. She has several publications. She taught American Studies, Women's Rights, and Human Rights at the Higher Institute of Languages in Tunis. She joined civil society in the late 1980s where she worked to promote environmental concerns and feminist issues. She founded and chaired ADPE, an environmental organization. She became the Secretary General of the Association of Tunisian Women for Research on Development and is a member of the Tunisian Association of Democratic Women, Amnesty International, a founding member of the Coalition against the Death Penalty, and the Tunisian Association of the United Nations. In 2012, following the trial of Dean Habib Kazdaghli—who was wrongly accused of slapping a girl wearing a niqab—she joined the Tunisian Association of Defense of University Values. In 2005, she was a Fulbright Visiting Scholar at Lake Forest College, Illinois, in a program entitled "Direct Access to Islam." A PEACE activist, she is a member of the International Civil Society Action Network/Women's Alliance for Security Leadership.

Henry F. (Chip) Carey is Associate Professor of Political Science at Georgia State University. He is author and editor of a dozen books and many articles on international law and human rights. Most recently, he is the co-author with Stacey M. Mitchell of *Legalization of International Law and Politics: Multi-Level Governance of Human Rights and Aggression* (Palgrave 2023); editor of *Understanding Contemporary Latin America* (Lynne Rienner 2022) and *Peacebuilding Paradigms: The Impacts of Theoretical Diversity on Implementing Sustainable Peace* (Cambridge 2022). He is the outgoing chair of the International Law section of the International Studies Association.

Roland Djieufack is Associate Professor of Laws in the Department of Law in the Higher Technical Teachers' Training College, The University of Bamenda, Cameroon. He is currently the Head of Department of Law in the same College in The University of Bamenda, Cameroon. He is Visiting Professor in the Faculties of Laws in the University of Buea and Dschang, Cameroon. He was a Research Fellow at the Radboud University, The Netherlands, the International Institute for the Unification of Private Law (UNIDROIT) in Rome, and Tulane Law School, USA. He has extensively published books and articles on Commercial law, e-Commerce Law, Consumer Law, and Environmental Law in high-impact publishing houses and journals, respectively.

Shannon M. Gibson received her PhD in Criminology and Criminal Justice from Florida State University. Her doctoral dissertation used Institutional Anomie Theory to explain comparative homicide rates between developed and developing countries. Her areas of research and writing include the impacts of residential substance abuse treatment programs on recidivism, international financial crimes, comparative criminal justice systems, and the impact of prison programs on recidivism.

Miao-ling Lin Hasenkamp is Senior Research Associate at the Institute for Political and Administration Sciences (IPV), Centre for Eurasian and Russian Studies (ZEUS) at the Universität Rostock in Germany. She has published in the areas of human rights, the COVID pandemic, peace missions in Africa, transitional justice regimes, and the impact of globalization on East Asian relations. Her recent publications include "Governing Uncertainties during the Covid-19 Pandemic: Change of the Science-Policy Interfaces and Its Impacts upon Gender in Europe," in *Uncertainty in Global Politics* (Routledge, 2023/2024) and a co-authored piece, "Rethinking Human-Nature Relationships: Daoism's Contribution to Transcultural Sociotechnical Imaginaries," *Special Issue: of Professional Geographer: Geographies of Imaginaries and Environmental Governance* (2022).

Yue Lin is a PhD candidate in the Travers Department of Political Science at the University of California, Berkeley, with a Designated Emphasis on Political Economy. Her main research interests cover political economy, economic security, US Congress and legislative behavior, and multinational corporations. Her dissertation project examines the domestic and international origins of economic security in Western democracies, and the social impacts of securitization, such as voter attraction. Her research has received funding from Berkeley Economy and Society Initiative, Berkeley Social Science Data Laboratory, and the Geoeconomics Society. Prior to doctoral studies, she gained experience at the American Enterprise Institute, the Center for Strategic and International Studies, and the Institute of New Structural Economics at Peking University. She earned her Master of Arts degree in International Economics and International Relations from Johns Hopkins University, Paul H. Nitze School of Advanced International Studies, and Bachelor of Social Sciences (First Class Honors) in Government and International Relations from Hong Kong Baptist University.

Stacey M. Mitchell is Associate Professor of Political Science at Georgia State University's Perimeter College. She received her PhD in Political Science with a specialization in Comparative Politics in 2007 from the University of Georgia's School of Public and International Affairs. Her areas of research and publication include human rights, democratization in African countries, genocide, international law, and transitional justice regimes. Her recent publications include *Legalization of International Law and Politics: Multi-level Governance of Human Rights and Aggression* (co-authored) (London: Palgrave Macmillan, January 2023) and "Institutional Legacies and the Decision to Commit Genocide," *Genocide Studies and Prevention* 17(1) (June 2023).

Jean-Francois Koly Onivogui is Assistant Professor of Political Science at Georgia State University's Perimeter College. He obtained his BA with Research Honors in Political Science from Georgia State University's Honors College in May 2010. Onivogui obtained his master's and doctorate in Comparative Politics at Georgia State University. His doctoral dissertation, "Understanding the Dearth of Contacts Between African Citizens and their Members of Parliaments" under Dr. Carrie Manning, Dr. Charles Hankla, Dr. Sean Richey, and Dr. Jeffrey R. Young was accepted in 2018.

Veraline Nchotu is Research Fellow at Northeastern Illinois University's Genocide and Human Rights Research in Africa and the Diaspora Center. She is a senior lecturer in international law, international human rights, and humanitarian laws and genocide. She was a scholar at the June 2022 Summer Institute for the Study and Prevention of Atrocity Crimes at Keene State College, New Hampshire, USA, the Adama Dieng African Genocide Scholars Studies Forum on Mainstreaming Genocide and other Atrocity Crimes, and the African Institute of International Law. Her research interests include international law, international human rights law, humanitarian law, conflict resolution, women's rights, minority rights, and genocide studies. Dr. Nchotu is a consultant of the Network of Human Rights Defenders in Central Africa (RHEDAC), where she has designed and implemented the use of organic tools for conflict resolution, healing, peacebuilding, and atrocity prevention in several parts of Cameroon. She is a consultant of the Foundation of Environment and Development (FEDEV) and an active civil society actor. She is a member of the International Federation of Women Lawyers (FIDA) Cameroon.

Kholisani Solo is Law Lecturer at the University of Botswana, Department of Law. He has a Bachelor of Laws degree from the University of Botswana, Master of Laws degree from the University College London, Master of Arts Degree from University of Kassel/Berlin School of Economics, and a Doctorate from the University of Cape Town. He has practiced and taught law for more than 15 years, and has published numerous articles, books, and technical reports. He was appointed to a Presidential Commission and has chaired several committees of inquiry. He has acted in various categories as a judicial officer. He has also participated in several consultancies related to law and human rights.

Introduction to Legalization of Human Rights in Africa

Stacey M. Mitchell, Veraline Nchotu, and Lem Lilian Atanga

Most countries on the African continent have ratified or acceded to several human rights treaties, including the Convention Against Torture and Other Cruel, Inhuman or Degrading Treatment or Punishment (Torture Convention), the International Covenant on Civil and Political Rights (ICCPR), and the African Charter on Human and People's Rights (Banjul Charter).[1] There are a variety of reasons why states ratify treaties. Sincerity of purpose has been put forth as one rationale, material incentives, another. With respect to the former, Çali, Ghanea, and Jones note that it is difficult to empirically determine whether states' motives for ratification are sincere or not, because "UN human rights treaties are complex legal texts with multiple provisions, [consequently] states may have a sincere intent with regard to some provisions at the time of ratification, while others may not."[2]

The contributors to *Legalization of Human Rights in Africa: The Institutionalization of Laws Prohibiting State Sanctioned Violence and Torture* go beyond the ratification puzzle to assess the progress African governments have made in the domestic legalization of human rights laws prohibiting torture, extrajudicial killings, and disappearances. It has been over 30 years since the transition to multiparty democracy began on the continent, during which time several African States became parties to the Torture Convention and other human rights treaties. Examining the progress made by these States in their protection and promotion of human rights laws prohibiting violence represents a test of the extent to which democratic rule has consolidated across the continent and can explain variations in consolidation between and within countries over time.

While there are examples of success in legalizing and implementing international human rights prohibitions on violence, there are also plenty of African states that continue to experience state-sanctioned violence. A government's proclivity toward bloodshed has repercussions that extend regionally. Studies written about African political stability emphasize the importance that regional politics has on domestic politics and vice versa.[3] For this reason, this volume also considers the influence of regional dynamics on a government's ability to legalize human rights laws domestically.

DOI: 10.4324/9781003471677-1

The decision of the editors and contributors to this volume to focus on the crimes of torture, disappearances, and extrajudicial killings stems from the fact that all three represent *jus cogens* violations. The perpetration of these acts is considered a violation of norms of international law and as such they are forbidden *regardless* of whether a State is a party to a treaty that prohibits their commission or not.[4] Moreover, these offenses represent life integrity violations, the widespread and systematic perpetration of which constitute a crime against humanity as defined by Article 7(1) of the Rome Statute of the International Criminal Court (ICC),[5] or depending on intent, genocide.[6]

A greater understanding of the factors that impair the legalization of international human rights laws prohibiting state-sanctioned violence contributes to the growing field of studies that focus on identifying risk factors for the commission of mass violence.[7] The extent to which economic downfall or sanctions harms the process of the domestication of human rights in a state creates a set of "red flags" to alert international policymakers about those conditions in a country most in need of international assistance.[8] *Legalization of Human Rights in Africa* demonstrates that a government's inability to institutionalize essential human rights laws that restrain that government from violently repressing its citizenry represents part of a larger temporal process that can eventually have dire consequences if left unchanged.

Although most African States are party to the ICCPR, the Banjul Charter, and the Torture Convention, fewer are party to the Optional Protocol to the Convention Against Torture and other Cruel, Inhuman or Degrading Treatment or Punishment (OPCAT),[9] and the Optional Protocol to the International Covenant on Civil and Political Rights (OP I).[10] Fewer still belong to the International Convention for the Protection of all Persons from Enforced Disappearance (Disappearances Convention).[11]

Most African States have codified the provisions of the treaties they ratified into their domestic statutes, and many have complied with international and domestic oversight mechanisms. However, practices of torture, extrajudicial killings, and disappearances continue to prevail across the continent.

These practices demonstrate that simply acceding to/ratifying an international agreement that prohibits various forms of political violence is not enough to demonstrate a State's "credible commitment" to constrain a government's use of force.[12] Whether or not this observation indicates that domestic legalization has completely failed, however, creates a host of questions that are worthy of further examination. How do we know when an international law is legalized domestically? What factors account for variation in the domestic legalization of international laws between countries? These questions point to a recurring issue in International Relations (IR) literature about what "legalization" means and how it is best measured.

Like Brunnée and Toope,[13] Adler and Pouliot,[14] and others, the contributors to this volume contend that legalization is more appropriately framed as a matter of practice which upholds the concept of legality. Before addressing the concept of legalization used by this book, this chapter focuses on the relative rise in authoritarianism across the continent, exemplified by the recent coups d'état in West Africa as well as the collapse of democratization in Tunisia. This discussion shows that domestic legalization of human rights is never a finished product.

Next, this chapter introduces a model that incorporates the criteria necessary for a practice to assume obligatory status and which focuses specifically on the relationship between and among public and private actors as constituting an essential component of the process. Lon Fuller's eight criteria of legality are introduced, with a special focus placed on criterion eight, *congruence*. *Congruence* is framed as an interactive variable that measures the efforts of government and the public to shape the law and its implementation.[15] The main hypothesis of this study is presented and the types of contextual factors that the contributors to this volume hypothesize influence *congruence* introduced. These factors include the role of women in government, economic stability, terrorism, and international involvement through peace missions, among others. The relationship between these independent variables and *congruence* is tested with an integrative model, combining qualitative and quantitative features.

This chapter then synopsizes the other chapters in this book, including those which provide broader analyses of the legalization of prohibitions against torture and other forms of political violence across African states, and those which focus more closely on the process of legalization in individual states. This chapter concludes with discussion of the value of the integrative model used by this study as a tool for conducting systematic cross-country comparisons to better account for variations in legalization processes, as well as its contribution to the extant legalization and risk assessment literatures in the political science discipline and to the literature about human rights development in Africa.

An Illiberal Trend in Africa

Between 2014 and 2024, only a few of the 23 African governments that were ranked as being authoritarian ("not free") by Freedom House transitioned to semi-democracies. In other instances, states slipped backward from partly free to not free.

Botswana, Namibia, South Africa, Lesotho, Cabo Verde, Ghana, São Tomé and Príncipe, and Mauritius are ranked by Freedom House as "free" countries, enjoying appreciably higher levels of civil liberties and political rights compared to other African states.[16] However, even in some of these more democratic countries, backsliding in the protection of human rights has transpired. For example, over the past few years in Cabo Verde, the use of torture has become more frequent.[17] The lethal use of force by police in South Africa remains widespread, and the use of torture by the government increased over the past few years.[18] The continued use of force creates problems which will likely impair the legacy of the African National

Congress government and may hamper its work in the new coalition government.[19]

The outbreak of the COVID-19 pandemic partially accounts for some of the recent backsliding.[20] Government lockdowns led to increases in gender-related violence, and violence perpetrated by the police. Moreover, lockdown policies and other restrictions were used by some governments to justify policies of eviction and incarceration of opponents.[21]

Government responses to the COVID pandemic are part of a larger story about the relative decline in democracy in countries around the world. Scholars such as Ginsburg, Hopgood, Fawcett, and others have noted a general decline in the protection of civil liberties and rights by governments around the world, accompanied by a rise in support for populist leaders.[22] In its 2022 report on the state of world democracy, Freedom House referred to a "rot in democracy," wherein

> undemocratic leaders and their supporters in democratic environments [...] worked to reshape or manipulate political systems, in part by playing on voters' fears of change in their way of life and by highlighting the very real failures of their predecessors.[23]

Conflicts in Sudan and Ethiopia continue to create humanitarian emergencies and many states in Africa that were once considered "free" have experienced a sharp decline and sometimes complete reversal of all democratic progress. The Arab Spring died in Tunisia when President Kaïs Saïd seized control of the government in July 2021 and immediately began to dismantle Tunisia's democratic institutions.[24] Mali and Burkina Faso have also seen sharp declines in democracy.[25] What progress Mali made in political liberalization and the protection and promotion of human rights in the early 2000s vanished nearly overnight.[26] Presently, the military is suspected of several egregious human rights violations,[27] and groups including the Islamic State in the Sahel (ISIS), the Group for the Support of Islam and Muslims (GSIM), not to mention foreign troops and militias, are responsible for similar offenses.[28]

The July 2023 coup in Niger launched by members of the Presidential Guard continues to threaten regional stability.[29] Like the other coups in the region, Niger's coup is an "anti-Western" one, intended (at least partially) to sever ties with France and establish closer ties to Russia.[30] The warnings issued by the Economic Community of West African States (ECOWAS) to the military junta in Niger to stand down and reestablish the Bazoum government led to counter threats from Mali and Burkina Faso that "they would join forces to defend Niger's new military junta" should ECOWAS (or anyone else) intervene militarily.[31]

It is a rather sobering fact that as of the time of this writing several of the countries considered by the Early Warning Project (EWP) to be most at risk for mass violence are located on the African continent. These countries include Sudan (5.7% risk), Ethiopia (5.1% risk), Guinea (4.5% risk),

Somalia (3.8% risk), and Nigeria (3.2% risk).[32] The Democratic Republic of Congo (DRC) has a risk of 2.7%. Although this marks a decrease from previous years, the renewed conflict that erupted in the Kivu region of the DRC in 2022 has increased civilian fatalities and instability.[33]

An Alternative Measure of Legalization

From Oette's perspective, the legalization of international human rights laws prohibiting torture, for example, requires a great deal of action on the part of a government. For instance,

> Legislative measures to be taken to this end cover provisions that (i) implement, wholly or partially, the prohibition against torture; (ii) constitute best practices in combating torture, such as providing for custodial safeguards; (iii) close loopholes that may enhance recourse to torture, such as the use of evidence that may have been obtained as a result of such treatment for security purposes; (iv) remove obstacles to accountability and justice; and (v) deal with other systemic factors that facilitate torture or perpetuate impunity.[34]

These actions must also include government efforts toward transparency, such as permitting access for nongovernmental organizations (NGOs) and other investigatory institutions to inform the public and hold the government accountable for its noncompliance with these laws.[35]

Regardless of why political elites choose to ratify or accede to a treaty, the achievement of "rule consistent behavior" by the leaders and officials of the ratifying State is clearly another matter altogether. The extent to which States report on their progress in implementing international human rights laws to various treaty bodies or permit in-country visits is part of a larger process that involves international pressure and the behavior of governing officials and the public in domestic settings.

The contributors to this volume contend that the process of legalization is more than just how precisely these international prohibitions are codified in domestic statutes, or for that matter, the fact that interpretation of these laws is assigned to the judiciary of a state. The institutionalization of these human rights cannot be characterized as a finished product. Rather, the legalization of human rights is constantly changing with the ever-changing conditions in a country.

Our conceptualization of legalization differs from how legalization is defined in IR literature. From realist and institutionalist (neoliberalist) perspectives, legalization of international laws is a consequence of rational action. For realists, it's a matter of the fit of human rights with national security interests or agendas of leaders. Institutionalist scholars frame legalization as a top-down, non-reflexive process (largely international) which varies in degrees of compliance, given the strength of the obligations involved, the specificity of the laws in question, and the manner with which implementation—violations or questions of the law—is handled.[36] Cosmopolitans focus on the ever-growing global village and the desire of states to improve life for all as being the impetus to legalization. To feminists, a failure to legalize and comply with human rights laws is attributable to the exclusive nature of the communities of practice involved in the lawmaking processes. Constructivists suggest that legalization is a process in which norm entrepreneurs and transnational advocacy networks strive to achieve norm diffusion. None of these paradigms, however, adequately explains *how* human rights norms create obligation, and none can adequately account for why legalization seems to decline in so many cases.

The contributors to this volume suggest that legalization is best framed as an interactive, comprehensive process involving many players, including political elites, NGOs, the public, and local and/or traditional institutions, who debate and shape the law, its application, and perceptions of its legitimacy. The concept of legalization utilized in this book is grounded in Fuller's criteria of legality, specifically, his eighth criterion, *congruence*, which represents legality as a reciprocal process which impacts and is impacted by those involved in the lawmaking and accountability processes.[37]

The concept of *congruence* used by the contributors to this volume expands on Fuller's concept to include the ways in which citizens meaningfully influence the policymaking process. The dependent variable of this study—*congruence*—is conceived of as an interactive composite variable that includes public information access (including use of social media), the activity of local and/or traditional institutions, and the role of civil society, along with Fuller's original components, judicial independence, access to justice, and corruption.

All of these components of *congruence* (separately or together) are considered by democratization studies and/or those which focus on the implementation of human rights in the developing world to be prerequisites for compliance with international human rights laws.[38] It is the idea that "UN human rights treaties have the most effect where there is strong and sustained elite leadership, civil society mobilization, and support by the domestic judiciary both during and after ratification."[39]

Taking these factors into consideration, this volume's primary hypothesis is as follows:

> The more inclusive the communities of practice involved in the legalization process—the greater their ability to freely operate and litigate for the creation and implementation of human rights laws prohibiting torture, disappearances, and extrajudicial killings—the more likely that these laws will become embedded in the governing system.

The real test of how embedded a human rights law is within a ruling system is how it is applied in practice by a government especially during hard times, in response to outside pressures, or most likely both. Institutional legacies associated with past regimes also inform the trajectory of policy implementation. The conceptualization of *congruence* used by this study grants the contributors to this volume the ability to test (quantitatively and qualitatively) a variety of factors that many studies suggest impact the human rights progress of countries. These factors include economic stability,[40] female inclusion in government,[41] conditions of internal political instability marked by terrorist attacks, civil wars and/or inter-state conflicts,[42] and international involvement through peace missions, foreign direct investment (FDI) and/or sanctions.[43]

The contributors to this volume suggest that these factors impact the inclusivity of the communities of practice that shape the law and their ability to function. Some insight into the legalization of international laws can be gathered from domestic codification of treaty provisions, reporting status, the reception of and reaction to on-site visits from special procedures mechanisms, and so forth. However, as measures of legalization, these actions are insufficient as they provide a superficial test of whether human rights laws are followed in practice. The real test, the contributors to this volume suggest, is the extent to which the lawmaking and accountability processes are fair and inclusive.

Part I: The Theory, the Model, and the International/Regional Regimes Regulating State-Sponsored Violence in African Countries

Chapter 1 examines extant explanations of the concept of legalization found in the IR literature in the political science discipline. Explanations of legalization from the Realist, Liberalist, Cosmopolitan, Feminist and Constructivist paradigms are assessed, with emphasis placed on the lack of attention these paradigms give to the notion of legalization as a complex, interactive, and multidirectional process. For a treaty to be legalized internationally, it must be legalized domestically. This becomes a matter of looking *inside* the state and assessing what contextual factors most impact the character of the communities of practice that make and assess the law, as well as their ability to operate effectively. Relying on practice theory, as well as the theory of historical institutionalism, the legalization of human rights is reframed as a moving target that is heavily influenced by several factors that are endogenous and exogenous to a country, some of them fortuitous, others deeply embedded in official practice.

Chapter 2 explains the integrative model used by the contributors to this volume. An integrative model—which includes qualitative and quantitative features—is valuable in that it permits the testing of multiple hypotheses at varying levels of analysis. This chapter also introduces the dependent variable of this study. *Congruence* is a composite variable that is intended to represent the extant communities of practice who debate and shape the law, its application, and perceptions of its legitimacy. Our general argument is that inclusive communities of practice surrounding the policymaking and implementation processes in a country and their ability to effectively operate bode well for the institutionalization of international laws. However, this inclusiveness is impacted by several factors. Editor and contributor Mitchell details each of the conditions that the contributing authors to this volume hypothesize impact the health of *congruence*, outlining a set of working hypotheses for each.

Chapters 3 through 5 address the legal framework for the Torture Convention, the ICCPR, and the Disappearances Convention, as well as examine the work of the charter-based UN bodies, including the Human Rights Council and the Security Council, as well as the African human rights regime. Emphasis is placed on governments' cooperation with these various mechanisms and the obstacles and controversies associated with these human rights regimes.

Part II: Continent-Wide Progress in the Legalization of Prohibitions against Torture, Disappearances, and Killings in African Countries

In Chapter 6 the editors of this volume quantitatively test a variety of factors which are believed to impact the process of the domestication of human rights prohibitions on torture and other forms of political violence in African states. They rely on a quantitative composite score for *congruence* which includes measures of all six components of the variable: *local authority, societal engagement, information access, access to justice, corruption*, and *independent judiciary*. The authors test all five of this study's hypotheses for the period 2012 to 2022. The results of the analysis suggest that *regional stability* and *international presence* have a significant positive impact on *congruence* while various aspects of *internal stability* have a significant negative impact on *congruence*.

In Chapter 7 Maio-ling Lin Hasenkamp and editor Mitchell focus on the impact peace missions have on the process of the domestic legalization of human rights prohibitions against political violence. The authors define "peace mission" as one that includes peacekeeping and peacebuilding missions, including the work of fact-finding missions and in some cases special rapporteurs. A focus is placed by the authors on the "Local/Comparative" IR paradigm to peacebuilding and the ways in which it improves on Realism, Liberalism, and other IR paradigms as a means of explaining how and why peace missions fail to contribute to the legalization process. Looking at examples of missions in Mali and Burundi the authors find evidence that suggests that the more closely peace missions incorporate local interests and agendas the greater the likelihood that the development of civil society and other institutions necessary to maintain rule of law will occur.

In Chapter 8 Yue Lin explores the potential for FDI to contribute to intrastate conflict and state-sanctioned violence in African countries. With an integrative model Lin focuses on the influence different sectoral investments from foreign countries have on social conflicts and state-sanctioned violence, as well as the impact of divergent weights of investment in each sector on same. Based on data from fDi Markets and the Armed Conflict, Location, and Event Project from 2013 to 2019, Lin uses a difference-in-difference method to quantitatively demonstrate the causal relationship between FDI and the likelihood of social conflicts and state-sanctioned violence (including torture and killings) in Africa. She also qualitatively compares Chinese oil investments in Sudan with Chinese construction and manufacturing investments in Ethiopia. Her results demonstrate that investment toward "inclusive" sectors, including the manufacturing and service sectors, mitigates host countries' social conflicts. These results have some positive implications for *congruence*, although Lin concludes that *congruence* is more likely impacted by the deeply embedded conditions of structural violence that prevail in many African countries.

Part III: Case Studies and Conclusions

In Chapter 9 Roland Djieufack focuses on Cameroon. Disappearances, inhumane and degrading treatment, torture, and extrajudicial killings are a characteristic feature of life in contemporary Cameroon, a country which continues to endure the consequences of regional instability, including refugee inflows.[44] The mounting threat of secession by an Anglophone insurgency group seeking to create a new state of Ambazonia makes the achievement of political stability increasingly untenable.[45] Djieufack demonstrates that a lack of judicial independence and access to justice in Cameroon and the misuse of social media only contribute further to a country on the brink of collapse.

In Chapter 10 Jean Francois Koly Onivogui assesses the extent to which successive waves of state-sponsored violence have shattered citizens' democratic attitudes in Guinea and their willingness to engage with the government. Political development in Guinea has been marked by several institutional critical junctures, all of which were accompanied by violence as a means of maintaining authoritarian rule. Drawing on narratives from national and international human rights NGOs and quantitative data from the *Afrobarometer* surveys, Onivogui demonstrates that cyclical state-sponsored violence in Guinea has created a traumatized and alienated citizenry. Guineans' deeply rooted and pervasive institutional and interpersonal distrust, coupled with their abysmal democratic expectations, represent one part of a larger damaged community of practice that includes a dysfunctional judiciary and a foundationally corrupt governing system.

In Chapter 11 Khedija Arfaoui addresses the work of the men and women involved in the process of institutionalizing human rights protections in Tunisia, specifically their work through human rights organizations like the Tunisian League of Human Rights (LTDH). The communities of practice surrounding the legalization of human rights in Tunisia narrowed dramatically in recent years as the Saïd government continues to destroy the progress that was made in the Arab Spring. Using the theory of historical institutionalism Arfaoui demonstrates that a legacy of violence persists in Tunisia along with a legacy of social activism. Civil society, although hobbled, continues to operate, shining a light on the consequences associated with the collapse of public engagement in the policymaking process and their ability to effectively hold government accountable.

In Chapter 12 criminologist Shannon M. Gibson applies a revised version of Institutional Anomie Theory (IAT) to examine whether civil society or the public through social media, protests, and other nonviolent actions has the will to push forward to progressively impact the policymaking process in Zimbabwe. Gibson shifts the focus of IAT to the legacy of violence and misrule by the ZANU-PF and the role that widespread corruption and politics as usual have on public's willingness to constructively engage with the government. Like the chapter by Onivogui, Gibson looks at the behavior of the public, partially demonstrated by their attitudes toward the ZANU-PF regime, corruption, their economic well-being, and the viability of the political opposition, to suggest that a desire to "tune out" the government may be emerging as a form of self-preservation for many in Zimbabwe.[46]

In Chapter 13 Hasenkamp addresses the influence of regional dynamics on the process of the domestication of international human rights prohibitions against torture and political violence in Mali. The fragile political, socioeconomic, and legal environments in Mali pictorially mirror the dynamics of the emergence and transformation process of a new regional imaginary in the "wider Sahel region" in which cross-border practices of state, non-state actors, and informal institutions shape the region's fuzzy political reality. What this means for *congruence* in lawmaking pertaining to prohibitions on political violence is unclear as legalization is a changing and moving target. For non-state actors, however, Hasenkamp writes that a type of *congruence*—"*mis-congruence*"—exists wherein these non-state actors are creating their own systems of rules to govern (really control) local populations. These patterns of *mis-congruence* only further exacerbate tensions and fragility in Mali.[47]

In Chapter 14 Kholisani Solo assesses the legalization process in Botswana. Since independence in 1966, Botswana has held regular, free, and fair elections. Botswana continues to thrive economically from the diamond, beef, and tourism industries. However, Solo suggests that beneath the façade, there are mounting concerns about political intolerance, official use of torture, intrusion into press freedom, economic inequality, and growing unemployment. At the same time and relative to most countries on the continent, IDEA data indicate that on all of the indicators of *congruence* used by this study (*societal engagement*, *access to justice*, etc.) the communities of practice surrounding the legalization of international human rights laws prohibiting political violence should be more successful than it is in practice. One constant in Botswana's post-independence past is the Botswana Democratic Party (BDP). Solo's chapter uses historical institutionalism to explore what impact rule by the BDP has on the process of the legalization of human rights prohibitions against torture, lethal force and other forms of violence in Botswana. Solo's chapter perhaps most clearly demonstrates that the legalization of human rights is a process, never a finished product.

In the concluding chapter of this book, Mitchell, Atanga, and Hasenkamp take stock of the progress African states have made toward the legalization of human rights laws prohibiting political violence. They argue that each of the chapters included in this volume demonstrates that legalization is an incredibly complex process that cannot be reduced to the precision of the law, the obligation it creates, or how it is adjudicated. Rather, legalization is a continually evolving process that does not merely include the legal community or politicians, but also civil society organizations and society at large through their ability to influence the lawmaking and law implementing processes. Discussion is also provided about future areas of research using this model.

Conclusions

Over the past decades, the literature about the progress of human rights on the African continent has expanded, particularly in contributions by African authors. *Legalization of Human Rights in Africa* adds to this literature. *Human Rights in Africa* by Bonny Ibhawah, *Expanding Perspectives on Human Rights in Africa* edited by M. Raymond Izarali, Oliver Masakure, and Bonny Ibhawoh, Frans Viljoen's *Human Rights Law in Africa*, and George William Mugwanya, *Human Rights in Africa: Enhancing Human Rights Through the African Regional Human Rights System* provide valuable insight into the variety of factors that impact human rights implementation and compliance.[48] *Human Rights in Africa* by Ibhowah focuses on the history of the human rights struggle on the continent. While very insightful and well written, *Human Rights in Africa* does not provide a basis for systematic comparison between the African countries, nor does it include a measurable concept of legalization. Likewise, *Expanding Perspectives on Human Rights* provides an excellent analysis of several facets of human rights in Africa, including analysis of the work of the ICC, and current human rights controversies in Africa, yet it does not provide a clear concept of legalization that is testable. A similar argument applies to Viljoen's book which does include a chapter on legalization but does not rely on a model that is testable across cases.

Enhancing Human Rights Through the African Regional Human Rights System compares other regional human rights regimes to the African regime, highlighting the importance of national agency in human rights compliance in African states. This book provides some useful anecdotal examples of human rights practices but lacks a systematic analysis of how these human rights gain legitimacy in African states (or in any state). *Legalization of Human Rights in Africa*, by contrast, more closely explores how human rights become institutionally embedded within a state.

Each chapter in our volume provides a thorough analysis of how *congruence* changes over time and what factors contribute to this change. Taken together, the quantitative and/or qualitative analyses provided in these chapters shine a light on the complexity of the legalization process and emphasize that it is a long-term project requiring sustained commitment on the part of *all* stakeholders, regardless of a change in economic or political stability. From this perspective, the protection and promotion of human rights is never a finished product that we can walk away from. The example of the progress and regress of human rights in Africa mirrors the ebb and flow of human rights protections around the world.

Understanding those factors that impact the domestic legalization of human rights laws contributes to the constructivist scholarship by adding another layer to their arguments about those factors that contribute to the process of norm acceptance and or "rule consistent behavior."[49] Legalization is conceived of as something dependent on the degree to which the interactions between and among those actors that make up the communities that create and implement the law are fair and inclusive. Moreover, the contributors to this volume are explaining *how* the actual practice of legality surrounding the domestication of international prohibitions on torture, disappearances, and political killings works. In doing so, they are expanding on constructivist studies and (neo)liberal/institutionalist studies which explicate the outcomes and progress of human rights compliance by fleshing out the process.

A greater understanding of the factors that impair the domestic legalization of international human rights laws prohibiting torture, disappearances and extrajudicial killings also contributes to the risk assessment literature,[50] as it creates a model that will enable scholars to more clearly explain *how* certain contextual factors induce states to perpetrate violence. Many quantitative risk studies show that economic strife, or coups, for example, predict mass violence. However, how this occurs and why requires greater attention to avoid false positives or negatives. *Legalization of Human Rights in Africa* shines a light on an essential aspect of violence prevention that more accurately explains and perhaps predicts state violence on a mass scale. The ability to focus more closely on what makes those factors commonly considered by the literature to be red flags for mass violence is crucial for a literature that seeks to prevent the widespread and systematic perpetration of mass atrocities.

Notes

1 UN General Assembly, *Convention Against Torture and Other Cruel, Inhuman or Degrading Treatment or Punishment*, 10 December 1984, United Nations, Treaty Series, vol. 1465, 85, available at: https://www.refworld.org/docid/3ae6b3a94.html; UN General Assembly, *International Covenant on Civil and Political Rights*, 16 December 1966, United Nations, Treaty Series, vol. 999,

p. 171, available at: https://www.refworld.org/docid/3ae6b3aa0.html; and Organization of African Unity, *African Charter on Human and Peoples' Rights* (Banjul Charter), 27 June 1981, CAB/LEG/67/3 rev. 5, 21 I.L.M. 58 (1982), available at: https://www.refworld.org/docid/3ae6b3630.html. All treaties accessed August 4, 2023.

2 Başak Çali, Nazila Ghanea, and Benjamin Jones, "Big Promises, Small Gains: Domestic Effects of Human Rights Treaty Ratification in the Member States of the Gulf Council," *Human Rights Quarterly* 38 (2016): 21–57, 24; see also Oona Hathaway, "The Promise and Limits of the International Law of Torture." In, *Torture: A Collection*. eds. Sanford Levinson and Alan M. Dershowitz (Oxford: Oxford University Press, 2004) and Richard A. Nielsen and Beth A. Simmons, "Rewards for Ratification: Payoffs for Participating in the International Human Rights Regime?" *International Studies Quarterly* 59(2) (2015): 197–208.

3 Gero Erdmann, "Party Research: Western European Bias and the 'African Labyrinth," *Democratization* 11 (2004): 63–87; Francis Stewart, "Horizontal Inequalities: A Neglected Dimension of Development." In *Wider Perspectives on Global Development: Studies in Development Economics and Policy* 101–135, UNU-WIDER, eds. (London: Palgrave Macmillan, 2005); and Jeffrey M. Davids, Rolando Ossowski and Annalisa Fedelino, *Fiscal Policy Formulation and Implementation in Oil-Producing Countries* (Washington, DC: International Monetary Fund, 2003). Moreover, Gudrun Østby, Ragnhild Nordås, and Jan Ketil Rød, for example, find that intraregional inequalities increase the potential for regional conflict in the sample of sub-Saharan African countries they consider. Gudrun Østby, Ragnhild Nordås and Jan Ketil Rød, "Regional Inequalities and Civil Conflict in Sub-Saharan Africa," *International Studies Quarterly* 53(2) (2009): 301–24.

4 Jutta Brunnée, "The Prohibition on Torture: Driving Jus Cogens Home?" *Proceedings of the Annual Meeting (American Society of International Law)* 104 (2010): 454–57. *Jus cogens* norms are non-derogable and obligate states to prosecute offenders. See Cherif M. Bassouni, "International Crimes: 'Jus Cogens' and 'Obligatio Erga Omnes'." *Law and Contemporary Problems* 59(4) (1996): 63–74, 66.

5 UN General Assembly, *Rome Statute of the International Criminal Court (last amended 2010)*, July 17, 1998, ISBN No. 92-9227-227-6, available at: https://www.refworld.org/docid/3ae6b3a84.html (accessed 4 August 2023).

6 UN General Assembly, *Rome Statute*, Art. 6; also, UN General Assembly, *Convention on the Prevention and Punishment of the Crime of Genocide*, December 9, 1948, United Nations, Treaty Series, vol. 78, available at: https://www.refworld.org/docid/3ae6b3ac0.html (accessed August 6, 2023). There is also abundant case law from the International Criminal Tribunal for Yugoslavia (ICTY) and the International Criminal Tribunal for Rwanda (ICTR) on the definition of torture as a war crime, sexual violence as a war crime, and the connection of torture to customary international law. See, for example, *Prosecutor v. Kunarac et al.* Appeals Judgement, IT-96-23/IT-96-23/1-A (June 12, 2002), paras. 142, 153, 155; *Prosecutor v. Athanase Seromba*, Appeals Judgment, ICTR-2001-66-I, March 12, 2008, para. 46 (sexual acts as torture); *Prosecutor v. Jean-Paul Akayesu*, Trial Chamber, ICTR-96-4, September 2, 1998, para. 595 (torture as a crime against humanity) and paras. 597, 687 (rape as torture), para. 731 (rape as tool of genocide).

7 Hollie Nyseth-Brehm (Nzitatira), "Re-Examining Risk Factors of Genocide," *Journal of Genocide Studies* 19(1) (2017): 61–87; Benjamin Valentino, "Triggers of Mass Killing," Report on a Research Project for the Political Instability Task Force (Hanover: Dartmouth College, February 2016); Benjamin E. Goldsmith

and Charles Butcher, "Genocide Forecasting: Past Accuracy and New Forecasts to 2020," *Journal of Genocide Research* 20(1) (2018): 90–107. It is also helpful here to refer to the work of James Waller, including his 2016 book, *Confronting Evil: Engaging our Responsibility to Prevent Genocide* (Oxford, UK: Oxford Univ. Press, 2016).

8 This suggestion raises a host of issues associated with the extraterritoriality of human rights obligations, which are beyond the scope of the present study. For more information on this point, see Sigrun Skogly and Mark Gibney, "Transnational Human Rights Obligations," *Human Rights Quarterly*, 24(3) (August 2002): 781–798.

9 UN General Assembly, *Optional Protocol to the Convention Against Torture and other Cruel, Inhuman and Degrading Treatment or Punishment*, January 9, 2003, A/RES/57/199, available at: https://www.refworld.org/docid/3de6490b9.html (accessed 4 August 2023).

10 UN General Assembly, *Optional Protocol to the International Covenant on Civil and Political Rights*, December 19, 1966, United Nations, Treaty Series, vol. 999, available at: https://www.refworld.org/docid/3ae6b3bf0.html (accessed 4 August 2023).

11 UN General Assembly, *International Convention for the Protection of All Persons from Enforced Disappearance*, August 3, 2017, A/72/280, available at: https://www.refworld.org/docid/59ad5e094.html (accessed August 4, 2023).

12 Beth Simmons and Allison Danner, "Credible Commitments and the International Criminal Court," *International Organization* 64 (2010): 225–256.

13 Jutta Brunnée and Stephen J. Toope, *Legitimacy and Legality in International Law: An Interactional Account* (Cambridge: Cambridge Univ. Press, 2010).

14 Emanuel Adler and Vincent Pouliot, "International Practices: Introduction and Framework." In *International Practices*, ed. Emanuel Adler and Vincent Pouliot, 3–35 (Cambridge: Cambridge Univ. Press, 2011).

15 Lon Fuller, *The Morality of Law*, Rev. ed. (New Haven, CT: Yale Univ. Press, 1964).

16 Freedom House, *Freedom in the World, 2024: The Mounting Damage of Flawed Elections and Armed Conflict*, at FIW_2024_DigitalBooklet.pdf (freedomhouse.org) (accessed May 27, 2024).

17 David L. Cingranelli and Clay K. Richards, "The CIRI Human Rights Dataset, Version 2014.04.14," (2021) at https://doi.org/10.7910/DVN/UKCPXT, Harvard Dataverse, V1, UNF:6:+N2W6SCqRsXxIn6+qCBSyg== [fileUNF] (accessed August 4, 2023).

18 Cingranelli and Richards. "CIRI."

19 The ANC lost its majority for the first time in June 2024 elections. Although President Cyril Ramaphosa was re-elected, the coalition government in which the ANC shares power with 15 other parties, including Inkatha Freedom Party, is a fragile one. John Eligon and Lynsey Chutel, "Ramaphosa Gets Second Term in South Africa, but Coalition is Fragile," (June 13, 2024), *The New York Times* at South Africa Re-elects Ramaphosa, but Coalition Is Fragile – The New York Times (nytimes.com) (accessed June 30, 2024).

20 Wolfgang Merkel and Anna Lührmann. "Resilience Of Democracies: Responses To Illiberal And Authoritarian Challenges," *Democratization* 28 (2021): 869–884.

21 Marshal Olal Johnson Limong, "Africa: Lessons Learned from the COVID-19 Pandemic," *Medical Research Archives: Report, European Society of Medicine* (January 31, 2023), at DOI: 10.18103/mra.v11i1.3486 (accessed March 1, 2023).

22 Edmund Fawcett, "Facing Illiberal Democracies," *The Political Quarterly* (2022); Tom Ginsburg, "AUTHORITARIAN INTERNATIONAL LAW?" *The American Society of International Law*, 2020, at doi:10.1017/ajil.2020.3; Stephen

Hopgood, *The End Times of Human Rights* (Ithaca-USA; London-ENG: Cornell University, 2013)."

23 Sarah Repucci and Amy Slipowitz, *Freedom of the World 2022: The Global Expansion of Authoritarian Rule* (Freedom House, Feb. 2022) at FIW_2022_PDF_Booklet_Digital_Final_Web.pdf (freedomhouse.org) (accessed May 1, 2022, 6–7).

24 Human Rights Watch, "Tunisia; President Intensifies Attacks on Judicial Independence," February 27, 2023, at Tunisia: President Intensifies Attacks on Judicial Independence | Human Rights Watch (hrw.org) (accessed February 27, 2023).

25 According to Freedom House, Burkina Faso witnessed the sharpest decline in democracy of any other country in 2022, a drop of 23 points, moving Burkina Faso from "Partly Free" to "Not Free." Freedom House, *World Report*, 2023, 3–4.

26 According to Freedom House, over the past decade Mali's aggregate democracy score declined 40 points. Repucci and Slipowitz, *Freedom of the World 2022*, 16.

27 Amnesty International, "Human Rights in Mali, 2022," at Human rights in Mali Amnesty International (accessed March 2, 2023).

28 Amnesty, "Mali." See William Rampe, "What is Russia's Wagner Group Doing in Africa?" *Council of Foreign Relations Brief* (May 23, 2023) at What Is Russia's Wagner Group Doing in Africa? | Council on Foreign Relations (cfr.org) (accessed July 12, 2023). French forces have also faced allegations of war crimes in Mali. Jonathan Pedneault, "Lessons for French Forces in Mali: European Court of Human Rights Reiterates Obligation to Investigate Alleged War Crimes," Human Rights Watch, March 11, 2021 at Lessons for French Forces in Mali | Human Rights Watch (hrw.org) (accessed August 1, 2023).

29 Boureima Balima and Moussa Askar, "Niger's Army Command Declares Support for Military Coup," *Reuters*, July 27, 2023, at Niger's army command declares support for military coup | Reuters (accessed July 27, 2023).

30 Declan Walsh, Elian Peltier and Donne Searcey, "Europeans Evacuate Niger Amid Risks of Wider Conflict," *The New York Times* (August 1, 2023), at France Prepares Niger Evacuation Amid Risks of Conflict – The New York Times (nytimes.com) (accessed August 1, 2023).

31 Walsh et al., "Europeans."

32 Early Warning Project, "Countries at Risk for Mass Killing, 2022–2023: Statistical Risk Assessment Results" (Washington, DC: Simon-Skodjt Center for the Prevention of Genocide, United States Holocaust Museum; Hanover, NH: Dartmouth College, November 2022), 8.

33 Early Warning, "Countries," 17–18.

34 Lutz Oette, "Implementing the prohibition of torture: The contribution and limits of national legislation and jurisprudence," *The International Journal of Human Rights*, 16(5) (2012): 717–736, 718.

35 Ozette, "Implementing," 718–719.

36 *International Organization* 54(3) (Summer 2000).

37 Fuller, *Morality of Law*.

38 Çali, et al., "Big Promises," 21–57; Lance Minkler and Shawna Sweeney, "On the Indivisibility and Interdependence of Basic Rights in Developing Countries," *Human Rights Quarterly* 33(2) (May 2011): 351–396; David L. Cingranelli & David L. Richards, "Measuring Government Effort to Respect Economic and Social Human Rights: A Peer Benchmark." In *Economic Rights Conceptual, Measurement, And Policy Issues*, Shareen Hertel and Lanse Minkler eds. (Cambridge, UK: Cambridge Univ. Press, 2007); Michael Bratton and Nicolas van de Walle, *Democratic Experiments in Africa: Regime Transitions in Comparative Perspective* (Cambridge, UK: Cambridge University Press, 1997).

39 Çali, Ghanea, and Jones, "Big Promises," 25.
40 Lance Minkler and Shawna Sweeney, "On the Indivisibility and Interdependence of Basic Rights in Developing Countries," *Human Rights Quarterly* 33(2) (May 2011): 351–396; also, Neil Mitchell, and James McCormack, "Economic and Political Explanations of Human Rights Violations," *World Politics*, 40 (1988): 476–498.
41 See Li-Ju Chen, "Female Policymakers and Educational Expenditures: Cross-Country Evidence," *European Journal of Law and Economics* 51(1): 129–155.
42 Nzitatira, "Re-Examining Risk"; Nils Petter Gleditsch, Håvard Hegre and Håvard Strand, "Democracy and Civil War 1." In *Handbook of War Studies III*, Manus Midlarsky, ed. (Ann Arbor, MI: University of Michigan Press, 2007); and Carl Henrik Knutsen, and Håvard Mokleiv Nygård. "Institutional Characteristics and Regime Survival: Why are Semi-Democracies Less Durable Than Autocracies And Democracies?" *American Journal of Political Science* 59 (2015): 656–670.
43 See, for example, Matthew Krain, "The Effect of Economic Sanctions on the Severity of Genocides or Politicides," *Journal of Genocide Research* 19(1) (2017): 88–111.
44 Manu Lekunze and Ben Page, "Security in Cameroon: A Growing Risk of Persistent Insurgency," *Canadian Journal of African Studies / Revue Canadienne Des Études Africaines*, 57(1) (2023): 219–236. https://doi.org/10.1080/00083968.2022.2120507, 228.
45 The increases in insurgency movements are a consequence of various policies followed by the Biya governments that are intended to preserve his rule and reinforce the status quo. Among these policy strategies, according to Lekunze and Page, were efforts to divide the people as much as possible to prevent their successful mobilization by reinforcing ethnic identities. Lekunze and Page, "Security," 226.
46 David Coltart suggested that the willingness of many Zimbabweans to continue supporting ZANU-PF after Mugabe's downfall, despite the legacies of violence and misrule, was analogous to Stockholm Syndrome. David Coltart, "After Mugabe: Mnangagwa's Choice," *Policy* 34(1) (2018): 51–54, 53.
47 Elisa Lopez-Lucia, "Security Politics and the 'Remaking' of West Africa by the European Union: From Bounded to Fuzzy Regions," in *The Multidimensionality of Regions in World Politics* 1st ed. by P.J., Kohlenberg and N. Godehardt (London: Routledge, 2020); John Kotsopoulos and Frank Mattheis, "A Contextualisation Of EU–Africa Relations: Trends And Drivers From A Reciprocal Perspective," *South African Journal of International Affairs* (2018): 25(4), 445–460; and Philippe Le Billon ed., *The Geopolitics of Resource Wars: Resource Dependence, Governance and Violence* (London: Routledge, 2017).
48 Bonny Ibhowah, *Human Rights in Africa* (Cambridge, UK: Cambridge Univ. Press, 2018); *Expanding Perspectives on Human Rights in Africa* edited by M. Raymond Izarali, Oliver Masakure, and Bonny Ibhawoh (London: Routledge, 2019) and George William Mugwanya, *Human Rights in Africa: Enhancing Human Rights Through the African Regional Human Rights System* (New York: Transnational Publishers, 2003); and Frans Viljoen, *International Human Rights Law in Africa* 2d (Oxford: Oxford Univ. Press, 2012).
49 Thomas Risse and Kathryn Sikkink, "The Socialization of International Human Rights Norms into Domestic Practices: Introduction." In *The Power of Human Rights: International Norms and Domestic Change*, ed. Thomas Risse et al. (Cambridge: Cambridge Univ. Press, 1999).
50 Nzitatira, "Re-Examining Risk"; Goldsmith and Butcher, "Genocide Forecasting," and Waller, *Confronting Evil.*

Part I

The Theory, the Model, and the International/Regional Regimes Regulating State-Sponsored Violence in African Countries

1 What Is "Legalization"?

Stacey M. Mitchell

Introduction

The present chapter focuses first on the ways in which *legalization* is defined by the International Relations (IR) paradigms of the political science discipline: Realism, Constructivism, Neo-Liberalism/Institutionalism, Feminism, and Cosmopolitanism. One of the many difficulties associated with these definitions is that they frame the legalization of human rights laws as a terminal goal and/or as a top-down process states engage in to improve their relations with other states or to solve collective problems. Legalization is largely depicted as unidirectional, except for constructivism, which does account for domestic backsliding. Moreover, constructivism pays greater heed to the extent to which international laws are considered legitimate by a government's ruling elites. Yet, constructivist explanations do not clearly explain *how* these laws gain legitimacy or create a sense of obligation in states. This volume's authors suggest that greater focus is needed on the role of the communities of practice surrounding the creation and application of these laws domestically.

A general observation that applies to all these studies of legalization is their lack of consideration of the influence that formal and informal institutional experiences and belief systems have on legalization. This chapter provides an alternate explanation of legalization that reframes legalization as an interactive, comprehensive process involving many players, including political elites, nongovernmental organizations (NGOs), and the public, who debate and shape the law, its implementation, and perceptions of its legitimacy. This concept of legalization is heavily grounded in Lon Fuller's eighth criterion of legality, *congruence.*[1] *Congruence* represents a process that is reflexive. Rather than an endpoint, the legalization of human rights is more rightly conceived of as a moving target that is heavily influenced by several factors that are endogenous and exogenous to a country. What's preferable, not to mention more realistic, is conceiving of legalization as an ongoing course of action in which states progress or regress in their protection and promotion of international human rights laws depending on who is allowed to take part in the policymaking process.

DOI: 10.4324/9781003471677-3

If institutional development is a path-dependent process, then the communities of practice involved in the domestication of international human rights laws prohibiting torture, extrajudicial killings and disappearances impact the directions in which these paths develop over time—if they are allowed to operate freely, that is. The concept of path dependency is rooted in the theory of Historical Institutionalism from the Comparative Politics discipline of political science. The contributors to *Legalization of Human Rights in Africa* contend that historical institutionalism is useful as a means of explaining the course of human rights development in states and the institutional challenges that communities of practice face on their way to altering state behavior. The assumptions of the theory and its fit with the practice theory of legalization on which this study relies are discussed in detail below.

This chapter concludes with some final observations about how the theory used by the contributors to this volume improves extant explanations of legalization from the political science literature. This section also includes discussion about how the theory and model utilized by this study contribute to the risk assessment literature that seeks to predict mass violence and genocide. This latter contribution is especially noteworthy given the contemporary challenges to democracy in Africa (and elsewhere around the globe) and the increased prevalence of political violence.

Existing Explanations of Legalization

Legalization is a concept that has been framed by political science scholars largely as an endpoint, measurable by what is required to achieve it. In the summer 2000 issue of *International Organization* scholars argued that legalization is best "characterized by three components: obligation, precision, and delegation."[2] In this context, what matters is the extent to which rational states achieve these three goals.

Adamson and Sriram sum up the realist position on international law as being

> *epiphenomenal* [italics in original] to state power, [...] that the contours of international law and its effectiveness are a product of the interests of powerful states or the balance of power among states, but that international law does not exert an independent effect on states.[3]

Everything is reducible to states' interests. As Mearsheimer and other realists suggest, these interests are short-term ones, having largely to do with national security.[4] Traditionally, realists place human rights laws and obligations rather low on the totem pole of a government's priorities, and rightly so, given their view that adherence to such obligations places states in a vulnerable position in the extant system of international anarchy (Neorealism) or among other self-interested leaders (Classical Realism).[5]

As Goldsmith and Posner contend, measures of the "efficacy of international norms" mentioned by constructivists, cosmopolitans, liberals, and so on as explanations as to why states comply with their international treaty obligations, falsely attribute motives to these states that cloak their real motivation: self-interest.[6] This observation certainly flies in the face of cosmopolitan arguments which emphasize an "imagined just world order."[7] In a realist world stability in the international system is prioritized as is the national security of the sovereign states that constitute the system. In such a world the domestic legalization of international human rights laws is shallow at best.

Admittedly, the behavior of states seems to reinforce this notion. One only need consider the problems associated with the international response to countries that are experiencing egregious human violations. Gibney refers to, "the myriad of cases where widespread human suffering has either elicited no response by the international community or else the efforts were inadequate compared to the humanitarian disaster at hand."[8]

Selective compliance with international human rights laws is commonplace around the world, particularly in dualist states like the United States. A simple look at the changes made to US torture policy over the past 20 years demonstrates that national security interests prevail in determining how international human rights are defined domestically and the extent to which their implementation conforms to the letter or spirit of the law. The torture policies of the administration of President George W. Bush, for example, were based on a very narrow reinterpretation of the US torture statute that raised the bar for what was considered torture incredibly high. This reinterpretation permitted the use of waterboarding, hooding, and a variety of other brutal methods of extracting information from terrorism suspects.[9]

To realists and institutionalists, the world is occupied by rational states. For realists the choice to comply with international laws is strictly contingent upon more immediate national interests. However, as Franck contends, the perceptions of states (and their behavior) indicate otherwise: "In the interstate community, the belief that *pacta sunt servanda*—that treaties, all treaties, are binding, and not just when they are convenient or advantageous—is what keeps the bumblebee of international law aloft."[10] Just because infractions of the law occur—and they do, regularly—does not mean international rule of law is absent if the perception that it exists prevails. In practice, the fact that states continue to "work around" various political obstacles in the international system to effectively comply with international legal obligations indicates that international law has legitimacy; that "law can adapt new circumstances while retaining the determinacy that underpins its perceived legitimacy."[11]

For institutionalists like Krasner, Simmons, Keohane, Abbott, and others, international law is a consequence of a rational consensus between states, based on the notion that states are better off cooperating than resorting to force as a means of resolving differences.[12] International law exists as a necessary and valuable entity that serves the interests of states who understand that "compliance is not just the consequence of strategic calculation by parties to a particular agreement[,] [...] compliance is to their advantage."[13] Neoliberalism offers a longer-term perspective that assumes cooperation is an outcome of "independent variables such as balances of power, interests of various actors, and institutions."[14]

Many of these scholars agree on how "legalization" should be defined, or at the very least, how it should be measured: as "a form of institutionalization characterized by three components: obligation, precision, and delegation."[15] "Obligation" refers to the extent to which states feel bound by a set of laws; "precision," is the clarity of these laws, and "delegation," the granting of "authority to implement, interpret, and apply the rules; to resolve disputes; and (possibly) to make further rules" to a third party, which in this example, refers to international institutions with regulatory authority.[16] The typology created by these authors categorizes international legal regimes—the Rome Statute of the International Criminal Court, the Montreal Protocol, the Vienna Ozone Convention and others—by their achievements on each of these measures. In creating this conceptualization of legalization, the authors demonstrate that adherence to international law is less a matter of force, and more a matter of the ways in which these laws are constructed and applied.[17]

While this conceptualization is useful as a means of explaining *why* states vary in their compliance with and implementation of international laws, it is not without its critics. As Carey and Mitchell contend, "this conceptualization of legalization did not count illiberal uses of international law, and it largely [overlooks] the sphere of activity where most international law is implemented and enforced, by domestic (internal) state political-legal systems."[18] Instead, legalization is portrayed by institutionalists as an essentially top-down, non-reflexive process which varies in degrees of compliance, given the strength of the obligations involved, the specificity of the laws in question, and the manner with which implementation of the law is dealt. It is an approach that pays little attention to how these laws directly and/or indirectly impact domestic societies.

Other studies specifically address the compliance gap, or the gap between what a state promises the international community (and its own) and what it does. The studies by Bueno de Mesquita, Downs and Smith, Cingranelli, Mark and Sadykova-DuMond, and Bell, Clay, and Murdie, for example, demonstrate that state leaders comply (or not) with international law for several reasons, including regime type, regional dynamics, naming and shaming by human rights NGOs, and international pressures.[19] Implicit in these arguments (although not adequately addressed) is the assumption that political elites do not comply with international laws because these laws have not been fully institutionalized domestically. A constant feature of these studies is the insufficient connection made between the international system, domestic institutions, and societal norms.

However, scholars like Simmons, more closely examine the specific effects of treaty membership on a polity, including the impact treaty membership has on mobilizing political dissent in a country.[20] In *Mobilizing for Human Rights*, Simmons addresses the puzzle of why leaders of sovereign states who ratify or accede to treaties that demand greater official accountability follow through on at least some of their commitments in practice, especially when these commitments go against their perceived interests. She pushes back against the more realist arguments that contend that the frequency of egregious violations of human rights laws by states around the world makes these laws essentially worthless.[21]

She considers a variety of human rights ranging from civil and political (including torture) to the economic, social, and cultural, and finds evidence that indicates that the international human rights regime has had a positive impact on changing the behavior of state leaders, particularly in those states that have independent legal systems, greater governmental transparency, not to mention greater resources, and greater stakeholder agency (for political and nonpolitical actors) in the policymaking process. Success is also a matter of the right or set of rights in question (e.g., children's rights versus prohibitions on torture, the latter of which are more frequently violated for national security reasons).

With respect to the work of domestic actors her argument that "treaties assist in the process of political mobilization of groups who stand to gain from their provisions" is relevant to the present study.[22] She goes on to state that,

> [i]n many countries – especially those that are at least partially democratic and are based on the rule of law – ratified treaties provide highly legitimate focal points that help to clarify reasonable demands, support the legitimacy of those demands, and contribute to the political and legal resources stakeholders can bring to bear in the quest to realize treaty rights.[23]

She addresses many of the same components that the contributors to this present volume argue constitute *congruence* between the law as written and the law as it is practiced (which she summarizes as "the nature of public demands, institutions, and capacities").[24]

Our study differs in that we examine those factors that directly impact *congruence*, not what impacts torture practices, disappearances, and political killings in a country. For example, does political conflict negatively impact the relationship between domestic NGOs and the governing system and what does this mean for the ability of NGOs to hold leaders accountable? Likewise, is the public's access to information being stifled because of internal conflict, and if so, how does this impact their willingness to criticize their government or even attempt to litigate their demands? One could make the argument that our dependent variable, *congruence*, is a measure of democracy. To that point, addressed in further detail below, the authors of this study argue that *congruence* is not synonymous with democracy. Rather, it is a foundation necessary for democracy to succeed.

Cosmopolitans suggest that the Neoliberal/Institutionalist and Realist paradigms (and Constructivist to some extent) are embedded in the normative traditions of the Westphalian order which continue to dominate the decision-making of international and domestic elites. Wars, various other types of conflicts, economic agreements, and security arrangements reinforce the logic of extant international power structures wherein the interests of the most powerful states prevail.

Cosmopolitanism suggests that the need of states to create and comply with international laws stems from their desire to improve the human condition. Cosmopolitanism finds its roots in Immanuel Kant's notion of perpetual peace.[25] In a world of sovereign states complete with wars, squabbles, and desires for expansion, Kant advocated for a body of norms—public rights—that were not derived from natural law per se, but which emanated from like-minded reasonable states "dedicated to the establishment of a more rightful condition" for mankind.[26] Although cosmopolitanism and what Brown refers to as "international liberalism" share in the idea of democracy as a preferred form of governance to ensure for a peaceful global coexistence, cosmopolitanism looks beyond the state as the primary actor to a larger global community and loftier goals of universal justice.[27]

The focus of cosmopolitans is the global collective.[28] They embrace the idea that the problems of humankind—environmental deterioration, the spread of artificial intelligence, war, disease pandemics, poverty—are universal and must be solved collectively through a more egalitarian process. They emphasize the work of global communities of practice consisting of NGOs, politicians, individuals, and human rights groups who advocate for universal human rights, economic equality, and justice.

However, whether global democracy is possible or not is another question altogether. As Baynes notes, cosmopolitanism has been criticized for presupposing a world order that can be changed to fit the cosmopolitan ideal which is to say an order in which institutions can be altered, perhaps absent a democratic procedure of sorts to determine which institutions are changed, who makes these changes, and to what extent.[29] Others advocate the Kantian notion of like-minded states coming together "to share a normative vision."[30] Baynes argues that a reconceptualization of cosmopolitanism to focus more closely on the practice of international law between and within states (in institutions of "public reasoning") and less on where this law emanates is useful to understanding that international rule of law can (and does) prevail and with it the emergence of a kind of democratic entitlement, even institutions of deliberative democracy.[31] It is nevertheless a slow process and a matter of the continued interaction between actors and institutions at the national and international levels. An excellent analogy of international law is provided by Waldron, who refers to a "dense thicket of twisted and interlocking laws, treaties, regulations and applied norms"[32] that guides state behavior.

However, even if we assume a more pragmatic institutionalist cosmopolitan perspective, we cannot ignore the challenges that persist with the domestic legalization of international laws, a consequence of the messy sphere of internal politics, power structures, and nationalist ideals.[33] With cosmopolitanism, legalization is a phenomenon that takes place at the international level, where there is a perceived agreement on the "universality of human worth," which "cannot be overruled by local commands or decrees," normatively speaking.[34] However, legalization of international laws starts at the state level. For cosmopolitanism, the process by which international laws become embedded in domestic venues is vague and demands further clarification. Assuming an ideal world in which all states are democratic still does not explain how politics, power, even culture impact policymaking, nor does it necessarily account for the variations in compliance and implementation of human rights that we know transpire among democratic states.

One area of IR studies that deals directly with issues of power is feminist studies. Feminist theories range from postcolonial feminism to liberal feminism to ecofeminism, each with its emphasis placed on various gender experiences. One common thread linking these schools of thought is that law, whether international or domestic, is imbued with a masculine perspective. The dominant patriarchal system that has existed since the beginning of time marginalizes women and girls (and other vulnerable groups) and prevents them from participating in the policymaking process, certainly as this pertains to the domestication of international human rights laws. The work of Enloe and Cohen suggests that greater inclusion of female perspectives in policymaking processes would improve the strength of human rights.[35] These studies and the work of Collins et. al., Altan-Olcay, and Corredor provide valid critiques of the male-dominated international system of human rights laws and legal practices.[36] The contributors to the present volume seek to test some of the assumptions of these feminist theories to determine whether the inclusion of greater female representation (at least domestically) has an impact on the legalization of human rights norms prohibiting torture and other forms of state-sanctioned violence.

Constructivist studies also address the influence of norms, but from the perspective that greater focus should be placed on the fit of international laws with extant norms and belief systems within countries.[37] How precise a law is or whether there is an institution to enforce the law is dependent upon the perceived legitimacy of these laws by a society:

> [This] broader view of laws [...] encompasses features and effects of legitimacy, including the need for congruence between law and underlying social practice. It attends to the purposive construction of law within inherited traditions, the way participating in law's construction contributes to legitimacy and obligation, and to the continuum of legality from informal to more formal norms.[38]

When the conversation turns to international human rights treaty obligations, the fit between these laws and local systems gains importance.

Agreements that require states to extend to their citizenry individual freedoms and protections can result in substantial resistance. Constructivists suggest this pushback is part of a larger process that eventually results in "rule-consistent behavior" by the rule-breaking states. What is at stake is the success of the normative shift on the part of government and society toward embracing human rights. However, the legitimacy of international law is often a "contested ideological terrain," much like collective memory or political discourse more broadly conceived.[39] Different groups within a society will have different conceptions of what legitimacy is.[40]

For example, as part of the "denial" phase of the socialization of human rights norms (e.g., the "spiral model"), Risse, Ropp, and Sikkink argue that elites frequently frame the validity of human rights norms as a form of outside intervention, and justify their noncompliance based on national security, culture, and/or sovereignty.[41] For whatever reason the state denies the legitimacy of these norms, the fact they are engaging in dialogue with human rights advocates is seen by these scholars as indicating that the "process of socialization is already under way."[42]

Constructivists point to the work of "norm entrepreneurs" as a conduit for change in domestic human rights practices.[43] Norm entrepreneurs are actors who embrace particular norms and seek to convince the leaders of states to modify their perspectives and their policymaking behavior, with the end goal being the institutionalization of the norm or norms in question. Finnemore and Sikkink contend that

> Norm entrepreneurs attempt to convince a critical mass of states (norm leaders) to embrace new norms. The second stage [of the spiral model] is characterized more by a dynamic of imitation as the norm leaders attempt to socialize other states to become norm followers. The exact motivation for this second stage where the norm "cascades" through the rest of the population (in this case, of states) may vary, but we argue that a combination of pressure for conformity, desire to enhance international legitimation, and the desire of state leaders to enhance their self-esteem facilitate norm cascade.[44]

In this respect, leaders are also acting strategically, at least initially. Over time, however, the international human rights laws become embedded throughout the domestic political system and society at large and leaders no longer question the legitimacy of these laws.

Brunnée and Toope argue, however, that the cycle of norm diffusion described by these scholars illustrates the origin of a norm, the actors involved, and the beginnings of the process. It does not explain *how* exactly these norms create obligation, or, as they describe it, "the interactional roots of shared understandings."[22] Additionally, as Gonzales-Ocantos points out, norm entrepreneurs are depicted as having a clear idea about what the changes should be in a ruling system, which may or may not grant agency to domestic actors.[45] "Communicative entrepreneurs" (his term), on the other hand, are more ready to engage in a productive dialogue with domestic actors to create more mutually acceptable outcomes.

In his work on the cooperation of member States with the Inter-American Court for Human Rights (IACtHR), for example, Gonzales-Ocantos suggests that the IACtHR simply dictating orders to national courts is counterproductive and ignores the fact that the context within each member State varies and requires a more nuanced approach on the part of the IACtHR to achieve compliance. A better alternative is creating an "open-ended dialogue [...] to provide a playing field conducive to genuine discussion. Norm development [...] becomes a multidirectional, consensual, and participatory process."[46] Gonzalez-Ocantos recommends that IACtHR judges use "nudges" to forge a dialogue with local judicial actors, such as referring specifically to a national court or other judicial institution in a country in their rulings, which serves the purpose of "treating [...] [the local bodies] as distinct entities."[47]

To more fully comprehend how legalization occurs, the scope of analysis must be broadened to include not only a fuller assessment of the context of change, but also the influence that domestic actors and institutional legacies have on the process. What this suggests is a reconceptualization of legalization as an ongoing process that is always a work in progress (or regress in certain instances). Here, the decision-making surrounding the institutionalization of norms prohibiting political violence is shaped by historical and current events and a mutual interaction between non-state and state actors.

An Alternative Explanation of Legalization

Whether the focus is on norm entrepreneurs or communicative ones, legalization is presented by the contributing authors to this volume as an interactive, comprehensive process involving many players, including political elites, advocacy organizations, the public, and traditional leaders, who debate and shape the law and perceptions of its legitimacy. To Brunnée and Toope, "legality is tethered to broader social practices, in part because, to understand law's guidance, citizens and law-applying officials must first of all share a basic repertoire of common reference points—'implicit rules'—that are embedded in social practice."[48]

Whose conception of legitimacy wins out is a function of several factors, including power, persuasion, but also effectiveness, existing "norms that shape social identities and situations," and all of the above.[49] The legitimacy of international laws prohibiting a state's use of violence faces stiff challenges from those within a government who defend violent state practices on the basis of national security interests.[50] Much of the violence perpetrated by official agents of a government is frequently justified as being a response to terrorism, an effort to restore stability, achieve freedom for their people, and/or maintain territorial sovereignty. For example, in response to the uprising of the Tigrayan People's Liberation Front in 2021, Ethiopian Prime Minister Abiy Ahmed called on the "Ethiopian children, [...] [to] rise up for [their] country today," in what he characterized as an "existentialist war to save Ethiopia."[51]

Adler and Pouliot focus on *law as practice* to measure legalization. Perceptions of legitimacy are relevant, but they are one aspect of a larger process that embodies performance, patterns of behavior, competency, and background knowledge.[52] The authors define "practice" as "socially meaningful patterns of action, which, in being performed more or less competently, simultaneously embody, act out, and possibly reify background knowledge and discourse in and on the material world."[53] How international laws are legalized domestically becomes a matter of context and the continuing interaction between relevant actors and their environment and how their behaviors impact background knowledge, the latter of which refers to the extent to which certain norms, institutional legacies, and belief systems are embedded in society.[54]

In many ways, practice theory fits with historical institutionalism.[55] Scholars such as Thelen, Mahoney, Steinmo, Streeck, and Hall and Taylor argue that institutions filter the impact of national crises that occur and in so doing shape the impressions of political and social elites, party members, and the public.[56] Institutions are the "*building-blocks of social order* [italics in original]: they represent socially sanctioned [...] collectively enforced expectations with respect to the behavior of specific categories of actors or to the performance of certain activities."[57] They also fuel the creation of political paradigms that justify or reinforce policymaking behavior. The influence that institutions have on individual preferences extends to leaders' interpretations of the legitimacy of existing power relationships and the appropriateness of political reforms, including the domestication of international human rights laws.

Historical institutionalism's notion that path-dependency—the idea that once institutions are formed, they lock in or follow a certain trajectory—has become more nuanced in recent years.[58] Critical junctures, which are defined by Hall and Taylor as "moments when substantial institutional change [creates] [...] a 'branching point' from which historical development moves onto a new path,"[59] are no longer assumed to consist of "punctuated equilibrium" types of events (a stock market crash, a civil or inter-state war, a coup d'état, etc.). Rather, Streeck and Thelen suggest that the focus of institutionalist literature on the punctuated equilibrium model has led scholars to misinterpret incremental institutional change as being less significant than it is. They argue that even gradual institutional change—or change constrained and influenced by existing institutional structures—can and does exert a significant impact on societies. Consequently, the outcome of incremental change can be either institutional adaptation or institutional transformation over time. In terms of the latter, the results often entail a drastic long-term shift in previous institutional arrangements.[60]

Regardless of the type of critical juncture, the agents involved with the extant institutions affected by change must readjust and modify their expectations. They can also resist change entirely. It is the institutional legacies of that state which influence the direction in which change unfolds and how actors respond.[61]

Applying this argument to the domestication of international human rights laws prohibiting political violence, the changes in policymaking behavior that come about most often appear negligible at first. Over time it is hoped legalization will create rule-consistent behavior. If the ratification of/ accession to the Torture Convention, the Disappearances Convention, the ICCPR, their related optional protocols, and the Banjul Charter represents a critical juncture, the chapters in this study demonstrate that similar critical junctures impact states differently depending on their interaction with various internal political processes.[62]

Streeck and Thelen account for five main types of gradual institutional change: displacement, layering, drift, conversion, and exhaustion. "Displacement" refers to the rising influence that alternative (subordinate) institutions come to have in a society, which can lead many to defect from extant dominant institutions. "Layering" refers to the layering of new institutional structures or features over old ones; the result, the destruction of the old institutions by these new "layers." "Drift" simply means institutional change as an eventual consequence of institutional neglect. "Conversion" involves the redirection of old institutions largely through reinterpretation of their purposes and logics. Lastly, "exhaustion" refers to a "[g]radual breakdown (withering away) of institutions over time."[63] Pouliot argues that historical institutionalism's concept of layering, or the process of grafting new policies onto old ones, is a result of the expansion or reformation of extant communities of practice.[64]

Communities of practice are not merely groups of individuals, but "a social process of negotiating competence in a domain over time.[65] That this process ends up structuring social relationships among people involved in various ways is a secondary phenomenon."[66] The concept is based on the notion that social learning and negotiation occurs between actors within this domain, which Wenger-Trayner suggests is "the area in which a community claims to have legitimacy to define competence."[67]

The basis of community is "mutual engagement," not shared values and perspectives necessarily. Actors recognize there is a problem that needs to be addressed. Through their engagement, given their background knowledge, norm diffusion occurs. With respect to legalization, Brunnée and Toope argue that

> When norm creation meets [Fuller's] criteria and is matched with norm application that also satisfies the legality requirements—when there exists what we call a "practice of legality"—actors will be able to pursue their purposes and organize their interactions through law.[68]

Communities of practice ideally *should* consist of actors who freely negotiate and re-negotiate group understandings of the world. But this does not always occur, nor are communities of practice beyond manipulation.[69] Voeten writes that while formal institutions may guide decision-making in certain directions, it is really background knowledge that serves political actors well in their efforts to push their agendas forward. In this respect, background knowledge "weaves together discursive and material worlds and, most importantly, [...] it stresses that there are patterns of rhetoric and actions that create path dependency. These patterns shape beliefs that actors have about each other."[70] Whether these negotiations are subject to manipulation or not, they are grounded in context and informed by "reference points," which can be cultural or historical experiences, and/or extant or preexisting institutions.[71]

For example, in Rwanda the 1994 genocide is frequently used by politicians and elites as a reference point in their dialogue about calls for political reform. The Kagame regime reinforces the idea that challenges to the regime—calls to open the political process, protect civil liberties and rights—are made by those who seek to create instability in Rwanda, who deny the genocide, and/or who seek a return of absolute Hutu rule.

This study contends that the extent to which the communities of practice involved in the policymaking process of a state are inclusive indicates the degree to which the legalization of prohibitions against torture, disappearances, and political killings is fair and just. Fuller's criteria of legality are extremely useful in this regard. As stated above, they also serve as the basis of the concept of legalization used by Brunnée and Toope in their 2010 study (and others) about legality as practice.[72]

Fuller suggested eight criteria for legality, the absolute failure of any one of which "does not simply result in a bad system of law; it results in something that is not properly called a legal system at all."[73] These criteria are: (1) the existence of a body of law, (2) that is made public, (3) does not include ex post facto rules, (4) is clear and understandable, (5) is not contradictory, (6) does "not require conduct beyond the powers of the affected party," (7) is changed infrequently, and (8) is congruent with actual administration (the law is as it is applied).[74]

This study's conception of *congruence* differs from Fuller's in that the actors who engage in the creation and implementation of the law are expanded to include NGOs, local politicians, and the public at large.[75] Each of these additional components of *congruence* is unpacked further in Chapter 2 of this volume. For clarity, the authors of this study assess *congruence* by the inclusiveness of the communities of practice surrounding the lawmaking and law implementation processes. The more limited in scope these communities are, the less likely "citizens [...] [can] expect that the government will abide by and apply these rules."[76] Citizens cannot always take leaders at their word. Without having any impact on the policymaking process, rule of law—*congruence*—becomes a moot point.

In her assessment of the impact that non-state actors have on application of human rights laws at the international level, Lane writes that, "States are no longer the only actors adopting instruments aimed at implementing or developing international law (including aspects of international human rights law). Non-State actors are becoming increasingly involved in global governance."[77] Of course, this is not always an absolute good. Armed rebel groups and terrorist organizations are non-state actors as well.

Although Lane's focus remains at the international level, it is nevertheless a valid question to ask whether these types of non-state actors could or should be included in the communities of practice surrounding the domestication of international human rights laws. Lane argues that these actors are indirectly horizontally bound to meet basic international human rights standards as they usually operate in a quasi-public capacity.[78] That being said, it is still the governing state to which human rights obligations are attributed by the international treaty monitoring bodies. However, the use of torture and other forms of violence by members of rebel groups or terrorist organizations will be considered by the contributors to *Legalization of Human Rights in Africa* as a force contributing to conditions of instability in a country. These organizations will not be considered as members of the communities of practice surrounding the domestic legalization of human rights laws *unless* they have been incorporated into a political system in some way.[79]

The practice of legality is affected by power differentials between states, much of which are rooted in legacies of colonialism and exploitation.[80] In most of the countries examined by the contributors to *Legalization of Human Rights in Africa* stark power differentials prevail *within* states between citizenry and the government. Whether these divisions are based on ethnicity, religion, or any number of other identity sources, they tend to be deeply embedded in that country's economic, social, and political institutional structures. To overcome these differentials, to expand the communities of practice that surround the policymaking and implementation processes, greater dialogue between rulers and ruled is necessary and essential.

The entire process surrounding the domestication of international laws does not occur in a vacuum. Economic crises or terrorist attacks create conditions of internal instability that lead governments to "crack down" on public expressions of dissent, including access to reliable information and use of the internet.

The relationship between exogenous and endogenous factors, historical institutional legacies, and the process of legalization is as follows (Figure 1.1):

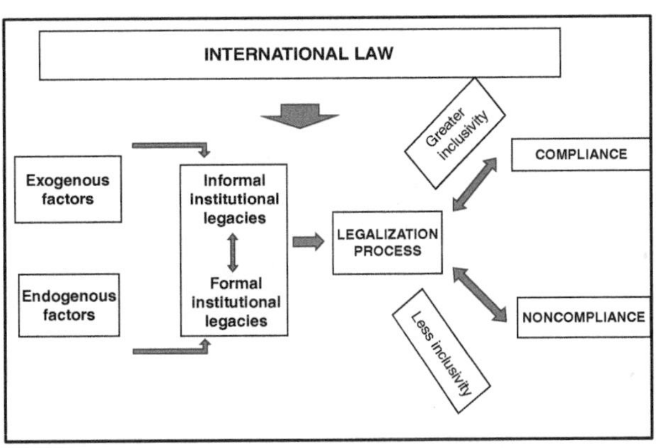

Figure 1.1 Law as practice.

Compliance in this framework means that a government's use of torture, disappearances, and political killings is minimal. Noncompliance means the opposite. The contributors to this volume argue that compliance is part of the legalization process in that how a state complies with its obligations reverberates back on the inclusiveness of the communities of practice involved in the policymaking process. Compliance or noncompliance feeds into the background knowledge that informs the institutionalization of the law.

Many of the states referenced in this volume demonstrate noncompliance. Whether we're talking about Sudan or Ethiopia or Tunisia, governments can and do restrict human rights, especially during periods of national emergency. There are also factors that mitigate the extent to which this happens.

For example, more female legislators may serve as a buffer, although, as author Khedeji Arfaoui contends in Chapter 11, this has not happened in Tunisia. Similarly, a strong international presence may help relieve some of the negative impacts of national crises, but, as Miao-ling Lin Hasenkamp and Stacey M. Mitchell write in Chapter 7, this is certainly not a given. The contributors to this volume argue that the extent to which communities of practice surrounding the creation and implementation of human rights laws in states are inclusive and able to effectively operate is influenced by national crises. Depending on the institutional legacies present, these crises are hypothesized to negatively impact the willingness of political elites to broaden the scope of these communities of practice and to permit them to operate undeterred.

Conclusions

Legalization is an ongoing, multidirectional process that involves more than just the legal community within a state, but also includes nongovernmental actors. All parties included in the communities of practice pertaining to the domestication of international laws continuously interact to make sure that the rule of law is upheld; that citizens and rulers alike abide by the law and hold one another accountable for its infraction. The rule of law is not merely followed for rational purposes as realism or institutionalism suggests, but because it is the essence of a democratic society. As Brunnée and Toope contend, "the criteria of legality are not merely signals, but are conditions for the existence of law."[81]

From the creation of and adherence to the law by all parties comes a sense of obligation that is organic rather than something imposed on a state by the international community through treaty monitoring processes and other similar forms of engagement. The contributors and editors of *Legalization of Human Rights in Africa* strongly suggest that this organic quality of obligation explains in greater detail how the constructivist's "spiral model" can lead to rule-consistent behavior by leaders in a country or not, depending on the situation.[82] Societies feel an obligation to adhere to the rules when they conform to Fuller's criteria of legality *and* are subject to public critique and input.

Moreover, the focus on the work of practitioners—members of the law-making communities of practice—resolves some of the agency problems that historical institutionalist models tend to encounter. "In this formulation, actors figure as agents not just in their rational, goal-seeking pursuits, but within a culturally and temporally bounded social context," influenced by past institutional arrangements and normative belief systems.[83] One of the difficulties Duvall and Chowdury note with respect to the relationship between competency and practice is the idea that the former may prevent change. In historical institutionalist terms competent performance becomes path dependent. In response, they contend that if focus is placed on the temporal significance of certain practices and their clash with other practices, this can change the conversation between members of an extant community of practice or even expand that community.[84]

The significance and meaning of certain practices change over time. Not to mention the fact that incompetency does shine a light on areas of the law much in need of substantial reform. For example, the murder of George Floyd by police officers in Minneapolis, Minnesota, in 2020, as well as the murders of many other African American men and women by police in the United States over the past few years, has expanded the dialogue surrounding what is and is not proper police conduct. The militarization of police forces in the United States has had to confront a strong undercurrent of deeply embedded racism that defies the very principles of due process and equality under the law.

There is a certain sense of urgency in the need for a reframing of the concept of legalization. The rise in authoritarian practices around the world over the past few years has created a need to refocus our attention on what the rule of law means and how it is best protected. This is an observation perhaps best expressed by Hunt in her critique of current political theory:

> If political theory fails to address this truly urgent problem in our own time, we risk losing the liberal democratic constitutional protections that ensure the equal rights upon which a free society—characterized by freedom of speech, association, thought, academic work, religion, and the press—depends.[85]

Risk assessment studies from the genocide and conflict literatures address the rise in authoritarianism as a warning sign that could lead to episodes of mass violence, even genocide, if left uncorrected. The studies by Butcher, Goldsmith, Harff, Mayersen, Nzitatira, Straus, Ulfelder, and Valentino empirically demonstrate further that crisis events further exacerbate unfavorable conditions in a country and lead governments to commit more violence.[86]

However, those studies that are quantitative tend to encounter issues of accuracy and agency, their nearly exclusive reliance on quantitative data being said to "erase lived experiences, and privilege violence that is easily quantified."[87]

Legalization of Human Rights in Africa adds to these studies in that it provides a perspective on violence that is more deeply grounded in historical and contemporary institutional experiences and explains how crises and other factors make it more or less possible for a government to rely on the use of violence against its population as a means of maintaining stability. As the author of this chapter has indicated in past work,

> a greater focus on institutions within a country—how and why they were constructed in a particular manner, how they change over time, who changes them—is essential to understanding why many societies become vulnerable to genocide and others do not.[88]

The communities of practice involved in the policymaking and implementation of laws in a state consist of many informal institutions that together interact with the governing system to improve human rights conditions. This volume shows that these informal institutions, their ability to work, and their membership reflect a country's institutional past, including its colonial history and contemporary conditions in that country.

Notes

1 Lon Fuller, *Morality of Law*, Rev. ed., (New Haven and London: Yale University Press, 1964).
2 Kenneth W. Abbott, Robert O. Keohane, Andrew Moravcsik, Anne-Marie Slaughter and Duncan Snidel, "The Concept of Legalization," *International Organization* 54(3) (2000), 401.
3 F. B. Adamson and C. L. Sriram, "Perspectives on International Law in International Relations." In *International Law for International Relations* ed. B. Çali (Oxford: Oxford University Press, 2010), 27.
4 John Mearsheimer, "The False Promise of International Institutions," *International Security* 19 (1994/95): 5–49.
5 An excellent example of the former school of thought is Kenneth Waltz's *Man, The State and War: A Theoretical Analysis* (New York, NY: Columbia Univ. Press, 1959); the latter, Niccolò Machiavelli's *The Prince* (Penguin Classics, 2003).
6 Jack L. Goldsmith and Eric A. Posner, *The Limits of International Law* (New York: Oxford University Press, 2005).
7 Terry Nardin, "Realism, Cosmopolitanism and the Rule of Law," *Proceedings of the Annual Meeting (American Society of International Law* 81 (April 8–11, 1987): 416–420, 416.
8 Mark Gibney, "Universal Duties: The Responsibility to Protect, the Duty to Prevent (Genocide) and Extraterritorial Human Rights Obligations," *Global Responsibility to Protect* 3(2) (2011): 123–151, 125.
9 These patterns of policymaking behavior are what Franck refers to as the "self-fulfilling prophecy" associated with realist views of international law. Thomas M. Franck, "The Power of Legitimacy and the Legitimacy of Power: International Law in an Age of Power Disequilibrium," *The American Journal of International Law* 100(1) (Jan. 2006): 88–106, 90. The torture policy of the Bush administration was based on the notion that the Taliban and al Qaeda terrorism detainees were not protected by the Geneva Conventions and therefore could be subjected

to torture. The legality of the use of "enhanced interrogation" techniques stemmed from two memoranda written by then Deputy Assistant Attorney General John Yoo. See M. Cheríf Bassiouni, "Reflections on The Torture Policy of The Bush Administration (2001–2008)." In *Looking to the Future*, eds. Mahnoush H. Arsanjani, Jacob Katz Cogan, Robert D. Sloane and Siegfried Wiessner (Brill, 2010); also, Jeffrey P. Fontas, "The Bush Administration Torture Policy: Origins and Consequences," *Inquiries Journal* 2 (2010).

10 Franck, "Power of Legitimacy," 92.

11 Franck, "Power of Legitimacy," 105. See also Beth A. Simmons, *Mobilizing for Human Rights: International Law in Domestic Politics* (Cambridge, UK: Cambridge Univ. Press, 2009), 125.

12 Stephen D. Krasner "Structural Causes and Regime Consequences: Regimes as Intervening Variables." In *International Law and International Relations*, 3–17; Beth A Simmons and R. H. Steinberg eds., (Cambridge: Cambridge Univ. Press, 2006); and Peter Katzenstein et al., "*International Organization* and the Study of World Politics," *International Organization* 52(4) (1998): 645–685.

13 Franck, "Power of Legitimacy," 91.

14 Jutta Brunnée and Stephen J. Toope, "International Law and the Practice of Legality: Stability and Change," 49 *Virginia Univ. of Wellington Law Review* 429 at 431 (2018).

15 Abbott, et al. "The Concept," 401.

16 Abbott et al., "The Concept," 401; also 128. "Precision" in this instance is akin to Franck's concept of "determinacy." See Franck, "Power of Legitimacy," 94.

17 This is a response to the positivist philosophy of law, exemplified by the works of H.L.A. Hart and Hans Kelsen. Positivism holds that law represents a "one-way projection of authority," which does not concern how the law works, or the actors involved in making it work in application, but rather which authority makes the law. See Abbott et al., "The Concept," 403.

18 Henry F. Carey and Stacey M. Mitchell, "Introduction: Re-Conceptualizing Legalization—The Positive and Negative Uses and Effects of International Law." In *Legalization of International Law and Politics* eds. Carey and Mitchell (Cham, Switzerland: Palgrave/MacMillian, 2023), 5.

19 Bruce Bueno de Mesquita, George W. Downs and Alastair Smith, A., "Thinking Inside the Box: A Closer Look at Democracy and Human Rights," *International Studies Quarterly* 49(3) (2005): 439–457. doi:10.1111/j.1468-2478.2005.00372.; David L. Cingranelli, Skip Mark and Almira Sadykova-DuMond, "Democracy, Capacity, and the Implementation of Laws Protecting Human Rights," *Laws.* 2(1) (2023): 1–19. https://doi.org/10.3390/laws12010006 and Sam R. Bell, Chad Clay, and Amanda Murdie, "Join the Chorus, Avoid the Spotlight: The Effect of Neighborhood and Social Dynamics on Human Rights Organization Shaming," *The Journal of Conflict Resolution* 63(1) (2019): 167–193. https://www.jstor.org/stable/48596924.

20 Simmons, *Mobilizing*, 113.

21 On this point Simmons states that these "violations no more prove the absence of effective international law than do headlines about murder on the streets of Boston or Los Angeles prove the absence of effective law [in the US]." Simmons, *Mobilizing*, 350.

22 Simmons, *Mobilizing*, 357.

23 Simmons, *Mobilizing*, 357.

24 Simmons, *Mobilizing*, 373.

25 Immanuel Kant, "Perpetual Peace: A Philosophical Sketch." In *Kant's Politics Writing* ed. H. Reiss (Cambridge, UK: Cambridge Univ. Press, 1970).

26 Garrett Wallace Brown, "Moving Cosmopolitan Legal Theory to Legal Practice: Models of Cosmopolitan Law," *Legal Studies* 28(3) (Sept. 2008): 430–451, 435.

For further discussion of Kant's cosmopolitanism, including his five laws of hospitality, see Brown, "Moving," 434–438.

27 Brown, "Moving," 440. When Brown refers to "international liberalism" he means classical liberalism. His observation also applies to neoliberalism/institutionalism in that this philosophy also sees states as primary actors and focuses on the notion that democracy and a free-market economy are the best ways to achieve domestic growth and stability.

28 Falk may be the most famous (or infamous depending on who you ask) of the cosmopolitans. Richard A. Falk, "A Pluralist Cosmopolitanism for the Twenty-First Century." In *Peacebuilding Paradigms: The Impact of Theoretical Diversity on Sustainable Peace*, ed. Henry F. Carey (Cambridge University Press, 2020), 147-159; Richard Falk, "Revisioning Cosmopolitanism." In *For Love of Country: Debating the Limits of Patriotism* eds. Martha C. Nussbaum and Joshua Cohen (Boston: Beacon Press, 1996), 53–60; Others include: David Held, *Global Covenant: The Social Democratic Alternative to the Washington Consensus* (Cambridge, UK: Polity Press, 2004), Garrett Wallace Brown and David Held eds., *The Cosmopolitan Reader* (Cambridge, UK, Polity Press, 2010); J. Brecher, J.B. Childs and J. Cutler eds., *Global Visions: Beyond the New World Order* (Boston: South End Press, 1993); N. Dower and J. Williams eds., *Global Citizenship: A Critical Reader* (London: Routledge, 2002); Y.F. Tuan, *Cosmos and Hearth: A Cosmopolite's Viewpoint* (Minneapolis MN: Univ. of Minnesota Press, 1996); and K.A. Appiah, *Cosmopolitanism: Ethics in a World of Strangers (Issues of Our Time)* (New York, NY: W.W. Norton & Company, 2010).

29 This argument is a restatement of William Scheuerman's critique of Held's proposals for a global world order. Kenneth Baynes, "Cosmopolitanism and International Law," *Moral Universalism and Pluralism* 49 (2009): 219–239, 220. For more on Scheuerman's observations, see William Scheuerman, "Cosmopolitan Democracy and the Rule of Law," *Ratio Juris* 15 (2002): 439–457.

30 Brown, "Moving," 443.

31 Baynes, "Cosmopolitanism," 232–235.

32 Brown, "Moving," 442.

33 Nationalism stands as one of the chief obstacles to a domestic pursuit of more globally oriented policies. See Kok-Chor Tan, "Cosmopolitanism and Nationalism," *The European Union, Nationalism and Cosmopolitanism* 77(3) (2012): 188–205.

34 Brown, "Moving," 431. Simmons characterizes this perspective as "[representing] a justified sensitivity to global values that run roughshod over local distinctiveness." Simmons, *Mobilizing*, 371.

35 Cynthia Enloe, *Bananas, Beaches and Bases: Making Feminist Sense of International Politics* 2nd ed. (Berkeley: University of California Press, 2014), *Maneuvers: The International Politics of Militarizing Women's Lives* (Berkeley: University of California Press, 2000) and *The Big Push: Exposing and Challenging Persistent Patriarchy* (Myriad, UK, and Univ. of California Press, US, 2017); Carol Cohen, "Sex and Death in the Rational World of Defense Intellectuals," *Signs* 12(4), 168–178 and Carol Cohen and S. Ruddick, "A Feminist Ethical Perspective on Weapons of Mass Destruction," *Boston Consortium on Gender, Security and Human Rights, Working Paper* 104 (2012): 3–33.

36 Dana Collins, Sylvanna M. Falcón, Sharmila Lodhia, and Molly Talcott. "New Directions in Feminism and Human Rights," *International Feminist Journal of Politics* 12 (2010): 298–318; Özlem Altan-Olcay, "Making and Unmaking Culture: Gender Experts, Faith, and the International Governance of Gender," *International Feminist Journal of Politics* 24 (2021): 286–309; Elizabet S. Corredor, "Unpacking 'Gender Ideology' and the Global Right's Antigender Countermovement," *Signs: Journal of Women in Culture and Society* 44 (2019): 613–638.

37 Martha Finnemore and Stephen J. Toope, "Alternatives to 'Legalization': Richer Views of Law and Politics," *International Organization* 55(3) (2001): 744.
38 Finnemore and Toope, "Alternatives."
39 Bo Rothstein, "Trust, Social Dilemmas and Collective Memories," *Journal of Theoretical Politics* 12(4) (2000): 494. As Wendt contends, systemic change can be inhibited by a variety of factors, not least of all which are the interests and identities of actors." Alexander Wendt, "Anarchy is What States Make of It: The Social Construction of Power Politics," *International Organization* 46(2) (1992): 391–425, 411.
40 Constructivism has been compared to cosmopolitanism, both of which assert that the state is a social construction. N.J. Reggner, "On Cosmopolitanism, Constructivism and International Society: Some Reflections on British International Studies at the Fin de Siècle," *Zeitschrift für Internationale Beziehungen* 3(1) (June 1996): 183–199, 193.
41 Thomas Risse and Kathryn Sikkink, "The Socialization of International Human Rights Norms into Domestic Practices: Introduction." In *The Power of Human Rights: International Norms and Domestic Change* ed. Thomas Risse et al., (Cambridge: Cambridge Univ. Press, 1999), 22–24.
42 Risse and Sikkink, "Socialization," 23. This observation extends also to the realist and institutionalist explanations of legal obligation. Without taking into consideration the political processes within a country, it becomes impossible to explain *why* a state agrees to be bound by a certain set of international rules.
43 Roger Alford, "The Nobel Effect: Nobel Peace Prize Laureates as International Norm Entrepreneur," *Virginia Journal of International Law* 49(1) (2008): 61–153 and N. Deitelhoff, "The Discursive Process of Legalization: Charting Islands of Persuasion in the ICC Case," *International Organization* 63(1) (2009): 33–65.
44 Martha Finnemore and Kathryn Sikkink, "International Norm Dynamics and Political Change," *International Organization* 52(4) (1998): 887–917, 895.
45 Ezquiel Gonzalez-Ocantos, "Communicative Entrepreneurs: The Case of the Inter-American Court of Human Rights' Dialogue with National Judges," *International Studies Quarterly* 62 (2018): 737–750.
46 Gonzalez-Ocantos, "Communicative," 740.
47 Gonzalez-Ocantos, "Communicative," 740.
48 Jutta Brunnée and Stephen J. Toope Toope, *Legitimacy and Legality in International Law: An Interactional Account* (Cambridge: Cambridge Univ. Press, 2010)., 66.
49 Martha Finnemore, "Fights about Rules: The Role of Efficacy and Power in Changing Multilateralism." In *Force and Legitimacy in World Politics* ed. David Armstrong et al. (Cambridge: Cambridge Univ. Press, 2005), 201–202; David Armstrong and Theo Farrell, "Force and Legitimacy in World Politics: Introduction," in Armstrong et al. *Force*, 10.
50 These incidentally are three "-isms" or the "three evils" that Ginsburg cites to as the most common justifications cited by states for the use of authoritarian practices. Tom Ginsburg, "Authoritarian International Law?" *The American Society of International Law*, (2020), DOI.10.1017/ajil.2020.3.
51 Anver Versi, "We Must Stop Ethiopia Tearing Itself Apart," *New African*, December 21, 2021.
52 Emmanuel Adler and Vincent Pouliot, "International Practices," *International Theory* 3(1) (2011): 1–36, 6–9.
53 Adler and Pouliot, International Practices," 6. Karp distinguishes Adler and Pouliot's concept of practice from "a practice," the latter of which he defines as a specific set of activities that can be labeled and which exist within an institution of sorts. David Jason Karp, "The Location of International Practices: What is

Human Rights Practice?" *Review of International Studies* 39(4) (October 2013): 969–992, 974.

54 See also Ilias Bantekas and Lutz Oette, *Human Rights in Law and Practice* 3rd ed. (Cambridge UK: Cambridge Univ. Press, 2030). Practice theory has been around for some time. Turner in his seminal book, *The Social Theory of Practices*, called for a change in the way social sciences perceive "practice." Rather than as a distinct entity, practices to Turner are more appropriately considered as social action that is recurrent, ongoing, and embedded in tacit knowledge. Stephen Turner, *The Social Theory of Practices: Tradition, Tacit Knowledge, and Presuppositions* (Chicago: University of Chicago Press, 1994); also, James Davis, *Terms of Inquiry on the Theory and Practice of Politics* (Baltimore: Johns Hopkins Univ. Press, 2005).

55 Vincent Pouliot, "Historical Institutionalism Meets Practice Theory: Renewing the Selection Process of the United Nations Secretary-General," *International Organization* 74 (2020): 742–772.

56 Kathleen Thelen, "Historical Institutionalism in Comparative Politics," *Annual Review of Political Science* 2 (1999), 369–404; Kathleen Thelen and James Mahoney, "Comparative-Historical Analysis in Contemporary Political Science," in *Advances, Comparative-Historical Analysis* eds. James Mahoney and Kathleen Thelen (Cambridge: Cambridge Univ. Press, 2015); Peter Hall and R.C.R. Taylor, "Political Science and the Three New Institutionalisms," *Political Studies* 44 (1996): 936–957; Wolfgang Streeck and Kathleen Thelen, eds., *Beyond Continuity: Institutional Change in Advanced Political Economics* (Oxford: Oxford Univ. Press, 2005).

57 Streeck and Thelen, *Beyond Continuity*, 9. Institutions are now depicted as being broader and deeper than a simple structure. They still concern rules, but these can be informal and formal rules, they are multidimensional and "sometimes overlap, can be ambiguous and contain contradictory logics." Sven Steinmo, "Historical Institutionalism and the Cognitive Basis of Cooperation," *Public Performance and Management Review* 44(5) (2021): 1140–1159, 1142.

58 Stephen D. Krasner, "Approaches to the State: Alternative Conceptions and Historical Dynamics," *Comparative Politics* 16(2) (1984): 240–244, 235; also, Stephen D. Krasner, "Sovereignty: An Institutional Perspective," *Comparative Political Studies* 21(1) (1988): 77–80.

59 Hall and Taylor, "Political Science," 942.

60 Streeck and Thelen, *Beyond Continuity*, Ch. 1.

61 See Bannerman and Blayne Haggart's discussion about bricolage. Sara Bannerman and Blayne Haggart, "Historical Institutionalism in Communications Studies," *Communication Theory* (2015): 1–22, 14–15.

62 Richard M. Locke and Kathleen Thelen, "Apples and Oranges Revisited: Contextualized Comparisons and the Study of Comparative Labor Politics," *Politics and Society* 23(3) (1995), 328.

63 Streeck and Thelen, *Beyond Continuity*, 19–30.

64 Pouliot, "Historical Institutionalism." The effort to expand historical institutionalism's focus to incorporate communities of practice is part of a larger attempt to address the theory's problem of agency, in which institutions appear to predetermine the thought processes and policymaking decisions of political actors. On this point see B. Guy Peters, Jon Pierre, and Desmond S. King, "The Politics of Path Dependency: Political Conflict in Historical Institutionalism," *The Journal of Politics* 67(4) (2555): 1275–1300. Some good examples of efforts to rework historical institutionalism to incorporate greater agency include Stacey M. Mitchell, *Institutional Legacies, Decision Frames and Political Violence in Rwanda and Burundi* (London: Routledge, 2018) and Toby S. James,

"Neo-Statecraft Theory, Historical Institutionalism and Institutional Change," *Government and Opposition* 51(1) (Jan. 2016): 84–110.

65 Communities of practice are also international. In fact, most of the examples provided in Adler and Pouliot's edited volume, *International Practices*, are international ones.

66 Valerie Farnsworth, Irene Kleanthous and Etienne Wenger-Trayner (2016) "Communities of Practice as a Social Theory of Learning: A Conversation with Etienne Wenger," *British Journal of Educational Studies*, 64(2): 139–160.

67 Farnsworth, Kleanthous and Wenger-Trayner, "Communities," 143.

68 Brunnée and Toope, *Legitimacy*, 6–7. David Luban offers a similar interpretation of Fuller's argument. See David Luban, "The Rule of Law and Human Dignity," 2 *Hague Journal on the Rule of Law* 29 (2010): 43.

69 Jutta Brunnée and Stephen J. Toope "Interactional International Law and the Practice of Legality." In *International Practices*, ed. Emanuel Adler and Vincent Pouliot (Cambridge: Cambridge Univ. Press, 2011) 112; Erik Voeten, "The Practice of Political Manipulation." In *International Practices*, ed. Emanuel Adler and Vincent Pouliot, 255–279 (Cambridge: Cambridge Univ. Press, 2011), 257.

70 Voeten, "The Practice."

71 Adler, *Communitarian*, 5.

72 Brunnée and Toope, *Legitimacy*, 69.

73 Fuller, *Morality*, 39.

74 Fuller, *Morality*.

75 Luban, "Rule of Law," 43.

76 Brunnée and Toope, "Interactional," 114.

77 Lane, "Horizontal," 8.

78 Armed groups can be held directly responsible by a treaty monitoring body for human rights violations perpetrated in territorial areas in which these groups exercise control. When it comes to the application of international criminal law, including the laws of war, armed groups can and are held criminally liable for violations.

79 The research by Manning, Smith, and Tuncel demonstrates that once rebel groups *are* incorporated as parties into a political system and can compete in elections, the likelihood of a return to conflict lessens. See Carrie Manning, Ian O Smith and Ozlem Tuncel, "Rebels with a Cause: Introducing the Post Rebel Electoral Parties Dataset," *Journal of Peace Research* 61(2) (2024): 294–303; https://doi.org/10.1177/00223433221126552.

80 Brunnée and Toope, "Interactional," 119.

81 Brunnée and Toope, "Interactional," 115.

82 Obligation is "the 'value added' of law, distinguishing it from social desiderata or the rationalist proposition that 'obligation' is a mode of action chosen by actors to signal credible commitment," Brunnée and Toope, "Interactional," 115–116.

83 Raymond D. Duvall and Arjun Chowdury, "Practices of Theory." In *International Practices* ed. Emanuel Adler and Vincent Pouliot. 335–354 (Cambridge: Cambridge Univ. Press, 2011), 337.

84 Duvall and Chowdury, "Practices of Theory," 347; 342–343.

85 Eileen M. Hunt, "The Past, Present, and Future States of Political Theory," *Society* 59 (2022): 119–128, 122.

86 Hollie Nyseth Brehm (Nzitatira), "Moving Beyond the State: An Imperative for Genocide Prevention," *Genocide Studies and Prevention* 13(3) (2019): 64–78; Hollie Nyseth Nzitatira, "Re-Examining Risk Factors of Genocide," *Journal of Genocide Research* 19(1) (2017): 61–87; Deborah Mayersen, "On the Timing of Genocide," *Genocide Studies and Prevention* 5(1) (2010): 20–38; Benjamin

Valentino, "Triggers of Mass Killing: Report on a Research Project for the Political Instability Task Force" (Hanover: Dartmouth College, February 2016), at https://bpbus-e1.wpmucdn.com/sites.dartmouth.edu/dist/b/1324/files/2019/05/PITF-triggers-report-2-1-2016-webversion.pdf (accessed June 8, 2023); Scott Straus, "Triggers of Mass Atrocities," *Politics and Governance* 3(3) (2015): 5–15; Benjamin E. Goldsmith and Charles Butcher, "Genocide Forecasting: Past Accuracy and New Forecasts to 2020," *Journal of Genocide Research* 20(1) (2018): 90–107; Barbara Harff, "No Lessons Learned from the Holocaust? Assessing Risks of Genocide and Political Mass Murder Since 1955," *American Political Science Review* 97(1) (2003): 57–73 and Jay Ulfelder and Benjamin Valentino, Assessing Risks of State-Sponsored Mass Killing, *SSRN* (February 1, 2008), at https://papers.ssrn.com/sol3/papers.cfm?abstractid=1703426 (accessed November 23, 2021).

87 Stacey M. Mitchell, "Institutional Legacies and the Decision to Commit Genocide," Genocide Studies and Prevention 17(1) (2023): 1-24, 3, quoting Hollie Nyseth-Brehem, "Moving Beyond," 67.

88 Mitchell, "Institutional," 4.

2 An Integrative Model for the Assessment of Legalization as Congruence

Stacey M. Mitchell

Introduction

The present chapter introduces the model on which this study relies to explain the domestication of international prohibitions on torture, disappearances, and the official use of lethal violence. In the first section, the contributors' choice to use an integrative model is discussed. Emphasis is placed on the value an integrative model has for explicating complex phenomena like the institutionalization of international laws in domestic systems.

The use of process-tracing is a common feature in all the chapters of *Legalization of Human Rights in Africa*. For the qualitative chapters this technique provides useful insights into the perspectives that political and nonpolitical actors have of the progress of legalization in their country and what local factors have worsened or improved conditions on the ground. They complement the large-*n* studies by providing more comprehensive explanations of the process of *congruence* as it is taking place in individual states.

In the second section of this chapter, the dependent variable *congruence* is introduced. *Congruence* is a composite variable which includes civil society engagement, corruption, public access to and use of media sources, the public's ability to utilize domestic mechanisms of justice to litigate their demands for government accountability, the ability of these judicial mechanisms to operate independently of government control, and the work of local institutions of authority, both political and indigenous. As several studies written about human rights practices in Africa and elsewhere around the world indicate, they are all significant aspects of the process.[1]

The various components of *congruence* are measured quantitatively and qualitatively. The sources of data for these components are included in this discussion, with emphasis placed on this volume's use of the Institute for Democracy and Electoral Assistance's (IDEA) Global State of Democracy (GSoD) database.

This chapter then introduces the endogenous and exogenous factors which several studies suggest influence human rights domestication in states. These factors range from civil war to economic collapse to female representation in

DOI: 10.4324/9781003471677-4

government. The sources of data for each of these contextual factors are addressed, and hypotheses made about their relationship to *congruence*. This chapter concludes with final comments about this model's usefulness as a means of comprehensively explaining variation in human rights practices between and within countries.

The Value of an Integrative Model

In *Legalization of Human Rights in Africa*, the contributors rely on qualitative and quantitative methods to examine the factors that impact the *congruence* between the law as it is written and the law as applied. A reliance on macro-level factors alone to explain variation in *congruence* would not provide a clear explanation of how contextual factors like terrorist attacks or economic crises translate into specific policy choices made by political leaders, especially those having to do with limiting the ability of the courts or local authorities to act as a watchdog on a government's use of violence. Rather, institutions assume the form of a "black box" and outcomes appear devoid of agency. As Mahoney and Snyder argue, this quality of macro-level studies "creates a strong bias for emphasizing long-term, impersonal processes and for overlooking the possibility that actors may have margins of maneuverability during periods of regime change [the topic of their analysis]."[2]

For quantitative studies, especially large-*n* studies, additional questions surround the measurement of the variables employed and the overall "fit" of the model to the research question it is trying to explain. On the one hand, there is the potential for conceptual overreach. Some of these problems are resolved to the extent that the contributors to this volume are focusing on one continent. Of course, we are not making the argument that all African countries are alike. However, these countries warrant comparison because most experienced the transition to democracy at or around the same time. Most have had to contend with IMF austerity measures and the advent of contingent development aid, not to mention the rise in authoritarian tendencies in recent years.[3]

On the other hand, one could inquire about the feasibility of measuring a complex concept like *congruence* quantitatively. After all, congruence is a human endeavor that encompasses a variety of moving parts, each of which captures a snapshot of rule of law at certain moments in time. Moreover, questions can be raised as to whether the components of *congruence—societal engagement, local authority, access to justice, corruption, independent judiciary, information access*—are valid representations of what they are intended to measure.

Turning to the use of qualitative methods, the use of a smaller number of cases or even a single case—as is done in many of the chapters in this book—permits more comprehensive explanations of what *congruence* means to a particular state and how it varies over time. The use of a case study or studies is useful as it permits an inside view of how *congruence* plays out at the local level, particularly how it influences the perceptions, interests, and behavior of domestic state and non-state actors.

Of course, single-case studies encounter their own set of problems. For studies that rely on thicker explanations of behavior, individual observations of complex phenomena are emphasized and grounded in context. Can generalizations be reached from studies that are more idiosyncratic? What can the relationship between indigenous resolution mechanisms and the domestic legalization of international human rights laws in Burundi, for example, tell us about the relationship of traditional institutions to rule of law in the wider world?

Studies that focus on a single case study are said to lose "leverage," compared to large-*n* analyses.[4] They face problems associated with an overdetermination of the significance of anecdotal evidence as a measure of a particular phenomenon, not to mention a degrees of freedom problem.[5] In this latter instance, more inferences exist than observations and, as a result, a research model is created that is largely indeterminate.

To avoid these methodological issues, an integrative study becomes an ideal solution. King, Keohane, and Verba and others contend that the combination of elements of both in an analysis is often preferable, because, [i]n the same research project, some data may be collected that is amenable to statistical analysis, while other equally significant information is not. [...] If we are to understand the rapidly changing social world, we will need to include information that cannot be easily quantified as well as that which can."[6]

With respect to the study of regime change, Mahoney and Snyder contend that an integrative approach is useful. An integrative approach is

> defined by [the] use of both subjective evaluations of actors *and* objective conditions as primary causal variables; a focus on temporally proximate *and* remote factors; a methodological concern with case-specific *and* general causes of regime change; and an emphasis on multi-level explanations that span micro *and* macro levels of analysis.[7]

Although this study does not incorporate a formal micro-level type of analysis (such as the inclusion of a decision-making model) to systematically test the significance of individual perceptions and beliefs, what it does do is include statements of local actors involved in the lawmaking process in a particular state as well as historical evidence and current reports about human rights conditions to more closely connect the impact that larger-scale environmental factors have on the domestic policymaking processes in individual countries.

Institutional reform—the ratification of a human rights treaty, its codification into law, its application in practice—marks a critical juncture in a state's institutional development. Critical junctures may or may not be crisis events; neither are they necessarily brief or fortuitous. Rather, policymaking that takes place over a lengthy period can also culminate in a critical juncture. In all the cases included in this volume, what is transpiring in these countries is a process of institutional change through the expansion and/or contraction of the communities of practice that are involved in the policymaking process.

Mahoney and Snyder suggest that when a country experiences a critical juncture of this sort, agency is demonstrated.[8] Critical junctures become the link between larger-scale phenomena and human behavior. To assess the influence that environmental factors have on the process of *congruence*, the contributors to this volume rely on the technique of process-tracing. Beach and Pedersen, Schulte-Mecklenbeck, Kühberger and Johnson, Mahoney and Snyder, Gerring, Collier, Bennet, and Checkel all consider process-tracing to be an invaluable way of explaining how larger phenomena, like war or economic collapse, impact the policymaking behavior of actors in certain contexts.[9] Beach and Pedersen contend that

> process-tracing methods are arguably the only method that allows us to study causal mechanisms. [...] [Which] [...] enables the researcher to make strong within-case inferences about the causal process whereby outcomes are produced, enabling us to update the degree of confidence we hold in the validity of a theorized causal mechanism.[10]

There are different ways to do this, depending on a study's research question. Bennet and Checkel suggest that process-tracing can be done inductively or deductively. Beach and Pedersen suggest three ways that the mechanism of process-tracing can be used: to test a theory (deductively); to build a theory "that can be generalized to a population of a given phenomenon" (inductively); and thirdly, process-tracing can be used to solve an historical puzzle.[11]

The primary use of process-tracing for this volume is deductive. Many of the contributors to this volume examine the impact of specific sets of phenomena on *congruence* to test several hypothesized relationships about phenomena that are believed to weaken or strengthen a state's compliance with and implementation of international human rights laws domestically.

However, others, including Kholisani Solo in his chapter about Botswana and Miao-Ling Lin Hasenkamp and Stacey M. Mitchell in their contribution about peace missions and *congruence* in host states, approach their research topics by using the third approach, which is to say, they use process-tracing to explain a puzzle of sorts; an outcome that should *not* occur given a hypothesized relationship between a causal factor and *congruence*.[12]

The causal variables considered by this study are those familiar to scholars who explain democratization, political and mass violence in the developing world, and a variety of other institutional outcomes.[13] In our case, the contributors to this volume seek to explain how these crisis events expand or contract the communities of practice that surround the law as practice in a particular state.

Congruence and Its Components

Congruence is the dependent variable of this study. Each of its components is measured qualitatively and quantitatively. For quantitative data the authors in this volume rely heavily on data gathered from IDEA's GSoD. The decision to utilize IDEA data stems from the fact that their data comprise a variety of different measures of democracy that together demonstrate the complexity and nuances of the democratization process at the state level. IDEA's concept of democracy is a broad one that is based on the notion of democracy as "popular control of public decision-making and political equality."[14]

It is important to acknowledge the fact that the GSoD has a variable that measures rule of law in a state. "Rule of Law" is a larger composite variable that shares some of the components of our dependent variable *congruence*, such as independence of the judicial system and corruption, but also includes "Personal Integrity and Security" and "Predictable Enforcement." The contributors to this volume suggest that IDEA's "Rule of Law" variable is close to Fuller's original concept, but with a greater emphasis on *outcome* rather than *process*. Because we seek to focus more closely on the actual *process* of legalization and what impacts this process, we rely on our version of *congruence*.

Societal Engagement

The relationship between civil society, social capital, and democratization has repeatedly been the focus of many studies.[15] The basic argument contends that greater public involvement in community organizations, including non-governmental organizations (NGOs), creates bridging social capital, which is generally defined as social capital that exists among members of different communal groups. In this context, the creation of social capital between groups is analogous to the creation of cross-cutting cleavages in society. The trust generated between diverse groups within these associations leads to greater tolerance and a greater desire to collaborate in problem-solving endeavors.

Putnam has acknowledged, however, that "[l]ife does not exempt us from the need to worry about how [a] community is defined—who is inside and thus benefits from social capital, and who is outside and does not."[16] What arises from exclusionary networks is bonding social capital, which binds together individuals who are already alike in some way. Because it is based on social exclusion, bonding social capital is assumed to lead to the creation of reinforcing cleavages within societies.[17] For a government to promote and protect human rights in its country, the communities of practice must be inclusive, representing the viewpoints of a cross section of members of society.

In this process the work of domestic civil society organizations is especially essential.[18] This study relies on *societal engagement* to tap into the inclusiveness of civil society in a country and its ability to freely participate in the policymaking process. Much of the focus of current civil society (and democratization) literature has been placed on Africa.[19] The present study assumes that the type of civil society that prevails in African countries impacts the shape and character of the laws passed by a government as well as how they are implemented in society.

The work of civil society as a component of *congruence* is measured by the contributors to this volume quantitatively using the IDEA data as well as qualitatively.[20] Contributing authors also look to the reports generated by the oversight bodies for the Torture Convention, ICCPR, the Disappearances Convention, and the Banjul Charter,[21] which provide a wealth of information about the ability of civil society organizations to operate freely as watchdogs on government. Additionally, authors rely on survey data from *Afrobarometer* and the *World Values Survey* about citizens' perceptions of trust in government and society as measures of *societal engagement.*

Local Authority

LaMonica has written that local governance is the key to achieving a better functioning national system in African countries.[22] Local governments are the institutions that citizens historically go to first to address their immediate concerns—security, order, land tenure, record keeping, and so forth. To generate greater political liberalism at the top, a greater focus on the crucial role that local institutions have as agents of liberalization at the grassroots level is desirable and necessary or so the argument goes.[23]

Others, including Vedeld, Johnson, and Crawford, note that the link between poverty reduction and local government is smaller than hypothesized, that various preconditions need to be in place for local governing institutions to work effectively, and/or that democratic decentralization reduces the significance of traditional local leaders.[24] This study does not seek to resolve this issue. Rather, the inclusion of *local authority* as an important component of *congruence* rests on the notion that, at the very least, it demonstrates the existence of some public agency in the governing process.

Local authority includes not just formal structures but traditional ones also. Several scholars have written about the impact that indigenous institutions have (or could have) on the democratization process in countries in Africa and elsewhere around the world.[25] The removal of these institutions or their weakening, as with the chieftaincies in the rural areas in Cameroon because of government restructuring policies, deprives local populations of trusted allies.[26]

Quantitative data for *local authority* are derived from the GSoD variable for "Local Democracy." This indicator measures the occurrence of local elections in a country and the ability of local governing bodies to act independently of the higher governing body in that country. These data are also accompanied by historical qualitative assessments of local government and indigenous institutions in Africa and reports from sources such as the United Nations Development Programme (UNDP) and the African Union about the role and significance of local institutions as a voice of the people, especially for communities in rural areas, as well as the challenges local institutions face.[27]

Independent Judiciary

The value of an independent judiciary has long been considered as essential to the political and economic development of a country. The ICCPR and the Universal Declaration of Human Rights contain provisions requiring an independent judiciary for the full realization of the rights embodied within these documents.[28]

As Shetreet remarks

> [j]udicial independence is a significant component of the political culture in every country. It is shaped by the relations between the branches of government and is one of the basic values which lie at the foundation of the administration of justice.[29]

Judicial independence ensures for the fair adjudication and application of the law which in turn fosters the rule of law which is essential for the development of democracy and economy in a country.[30] The opposite spells a decline in democracy and individual freedoms.[31]

Masengu, Peter and Wambali, Madhuku, and Mariam, among others, argue that control of the courts by high-ranking elites in many African states creates a deficit of democracy.[32] Others, including Vondoepp, write that judicial assertiveness against the executive does take place in some African states and that a closer look at political cultures and institutions is warranted.[33]

This study relies on IDEA's variable for "Independent Judiciary" from the GSoD. "Independent Judiciary" is one of the sub-attributes of their larger "Judicial Independence" variable,[34] and it measures "the extent to which the judiciary is independent of control from other sources, such as another branch of government or the military."[35]

A great deal of the qualitative data authors rely on to assess this variable are generated by sources which include reports from international human rights NGOs, such as Lawyers without Borders, Human Rights Watch, Penal Reform International, as well as UN reporting data and African and non-African scholarship.

Access to Justice

To Fuller access to justice is one of the "procedural devices designed" to maintain congruence.[36] In this sense, due process, including the right to habeas corpus, the ability to examine witnesses and evidence, and the right to an appeal are essential components of the law as practice, without which exists "a broken and arbitrary correspondence between the Constitution and its realization."[37] To Shetreet, access to justice is another of the fundamental values of a judiciary as it

> includes the provision of judicial services to the public at reasonable cost, provision of the means to go to court for those unable to pay the cost, as well as increasing the awareness of the community so that citizens within the community appreciate that they are entitled to turn to the courts in order to defend their rights.[38]

States parties to the ICCPR and the Disappearances and Torture Conventions are obligated to grant citizens access to the courts and investigatory mechanisms to achieve justice.[39] For purposes of this study, *access to justice* does not include traditional forms of justice, mediation devices, or truth and reconciliation mechanisms. Although these have been shown to be extremely useful as a way of resolving lower-level disputes and, when implemented on a larger-scale, addressing egregious human rights violations,[40] for this volume the editors and contributors are concerned solely with those mechanisms responsible for the domestic prosecution of accused perpetrators of torture, disappearances, and extrajudicial killings.

Quantitatively, this study relies on data from the GSoD, and adopts their variable, "Access to Justice," which is a sub-attribute of their larger "Rights" variable. GSoD's "Access to Justice"

> denotes the extent to which the legal system is fair (i.e., citizens are not subject to arbitrary arrest or detention and have the right to be under the jurisdiction of, and seek redress from, competent, independent and impartial tribunals without undue delay).[41]

Qualitatively, contributors rely on historical evidence, testimonials, and the wealth of qualitative evidence provided by international NGOs and other sources, to measure access to justice.

Corruption

Corruption in Africa has been the subject of many studies, including recent studies by Anzanilufuno, Mbaku, Agang, Jones, and Pillay, and many others.[42] In his study about the Jacob Zuma regime in South Africa, for example, Titus writes, "[c]orruption was taking place in broad daylight; corruption took place in the face of human rights."[43] Many scholars associate corruption with traditional institutions (kinship, patrimonial) and culture.[44] Its deeply embedded qualities make it a challenge to overcome, particularly given the administrative weaknesses associated with the extant political systems in many of these states.[45]

One of the measures of *corruption* the contributors to this volume rely on is IDEA's variable "Absence of Corruption" from the GSoD. "Absence of Corruption" measures "the extent to which the executive and the public administration, more broadly, do not abuse their office for personal gain."[46] Data from surveys like the *Afrobarometer* surveys are also used to gauge citizens' perceptions of corruption. For qualitative assessment, the yearly reports issued by Transparency International shine a light on the deleterious impact corruption has on the ability of political systems to function fairly and at times function at all. As their 2022 annual review of corruption in sub-Saharan Africa states, "intertwined paths of democracy, security and development in Sub-Saharan Africa are eroded by corruption."[47] Just as governments struggle to effectively respond to corruption, they face an uphill battle thanks to prevailing conditions of political instability, fights against terrorism, as well as lingering effects of the COVID pandemic.

Information Access

The use of Facebook, Twitter (X), WhatsApp, and other social platforms has become especially important, "in times of insecurity and or increased repression of the media."[48] As Kakerwaivanane and Mare demonstrate in the case of the *#ThisFlag* social media campaign in Zimbabwe, for example, social media was an extremely important tool with which to pass on information about government misdeeds when other information outlets prove unreliable.[49] Hove and Chenzi write that "the proliferation of online platforms available to the Zimbabwean general public led to the spiraling of cyber-communities which challenged ZANU-PF's political hegemony, both in cyber-space and in the real world."[50]

The use of social media during the Arab Spring in 2010/2011 became a catalyst for political reform in North Africa and elsewhere in the Middle East. Waetchter observes that young people in these countries relied on social media to initialize the protests and mobilize the older populations.[51] Several studies written about the connection between social media and the process of political reform in the Middle East (and elsewhere) suggest that social media played a key role in "energizing democracy."[52] Others suggest the impact of social media is more nuanced.[53] This volume focuses on the public's access to and use of social media as a means of becoming better informed about government rule and as a way of voicing opposition to or support for the policy-making process.

Although internet access tends to reflect domestic resources and infrastructure concerns, legal limitations on access to content and internet use is another matter. Kenya, for example, showed an improvement in internet freedom according to Freedom House's report, yet some regulations and misuse of content persist. Kenya, like other countries, has experienced a rise in hate speech some of it coming in the form of approved political[54] Similarly, Roland Djieufack, in his chapter about Cameroon, explains the use of social media by government and nongovernment actors as a tool for misinformation and intimidation.

The variable *information access* is quantitatively measured by the KOF Globalization Index created by Gygli, Haelg, and Sturm.[55] The contributors to this volume also rely on qualitative data including interviews, human rights reports, and scholarly assessments of media access and use in Africa to corroborate and expand on this KOF composite measure.

Figure 2.1 provides a visual representation of this study's concept of *congruence*.

This study's primary hypothesis is as follows:

> The more inclusive the communities of practice involved in the legalization process—the greater their ability to freely operate and litigate for the creation and implementation of human rights laws prohibiting torture, disappearances, and extrajudicial killings—the more likely that these laws will become embedded in the governing system.

This argument is rooted in the International Relations (IR), democratization, and human rights literatures, all of which suggest that greater societal involvement in the legislative and governing processes and greater

Figure 2.1 Legalization as Congruence.

independence of the judiciary are prerequisites for compliance with international human rights laws.[56]

Independent Variables

Economic Health

The influence of economic status on the ability of countries to implement and comply with international human rights laws has been a focus of numerous studies.[57] The contributors to this volume consider several measures of economic vulnerability, including aggregate GDP growth, the GINI coefficient, trade imbalances, and public debt. One or all these measures are used to test the following hypothesis:

> H1: The greater the economic health of a country, the more inclusive the communities of practice involved in the policymaking and implementation processes, the more likely international human rights laws prohibiting torture, political killings, and disappearances will be legalized.

A more economically stable and prosperous country should have more inclusive communities of practice involved in policymaking and implementation. Data for all economic health measures are obtained from the World Bank and qualitative sources.

Internal Stability

The contributors to this volume assess the impact that events like coups d'état, terrorist attacks, and influxes of large refugee populations have on *congruence* quantitatively and qualitatively. Quantitative data are accessed from sources including the Polity Data Project and the Global Terrorism database.[58] For the qualitative chapters these data are frequently used as a baseline for qualitative assessment using historical data, policy statements, human rights reports, UN reporting data, and so forth.

These types of internal disruptors create situations conducive to both political and economic deterioration and a subsequent need for outside intervention per the global Responsibility to Protect (R2P) doctrine.[59] These measures are used to test the following hypothesis:

> H2: The more internally stable the country, the more inclusive the communities of practice involved in the policymaking and implementation processes, the more likely international human rights laws prohibiting torture, political killings, and disappearances will be legalized.

One of the major insights that can be gained from the conflict literature is that a deterioration of conditions of internal stability leads to a rise in opposition movements, restrictions on civil liberties, and a breakdown of constraints on a government's use of force, particularly when the regime in question is a hybrid one.[60] These crises are deleterious to the legalization of human rights generally, and with respect to prohibitions on a government's use of torture, lethal force, and disappearances, specifically.

Regional Stability

As Niang has written: "Since 2012, the Sahel has been plunged into a permanent state of warfare and been turned into a transnational battleground as well as a field of experimentation for various modes of military intervention."[61] The spread of ISIS and similar groups, political crises, and refugee inflows and outflows prevail in entire regions of Africa. It would be understating the obvious to suggest that *regional stability* is a crucial factor that must be considered when making any effort to assess the political conditions in any one African country.[62]

Quantitatively the present volume measures *regional stability* with a regional index developed from data from the CIRI Dataset, specifically their Physical Integrity and Rights Index (PIRI), which includes data on torture, disappearances, and killings for each country for each year. Our version is a modified version of the scale used by Bell, Clay, and Murdie to capture neighborhood PIRI.[63]

Qualitatively, the contributors to this volume utilize the abundance of documentary evidence about patterns of regional political and economic development to trace the influence that regional location has on the states that make up that region.

These indicators are used to test the following hypothesis:

> H3: The greater the regional stability, the more inclusive the communities of practice involved in the policymaking and implementation processes, the more likely international human rights laws prohibiting torture, political killings, and disappearances will be legalized.

International Presence

Studies have shown that international presence and/or pressures on a state can have a positive impact on a state's compliance with international human rights treaties, a negative impact, and sometimes a bit of both.[64] Paris has stated that "in spite of their many flaws, [peace missions] have done more good than harm."[65] Once seen as a fix-all for developing war-torn countries, peace missions are now perceived by many as entirely futile and a waste of resources. For purposes of this study, the contributors accept Paris' position that liberal peace missions are valuable, albeit very much in need of reform,[66] and tentatively suggest that greater international involvement in a country, including the presence of an international or regional peace mission, the work of tribunals, special rapporteurs, and the use of sanctions against a state, exerts a positive impact on a state's progress toward legalizing laws prohibiting political violence.[67]

With these measures, the following hypothesis is tested:

> H4: The greater the international presence in a country, the more inclusive the communities of practice involved in the policymaking and implementation processes, the more likely international human rights laws prohibiting torture, political killings, and disappearances will be legalized.

Data for these components of *international presence* are derived qualitatively from several sources, including scholarly studies, human rights reports, reporting data and interviews as well as quantitatively from databases including the KOF Index,[68] the UN peacebuilding and peacekeeping sites[69] and the Global Sanctions Database.[70]

Female Representation

The last of the independent variables this volume considers is the impact that women in government have on the domestication of human rights. Several studies suggest that the presence of female policymakers has a positive impact on legislation that benefits the establishment of quality-of-life rights, including access to safe drinking water, education, and childcare.[71] However, to our knowledge no study has tested to see what impact female politicians have on the process of legalization of human rights as it is measured by this study. *Female representation* is included to test the following hypothesis.

> H5: The greater representation of female legislators at the national level, the more inclusive the communities of practice involved in the policymaking and implementation processes, the more likely international human rights laws prohibiting torture, political killings, and disappearances will be legalized.

The impact of *female representation* is assessed qualitatively and quantitatively. Quantitatively, data were obtained from IPU Parline.[72] Qualitative data on the importance of women in African governments are obtained from sources which include scholarly research, human rights reports, and reports from sources such as UN Women.[73]

Figure 2.2 demonstrates the relationship between the independent and dependent variables suggested by this study. All the hypothesized relationships between *congruence* and the independent variables are included in Table 2.1.

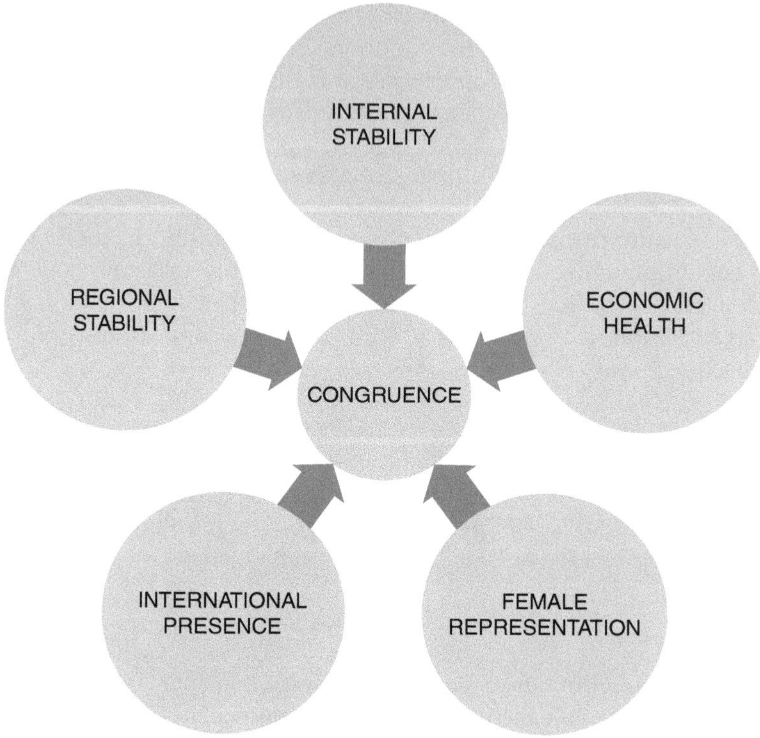

Figure 2.2 Contextual Factors That Impact Congruence.

Table 2.1 Expected Outcomes

Hypotheses	*Expected Outcome*
H1: Economic health and congruence	**Positive**
H2: Internal stability and congruence	**Positive**
H3: Regional stability and congruence	**Positive**
H4: International presence and congruence	**Positive**
H5: Women in government and congruence	**Positive**

Concluding Thoughts

The contributors to this volume strive to provide a more comprehensive explanation of how legalization works. Reframing legalization as a complex process deeply enmeshed in local dynamics and constitutive interactions between rulers and the ruled contributes to a greater understanding of how law becomes embedded, and, to some extent, the shape that embeddedness acquires. It is not simply a matter of foreign aid or intervention, unless these are geared toward enabling the communities of practice involved in the institutionalization of human rights to become more inclusive and to function better.

Our model improves on the work of legalization as practice scholars because it: (a) relies on the use of a broader, more comprehensive concept of *congruence* and (b) creates a model that is testable and replicable in other states around the world. For example, our model could be used to assess the progress of the domestic legalization of international human rights laws in Latin American states, each of which has been experiencing their own share of instability and economic strife in recent years; the most recent example of which is a failed coup in Bolivia in June 2024.[74]

El Salvador, Honduras and Guatemala, Ecuador and Bolivia, Venezuela, Brazil, and the Dominican Republic have experienced increases in political instability and economic distress that have been accompanied by an increase in the use of state-sanctioned violence. These practices have occurred despite the "norms cascade" that Lutz and Sikkink suggest accounts for the progress in the legalization of prohibitions against torture, disappearances, and the right to democratic governance that Latin American states made in past decades.[75] The model used by this book would be helpful as a means of re-examining why and how these trends have occurred both quantitatively and qualitatively.

Notes

1 In addition to the studies explained in greater detail in sections of this chapter, see Bonny Ibhawoh, *Human Rights in Africa* (Cambridge, UK: Cambridge Univ. Press, 2018); *Expanding Perspectives on Human Rights in Africa* edited by M. Raymond Izarali, Oliver Masakure, and Bonny Ibhawoh (London: Routledge, 2019) and Rachel Murray, *Human Rights in Africa: From the OAU to the African Union* (Cambridge, UK: Cambridge Univ. Press, 2004).

2 James Mahoney and Richard Snyder, "Rethinking Agency and Structure in the Study of Regime Change," *Studies in Comparative International Development* 34 (1999): 3–42, 5; for their full discussion on the metatheoretical bases of structural and voluntarist theories, see 5–11.

3 Structural adjustment plans (SAPs) are austerity measures that countries must put in place in order to receive loans from the IMF. See International Monetary Fund, *IMF Conditionality*, at IMF Conditionality (accessed July 25, 2023). SAPs have been criticized for their impact on political stability in participating states. See the work of the late scholar Thandika Mkandawire; for example, "Crisis Management and the Making of 'Choiceless Democracies'." In *State, Conflict, and Democracy in Africa*, ed. Richard Joseph, 119–136. (Boulder: Lynne Reinner Publishers, 1999).

4 Maximizing leverage requires the researcher to explain "as much as possible with as little as possible" to increase the significance of what is being explained. Gary King, Robert O. Keohane and Sidney Verba, *Designing Social Inquiry: Scientific Inference in Qualitative Research* (Princeton, NJ: Princeton University Press, 1994), 29; see also Arend Lijphart, "Comparative Politics and the Comparative Method," *American Political Science Review* 65(3) (1971): 682–689.

5 See Lijphart, "Comparative," 685; also King, Keohane, Verba, *Designing*, 119–122; David Collier, "The Comparative Method: Two Decades of Change," in *Comparative Political Dynamics: Global Research Perspectives*, eds. Dankwart

A. Rustow and Kenneth Paul Erikson, 7–31 (New York: Harper Collins, 1991); James Mahoney, "Strategies of Causal Assessment in Comparative Historical Analysis." In *Comparative Historical Analysis in the Social Sciences*, ed. James Mahoney and Dietrich Rueschemeyer, 337–372 (Cambridge, UL; New York: Cambridge Univ. Press, 2003) and Dietrich Rueschemeyer, "Can One or a Few Cases Yield Theoretical Gains?" In *Comparative Historical Analysis in the Social Sciences*, ed. James Mahoney and Dietrich Rueschemeyer, 305–336 (Cambridge, UL; New York: Cambridge Univ. Press. 2003).

6 King, Keohane, Verba, *Designing*, 51.

7 Mahoney and Snyder, "Rethinking," 11.

8 Mahoney and Snyder, "Rethinking," 11.

9 Studies use process-tracing to explain a variety of vastly different phenomena. For example, Wenxiao Yan, "An Introduction to Process-Tracing as an Innovative Qualitative Research Method to Explore Affective Variables in SLA," *Frontiers in Psychology* 13 (2023): 1–7; Pratyush Paras Sarma, "Process Tracing and Professionalization of Political Campaigns," *Journal of Liberty and International Affairs* (JLIA) 9(1) (January 1, 2023): 220–235; and Kyriakos Moumoutzis and Sotirios Zartaloudis, "Europeanization Mechanisms and Process Tracing: A Template for Empirical Research," *Journal of Common Market Studies* 54(2) (2016): 337–352.

10 Derek Beach and Rasmus Brun Pedersen, *Process-Tracing Methods: Foundations and Guidelines* (Ann Arbor, MI: Univ. of Michigan Press, 2013), 1–2. See also the work of Andrew Bennett, including Bennett and Jeffrey T. Checkel, *Process Tracing: From Metaphor to Analytical Tool* (Cambridge: Cambridge Univ. Press, 2015), Bennet, "Process Tracing and Causal Inference." In *Rethinking Social Inquiry: Diverse Tools, Shared Standards*, 2nd, eds. Henry E. Brady and David Collier 207–220 (Lanham, MD: Rowman and Littlefied, 2010); Andrew Bennett, "Process Tracing: A Bayseian Perspective." In *The Oxford Handbook of Political Methodology* eds. Janet M. Box-Steffensmeir, Henry E. Brady and David Collier, 702–721 (Oxford: Oxford University Press, 2008), and Andrew Bennett and Colin Ellman, "Qualitative Research: Recent Developments in Case-Study Methods," *Annual Review of Political Science* 9 (2006): 455–476; Jeffrey T. Checkel, "Tracing Casual Mechanisms," *International Studies Review* 8(2) (2008): 362–370; also David Collier, Henry E. Brady and Jason Seawright, "Sources of Leverage in Causal Inference: Toward and Alternative View of Methodology." In *Rethinking Social Inquiry: Diverse Tools, Shared Standards*, 2d, eds. Henry E. Brady and David Collier 161–200 (Lanham, MD: Rowman and Littlefield, 2010); John Gerring, *Case Study Research* (Cambridge: Cambridge Univ. Press, 2007). Lastly, see Michael Schulte-Mecklenbeck, Anton Kühberger and Joseph G. Johnson, *A Handbook of Process Tracing Methods*, 2d (New York; London: Routledge, 2019).

11 Beach and Pedersen, *Process-Tracing*, 10–12. The authors refer to the first two uses of process-tracing as "theory-centric," and the last use as "case-centric." Beach and Pedersen, *Process-Tracing*, 12.

12 The best examples of these are most similar and most different comparative models. See Lijphart, "Comparative," 687–690.

13 See, for example, Theodore R. Gurr, *Handbook of Political Conflict: Theory and Research* (New York: Free Press, 1980); Thedore R. Gurr and Barbara Harff, *Ethnic Conflict in World Politics* (Boulder: Westview Press., 1994); and Barbara Harff, "No Lessons Learned from the Holocaust? Assessing Risks of Genocide and Political Mass Murder since 1955," *American Political Science Review* 97(1) (2003): 57–73. Other studies include Håvard Hegre, Tanja Ellingsen, Scott Gates, and Nils Peter Gleditsch, "Toward a Democratic Civil Peace? Democracy, Political

Change, and Civil War, 1816–1992," *American Political Science Review* 95(1) (2001): 33–48; Matthew Krain, "State-Sponsored Mass Murder: The Onset and Severity of Genocides and Politicides," *The Journal of Conflict Resolution* 41(3) (1997): 331–360; Tanja Ellingsen and Nils Peter Gleditsch, "Democracy and Armed Conflicts in the Third World." In *Causes of Conflict in Third World Countries*, eds. Ketil Volden and Dan Smith. 69–81. (Oslo: North-South Coalition and International Peace Research Institute, 1997); Tanja Ellingsen, "Colorful Community or Ethnic Witches' Brew? Multiethnicity and Domestic Conflict During and After the Cold War," *The Journal of Conflict Resolution* 44(2) (2000): 228–249; Benjamin Valentino, "Triggers of Mass Killing," *Report on a Research Project for the Political Instability Task Force* (Hanover: Dartmouth College, February 2016); Benjamin E. Goldsmith and Charles Butcher, "Genocide Forecasting: Past Accuracy and New Forecasts to 2020," *Journal of Genocide Research* 20(1) (2018): 90–107.

14 IDEA, "Frequently Asked Questions," at FAQs | The Global State of Democracy Indices (idea.int) (accessed March 19, 2022). IDEA ranks its measures for "Civil Society/Civic Engagement," "Judicial Access," "Local Government," and "Independent Judiciary" similarly, rating each on a scale between "0" and "1" with "1" indicating strength. IDEA derives the data for these scores from a variety of sources, including surveys of relevant actors in a country and government and NGO data. Yves Leterme, "Elections in International Democracy Assistance," *Brown Journal of World Affairs* 24(2) (2018): 81–95.

15 Robert Putnam, *Making Democracy Work* (Princeton, NJ: Princeton Univ. Press, 1993b), also *Bowling Alone* (New York: Simon and Schuster, 2000), and *Democracies in Flux: The Evolution of Social Capital in Contemporary Democracies* (Oxford: Oxford Univ. Press, 2002). Putnam and his theories of social capital have not been above criticism. See Derik Gelderblom, "The Limits to Bridging Social Capital: Power, Social Context and the Theory of Robert Putnam," *The Sociological Review* 66 (2018): 1309–1324. For other examples of work on the importance of social interaction and social capital, see Jan Aart Scholte, "Civil Society and Democracy in Global Governance," *Global Governance: A Review of Multilateralism and International Organizations* 8 (2002): 281–304; Timm Beichelt, Irene Hahn-Fuhr, Frank Schimmelfennig and Susann Worschech, *Civil Society and Democracy Promotion* (Springer: 2014); Erich J. Sommerfeldt, "The Civility of Social Capital: Public Relations in the Public Sphere, Civil Society, and Democracy," *Public Relations Review* 39 (2013): 280–289; Bernard Enjolras and Karl Henrik Sivesind eds., *Civil Society in Comparative Perspective* (Bingley, UK: Emerald Group Publishing Ltd., 2013) and Carolyn Elliott, *Civil Society and Democracy: A Reader* (Cambridge, UK: Cambridge Univ. Press, 2003). As this theory is applied more specifically to Africa, see Michael Bratton and Nicholas van de Walle, *Democratic Experiments in Africa: Regime Transitions in Comparative Perspective* (Cambridge: Cambridge Univ. Press, 1997).

16 Robert Putnam, "The Prosperous Community: Social Capital and Public Life," *The American Prospect* 4(13) (1993a): 1–11, 11.

17 The difference between bonding and bridging social capital is comparable to the concepts of generalized and particularized trust. Ana Kopren and Hans Westlund, "Bridging Versus Bonding Social Capital in Entrepreneurs' Networks: The Case of Post-Conflict Western Balkans," *Sustainability* 13 (2021): 1–18, 4.

18 Beth A. Simmons, *Mobilizing for Human Rights: International Law in Domestic Politics* (Cambridge, UK: Cambridge Univ. Press, 2009), 371.

19 Ebenezer Obadare, ed., *The Handbook of Civil Society in Africa* (New York: Springer New York, 2014); D. Lewis, *Civil Society in Non-Western Context:*

Reflections on the 'Usefulness' of A Concept (Civil Society Working Paper, No. 13) (2001); Michael Bratton, "Civil Society and Political Transition in Africa," *Institute for Development Research Project* 11(6) (1994); Malang B.S. Bojang, "The Debate around Civil Society in Africa: A Replica of 'Western Civil Society'," *International Journal of Research and Innovation in Social Science* (IJRISS) 3(4) (April 2019): 422–426; and Obiora Chinedu Okafor, *The African Human Rights System: Activist Forces and International Institutions* (Cambridge, UK: Cambridge Univ. Press, 2007). Civil society is not a panacea for all that troubles democracy. As Hearn demonstrates with the cases of South Africa, Uganda and Ghana, civil society organizations can be subject to influence by powerful actors both inside and outside of a country. Julie Hearn, "The 'Uses and Abuses' of Civil Society in Africa," *Review of African Political Economy* 87 (2001): 43–54.

20 *Societal engagement* combines IDEA's measure "Civic Engagement" with "Civil Society" into one interactive variable. For further details, see Chapter 6 of this volume.

21 See UN General Assembly, *Convention Against Torture and Other Cruel, Inhuman or Degrading Treatment or Punishment*, December 10, 1984, United Nations, Treaty Series, vol. 1465, available at: https://www.refworld.org/docid/3ae6b3a94.html; UN General Assembly, *International Convention for the Protection of All Persons from Enforced Disappearance*, December 20, 2006, available at: https://www.refworld.org/docid/47fdfaeb0.html; UN General Assembly, *International Covenant on Civil and Political Rights*, December 16, 1966, United Nations, Treaty Series, vol. 999, available at: https://www.refworld.org/docid/3ae6b3aa0.html; and Organization of African Unity, *African Charter on Human and Peoples' Rights* (Banjul Charter), June 27, 1981, CAB/LEG/67/3 rev. 5, 21 I.L.M. 58 (1982), available at: https://www.refworld.org/docid/3ae6b3630.html. All treaties accessed August 4, 2023.

22 Christopher LaMonica, "Moving Beyond 'Illiberal Democracy' in Sub-Saharan Africa: Recalling the Significance of Local Governance," *African Journal of Political Science and International Relations* 9(7) (2015): 268–283.

23 LaMonica argues that one of the obstacles to focusing more on the role of local governments has been the perception that local governments drain the resources of the central government. LaMonica, "Moving," 270. See also Anjali Thomas Bohlken, *Democratization from Above: The Logic of Local Democracy in the Developing World* (Cambridge: Cambridge Univ. Press, 2015).

24 Trond Vedeld, "Democratic Decentralisation and Poverty Reduction: Exploring the Linkages," *Forum for Development Studies* 30 (2003): 159–203; Craig Johnson, "Local Democracy, Democratic Decentralisation and Rural Development: Theories, Challenges and Options for Policy," *Development Policy Review* 19 (2001): 521–532; and Gordon Crawford, "Decentralization and the Limits to Poverty Reduction: Findings from Ghana." *Oxford Development Studies* 36 (2008): 235–258.

25 Zelalem Tesfaye Sirna, *Ethiopia: When The Gadaa Democracy Rules In A Federal State: Bridging Indigenous Institutions Of Governance To Modern Democracy*, Master's Thesis, University of Tromsø, Norway (2012); Immaculate N. Kizza, *Africa's Indigenous Institutions In Nation Building: Uganda* (Mellon Press, 1999); Jo Beall and Mduduzi Ngonyama, "Indigenous Institutions, Traditional Leaders And Elite Coalitions For Development: The Case Of Greater Durban, South Africa," *Crisis Research Centre, Working Paper, No. 55* (2009); Bertha Z. Osei-Hwedie, *Botswana: Indigenous Institutions, Civil Society and Government in Peace Building in Southern Africa* (Core Open Access, 2010); Yahaya Yakubu and Abubakar Aliyu Maigari, "Towards Enduring Democratic Polities in Africa: Prospects, Challenges and Trajectories," *International Journal of Research and*

Innovation in the Social Sciences 2(3) (2018): 47–51; and Martin Odei Ajei, "Kwasi Wiredu's Consensual Democracy: Prospects for Practice in Africa," *European Journal of Political Theory* 15 (2016): 445–466.

26 For more on this point, see Manu Lekunze and Ben Page, "Security in Cameroon: A Growing Risk of Persistent Insurgency," *Canadian Journal of International Studies* 57(1) (2023): 219–236.

27 Excellent sources of data for this topic are the African Governance Reports issued by the AU and produced by the African Peer Review Mechanism or "APRM." These reports are accessible through the AU's website at Sectoral Reports | African Union (au.int). See also UNDP, *Local Governments in Eastern Africa: An Analytical Study of Decentralization, Financing, Service Deliveries and Capacities* (2012); UNDP, *Building Bridges Between the State and the People* (2010).

28 Shimon Shetreet, "Creating a Culture of Judicial Independence: The Practical Challenge and the Conceptual and Constitutional Infrastructure." In *The Culture of Judicial Independence: Conceptual Foundations and Practical Challenges* eds. Shimon Shetreet and Christopher Forsyth (Leiden, The Netherlands; Boston, MA: Martinus Nijhoff Publishers, 2012), 37 at fn. 75. For studies providing specific country-wide analyses, see Erik S. Herron and Kirk A. Randazzo, "The Relationship Between Independence and Judicial Review in Post-Communist Courts," *The Journal of Politics* 65 (2003): 422–438 and Oya Yeğen, "Judicial 'Empowerment' Through Constitutional Change: The Case of Chilean and Turkish Constitutional Courts," *Research and Policy on Turkey* 3 (2018): 40–67. For a broader view of judicial independence, see Christopher M. Larkins, "Judicial Independence and Democratization: A Theoretical and Conceptual Analysis," *American Journal of Comparative Law* 44 (1996): 605–626.

29 Shetreet, "Creating," 37.

30 Shetreet, "Creating," 21–22; see also Lutz Oette, "Implementing the Prohibition of Torture: The Contribution And Limits Of National Legislation And Jurisprudence," *The International Journal of Human Rights* 16(5) (2012): 717–736, DOI: 10.1080/13642987.2012.685316.

31 With respect to illiberal rule in Hungary and Poland, see Bień-Kacała, Agnieszka. "Legislation in Illiberal Poland," *The Theory and Practice of Legislation* 9 (2021): 276–294. See also Marcel Strome, "Independence of the Judiciary: The European Perspective." In *The Culture of Judicial Independence: Conceptual Foundations and Practical Challenges* eds. Shimon Shetreet and Christopher Forsyth, 85–95 (Leiden, The Netherlands; Boston, MA: Martinus ijhoff Publishers, 2012).

32 Tabeth Masengu, "The Vulnerability of Judges in Contemporary Africa: Alarming Trends," *Africa Today* 63(4) (2017): 3–19; Lovemore Madhuku, "Constitutional Protection of the Independence of the Judiciary: A Survey of the Position in Southern Africa," *Journal of African Law* 46(2) (2002): 232–245; C.M. Peter, and M.K.B. Wambali, "Independence of the Judiciary in Tanzania: A Critique," *Verfassung Und Recht in Übersee/Law and Politics in Africa, Asia and Latin America* 21(1) (1988): 72–87, at http://www.jstor.org/stable/43109730; and Alemayehu G. Mariam, "Human Rights Matters in the New Millennium: The Critical Need for an Independent Judiciary in Ethiopia." *International Journal of Ethiopian Studies* 3(2) (2008): 123–142.

33 Peter Vondoepp, "The Problem of Judicial Control in Africa's Neopatrimonial Democracies: Malawi and Zambia," *Political Science Quarterly* 120(2) (2005): 275–301, at http://www.jstor.org/stable/20202519.

34 Claudiu D. Tufis and Alexander Hudson, *The Global State of Democracy Indices, Version 7* (Stockholm, Institute for Democracy and Electoral Assistance, 2023), 152–156.

35 Tufis and Hudson, *Global State*, 156.

36 Fuller, *Morality*, 81.
37 Fuller, *Morality*, 81.
38 Shetreet, "Creating," 41.
39 For the Torture Convention, this obligation can be found in Articles 13 and 14. For the Disappearances Convention, there are several articles that contain provisions about due process and judicial access, including Articles 17, 18 and 22. Similarly, for the ICCPR, this can be found in Articles 2(3), 9(2) and 14 for example.
40 Some of the best sources for information about truth and reconciliation commissions include Haron Muhammed, *South Africa's Truth and Reconciliation Commission: An Annotated Bibliography* (African Political, Economic, and Security Issues Series. New York: Nova, 2009) and Priscilla B. Hayner, *Unspeakable Truths: Transitional Justice and the Challenges of Truth Commissions* (New York: Routledge, 2011).
41 Tufis and Hudson, *Global State*, 57.
42 Munyai Anzanilufuno, *Overcoming the Corruption Conundrum in Africa: A Socio-Legal Perspective* (Newcastle upon Tyne, UK: Cambridge Scholars Publishing, 2020); John Mukum Mbaku, *Corruption in Africa: Causes, Consequences, and Cleanups* (Lanham, MD: Lexington Books, 2007); Sunday Bobai Agang, Chris Jones, and Pregala Pillay, eds. *A Multidimensional Perspective on Corruption in Africa: Wealth, Power, Religion and Democracy* (Newcastle upon Tyne, UK: Cambridge Scholars Publishing, 2019); Aborisade, Richard Abayomi, "Approaches to Preventing and Fighting Corruption in Nigeria." In *Corruption and Development in Nigeria*. eds. Ọláyínká Àkànle and David O. Nkpe. 169–181 (London: Routledge, 2022); and Emad Ahmad and Lina A. Issa, "Key Determinants of Corruption in the Middle East and North Africa," *International Journal of Research in Business and Social Science (2147–4478)* (2022): 410–420.
43 Danny Titus, "Corruption in the Face of Human Rights." In *A Multidimensional Perspective on Corruption in Africa: Wealth, Power, Religion and Democracy* eds. Sunday Bobai Agang, Chris Jones, and Pregala Pillay, 2–18 (Newcastle upon Tyne, UK: Cambridge Scholars Publishing, 2019), 2.
44 Bratton and van de Walle, *Democratic Experiments*; Joseph Ouma Oindo, "The Cultural Foundations of Corruption in Kenya," *The International Journal of Humanities & Social Studies* 9(3) (2021): https://doi.org/10.24940/theijhss/2021/v9/i3/HS2103-008; Patrick Acquah and E. Owusu, "Corruption, Culture and National Development - An Interrogation of Africa's Experience," (2017); Daniel Jordan Smith, *A Culture of Corruption: Everyday Deception and Popular Discontent in Nigeria* (Princeton, NJ: Princeton University Press, 2007); and J. P. Olivier de Sardan, "A Moral Economy of Corruption in Africa?" *The Journal of Modern African Studies* 37(1) (1999): 25–52.
45 Ernest Harsch, "Accumulators and Democrats: Challenging State Corruption in Africa," *The Journal of Modern African Studies* 31(1) (1993): 31–48 and Eliska Drapalova, Alina Mungiu-Pippidi, Bonnie Jo Palifka, and Jon Vrushi, "Corruption and the Crisis of Democracy: The Link between Corruption and the Weakening of Democratic Institutions," *Transparency International* (2019). See also United Nations Press Office, "Opening Session on Corruption, General Assembly Adopts Political Declaration with Road Maps to Help Countries Tackle Bribery, Money Laundering, Abuse of Power," GA/12329 (June 2, 2021), at Opening Special Session on Corruption, General Assembly Adopts Political Declaration with Road Maps to Help Countries Tackle Bribery, Money-Laundering, Abuse of Power | UN Press (accessed June 30, 2023); Matos de Oliveira and Ana Luíza. "Exploring the Links Between Corruption and Human Rights Violations with a Focus on the

Private Sector," *Journal of Human Rights and Social Work* 8 (2022): 51–56; L. Cardona, Horacio Ortiz and Daniel Arias Vazquez, "Corruption and Human Rights: Possible Relations," *Human Rights Quarterly* 40 (2018): 317–341; and Prosper Simbarashe Maguchu, *Transitional Justice and Socio-Economic Rights in Zimbabwe* (Springer, 2019), 27–52.

46 Tufis and Hudson, *Global State*, 149. "Absence of Corruption" is a composite of measures obtained from the International Country Risk Guide (L.D. Howell, "International Country Risk Guide Methodology," Political Risk Services [PRS Group], 2011), Freedom House, and Bertelsmann Stiftung's Transformation Index (Bertelsmann Stiftung, *Bertelsmann Transformation Index: Towards Democracy and a Market Economy* [Gütersloh: Bertelsmann Stiftung, 2023]), 149.

47 Transparency International, "CPI 2022: For Sub-Saharan Africa: Corruption Compounding Multiple Crises," at CPI 2022 for Sub-Saharan Africa: Corruption... - Transparency.org (accessed June 2, 2023).

48 Stephanie Diepeveen, "A Familiar Refrain: Political Discourse in and Facebook Use in Kenya." In *Social Media and Politics in Africa: Censorship and Security* ed. Maggie Dwyer and Thomas Molony, 214–235 (London: Zed Books, 2019), 215.

49 George Kakerwaivanane and Admire Mare, "'We are not just Voters. We are Citizens'," in Dwyer and Molony *Social Media*, 43–65.

50 Mediel Hove and Vincent Chenzi "Social Media, Civil Unrest, and Government Responses: The Zimbabwean Experience," *Journal of Contemporary African Studies* 38(1) (2020): 121–137, 123.

51 Natalia Waechter, "The Participative Role of Social Media for the Disadvantaged Young generation in the Arab Spring," *Österreichische Zeitschrift für Soziologie* 44 (2019): 217–236.

52 Mildred Golden Pryor, Mark Wulf, Wajid Alazani, Nouf Ahlamad, and Oluwaseun Shomefun, "The Role of Social Media in Transforming Governments and Nations," *International Journal of Business and Public Administration* 2(2) (Summer 2014): 19–30, 22; Magdalena Karolak, "Social Media and the Arab Spring in Bahrain: From Mobilization to Confrontation." In *The Arab Spring, Civil Society and Innovative Activism* ed Cenap Çakmak, 81–119 (London: Palgrave Macmillian, 2017); and Emmanuel Ufuophu-Biri and Lucky Ogheneruemu Ojoboh, "Social Media as a Tool for Political Resistance: Lessons from the Arab Spring and the Nigerian Protests," *Academic Journal of Interdisciplinary Studies* 6 (2017): 61–66.

53 For the latter perspective, see Francesca Comunello and Giuseppe Anzera. "Will the Revolution be Tweeted? A Conceptual Framework for Understanding the Social Media and the Arab Spring," *Islam and Christian–Muslim Relations* 23 (2012): 453–470. However, governments can and do also use social media for the spread of misinformation. On this point, see Kylie Moore-Gilbert Kylie and Zainab Najim Abdul-nabi. "Authoritarian Downgrading, (Self)Censorship and New Media Activism After the Arab Spring," *New Media & Society* 23 (2021): 875–893 as well as many of the chapters in the present volume.

54 Adrian Shahbaz, Allie Funk, and Kian Vesteinsson, *Freedom on the Net 2022: Countering an Authoritarian Overhaul of the Internet* (Freedom House, 2022), at FOTN2022Digital.pdf.

55 See Savina Gygli, Florian Haelg and Jan-Egbert Sturm, *KOF Working Papers, No. 439*. (Zurich: KOF Swiss Economic Institute, February 2018). Data are available from KOF Globalisation Index – KOF Swiss Economic Institute | ETH Zurich (accessed March 22, 2022).

56 Cali et al., "Big Promises"; Lance Minkler and Shawna Sweeney, "On the Indivisibility and Interdependence of Basic Rights in Developing Countries," *Human Rights Quarterly* 33(2) (May 2011): 351–396; David L. Cingranelli and

David L. Richards, "Measuring Government Effort to Respect Economic and Social Human Rights: A Peer Benchmark." In *Economic Rights Conceptual, Measurement, and Policy Issues* eds, Shareen Hertel and Lanse Minkler, 214–232. (Cambridge, UK: Cambridge Univ. Press, 2007); and Bratton and van de Walle, *Democratic Experiments*.

57 Minkler and Sweeney, "On the Indivisibility"; also, Neil Mitchell, and James McCormack, "Economic and Political Explanations of Human Rights Violations," *World Politics*, 40 (1988): 476–498; Bruce Moon and William J. Dixon, "Basic Needs and Growth-Welfare Trade-offs," *International Studies Quarterly*, 36 (1992): 191–212.

58 Polity 5, "Regime Authority Characteristics and Transitions Datasets, Coup's d'état, 1946–2021," (Vienna, VA: Center for Systemic Peace, 2022) at INSCR Data Page (systemicpeace.org); Global Terrorism Database, University of Maryland National Consortium for the Study of Terrorism and Responses to Terrorism, 2009–2022), at GTD | Global Terrorism Database (umd.edu).

59 See International Commission on Intervention and State Sovereignty, *The Responsibility to Protect: The Report of the International Commission on Intervention and State Sovereignty* (Ottawa: International Development Research Centre, 2001), 33.

60 This is a rather voluminous literature. Some of the most significant studies are Hegre et al., "Toward a Democratic Civil Peace"; Håvard Hegre. "Democracy and Armed conflict," *Journal of Peace Research* 51 (2014): 159–172; Krain, "State-Sponsored"; Ellingsen and Gleditsch, "Democracy and Armed Conflicts"; Nils Petter Gleditsch, Håvard Hegre and Håvard Strand, "Democracy and Civil War." In *Handbook of War Studies III*, ed. Manus Midlarsky (Ann Arbor, MI: University of Michigan Press, 2007); and Carl Henrik Knutsen, and Håvard Mokleiv Nygård. "Institutional Characteristics and Regime Survival: Why are Semi-democracies less durable than Autocracies and Democracies?" *American Journal of Political Science* 59 (2015): 656–670.

61 Amy Niang, "Understanding Complex New Wars in Africa: The Example of the Sahel." In *Researching Peacebuilding in Africa: Reflecting on Theory, Fieldwork and Context*, eds. Ismail Rashad and Amy Niang, 131–148 (London: Routledge, 2020).

62 As this pertains to regional income inequality, see Gudrun Østby and Jan Ketl Rød. "Regional Inequalities and Civil Conflict in 21 Sub-Saharan African Countries, 1986–2004," *International Studies Quarterly* 53(2) (2009): 301–324.

63 Sam R. Bell, K. Chad Clay, and Amanda Murdie, "Neighborhood Watch: Spatial Effects of Human Rights INGOs," *Journal of Politics* 74(2) (2012): 354–368.

64 See, for example, Rebecca Brubaker and Thomas Dörfler, "UN Sanctions and the Prevention of Conflict," *United Nations University Centre for Policy, Research Conflict Prevention Series*, 4 (August 2017); also, Matthew Krain, "The Effect of Economic Sanctions on the Severity of Genocides or Politicides," *Journal of Genocide Research* 19(1) (2017): 88–111. For an argument against the ineffectiveness of sanctions, see Daniel W. Drezner, "The United States of Sanctions: The Use and Abuse of Economic Coercion," *Foreign Affairs* 100(5) (2021): 142–154.

65 Roland Paris, "Saving Liberal Peacebuilding," *Review of International Studies* 36(2) (April 2010): 337–365, 338; also 347–354.

66 The UN has since made several substantive reforms to the peace mission apparatus, including the creation of the Peacebuilding Commission and Support Office in 2005. UN Secretary General, 2019-SG-Report.pdf (un.org), accessed July 26, 2023; also United Nations Peacebuilding at PEACEBUILDING | (un.org) (accessed July 26, 2023) and UN Department of Peacekeeping Operations, at Department of Peace Operations | United Nations Peacekeeping (accessed July 26, 2023).

Sanctions are also frequently criticized for their inattention to the harmful impact they have on domestic societies. Robin Wright, "Why Sanctions Too Often Fail," *The New Yorker* (March 7, 2022). However, as with UN and other peace missions, the contributors to this volume adopt a pragmatic perspective on sanctions and suggest they are generally effective as a means of altering a state's behavior. For an excellent discussion about the challenges associated with the special rapporteur mechanisms, see the special issue of *The International Journal of Human Rights* (January 2011).

67 The contributors to this volume offer this suggestion even after considering the allegations of sexual misconduct made against UN and other peacekeepers, the insensitive way peace missions tend to be conducted, and a general disregard for the domestic consequences that accrue because of foreign direct investment (FDI). On these issues, see Skye Wheeler, "UN Peacekeeping has a Sexual Abuse Problem," *The Hill* (January 11, 2020) at UN Peacekeeping has a Sexual Abuse Problem | Human Rights Watch (hrw.org), accessed March 29, 2022; Henry F. Carey, *Peacebuilding Paradigms: The Impact of Theoretical Diversity on Implementing Sustainable Peace* (Cambridge: Cambridge University Press, 2020); Abutu Lawrence Okolo and Joseph O. Akwu, "China's Foreign Direct Investment in Africa's Land: Hallmarks Of Neo-Colonialism Or South–South Cooperation?" *Africa Review* 8 (2016): 44–59; Erik Beuck, Nourah Shuaibi and Wonjae Hwang, "Cross-border M&A, Greenfield FDI And The Onset Of Intrastate Conflict, 1990–2015," *International Trade, Politics and Development* 6(3) (2022): 90–106; and Farhan Ahmed, Imtiaz Ali, Shazia Kousar, and Saira Ahmed, "The Environmental Impact of Industrialization And Foreign Direct Investment: Empirical Evidence From Asia-Pacific Region," *Environmental Science and Pollution Research International* 29 (2022): 29778–29792.

68 KOF Globalisation Index – KOF Swiss Economic Institute | ETH Zurich, March 26, 2022.

69 Data on UN peacekeeping missions both past and present are available at United Nations Peacekeeping.

70 The Global Sanctions Database is a product of the Drexel University School of Economics, Hochschule Konstanz, University of Applied Sciences and Kiel Institute for the World Economy and is available from Global Sanctions Database – GSDB (accessed March 26, 2022).

71 Li-Ju Chen, "Female Policymakers and Educational Expenditures: Cross-Country Evidence," *European Journal of Law and Economics* 51(1): 129–155; Jamille Bigio and Rachel Vogelstein, "Women Under Attack: The Backlash Against Female Politicians," *Foreign Affairs* 99(1) (Jan/Feb 2020): 131–138; R. Chattopadhyay and E. Duflo, "Women and Policymakers: Evidence from a Randomized Policy Experiment in India," *Econometrica* 72(5) (2004): 1401–1443; and T. Besley and A. Case, "Political Institutions and Policy Choices: Evidence from the United States," *Journal of Economic Literature* 41(1) (2003): 7–73.

72 IPU Parline, Global Data on National Parliaments, at Parline: the IPU's Open Data Platform | Your one-stop-shop for information about national parliaments.

73 UN Women, at Welcome | UN Women – Headquarters.

74 Brenan O'Boyle and Daniel Ramos, "Bolivia Coup Fiasco Lays Bare a Divided Country in Political, Economic Crises, *Reuters* (June 27, 2024) at Bolivia coup fiasco lays bare a divided country in political, economic crisis | Reuters, accessed July 1, 2024.

75 Ellen L. Lutz and Kathryn Sikkink. "International Human Rights Law and Practice in Latin America," *International Organization* 54 (2000): 633–659.

3 The International Legal Framework for Prohibitions against Torture, Disappearances, and Extrajudicial Killings

Stacey M. Mitchell

Introduction

All African States that are parties to the international and regional treaties prohibiting torture, disappearances, and political killings are required to comply with the provisions of these treaties.[1] Given that the Torture and Disappearances Conventions, and the International Covenant on Civil and Political Rights (ICCPR),[2] create monitoring bodies to oversee compliance, obligate members to incorporate provisions of these treaties into their domestic legal systems, and pertain to many crimes that are *jus cogens* offenses, they could be characterized as approaching something like hard law, as opposed to soft law, which contains no such obligations, or, in the alternative, contains norms that are vague and leave "almost complete discretion to the parties as regards [...] implementation."[3] In this latter example, a treaty that is considered soft law is said to lack the requirements of precision, obligation, and likely delegation.[4]

The fact of the matter is that all three regimes are soft law regimes. Depending on the context, States incur few penalties for violating the rights embodied in each of these regimes, save for condemnation by the respective monitoring body and the international community at large. The Human Rights Committee or CCPR, the Disappearances Committee (CED), and the Committee Against Torture (CAT) are "quasi-judicial" bodies that have no power to enforce their recommendations.[5] At the same time, many scholars demonstrate that the reports and comments issued by these bodies do have a lasting impact on the institutionalization of norms prohibiting these offenses.[6]

These three treaty regimes represent areas of International Human Rights Law (IHRL), as opposed to International Humanitarian Law (IHL) which governs conflicts and wars. If extrajudicial killings, disappearances, and torture are perpetrated in the context of war or are widespread and systematic and target a group based on that group's identity, then depending on the context and intent, they move into the realm of war crimes, crimes against humanity, and genocide, the commission of which obligates States to punish the individual perpetrators of these offenses domestically or refer them to the International Criminal Court (ICC).[7]

DOI: 10.4324/9781003471677-5

In terms of their application, there are several obstacles associated with each of the three regimes, particularly for African States. Regarding torture, for example, there is the issue of whether parties to the Torture Convention are required to make the crime a distinct one in their criminal statutes. The CAT, for example, maintains that torture should be a separate offense under domestic law.[8] Others, however, contend that the more important matter is whether a government possesses the appropriate legal framework (e.g., due process provisions, jurisdictional and investigative capacity) to fully address instances of torture when they occur.[9]

The present chapter assesses the torture, disappearances, and ICCPR regimes and some of their related special mechanisms procedures. This chapter first considers member status for these UN regimes and their related protocols. The mandates and institutions of each of these UN treaty-based bodies are examined in detail, as well as the derogation and reservations processes. This chapter then addresses the Universal Periodic Review (UPR), a process that, although separate from the reporting processes mentioned in this chapter, does have some overlap. This chapter concludes with an assessment of the work of these regimes as per the International Relations (IR) paradigms of Realism, Neo-liberalism/Institutionalism, and Constructivism, and compares these arguments to the argument put forth by this study.

Treaty Membership[10]

As discussed in greater detail below, derogations have been made by some African States to some of the rights protected by these treaties and some refuse to participate in certain treaty procedures, such as the inquiry procedure under Article 20 of the Torture Convention (Table 3.1).

Data on membership to the Second Optional Protocol to the International Covenant on Civil and Political Rights (OP 2) which addresses the death penalty are also included.[11] Treaty ratification/accession is a significant step these countries have made. How much of a critical juncture treaty membership means in terms of a government's policymaking behavior is represented somewhat by the extent to which that State cooperates with the institutional framework of a treaty regime.

The UN Human Rights Regimes

International Covenant on Civil and Political Rights

The ICCPR contains 53 articles, the first 27 of which pertain to civil and political rights. Article 4 of the ICCPR permits derogation of certain rights during times of national crisis. The rights which State parties *cannot* derogate from include Articles 6 (right to life) and 7 (torture).

ICCPR *General Comment No. 29* provides specific details on what a derogation process must entail. These conditions include the declaration of a

Table 3.1 Treaty Membership Status

Country	*ICCPR*	*OP I*	*OP 2*	*TORTURE*	*OPCAT*	*DISAPP*	*BANJUL*
ALGERIA	x	x		x			x
ANGOLA	x	x	x	x			x
BENIN	x	x	x	x	x	x	x
BOTSWANA	x			x			x
BURKINA FASO	x	x		x	x	x	x
BURUNDI	x			x	x		x
CABO VERDE	x	x	x	x	x	x	x
CAMEROON	x	x		x			x
CENT. AFR. REP.	x	x		x	x	x	x
CHAD	x	x		x			x
COMOROS				x			x
CONGO REP.	x	x		x			x
COTE D'IVOIRE	x	x		x		x	x
DEM. REP. CONGO	x	x		x	x		x
DJIBOUTI	x	x	x	x			x
EGYPT	x			x			x
EQUAT. GUINEA	x	x		x			x
ERITREA	x			x			x
ESWATINI	x			x			x
ETHIOPIA	x			x			x
GABON	x		x	x	x	x	x
GAMBIA	x	x	x	x		x	x
GHANA	x	x		x	x		x
GUINEA	x	x		x			x
GUINEA BISSAU	x	x	x	x			x
KENYA	x			x			x
LESOTHO	x	x		x		x	x
LIBERIA	x		x	x	x		x
LIBYA	x	x		x			x
MADAGASCAR	x	x	x	x	x		x
MALAWI	x	x		x		x	x
MALI	x	x		x	x	x	x
MAURITANIA	x			x	x	x	x
MAURITIUS	x	x		x	x		x
MOROCCO	x	x		x	x	x	
MOZAMBIQUE	x		x	x	x		x
NAMIBIA	x	x	x	x			x
NIGER	x	x		x	x	x	x
NIGERIA	x			x	x	x	x
RWANDA	x		x	x	x		x
SAO TOME/PRIN.	x	x	x	x			x
SENEGAL	x	x		x	x	x	x
SEYCHELLES	x	x	x	x		x	x
SIERRA LEONE	x	x		x			x
SOMALIA	x	x		x			x
SOUTH AFRICA	x	x	x	x	x	x	x

(*Continued*)

Table 3.1 (Continued)

Country	*ICCPR*	*OP I*	*OP 2*	*TORTURE*	*OPCAT*	*DISAPP*	*BANJUL*
SOUTH SUDAN				x	x		x
SUDAN	x			x		x	x
TANZANIA	x						x
TOGO	x	x	x	x	x	x	x
TUNISIA	x	x		x	x	x	x
UGANDA	x	x		x			x
ZAMBIA	x	x		x		x	x
ZIMBABWE	x						x

state of emergency (SOE) by the State wishing to invoke Article 4, and the requirements that this SOE be temporally limited and nondiscriminatory in nature. The justification of an SOE must meet the criteria of a "public emergency which threatens the life of the nation," be necessarily related to the goals of the proclaiming State, be narrow in scope and proportional to the crisis in question, and be governed by the laws of the State.[12] Per Article 4(3), all parties to the ICCPR must be informed of this declaration of emergency by the UN Secretary-General. This notification "is essential not only for the discharge of the Committee's functions, [...] but also to permit other States parties to monitor compliance with the provisions of the Covenant."[13]

To date, some African States have issued declarations for SOEs, including Zambia, Gabon, South Africa, and Egypt. These SOEs have concerned internal conflicts, and/or the COVID pandemic.[14] Of the many problems associated with COVID pandemic derogations, in particular, is that many States invoked derogations from treaties that do not contain such provisions.[15] As a legacy of the post-9/11 period, States have increasingly relied on SOEs to deal with a variety of different internal problems, including political instability and terrorism.[16] These SOEs persisted in many cases for years and without the oversight of an international body like the CCPR.

Per Article 40 of the ICCPR, parties are obligated to report on their progress in implementing these rights to the CCPR. The CCPR also has the power to accept complaints that parties make against other parties for the latter's infraction of their obligations under the treaty (Article 41). However, this only applies to those States that have recognized the competence of the CCPR to hear interstate complaints.[17] The CCPR is also responsible for the issuance of general comments, monitoring interstate and individual complaints procedures,[18] and taking interim measures to "avoid irreparable damage to an alleged victim of a violation of the rights protected by the ICCPR."[19] No less important is the fact that the CCPR is the body that has the *final* authority over SOEs.[20]

Torture and extrajudicial killings are prohibited by the ICCPR. Disappearances are considered by the CCPR to be a violation of Article 6 of the ICCPR, and the CCPR has linked disappearances with torture and/or other cruel, inhuman, and degrading treatment.[21] Disappearances are also defined as a crime against humanity under Article 7(2)(i) of the Rome Statute.[22]

It should be noted that reservations to the ICCPR have been made by several States parties. As Redgwell contends, reservations "reveal the inadequacies of a reservations regime which is dependent on the individual responses of States, for these responses [are] inconsistent."[23] They also threaten the integrity of the treaty itself. Case in point, US reservations to Articles 6 and 7 of the ICCPR (among others).[24] The fact that sweeping reservations have been made to the ICCPR, most of which took place with little or no criticism by other parties, prompted the CCPR to issue *General Comment 24(52)* in 1994.[25] It is worthy of noting that *very* few African parties to these three conventions have entered reservations, declarations, or understandings.[26]

The individual complaints procedure is addressed by the First Optional Protocol to the ICCPR (OP I).[27] Article 2 of OP I states that "individuals who claim that any of their rights enumerated in the Covenant have been violated and who have exhausted all domestic remedies may submit a written communication to the Committee for consideration." There are a certain number of conditions that attach to the procedure, including that all available domestic remedies be first exhausted by complainants.[28] If these criteria are satisfied, the CCPR will be able to consider the substantive merits of the communication.

One of the major challenges for the CCPR is its limited ability to enforce its recommendations.[29] The fact that the CCPR is based on voluntary compliance is not a deal breaker per se. Most African States have complied with the reporting process. However, the lengths to which parties have gone in fulfilling the ICCPR's other requirements is another matter altogether.

Unlike the Torture Convention, there is no specific requirement in the ICCPR that parties prosecute offenses of torture, or violations of any of the other provisions of the ICCPR, including the violation of one's right to life or their freedom of movement (Article 12), for example, or that they criminalize any of these offenses.[30] For these reasons the ICCPR is accurately characterized as a soft law regime. A similar observation applies to the African Charter on Human and Peoples' Rights or the Banjul Charter,[31] although it is worth noting that State reporting to the CCPR exceeds that to the African Commission on Human and Peoples' Rights (ACHPR).[32]

Returning to the derogations issue, Fornaroli and Rettig associate the misuse of the process to the "unilateral character of the exercise of derogation."[33] Parties to the ICCPR (and other human rights treaties) make the determination of which rights will be suspended and when, with or without, it seems, the input or oversight of any of the human rights treaty bodies, practically speaking. Arguments that seek to justify derogation as a pragmatic necessity or a moral requirement fail to recognize the severity of consequences that arise when a suspension or alteration of human rights obligations takes place. In these cases, the consent of society is not required for derogation, nor is the derogation process clearly spelled out in Article 4 of the ICCPR (or any other human rights treaty).[34]

Moreover, when it comes to compliance with the ICCPR (and other human rights treaty regimes), there is the matter of resources and capacity, which limit a government's ability to fully comply with its treaty obligations.[35] Looking specifically at ICCPR compliance, Cole found that a State's bureaucratic capacity—its ability to logistically meet its obligations, particularly those involving substantial institutional reforms—has the strongest independent impact on that State's human rights behavior.[36] As he contends:

> Independently of ICCPR membership and other standard control variables, bureaucratic efficacy improves both physical integrity and empowerment rights outcomes. Effective, autonomous, and stable bureaucracies not only enable governments to fulfill "positive" empowerment rights, but they also empower them to protect "negative" physical integrity rights.[37]

Treaty implementation, therefore, may be *less* about a government's willingness to comply with its obligations, and more about its ability to do so. This is especially true for countries in transition. As Souillac contends, transitional communities with differing historical, political, social, and cultural backgrounds are a major challenge to the effective globalization of human rights norms. Whether because of local power and economic struggles, cultural and social challenges to human rights definitions, or competing strategies of implementation on the part of external agencies, clear communication on human rights issues seldom exists.[38] In cases like Somalia, the fact that the country's population had no security of person or land *before* the collapse of the Barre regime in 1992 means that the prospects for the institutionalization of human rights in Somalia today are rather dim.[39]

Many African governments are extremely politically fragile, the hold of government leaders on the reins of power tenuous at best. Often, leaders take the "logic of consequences" into account before anything else.[40] This has wider implications for explaining the noncompliance of many African governments with a range of human rights treaties. As the chapters in this book indicate, most African countries continue to experience a variety of internal conditions that only make compliance more difficult, including matters of economic and political instability.

UN data about reporting and visits from the Subcommittee on Torture (SPT) and related special procedures mechanisms[41] are not included in this chapter in efforts to save space.[42] For now, it is worth mentioning that UN reporting data indicate that most African member governments have engaged in the reporting process with the CCPR.[43] However, many of these reports were and are currently overdue.[44] Frequent reasons given for delay are insufficient resources and a lack of capacity due to conflict, poverty, and other related conditions of internal instability.[45]

Throughout the entire reporting process nongovernmental organizations (NGOs) and National Human Rights Institutions (NHRIs) play an essential role. NHRIs are officially accredited organizations that meet that *Paris Principles* and actively work to

> encourage and assist the State Party to meet its reporting obligations; provide the Committee with independent information on the national implementation of the Covenant; and work on follow-up to, and monitor implementation of, the Committee's concluding observations, views and other decisions.[46]

Nationally, NHRIs educate the public and government about human rights, including what is required for their implementation.[47]

NGOs also take part in the reporting and review processes. They provide reports to the CCPR (and other reporting bodies) detailing the status of human rights protections by a government, highlighting infractions and episodes of impunity or lack of accountability. NGOs contribute to the "constructive dialogue" between "States parties, United Nations entities and national human rights institutions."[48] NGOs have been referred to by Korey as fulfilling "the indispensable function, projected by Eleanor Roosevelt, of serving as the 'curious grapevine' that would enlighten everyone about their rights and channel information about human rights violations to the world community."[49] Whether we're talking about domestic NGOs or international ones, they serve as valuable advocates for human rights progress.[50] They also clarify reports and fill in any missing or incorrect information. As discussed throughout this volume, the ability of NGOs to function, to voice their opinions, to investigate abuses of the law, to fight the good fight as an essential part of the communities of practice that shape and impact the lawmaking process is extremely significant.

However, not all NGOs are pro-compliance with the decisions of monitoring bodies, like the CCPR or CAT. Van Staden found that "[c]ivil society's role is more Janus-faced," in that civil society groups "may also comprise 'pro-violation constituencies' that generate political pressure against compliance with human rights norms."[51] In the African context, groups like the Alliance for the Defense of Democracy in Nigeria and the Group of Malian Patriots in Mali, for example, work to bolster support for political actors (sometimes anti-government forces) through misinformation and intimidation, particularly through social media.[52] When these organizations come to have a greater influence over a government's decision-making behavior than their pro-compliance cohorts, civil society acts to reinforce noncompliant behavior.[53]

Efforts to restrict access to legitimate *pro*-compliance NGOs is part of a recent trend that Van De Velde has called "a new form of oppression by authoritarian governments and a means of restricting citizens' exercise of their fundamental civil and political rights."[54] Categorizing international NGOs as "foreign agents" through legislation, countries such as China,

Russia, Sudan, Georgia, Ethiopia, and Nigeria, for example, have hampered the work these NGOs can do, their ability to meet with government officials, and obtain overseas funding, all for the purposes of limiting government criticism and restricting citizens access to a valuable resource.[55] The shrinking public space for legitimate NGOs is alarming, much of it having to do with "the proliferation of counter-terrorism measures—often promoted by the west—that sweep civil society organizations into their embrace, either inadvertently or deliberately."[56]

Torture Regime

The UN torture regime is grounded in several international treaties and declarations, the most prominent of which are the Torture Convention and its Optional Protocol (OPCAT).[57] As Carey and Mitchell state,

> [t]he quarter century of activity by the Committee against Torture [...], clarified the full agenda of torture reform. However, the international torture regime also emerged from the relevant parts of treaties and soft (not technically legally binding but influential) law promulgations from European and American regional bodies, and the UN-Charter and treaty-based human rights bodies.[58]

Like the disappearances regime, the torture regime is a "single-issue regime."[59] The strength of this regime has increased over time. Donnelly considers the torture regime to be an example of an "implementation regime" or one in which parties are implementing provisions of a treaty, although, the treaty regime itself lacks a strong enforcement power.[60] At the same time, the torture regime is arguably the strongest of the three human rights regimes as it requires far more effort on the part of parties to ensure for compliance, particularly for those States that also ratified/acceded to the OPCAT.

Parties are obligated to report their progress to the CAT annually. The Convention makes it optional for parties to recognize the competence of the CAT to consider communications from a State party that is making allegations against another party for violation of the Convention (Article 21), to recognize the use of an inquiry procedure (Article 20), and to recognize the individual complaints procedure (Article 22). Presently of the 52 African States who are parties to the Torture Convention, only 11 recognize the competence of the CAT to hear individual complaints (Algeria, Burundi, Cameroon, Ghana, Guinea Bissau, Morocco, Senegal, Seychelles, South Africa, Togo, and Tunisia).[61] With respect to follow-up procedures on CAT decisions and to mandate compliance, CAT established a Special Rapporteur.[62]

OPCAT establishes the SPT. Representatives of the SPT conduct in-state visits to determine the status of persons housed in detention facilities when there is information that "persons are or may be deprived of their liberty, either by virtue of an order given by a public authority or at its instigation or with its consent or acquiescence." Since 2007, 17 reports documenting the prevalence of torture in detention facilities worldwide have been issued by SPTs.[63] Only a few African parties to OPCAT have had visits from the SPT as of the time of this writing. [64]

Articles 3 and 17 of the OPCAT require parties to create some type of National Preventive Mechanism (NPM). Per Article 19 the NPM's purpose is to

> regularly examine the treatment of the persons deprived of their liberty [...], to make recommendations to the relevant authorities with the aim of improving the treatment and the conditions of the persons deprived of their liberty ... [and] to submit proposals and observations concerning existing or draft legislation.[65]

The Office of the High Commissioner for Human Rights (OHCHR) touts the OPCAT as being the "only exclusively preventive international human rights treaty and the first instrument entrusting national bodies [...] with a role in the implementation of that international treaty."[66] NPMs are to be able to conduct unannounced visits to a wide range of detention facilities (prisons, police stations, military detention centers, etc.), be independent of State control, and have sufficient expertise and resources, not to mention freedom from harassment.[67] One of their purposes is to engage in meaningful dialogue with governments (and other relevant stakeholders) to ensure for progress on the prevention of torture.

There is also a UN Special Rapporteur on Torture. Created by the UN Human Rights Commission (the predecessor to today's Human Rights Council) via Res. 1985/33, the rapporteur works independently of CAT, but also collaborates with CAT in "exchanging information, reports and documents of common interest," as well as with the SPT to avoid duplication of work.[68] Unlike the CAT, and like the Special Rapporteur on Extrajudicial Killings, the Special Rapporteur on Torture investigates allegations of torture that take place in *any* member State of the UN and reports directly to the Human Rights Council. Additional information about these and other special procedures are included in Chapter 5 of this volume.

In practice, the problems associated with the application of the Torture Convention and OPCAT are similar, if not greater than, the CCPR as the creation of a NPM stands as one more institutional requirement that demands the use of a government's resources. States are required to create NPMs within one year after their ratification of OPCAT. Of the 25 African member States to OPCAT, only 12 have created a NPM as of the time of this writing. Most are past the required one-year deadline. Even counting for the funds available to parties (per Article 26 of OPCAT) to bolster their NPM's capacity, many have not met their obligations under OPCAT.[69]

Many African States could be considered to fit the category of the "delegative democracy," in that "other government branches delegate their oversight and checks and balances to the executive branch, which operates with autonomy and with law-breaking impunity."[70] This is especially the case when the use of torture enjoys popular support. Moreover, torture is often perpetrated by governments in secret and at times with the use of "stealth techniques" that evade detection.[71] In many of the countries that are the subject of this volume torture takes place in detention centers or camps far removed from the eyes of local communities.[72]

A related issue concerns how "torture" is defined in Article 1 of the Torture Convention, particularly as concerns the "lawful sanctions" clause, which considers torture to *not* include "pain or suffering arising from, inherent in or incidental to lawful sanctions." Reporting States will often take issue with what the CAT recommends about prison conditions, the use of corporal punishment, and a host of other practices which they consider to be lawful. Coracini writes about the vagueness of the phrase and the unwillingness of the CAT to rule definitively on what acts constitute lawful sanctions.[73] In a review conducted by the author of this chapter of all CAT annual reports from 2006 (the date of Coracini's piece) until today, the CAT's use of the term "lawful sanctions" rarely, if ever, came up.[74] Consequently, it is not shocking to find that the statutes of parties continue to include various forms of questionable punishment deemed to be lawful, like corporal punishment.

Simmons contends that the more democratic the regime—the more political experience that regime has with democratic traditions like rule of law—the more likely their compliance with the Convention (and other human rights treaties). To test this thesis, she examines the impact that extant legal traditions in a would-be ratifying State and the extent to which that State's neighbors have ratified the Torture Convention have on influencing whether that State chooses to become a member of the torture regime. Controlling for a host of factors, including the status of civil liberties protections in a State, the legality of the death penalty, the use of justice mechanisms, and internal conditions of political and economic instability, she finds that not all regimes that commit to the Torture Convention adhere to their promises.[75]

It is accurate to say that torture practices tend to be deeply embedded within a country's institutional history.[76] As stated in previous chapters, the contributors to this volume seek to go one step further than Simmons and test to see what impact environmental or contextual phenomena has on the inclusiveness of the communities involved in the creation of human rights legislation, specifically legislation prohibiting torture, disappearances, and extrajudicial killings, not to mention holding State actors accountable for their violations of these policies.

Disappearances Regime

As Sarkin writes

> [e]nforced disappearances regularly occur in Africa and remain one of the worst human rights violations. They infringe on many human rights, including the right to life, the right not to be tortured, the right to dignity, the right to a fair trial, and the right of access to justice.[77]

Similar to torture and extrajudicial killings, enforced disappearances are a violation of international humanitarian law and, if perpetrated in a widespread and systematic manner, international criminal law as well.[78] The crime of enforced disappearances has its roots in international humanitarian law stretching back before the work of the Nuremberg Tribunal; specifically, to the humanitarian function of protecting families during times of conflict.[79]

Disappearances have long been a subject of concern of the UN and its treaty bodies, including the CCPR. According to OHCHR, disappearances are "used as a strategy aimed at spreading terror within society."[80] However, despite the significance of the crime, few States are party to the Disappearances Convention.

The Working Group on Enforced or Involuntary Disappearances (WGD) estimates in its 2023 report that of the 47,774 active cases of enforced disappearances between 1980 and 2023, over 10 percent were in African countries, the bulk of them in Algeria (3,287 cases).[81]

The frequency of disappearances has been attributed by scholars to the fact that disappearances serve as a handy means for a government to get rid of its critics, opponents, and other *persona non grata* without having to kill them.[82] Payne and Abouharb suggest that there are less costs associated with enforced disappearances due to the difficulties in establishing the *ratione materiae* of the crime, not to mention who the responsible parties are for its commission.[83] Without a body there is no crime. Hence, many cases of disappearances remain unsolved.[84]

Article 2 of the Disappearances Convention defines "enforced disappearance" as "the arrest, detention, abduction or any other forms of deprivation of liberty by agents of the State or by persons or groups of persons acting with the authorization, support or acquiescence of the State," accompanied by a refusal of the State to acknowledge the disappearance or provide information regarding same.[85]

The Disappearances Convention has provisions requiring States parties to criminalize disappearances (Article 4), investigate the perpetration of disappearances (Article 3), to prosecute perpetration by nationals (Article 6), to extradite foreign perpetrators to the appropriate bodies (Article 10) or domestically prosecute them (Article 11), and to *not* engage in refoulement (Article 16), among other requirements.

Article 26 of the Disappearances Convention creates the CED, which receives and assesses reports from all parties to the Convention, makes observations and recommendations on these reports, and under Article 30 may receive "urgent" requests for investigation by family members of those disappeared, their counsel or representatives, and others who have a "legitimate interest," in a case. However, like the Torture Convention, States can opt out of recognizing the competence of the CED to receive communications from alleged victims (Article 31) as well as receive allegations of abuse made against that party by another party (Article 32).

Compared to the Torture and the ICCPR regimes, monitoring of disappearances in Africa is a far greater problem given the lack of membership to the Disappearances Convention and/or voluntary cooperation with the Working Group.[86] Moreover, for those States that do seek to investigate cases of disappearances (whether they are a party to the Disappearances Convention or not) there is still the matter of political will and government capacity.

Universal Periodic Review

Like other States around the world, African States are required to undergo a UPR every four years. The goal of the UPR is to encourage and promote the protection and promotion of human rights and do so by "assessing States' human rights records and addressing human rights violation whenever they occur," and providing States with the technical assistance to "enhance their capacity to deal effectively with human rights challenges and to share best practices in the field of human rights among States and other stakeholders."[87]

Etone has found that African States tend to comply *more* with the UPR process than with treaty bodies like CCPR, CAT, or CED.[88] Some of the reasons for this include the fact that African States respond more favorably to recommendations made by other African States (compared to non-African ones), as well as the fact that factors such as regionalism allow African States in the UPR to shield allies from harsh criticism.[89] Kälin has raised the issue of whether UPR compliance is more ritual than practice as the commission of torture, killings, and disappearances continue to prevail in these States.[90] Looking at the first cycle of reporting to the UPR, he suggests that its focus primarily on "non-confrontational" issues like treaty ratification or promoting a particular right without any further qualification did little to address the larger issues that require the greatest action in a particular country.[91]

Indeed, a review of the most recent reports issued by the Working Group of the UPR for States that are involved in protracted conflicts, such as Somalia and Sudan, demonstrates that the summary of each respective State's human rights progress is very limited and does not delve into issues of special concern including the use of torture or gender-related violence.[92] These reports include observations made by members of the Working Group as well as the Group's recommendations, neither of which devote much detail to the issues of concern, save for recommendations to ratify various human rights treaties and/or implement domestic policies.[93] The fact that so many areas of human rights are covered by the UPR mechanism simultaneously likely contributes to the lack of substantive content in these reports. However, this speaks directly to Kälin's argument about the process being more of a ritual that States engage in rather than producing any real changes.

Conclusions

When it comes to treaty membership and compliance, the three major paradigms in International Relations—Realism, Institutionalism/Liberalism, and Constructivism—differ with respect as to what drives the behavior of parties. Treaties limit sovereignty, so there are always costs involved in membership and compliance. To realists, "the extent of torture reform implementation correlates negatively with perceived national security threats."[94] African States over the past two decades have certainly experienced their share of attacks from groups such as *al Qaeda* in the Islamic Maghreb (AQIM), Islamic State in the Greater Sahara (ISGS), and *Boko Haram*; the list goes on. Realism would suggest that these States are merely protecting their internal security by using whatever means they have to investigate, prosecute, and/or detain individuals who pose a threat to the State.

From an institutionalist perspective, it is the monitoring processes of organizations like the CAT or CED that increase compliance and, in so doing, decrease incentives to use torture and/or other forms of violence as acceptable policy choices. From this perspective, to say how effective the CCPR, CAT, and CED are depends on the types of institutional reforms parties have made as per their treaty obligations as well as reducing their commission of these offenses. However, the road to institutional reform in many of these African States has been a long and difficult process, impacted heavily by history and the embeddedness of extant and preexisting domestic institutions, ongoing conditions of political turmoil, terrorism, and a lack of economic capacity.

To constructivists, the dialogue created through the engagement of States parties with international and national human rights NGOs, through the various reporting processes and in-country visits by the SPT or any number of special rapporteurs, is part of a longer process of socialization and internalization of norms prohibiting torture, extrajudicial killings, and disappearances. As Carey and Mitchell point out, however, there is a countervailing discourse propounded by the United States and other countries that suggests the "benefits accruing from torture could internalize a belief that torture is morally necessary against grave threats."[95] In this latter scenario, the strength and effectiveness of the torture and disappearances regimes and the ICCPR become conditional on the national security interests of a government, its ability to control the national narrative, and, consequently, its citizenry.

At the same time, torture is a long-standing policy for many States, reflective of deeply engrained traditions and styles of rule stretching back to colonial days that emphasize the use of coercion as a preferred means of social control. National security interests, the drive for greater cooperation, and the need for various policy reforms are filtered through these institutional experiences and explain why States vary to the extent they do in treaty compliance. Institutional legacies inform how States proceed in the legalization of international human rights laws, specifically as this pertains to the actors and organizations permitted to take part in the policymaking and implementation processes. As the chapters of this volume demonstrate, understanding the way *congruence* unfolds at the local and national levels is the key to explaining how and why legalization progresses or regresses over time.

Notes

1 This is the case whether a State is a monist or a dualist regime. Monist regimes are those in which international and national laws are seen as a single system of laws. For dualists, national law and international law are considered two separate systems, with the latter superseding the former. In a dualist system international law must be "transformed" into domestic law. Michelle Barnard, "Legal Reception in the AU against the Backdrop of the Monist/Dualist Dichotomy," *The Comparative and International Law Journal of Southern Africa* 48(1) (2015): 144–161, 153–154. For further discussion of monist and dualist regimes in Africa see Frans Viljoen, *International Human Rights Law in Africa*, 2nd ed. (Oxford: Oxford Univ. Press, 2012).

2 UN General Assembly, *Convention Against Torture and Other Cruel, Inhuman or Degrading Treatment or Punishment* (December 10, 1984), United Nations, Treaty Series, vol. 1465, available at: https://www.refworld.org/docid/3ae6b3a94.html; UN General Assembly, *International Convention for the Protection of All Persons from Enforced Disappearance*, December 20, 2006, available at: https://www.refworld.org/docid/47fdfaeb0.html; UN General Assembly, *International Covenant on Civil and Political Rights* (December 16, 1966), United Nations, Treaty Series, vol. 999, available at: https://www.refworld.org/docid/3ae6b3aa0.html.

3 IDEA, *Judicial Access*," at About the GSoD Indices | The Global State of Democracy. For the issues associated with torture as a *jus cogens* offense and extant treaty and domestic law, see Erika de Wet, "The Prohibition of Torture as an International Norm of jus cogens and Its Implications for National and Customary Law," *The European Journal of International Law* (15) (2004): 97–121.

4 As the scholars of the Summer 2000 Issue of *International Organization* would argue, the less precise a set of laws is, the weaker the obligations set forth for States, the lack of a strong (or any) adjudicative authority, the weaker the international treaty regime. Their framework for legalization is discussed in greater detail in Chapter 1 of this volume.

5 For purposes of this book, we use the UN's abbreviation for this oversight body, which is CCPR, likewise with the CED and CAT.

6 Averall Schmidt and Kathryn Sikkink, "Breaking the Ban? The Heterogeneous Impact of US Contestation of the Torture Norm," *Journal of Global Security Studies* 4(1) (2019): 105–122 and Lisbeth Zimmermann, Nicole Deitelhoff, Max Lesch, Antonio Arcudi and Anton Peez, *International Norm Disputes: The Link Between Contestation and Norm Robustness* (Oxford: Oxford University Press, 2023).

7 Per the Convention on the Non-Applicability of Statutory Limitations to War Crimes and Crimes Against Humanity, States can try cases of war crimes and crimes against humanity regardless of the date of their commission. UN General Assembly, *Convention on the Non-Applicability of Statutory Limitations to War Crimes and Crimes Against Humanity* (November 26, 1968), (A/RES/2391(XXIII)), available at: https://www.refworld.org/docid/3ae6b37818.html (accessed August 23, 2023). Universal jurisdiction for these crimes (as well as for genocide) is grounded in customary international law, the case law of the international tribunals, the statutes of these tribunals, and treaty law. M. Cherif Bassiouni, "Universal

Jurisdiction for International Crimes: Historical Perspectives and Contemporary Practice," 42 *Virginia Journal of International Law* 81 (2002). For the ICC definitions of these crimes, see Articles 6–8 of the UN General Assembly, *Rome Statute of the International Criminal Court* (last amended 2010), July 17, 1998, available at: https://www.refworld.org/docid/3ae6b3a84.html (accessed August 23, 2023).

8 Ezechieel A. Cirimwami, "Does the United Nations Convention Against Torture Oblige States Parties to Criminalize Torture in their Domestic Laws," *Perspectives* (January 2019); also, UN Committee Against Torture, *Convention Against Torture and Other Cruel, Inhuman or Degrading Treatment: General Comment No. 2* (January 24, 2008), (CAT/C/GC/2).

9 Matt Pollard, "Panel 1: Are Adequate Legal Frameworks in Place at the Domestic Level? Torture as a Specific Criminal Offense in Domestic Laws" (2009): 15–18, at r24351.pdf (corteidh.or.cr).

10 OHCHR, *Status of Ratification Interactive Dashboard*, at - OHCHR Dashboard (accessed October 12, 2023); also African Union, 36390-sl-african_charter_on_human_and_peoples_rights_2.pdf (au.int) (accessed October 12, 2023).

11 UN General Assembly, *Second Optional Protocol to the International Covenant on Civil and Political Rights, Aiming at the Abolition of the Death Penalty* (December 1989), (A/RES/44/128), available at: https://www.refworld.org/docid/3ae6b3a70.html (accessed August 22, 2023).

12 UN Human Rights Committee (CCPR), *CCPR General Comment No. 29: Article 4: Derogations during a State of Emergency* (August 31, 2001), (CCPR/C/21/Rev.1/Add.11), available at: https://www.refworld.org/docid/453883fd1f.html (accessed August 23, 2023); also, Alex Conte and Richard Burchill, *Defining Civil and Political Rights: The Jurisprudence of the United Nations Human Rights Committee (2nd ed.)*. (London: Routledge, 2016), Chapter 3. The authors go into detail about what derogation entails, how it is viewed by the CCPR and regional human rights bodies, what "national security" means, and so on. See also UN Human Rights Commission, *The Siracusa Principles on the Limitation and Derogation Provisions in the International Covenant on Civil and Political Rights* (September 28, 1984), (E/CN.4/1985/4), available at: https://www.refworld.org/docid/4672bc122.html (accessed August 23, 2023).

13 CCPR, *General Comment 29* at para. 17.

14 Center for Civil and Political Rights, Tracking Tool—Impact of States of Emergencies on Civil and Political Rights (April 1, 2020), at Tracking tool – Impact of States of Emergencies on ICCPR (ccprcentre.org).

15 Laurence R. Helfer, "Rethinking Derogations from Human Rights Treaties." *American Journal of International Law* 115(1) (2021): 20–40.

16 Helfer, "Rethinking," 24.

17 A great deal of the interstate complaint process is dependent on the voluntary compliance of the States parties involved. Article 42(1)(a) of the ICCPR, for example, permits the CCPR to form an ad hoc Conciliation Commission to resolve an interstate complaint if the parties to the complaint do not accept the initial decision of the CCPR. The creation of this commission is also subject to approval by the States involved.

18 Individual complaints procedures regard those states who are parties to OP I.

19 Conte and Burchill, *Defining*, 13. For greater detail about these five functions of the CCPR, see Conte and Burchill, *Defining*, 10–13. Many of the functions of the CCPR are identical to the functions of the CAT and CED.

20 Conte and Burchill, *Defining*, 45.

21 Human Rights Committee, *CCPR General Comment No. 6: Article 6 (Right to Life)*, April 30, 1982, available at: https://www.refworld.org/docid/45388400a.

html (accessed August 21, 2023); Conte and Burchill, *Defining*, 145; also, UN, *Enforced Disappearances, Fact Sheet 6, Rev. 4* (New York; Geneva: United Nations Human Rights Office of the High Commissioner ["OHCHR"], 2023) at Fact Sheet/6 Rev. 4 Enforced Disappearances (ohchr.org), 12.

22 UN General Assembly, *Rome Statute of the International Criminal Court (last amended 2010)*, ISBN No. 92-9227-227-6, UN General Assembly (July 17, 1998), https://www.refworld.org/legal/constinstr/unga/1998/en/64553 (accessed July 2, 2024), art. 7(2)(i).

23 Catherine J. Redgwell, "Reservations to Treaties and Human Rights Committee General Comment No. 24(52)," *International and Comparative Law Quarterly* 46 (April 1997): 390–412, 397.

24 The reservations to these non-derogable rights indicate that the US will follow these articles in so much as they do not contradict US law. Redgwell, "Reservations," 394–396. For an interesting discussion about the United States as an exceptionalist regime with regard to torture, see Henry F. Carey and Stacey M. Mitchell, *Legalization of International Law and Politics: Multi-Level Governance of Human Rights and Aggression* (Palgrave/Macmillan, 2023), 112–116.

25 *General Comment 24(52)* states: "The number of reservations, their content and their scope may undermine the effective implementation of the Covenant and tend to weaken respect for the obligations of States parties." This is especially the case if these reservations are unknown to other States parties. In a similar way, reservations to the Torture and Disappearances Conventions also threaten to undermine the effectiveness of these regimes. UN Human Rights Committee, *CCPR General Comment No. 24: Issues Relating to Reservations Made upon Ratification or Accession to the Covenant or the Optional Protocols thereto, or in Relation to Declarations under Article 41 of the Covenant* (November 4, 1994), (CCPR/C/21/Rev.1/Add.6), available at: https://www.refworld.org/docid/453883fc11.html (accessed August 22, 2023), para. 1. The ability of States parties to make reservations to the ICCPR was permitted as it was deemed necessary to garner greater ratifications. The flexible reservations system under Articles 19 to 23 of the Vienna Convention on the Law of Treaties was seen by the International Law Commission (ILC) to be preferable to encourage "widespread participation in treaties." Ibid., 392. See also United Nations, *Vienna Convention on the Law of Treaties*, May 23, 1969, United Nations, Treaty Series, vol. 1155, available at: https://www.refworld.org/docid/3ae6b3a10.html (accessed September 14, 2023), and UN Treaty Collection, Chapter IV Human Rights, 9. Convention against Torture and Other Cruel, Inhuman or Degrading Treatment, at UNTC (accessed August 22, 2023).

26 A few African States parties made reservations and/or interpretative declarations to the ICCPR. UNTC, Chapter IV: Human Rights, 4. International Covenant on Civil and Political Rights, at UNTC (accessed August 25, 2023). For explanations of why States make reservations to treaties, see Kelebrogile Zvobgo, Wayne Sandholtz and Suzie Mulesky, "Reserving Rights: Explaining Human Rights Treaty Reservations,' *International Studies Quarterly* 64 (2020): 785–797; Beth A. Simmons, *Mobilizing for Human Rights: International Law in Domestic Politics* (Cambridge, UK: Cambridge Univ. Press, 2009); Heather Elko McKibben and Shana D. Western, "'Reserved Ratification': An Analysis of States' Entry of Reservations Upon Ratification of Human Rights Treaties," *British Journal of Political Science* 50(2) (2020): 687–712. Data on treaty reservations, declarations and observations were gathered from the UN Treaty Collection, *Chapter IV Human Rights*, at UNTC (accessed August 22, 2023).

27 UN General Assembly, *Optional Protocol to the International Covenant on Civil and Political Rights*, 19 December 1966, United Nations, Treaty Series, vol. 999,

available at: https://www.refworld.org/docid/3ae6b3bf0.html (accessed August 23, 2023). For those States parties to the ICCPR who did not recognize the competence of the CCPR to hear complaints, this is nullified by Article 1 of the Op I (for those who are parties to the OP I).

28 Conte and Burchill, *Defining*, 20.

29 Christian Tomuschat, "International Covenant on Civil and Political Rights," *United Nations Audiovisual Library of International Law* (2008): 1–4; also, Eric Neumayer, "Do International Human Rights Treaties Improve Respect for Human Rights?" *Journal of Conflict Resolution* 49(6) (2005): 925–953 and Emilie M. Hafner-Burton, and Tsutsui Kiyoteru, "Human Rights in a Globalizing World: The Paradox of Empty Promises," *American Journal of Sociology* 110(5) (2005): 1373–1411.

30 Pollard, "Torture," 15.

31 There is no obligation within the Banjul Charter for States to criminalize or establish any legal framework for the prosecution of torture, nor any of the other crimes relevant to this study.

32 Organization of African Unity, *African Charter on Human and Peoples' Rights* (Banjul Charter), June 27, 1981, CAB/LEG/67/3 rev. 5, 21 I.L.M. 58 (1982), available at: https://www.refworld.org/docid/3ae6b3630.html (accessed August 4, 2023).

33 Giulio Fornaroli and Cristián Rettig, "Human Rights Under Emergency: A Normative Assessment of Derogation," *Social Theory and Practice* 49(3) (July 2023): 437–462, 438.

34 Fornaroli and Rettig, "Human Rights," 456.

35 Wade Cole, "Managing to Mitigate Abuse: Bureaucracy, Democracy, and Human Rights, 1984 to 2010," *International Journal of Comparative Sociology* 57(1–2) (2016): 69–97; T.A. Börzel and Thomas Risse, "Human rights in Areas of Limited Statehood: The New Agenda." In *The Persistent Power Of Human Rights: From Commitment To Compliance*, eds. Thomas Risse, T., Stephen C. Ropp, Kathryn Sikkink, 63–84 (Cambridge, UK: Cambridge University Press, 2013) and A. Anaya-Muñoz and Amanda Murdie, "The Will and the Way: How State Capacity and Willingness Jointly Affect Human Rights Improvement," *Human Rights Review* 23 (2022): 127–154.

36 Wade Cole, "Mind the Gap: State Capacity and the Implementation of Human Rights Treaties," *International Organization* 69 (Spring 2015): 405–441. Cole is referring to a government's ability to protect physical integrity rights (right to life, protection from torture, etc.) as well as empowerment rights (e.g., freedoms of speech and religion). Cole, "Mind," 414–416.

37 Cole, "Mind," 434.

38 Geneviève Souillac, "From Global Norms to Local Change: Theoretical Perspectives on the Promotion of Human Rights in Societies in Transition." In *Human Rights and Societies in Transition: Causes, Consequences, Responses*. eds Shale Asher Howowitz and Albrecht Schnabel, 77–99 (New York: United Nations University Press, 2004), 77–78.

39 F. Wafula Okumu, "Human Rights in Transition Societies: The Cases of Somalia and South Africa." In eds. Horowitz and Schnabel, *Human Rights*, 291–313.

40 The logic of consequences contends that post-conflict leaders are first concerned with maintaining stability and rebuilding their society rather than pursuing justice. Jack Snyder and Leslie Vinjamuri, "Principles Pragmatism and the Logic of Consequences," *International Theory* 4(3) (2012): 434–448.

41 These related mechanisms include a Special Rapporteur for Extrajudicial, Summary, or Arbitrary Executions. The mandate for this mechanism was established in 1982 through Economic and Social Council Resolution 1982/35. The

Special Rapporteur can examine cases of killings *regardless* of which treaties the State in question is a party.

42 The author of this chapter is more than happy to make this data available upon request. It is also available at OHCHR, UNTC, at tbinternet.ohchr.org/_layouts/15/TreatyBodyExternal/Countries.aspx.

43 The exceptions are Seychelles, Guinea-Bissau, São Tomé and Príncipe.

44 According to the UN's treaty reporting website, at present, all African States have overdue reports. See tbinternet.ohchr.org/_layouts/15/TreatyBodyExternal/LateReporting.aspx?Lang=en (accessed August 27, 2023).

45 Many of the reports submitted by parties to the CCPR frequently refer to unfavorable internal conditions such as civil war and poverty as contributing to the State's inability to perform not only its reporting functions, but also make policy reforms pursuant to ICCPR requirements.

46 CCPR, *Paper on the Relationship of the Human Rights Committee with National Human Rights Institutions, adopted by the Committee at its 106th session (October 15–November 2, 2012)*, (CCPR/C/106/3), 2. NHRI's are accredited by the International Coordinating Committee of National Institutions for the Promotion and Protection of Human Rights. The Paris Principles are rules or criteria that all NHRIs must meet. See European Network of National Human Rights Institutions (ENNHRI), "UN Paris Principles," at UN Paris Principles & Accreditation - ENNHRI (accessed August 1, 2023).

47 ENNHRI, "UN Paris."

48 CCPR, The Relationship of the Human Rights Committee with Non-Governmental Organizations, (CCPR/C/104/3) (June 4, 2012), 1.

49 William Korey, "Human Rights NGOs: The Power of Persuasion," *Ethics & International Affairs* 13 (1999): 151–174.

50 For further information about the legality of NGOs as participants, see Eduardo Szazi, *NGOs: Legitimate Subjects of International Law* (Leiden: Amsterdam University Press, 2012).

51 Andreas von Staden, "The Conditional Effectiveness of Soft Law: Compliance with the Decisions of the Committee Against Torture," *Human Rights Review* 23 (2022): 451–478, 470.

52 Carnegie Endowment for International Peace, *Fake Civil Society: The Rise of Pro-Government NGOs in Nigeria* (2021) at Fake Civil Society: The Rise of Pro-Government NGOs in Nigeria – Carnegie Endowment for International Peace (accessed September 14, 2023); Africa Center.org, Disinfo_chart (africacenter.org) (accessed September 14, 2023).

53 Africa Center.org, "Disinfo," 470. See also S. Cardenas, *Conflict and Compliance: State Responses to International Human Rights Pressure* (Philadelphia: University of Pennsylvania Press, 2007); Zoltan I. Búzás, "Is the Good News About Law Compliance Good News About Norm Compliance? The Case of Racial Equality," *International Organization* 72 (2018): 351–385 and B.B. Bernardi, "Transitional Justice and the Inter-American Human Rights System in Peru: The Role of Anti- and Pro-Compliance Constituencies." In *The Inter-American Human System: Impact Beyond Compliance*, ed. P. Engstrom, 221–246 (Cham, Switzerland: Palgrave Macmillan, 2019).

54 Jacqueline Van De Velde, "The Foreign Agent Problem': An International Legal Solution to Domestic Restrictions on Non-Governmental Organizations," 40 *Cardozo Law Review* 687 (2018): 691.

55 De Velde, "Foreign," 692.

56 Harriet Sherwood, "Human Rights Groups Face Global Crackdown 'Not Seen in a Generation'," *Guardian* (August 26, 2015), quoted in De Velde, "The Foreign," 694 at fn. 25.

57 UN General Assembly, *Optional Protocol to the Convention Against Torture and other Cruel, Inhuman or and Degrading Treatment or Punishment* (January 9, 2003), (A/RES/57/199), https://www.refworld.org/legal/agreements/unga/2003/en/17704 (accessed July 2, 2024). Other legal sources pertaining to torture prohibitions include *The Standard Minimum Rules for the Treatment of Prisoners*. Adopted by the First United Nations Congress on the Prevention of Crime and the Treatment of Offenders, held at Geneva on August 30, 1955, and approved by the Economic and Social Council by its resolutions 663 C (XXIV) of July 31, 1957 and 2076 (LXII) of May 13, 1977. This version is superseded by the UN General Assembly, *United Nations Standard Minimum Rules for the Treatment of Prisoners (the Nelson Mandela Rules): resolution/ adopted by the General Assembly*, (January 8, 2016), (A/RES/70/175), available at: https://www.refworld.org/docid/5698a3a44.html; UN General Assembly, *Declaration on the Protection of All Persons from Being Subjected to Torture and Other Cruel, Inhuman or Degrading Treatment or Punishment* (December 9, 1975), (A/RES/3452(XXX), available at: https://www.refworld.org/docid/3b00f1c030.html, and UN General Assembly, *Principles of Medical Ethics* (December 16, 1983), (A/RES/38/118), available at: https://www.refworld.org/docid/3b00f01464.html. All documents accessed August 24, 2023.

58 Carey and Mitchell, *Legalization*, 101. See also Matthew Lippmann, "The Protection of Human Rights: The Problem of Torture," *Universal Human Rights* 1(4) (1979): 25–55.

59 Jack Donnelly, *Universal Human Rights in Theory and Practice*, 3rd ed. (Cambridge: Cambridge Univ. Press, 2013), 179–190.

60 Donnelly, *Universal*, 194.

61 OHCHR, tbinternet.ohchr.org/_layouts/15/TreatyBodyExternal/Treaty.aspx?Treaty=CAT (accessed May 5, 2024). Von Staden writes that the individual complaint procedure for CAT has, as of 2021, generated at least 400 reports by the CAT on over 1,000 individual complaints. Von Staden, "The Conditional Effectiveness," 451.

62 This special rapporteur was created by Article 72 of the CAT's *Rules of Procedure*. The rapporteur follows up on the CAT's concluding observations and recommendations for a party and once a year reports to the CAT on the progress of that State party. OHCHR, *Follow-Up Procedure*, at Follow-Up Procedure | OHCHR, accessed September 1, 2023, and CAT, Rules of Procedure (July 5, 2023), (CAT/C/3/Rev.7), at tbinternet.ohchr.org/_layouts/15/treatybodyexternal/TBSearch.aspx?Lang=en&TreatyID=1&DocTypeID=65, (accessed September 1, 2023).

63 OHCHR, tbinternet.ohchr.org/_layouts/15/TreatyBodyExternal/TBSearch.aspx?Lang=en&TreatyID=12&DocTypeID=27, (accessed September 17, 2024).

64 To date seven countries have had visits from the SPT: Benin, Burkina Faso, Gabon, Liberia, Mali, Niger and Togo. See tbinternet.ohchr.org/_layouts/15/treatybodyexternal/TBSearch.aspx?Lang=en (accessed September 16, 2024).

65 NPMs are created by each member State. NPMs can take a variety of forms and are charged with ensuring that states' police forces meet their obligations per OPCAT. OHCHR, *Guidelines on National Preventive Mechanisms*, (December 9, 2010), at tbinternet.ohchr.org/_layouts/15/TreatyBodyExternal/Download.aspx?symbolno=CAT/OP/12/5&Lang=en (accessed July 1, 2023).

66 OHCHR, *Preventing Torture: The Role of the National Preventative Mechanisms, A Practical Guide, Professional Training Series No. 21* (Geneva: OHCHR, 2018), at NPM_Guide_EN.pdf (ohchr.org) (accessed August 29, 2023), iii.

67 OHCHR, *Preventing*, 7.

68 OHCHR, *Fact Sheet No. 17, The Committee Against Torture*, at FactSheet17en.pdf (ohchr.org), 6.
69 CAT, *Sixteenth Annual Report of the Sun-committee on Prevention of Torture and Other Cruel, Inhuman or Degrading Treatment or Punishment* (March 19, 2023), (CAT/C/76/2), 7.
70 Carey and Mitchell, *Legalization*, 121. "Delegative democracy" refers to O'Donnell's characterization of countries which are semi-democracies. See Guillermo O'Donnell, "Delegative Democracies," available at http://kellogg.nd.edu/publications/working.papers/WPS/172.pdf.
71 Adam S. Chilton and Mila Versteeg, "The Failure of Constitutional Torture Provisions," *Journal of Legal Studies* 44(2) (June 2015): 417–452, 421–422. In their analysis, the authors find no evidence that a constitutional prohibition on torture leads to less torture, controlling for various events like civil war and regime type. Chilton and Versteeg, "Failure," 446–448.
72 On this point, Simmons refers to the "decentralized way" in which torture is carried out. Simmons, *Mobilizing*, 259–260.
73 Celso Eduardo Faria Coracini, "The Lawful Sanctions Clause in the State Reporting Procedure before the Committee against Torture," *Netherlands Quarterly of Human Rights* 24(2) (2006): 305–318, 318.
74 The one exception is in the annual report CAT, (A/68/44), para. 91, which addresses links between indigenous justice mechanisms and the prevention of torture. CAT found that acts of spiritual justification and healing for persons punished by traditional mechanisms meet the qualification of "lawful." The term "lawful" is frequently used by the CAT in earlier reports to characterize government activity. (CAT, A/67/44).
75 Simmons, *Mobilizing*, 276.
76 See, for example, Howard Chitimira and Pontsho Mokone, "A General Legislative Analysis of Torture as a Human Rights Violation in Zimbabwe," *PER/PELJ* 20 (2017): 2–41. Philisiwe Hadebe and Nirmala Gopal, "When Torture Mocks the Law: Understanding Police Brutality in South Africa," *International Journal of Criminology and Sociology* 10 (2021): 231–243.
77 Jeremy Sarkin, "The Role of the International Criminal Court (ICC) in Reducing Massive Human Rights Violations such as Enforced Disappearances in Africa: Towards Developing Transitional Justice Strategies," *Studies in Ethnicity and Nationalism* 11(1) (2011): 130–142, 132.
78 Sarkin, "The Role," 551 and at fn. 85. F. Hampson, "Fundamental Guarantees." In *Perspectives on the ICRC Study on Customary International Humanitarian Law*, eds. E. Wilmshurst and S. Breau (Cambridge University Press, 2007), 282 and Brian Finucane, "Enforced Disappearance as a Crime Under International Law: A Neglected Origin in the Laws of War note," 35 *Yale Journal of International Law* 171 (2010).
79 Finucane, "Enforced Disappearance."
80 UN, *Enforced Disappearances, Fact Sheet* 6, Rev. 4 (New York; Geneva: United Nations Human Rights Office of the High Commissioner, 2023) at Fact Sheet/6 Rev. 4 Enforced Disappearances (ohchr.org) (accessed March 5, 2023), 7.
81 Human Rights Council, *Report of the Working Group on Enforced or Involuntary Disappearances* (August 8, 2023), (A/HRC/54/22).
82 Disappearances are also a way to dispose of migrant populations. Bernard Duhaime and Andreanne Thibault, "Protection of Migrants from Enforced Disappearance: A Human Rights Perspective," *International Review of the Red Cross* 99(2) (2017): 569–587 and Carlos Solar, "Forced Disappearances and the Inequalities of a Global Crime," *Alternatives: Global, Local, Political* 46(1) (2021): 17–22.

83 Caroline L. Payne and M. Rodwan Abouharb, "The International Covenant on Civil and Political Rights and the Strategic Shift to Forced Disappearance," *Journal of Human Rights* 15(20) (2016): 163–188, 165.
84 Under Article 2 of the Convention, States parties are obligated to investigate and prosecute these offenses with due diligence. UN, *Enforced Disappearances, Fact Sheet* 6, 11.
85 UN General Assembly, *International Convention for the Protection of All Persons from Enforced Disappearance*, 20 December 2006, available at: https://www.refworld.org/docid/47fdfaeb0.html (accessed September 1, 2023).
86 To be fair, this is an observation that applies to all working groups and special mechanisms.
87 OHCHR, *Basic Facts about the UPR*, at Basic facts about the UPR | OHCHR (accessed September 4, 2023).
88 Damien Etone, "African States: Themes Emerging from the Human Rights Council's Universal Periodic Review," *Journal of African Law* 62(2) (2018): 201–223.
89 This violates the principle of non-selectivity which is the foundation of the UPR. Damien, "African," 208–210.
90 Walter Kälin, "Ritual and Ritualism at the Universal Periodic Review: A Preliminary Appraisal." In *Human Rights and the Universal Periodic Review: Rituals and Ritualism*, 25–41. Hilary Charlesworth and Emma Larking eds. (Cambridge: Cambridge Univ. Press, 2014).
91 Kälin, "Ritual," 32.
92 The Working Group of the UPR, which consists of 47 member states of the Human Rights Council, reviews 14 states at a time in three sessions. OHCHR, *Universal Periodic Review Timeline*, at UPR TIMELINE NEW V.2 (ohchr.org) (accessed September 4, 2023). The second cycle began in 2012, the third in 2017, and the fourth in 2022. Forty-two States are reviewed each year of a five-year cycle.
93 See, for example, the Working Group's recommendations related to Somalia's reporting for the third cycle (A/HRC/48/11) and Sudan's (A/HRC/50/16).
94 Carey and Mitchell, *Legalization*, 98.
95 Carey and Mitchell, *Legalization*, 99.

4 The African Human Rights Regime

Stacey M. Mitchell and Lem Lilian Atanga

Introduction

This chapter reviews the work of the African human rights regime and various institutions that play a role in the human rights landscape in Africa. We focus on the work of the African Commission on Human and Peoples' Rights (ACHPR), the African Court on Human and Peoples' Rights (ACtHPR) and various subregional courts. Although these latter institutions also encounter obstacles with state compliance, their regional quality may place them in a better position to achieve greater norm dissemination and legalization.

The Banjul Charter and the Work of the African Commission and Court

The African Charter on Human and Peoples' Rights (Banjul Charter) was adopted in 1981 by the member States of the Organization of African Unity—the predecessor to the African Union (AU).[1] Article 4 of the Charter guarantees the right to life. The perpetration of torture, cruel, inhuman, and degrading treatment is prohibited under Article 5 of the Charter. Article 6 guarantees everyone "the right to liberty and to the security of his person."

Article 30 of the Charter establishes the ACHPR. Its mandate is spelled out in Article 45; specifically, it has an educative function, an interpretive function (of the Charter), and has the responsibility to "formulate and lay down, principles and rules aimed at solving legal problems relating to human and peoples' rights and fundamental freedoms upon which African Governments may base their legislation."[2] The ACHPR receives communications from State parties regarding violations of the Charter perpetrated by other parties (Article 47) and can also receive communications from individuals and NGOs (Article 55). Per Article 62 of the Charter, State parties are mandated to report to the ACHPR every two years from the date the Charter comes into force.

Zschrint notes that the Charter contains a number of "claw back clauses" which limit the protection of the human rights enshrined in the Charter in practice.[3] For example, Article 6 states that individuals can be deprived of

DOI: 10.4324/9781003471677-6

their freedom if preexisting legislation so requires, and the rights of freedom of assembly (Article 11) and movement (Article 12) are conditional on an individual's adherence to the laws of their state as well as the conditions that prevail within that country, including but not limited to national security, law and order, and morality, none of which are defined. Citizens also have a duty to not compromise the national security of their country (Article 29). Many of these provisions are certainly open to interpretation by a state. However, it is also worthy of noting that the Banjul Charter represents the efforts of the drafters to include traditional rights, such as family and communal rights, with individual ones.[4]

Most State parties to the Charter have complied with the reporting process, although not every two years. The reports of many members are overdue.[5] The only States that have not reported are Comoros, Equatorial Guinea, Guinea Bissau, São Tomé and Príncipe, Somalia, and South Sudan.[6]

The Robben Island Guidelines and Measures for the Prohibition and Prevention of Torture, Cruel, Inhuman or Degrading Punishment in Africa (Guidelines) were adopted by the ACHPR in 2002.[7] These guidelines are

> the first instrument adopted by the African Commission elaborating and providing guidance on states' obligations under Article 5 of the African Charter on Human and Peoples' rights [...], and devoting specific attention to the prevention of torture and other forms of ill treatment.[8]

Additionally, there is a Committee for the Prevention of Torture in Africa (CPTA) within the ACHPR. Established in 2004, the CPTA is intended to put the Guidelines into practice, and has been described as "instrumental in engaging States Parties to the African Charter on Human and Peoples' Rights (African Charter) to encourage and foster greater compliance with [...] Article 5 of the African Charter, including through the adoption of relevant legislation."[9] The CPTA is also mandated with issuing a progress report to the ACHPR every Ordinary session.[10] Unlike the Torture Committee or the ACHPR, States have no requirement to report to the CPTA and the CPTA *cannot* conduct regular visits to African countries.

Renzulli argues that a lack of clarity associated with several provisions of the Guidelines, magnified by certain acts by the CPTA, limits the effectiveness of the African torture regime. She cites several definitional and conceptual problems associated with the provisions of the Guidelines that hamper their implementation domestically. The absence of a definition of "torture," the lack of clarity surrounding what the obligations to "prevent" and "prohibit" torture entail, and the misguided efforts by the CPTA to "clarify" the concept of prevention by emphasizing the passage of domestic legislation and the creation of domestic monitoring systems (acts of prohibition) have muddied the waters further.[11] Acts of prohibition are "negative" in the sense that the State party has to refrain from torture and when it occurs, punish those responsible.[12] Prevention by comparison is both "negative" and "positive," as a government is also acting to address the conditions that make torture and other forms of violence possible.[13] By broadening its focus and re-prioritizing its goals, Renzulli suggests that the CPTA has the possibility of living up to its function as a body intended to effectively promote the *prevention* of torture on the continent.

Overall, the African human rights regime is what Donnelly would categorize as a "promotional" or at the very best, a "weak implementation" regime, meaning that the ACHPR and ACtHPR advocate for the protection of human rights, share information, encourage States to implement these rights, but their decisions have no real enforcement power.[14]

The ACHPR can bring cases before the ACtHPR pursuant to Article 2 of the Protocol to the African Charter on Human and Peoples' Rights on the Establishment of an African Court of Human and Peoples' Rights.[15] The ACtHPR has the mandate to issue advisory decisions and can deal with contentious disputes regarding the Charter and other human rights instruments. As of this date, 34 of the 55 member States of the African Union have ratified the Protocol.[16] Only eight of these recognize the competence of the Court to hear cases brought by individuals and NGOs pursuant to Article 34(6).[17] However, the fact that Rwanda withdrew from the Court's jurisdiction just as the ACtHPR was about to hear a case brought by opposition leader Victorie Ingabire indicates that the Court does have some influence.[18] As of the time of this writing, the ACtHPR has rendered over 400 decisions.[19]

Presently, the AU is perhaps the chief critic of the International Criminal Court (ICC), especially for the ICC's focus on prosecuting African heads of state/government, and for its focus on investigating Africa more generally. At present, 33 African States are party to the Rome Statute (the highest number of any region).[20] Many of these States gained membership early, including Senegal Leone (1999), Gabon (2000), and Ghana (1999).[21] Documents such as the 2001 Windhoek Plan of Action on the ICC Ratification and Implementation in the South African Development Community (SADC) demonstrate that cooperation between African governments and the ICC was of paramount importance initially.[22] However, over time opinions toward the ICC shifted. Recently, South Africa, Burundi, and Gambia filed written notices per Article 127 of the ICC Statute to withdraw from the Court.

Gambia's intent to withdraw was a result of the fear of possible prosecution of its president, Yahya Jammeh, for political violence. For South Africa, the intent to withdraw was partially fueled by the ICC's request for South Africa to arrest and detain Sudanese President Omar Hussein al Bashir at the AU Assembly in South Africa in June 2015 (which the government refused). Burundi's withdrawal request came after the ICC began investigating the political violence associated with the 2015 re-election of President Pierre Nkurunziza.[23] Although South Africa and Gambia withdrew their requests, Burundi did not.[24]

The AU's opinion is also demonstrated by the efforts of member States to pass the Malabo Protocol which grants additional powers of prosecution to an African Court of Justice and Human Rights, while also granting immunity for heads of state/government.[25] Moreover, the AU in 2018 sought a decision from the International Court of Justice regarding the issue of granting immunity to heads of state/government from prosecution by the ICC.[26]

The issue of immunity is considered by Clifford to reflect the "origins of violence and accountability on the continent, which are not remedied by prosecution but rather through efforts at peace and reconciliation."[27] The dissatisfaction with the ICC as a tool for justice is also reflected in a growing desire of States to place more emphasis on the work of regional and subregional courts.

Subregional Bodies

Aside from the ACtHPR, there is the Extraordinary African Chambers in Senegal,[28] the East African Court of Justice (EACJ), the Court of Justice of the Economic Community of West African States (ECCJ), the Court for the Common Market for Eastern and Southern Africa Court of Justice (COMESA Court of Justice), the Tribunal of the Southern African Development Community (SADC Tribunal), and the Court of Justice of the Economic Community of Central African States (ECCAS).[29] Similar to the ACtHPR, these bodies encounter problems of funding, mandates, overlapping jurisdictions, and issues of compliance. Human rights are mentioned specifically in some of these treaties, indirectly in others.

Ruppel writes that the integration of human rights into these treaties in one form or another stems from the fact that human rights, really democracy, plays "an essential role in economic development."[30] Moreover, the courts of regional economic communities, or RECs, work to monitor human rights practices and "can unquestionably contribute towards the promotion and protection of human rights, provided that decisions by regional judicial institutions are properly enforced at a national level."[31] As discussed below, enforcement at the national level remains problematic in many instances.

The Court of Justice of the Economic Community of West African States

The ECCJ is addressed in Article 15 of the Revised Treaty of the Economic Community of West African States.[32] Unlike the original ECOWAS Treaty (1975), the Revised Treaty references human rights and Article 4 of the Treaty recognizes the promotion of human rights in accordance with the Banjul Charter as a fundamental principle of ECOWAS.[33] Article 15 of the Revised Treaty makes the decisions reached by the ECCJ *binding* on all 15 Member States of the Economic Community of West African States (ECOWAS), institutions of ECOWAS, individuals, and corporations.[34] Cases can also be brought to the ECCJ by the ECOWAS Authority of Heads of State and Government (the Authority) (as per Article 7) as well as by the Council of Ministers (Article 10).[35] Per Articles 9(4) and 10(d) of Protocol (A/P.I/7/91) as revised by the Supplemental Protocol (A/SP.I/01.05), the ECCJ can hear cases concerning violations of human rights.

Although the ECCJ has a human rights mandate, problems arise with exercising this mandate in practice. As Ebrobrah contends, the ECCJ can hear cases referred to by State parties; however, the fact that it cannot sit as a court of appeal on rulings made by national courts makes its position as a court of human rights extremely weak.[36] There is also a lack of a right of appeal for those individuals who bring cases to the ECCJ.[37] Moreover, there are issues associated with which sources of law the ECCJ can rely on in human rights cases, although this is not as problematic as would seem. There are the ECOWAS instruments; other international instruments "indirectly or directly referred to" in these instruments and in ECCJ decisions; there is also the Banjul Charter, in which case jurisdictional issues could arise with the ACtHPR and the ACHPR.[38]

The ECCJ has made inroads in expanding its competence to rule on human rights regardless of their connection to economic rights, which contributes to a greater diffusion of human rights norms.[39] In their assessment of the ECCJ, Alter, Hefler, and McAllister contend that the ECCJ has taken a bold stand on human rights *despite* its limitations, noting that "the adjudication of human rights by the ECOWAS Court enhances, on balance, the clarity of international law and raises, not lowers, human rights protections in West Africa."[40]

The East African Court of Justice

Article 9 of the Treaty for the Establishment of the East African Community (EAC) creates the EACJ.[41] Located in Arusha, Tanzania the EACJ has a mandate to issue advisory opinions, rulings on the interpretation and application of the Treaty, arbitral awards, and unlike the ECCJ, the EACJ has an appellate body.[42] Articles 29 and 30 lay out the Parties that have standing in the EACJ, which include State parties, the Secretary-General of the EAC, and "Legal and Natural Persons" of a State party, including NGOs. Human rights are referenced throughout the Treaty, including in its Preamble, and are included as the foundational and operational principles of the EAC (in Articles 6 and 7, respectively). Article 27(2) gives the EACJ possible jurisdiction over matters of human rights, after additional protocols. As of the time of this writing, there have been no specific protocols spelling out the human rights jurisdiction of the Court. However, in practice, the EACJ has heard cases from States concerning human rights issues like arbitrary detention, ill-treatment, and freedom of the press.[43] The basis for jurisdiction of the EACJ in many of these cases is Article 27(1) of the Treaty, which grants the Court the power of interpretation of the Treaty.

One of the more consequential cases heard by the EACJ is the *Anyang Nyong'o v. Attorney General of Kenya* case, wherein the EACJ ruled against Kenya in Kenya's efforts to place a slate of candidates in a subregional legislature.[44] The EACJ ordered the EAC not to swear in these candidates "until the court ruled on the merits of the case."[45] As discussed below, Kenya's displeasure with this ruling led to changes made to the EACJ.

The Tribunal of the Southern African Development Community

The SADC Tribunal does not specifically have human rights jurisdiction spelled out in its mandate. Although the sources of law on which it can rule (Article 21) include "general principles and rules of law."[46] Articles 14 and 15 of the 2000 Protocol on the Tribunal address the basis and scope of the jurisdiction of the SADC Tribunal, respectively. Like the EACJ and ECCJ, the SADC Tribunal has jurisdiction over disputes between State parties as well as disputes involving natural or legal persons of a State (Article 15). The Tribunal interprets the SADC Treaty, any protocols or "subsidiary instruments" adopted by the SADC, as well as any agreements between States that grant the Tribunal jurisdiction (Article 14[a-c]). The SADC Tribunal also issues advisory opinions, like the other regional courts above. The jurisdiction of the Tribunal was expanded in 2007 to include an appellate division.[47]

The SADC has passed several declarations over the years, including a Charter of Fundamental and Social Rights, a Declaration on Agriculture and Food Security and a Declaration on HIV and AIDS that, although not legally binding, demonstrate the commitment of member States to the promotion and protection of quality-of-life rights.[48] Other instruments, such as the Protocol on Gender and Development are legally binding.[49]

Court for the Common Market for Eastern and Southern Africa Court of Justice and the Community Court of Justice of the Economic Community of Central African States

The COMESA Court of Justice was established in 1993 by Article 7(c) of the COMESA Treaty.[50] Although the COMESA does not specifically have jurisdiction over human rights matters as per the Treaty or the rules of the Court, the Treaty gives the Court jurisdiction over a variety of rights that easily fall under the rubric of human rights, including health (Chapter 14), the environment (Chapter 16), access to food, water, education, sanitation, and infrastructure (Chapter 18), promoting the role of women (Chapter 24), and free movement of persons (Chapter 28). Article 6e of the Treaty recognizes and the significance and applicability of the Banjul Charter.[51] The decisions of the COMESA Court are binding and supersede national courts' decisions.[52] Like the other bodies referenced above COMESA has an interpretive function as well as the ability to hear individual complaints and complaints between member States.

Although listed on the AU website for RECs as an institution of the ECCAS, the ECCAS Community Court of Justice has yet to be operational.[53] Article 29(3) of the revised Treaty of the ECCAS recommends a Court whose "statute, the composition, the jurisdiction, the procedure and other matters relating to the Court of Justice shall be specified in the Protocol relating thereto."[54]

Performance of Regional Courts

The regional courts have incurred some backlash because of their rulings against member States. In some respects, political leaders see the more proactive subregional courts as threats to state sovereignty.[55] As Gathii contends, State parties to the EACJ, for example,

> believe that the court's human rights decisions are creating new understandings of legality to which the states do not subscribe at home. These states are resisting allowing the court to conform their domestic affairs to international understandings of legality.[56]

In the examples of the EACJ, the SADC Tribunal, and the ECCJ, the success of any backlash launched against a Court varies depending at least partially on the strength of civil society but also the lengths to which a State proceeds in its efforts to refuse compliance.[57] In his comparison of State responses to particular rulings by these three judicial bodies, Helfer found that a ruling by the ECCJ against Gambia in two cases having to do with the arrest and detention of journalists prompted the government to make proposals seeking to limit the jurisdiction of the ECCJ. Thanks to strong reaction by NGOs and attorneys, these efforts failed.

In the Kenyan case before the EACJ referenced above, Kenya proposed a series of amendments to the EAC Treaty, that sought to

> alter the EACJ's structure, jurisdiction, and access rules. The revisions split the court into two divisions; expanded the grounds for removing or suspending EACJ judges facing misconduct allegations; clarified that the court could not hear cases in which the EAC Treaty confers jurisdiction on domestic actors; and added a two-month limitations period for filing complaints challenging national actions as contrary to the EAC Treaty.[58]

Kenya's efforts at hobbling the EACJ succeeded to some extent in the form of certain modifications made to the Treaty.[59]

Gathii suggests that the use of the EACJ by human rights NGOs and advocates has given the Court an "intermediate" level of authority.[60] These human rights and pro-democracy groups as well as some governments comply with the decisions of the Court, but more importantly, these EACJ cases serve as a means of naming and shaming member States for their human rights abuses.[61]

The last example Hefler considers concerns a case before the SADC Tribunal having to do with a Zimbabwean landowner whose property was confiscated by the Mugabe government.[62] The SADC Tribunal's ruling in favor of the plaintiff, Michael Campbell (and 78 others), led the Mugabe government to launch a campaign among more moderate member States that associated the case with "Western political attacks against African governments."[63] In so doing, he secured support for the "adoption of a new Protocol that, if it enters into force, will reconstitute the SADC Tribunal with a jurisdiction limited to interstate disputes."[64]

The Constitutional Court of South Africa ruled that President Jacob Zuma's signature on this 2014 Protocol was unconstitutional as the Protocol was in effect an amendment to the Treaty and the South African President (and the leaders of the *other* States who signed the Protocol) were seeking to amend the Treaty in a way that sought to undermine rule of law and democracy. This action was in violation of the South African Constitution which states that the President "may [...] not approve anything that undermines our Bill of Rights and international law obligations."[65] South Africa's President, Cyril Ramaphosa, has since withdrawn the signature from the Protocol. Tanzania followed suit for different reasons.[66] What the implications of these decisions have for participation in the SADC as well as in other courts are unclear.[67] To date, the 2014 Protocol has not received enough ratifications (two-thirds of States) to go into effect.

Overall, Alter, Hefler, and McAllister contend that subregional courts like the ECCJ (and others) have value for a variety of stakeholders, including easier access, quicker results, and a means for subregional courts to "expand their dockets, develop legal doctrine, and issue rulings that are relevant to stakeholders."[68] Viljoen contends that the closer economic, social, and political links between countries within a subregion make it possible for "faster response and improved implementation" of human rights laws, compared to international efforts."[69] However, at the same time, the work of these subregional courts (and the ACtHPR) is certainly a work in progress. If States parties continue to seek to alter these courts' jurisdictions when they receive decisions they do not like, the future of these mechanisms of justice in Africa may be in doubt.

Perhaps a more important facet for consideration is how apex domestic courts are addressing the rulings by African national and regional courts, the ACtHPR, as well as international treaties and decisions of the quasi-judicial human rights treaty bodies, the CAT, CED, and CCPR. Slaughter has referred to national courts as "the vehicles through which international treaties and customary law that have not been independently incorporated into domestic statutes enter the domestic legal systems."[70] The "transjudicial" communication between international and domestic courts is defined by Müller and Kjos, as occurring "when national and international judges construing or giving an effect to a particular norm look at how their colleagues in other states or international courts have construed the same or a similar norm."[71] Primarily their volume considers voluntary judicial dialogue, which is to say instances in which judges of higher domestic courts choose to incorporate the judicial decisions of external courts into their own rulings.[72] The extent to which this takes place is predicated on whether international human rights treaty laws are considered valid in the domestic legal order. Validity is indicated by the melding of these laws into domestic statutes and constitutions, as well as the importance these laws are granted by domestic courts.[73]

In Africa, there are examples of domestic courts relying on the rulings of external courts and references to international treaty law in their decision-making. South Africa is one of the best examples, as the discussion above regarding the controversy over the SADC Tribunal Protocol indicates.[74] Adjami, in her analysis of the common law countries Botswana, Namibia, Nigeria, South Africa, Tanzania, Zambia, and Zimbabwe, found that regardless of judicial independence and/or the status of the ruling regime (democratic, authoritarian, etc.), the national courts of these States tend to rely on the rulings of external courts (like the European Court of Human Rights) and international treaty law in their rulings. She considers this trend to be a positive sign that human rights are gaining a more solid footing in these countries.[75]

The examples she considers are States that include within their constitutions the protection of individual rights (a bill of rights) that makes reference to treaties like the Banjul Charter, the ICCPR, even the European Convention for Human Rights.[76] Judges in these African States use external decisions and on sources of law as means of "broadening the scope of indeterminate language that is used to define fundamental rights" and to "establish the substantive definition of particular rights."[77] In one particular ruling (*Catholic Commission for Justice & Peace in Zimbabwe v. Attorney-General*[78]), the Supreme Court in Zimbabwe relied on the opinions of the UN Human Rights Council on inhuman and degrading punishment in addition to the European Court of Human Rights and the US Supreme Court, among other sources.[79]

Conclusions

The African human rights regime could be considered to fit with the realist model of legalization in that from a more superficial perspective one could argue that national interests drive state behavior in several respects, including an emphasis on sovereignty and immunity from prosecution of heads of state/government.

At the same time, the issuance of declarations and the ratification of protocols that address human rights issues by the member States of the RECs could be seen as evidence of the fact that national interests of these States do include the promotion and protection of a life of dignity for their citizens. Moreover, as the preceding discussion about Africa's regional and domestic courts indicates, there are activist judges who seek to uphold international law even when the law works against the larger interests of their government leaders. The choice of African States to join one or more of the subregional courts belies the realist's position about the significance of national interests. The flip side to this, of course, are the efforts by Zimbabwe, Kenya, Gambia, and others to *limit* the jurisdiction of these courts when these courts issue decisions they do not like.

From a constructivist standpoint, the behavior of political and judicial elites in many African States can be interpreted as evidence of norm diffusion. From the perspective of the theory of legalization advanced by the authors of this volume, however, closer focus on the inclusiveness of the lawmaking communities of practice in these States as well as the influence of institutional legacies on the legalization process is warranted to explain why norm diffusion has taken place in some African States less so in others. The ensuing chapters in this volume will approach these tasks by expanding the investigative lens to include a wider range of actors and institutions.

Notes

1 Organization of African Unity (OAU), *African Charter on Human and Peoples' Rights (Banjul Charter)*, June 27, 1981, CAB/LEG/67/3 rev. 5, 21 I.L.M. 58 (1982), available at: https://www.refworld.org/docid/3ae6b3630.html (accessed September 13, 2023).

2 The Banjul Charter entered into force on October 21, 1986. AU, *African Charter on Human and Peoples' Rights*, at African Charter on Human and Peoples' Rights| African Union (au.int) (accessed September 3, 2023). The purpose of State reporting is to "establish a framework for constructive dialogue between the Commission and the States," which is seen as a tool for achieving the Charter's many goals. ACHPR, *State Reporting Procedures and Guidelines: II. Purpose of State Reporting*, at State Reporting Procedures and Guidelines|African Commission on Human and Peoples' Rights (au.int) (accessed September 5, 2023).

3 Steven Zschrint, "Locking in Human Rights in Africa: Analyzing State Accession to the African Court on Human and People's Rights," *Human Rights Review* 19 (2018): 97–119, 100.

4 See the discussion by Mirna E. Adjami, "African Courts, International Law, and Comparative Case Law: Chimera or Emerging Human Rights Jurisprudence?" 24 *MICH. J. INT'L L.* 103 (2002), 121–123.

5 For more information, see ACHPR, "States Reporting Status," at States Reporting Status | African Commission on Human and Peoples' Rights (au.int) (accessed September 5, 2023).

6 The Sahrawi Democratic Republic is not included in this number as it is only a partially recognized state. Morocco is not included because it is not a State party to the Charter.

7 ACHPR, *Robben Island Guidelines and Measures for the Prohibition and Prevention of Torture, Cruel, Inhuman or Degrading Punishment in Africa*, adopted 32rd ordinary session of ACHPR (2002).

8 Isobel Renzulli, "Strengthening the Preventative Role of the Committee for the Prevention of Torture in Africa," *International Human Rights Law Review* 7 (2018): 249–273, 250.

9 REDRESS, *Legal Frameworks to Prevent Torture in Africa: Best Practices, Shortcomings and Options Going Forward* (March 2016), 5, at 56e2d44e4.pdf (refworld.org) (accessed August 2, 2023).
10 ACHPR, Committee for the Prevention of Torture in Africa, at Committee for the Prevention of Torture in Africa | African Commission on Human and Peoples' Rights (au.int) (accessed September 6, 2023).
11 Renzulli, "Strengthening," 257–259.
12 Renzulli, "Strengthening," 260.
13 Renzulli, "Strengthening." Renzulli contends that these latter conditions include addressing conditions of detention (really "unequal power relations") that make some groups more vulnerable to torture than others in a society, as well as strengthening the role of the CPTA by broadening its focus. Her discussion of prevention touches on the conditions of structural violence that prevail within a country and which make certain groups vulnerable to state mistreatment. Renzulli, "Strengthening," 260–272.
14 Jack Donnelly, *Universal Human Rights in Theory and Practice* 3d (Ithaca, NY: Cornell Univ. Press, 2013) 161–162.
15 AU, *The Protocol to The African Charter on Human and Peoples' Rights on The Establishment of An African Court On Human And Peoples' Rights*, available at: <https://www.african-court.org/en/images/Basic%20Documents/africancourt-humanrights.pdf> (last accessed February 28, 2021). See also ACtHPR, *Rules of the Court*, Articles 34–39, at Rules-Final-Revised-adopted-Rules-eng-April-2021.pdf (african-court.org) (accessed September 6, 2023).
16 ACtHPR, "Basic Information," at Basic Information - African Court on Human and Peoples' Rights (african-court.org) (accessed August 8, 2023). "The AU refers to 55 members, this includes Western Sahara."
17 Burkina Faso, Gambia, Ghana, Guinea-Bissau, Mali, Malawi, Niger and Tunisia have all deposited a declaration acknowledging the Court's competence to hear individual cases.
18 Rachel Murray, "The Human Rights Jurisdiction of the African Court of Justice and Human Rights." In eds. C.C. Jalloh, K.M. Clarke and V.O. Nmehielle, *The African Court of Justice and Human and People's Rights in Context: Development and Changes*, 965–988 (Cambridge: Cambridge Univ. Press, 2019).
19 ACtHPR, "Cases: Statistics," at African Court Cases | Statistic (african-court.org) (accessed May 16, 2024).
20 UN General Assembly, *Rome Statute of the International Criminal Court (last amended 2010)*, ISBN No. 92-9227-227-6, UN General Assembly, July 17, 1998, https://www.refworld.org/legal/constinstr/unga/1998/en/64553 (accessed July 2, 2024).
21 States Parties to the Rome Statute, at States Parties - Chronological list | International Criminal Court (icc-cpi.int) (accessed October 7, 2022).
22 In the Windhoek Plan members who also were States parties to the Rome Statute agreed to prioritize the creation of implementing legislation of the Statute to ensure greater cooperation with the Court. Gerhard Kemp, "The Implementation of the Rome Statute in Africa." In *Africa and the International Criminal Court. International Criminal Justice Series*, vol 1. Eds. Gerhard Werle, Lovell Fernandez, and Moritz Vormbaum. 61–77. (The Hague: T.M.C. Asser Press, 2014).
23 Manisuli Ssenyonjo, "State Withdrawal Notifications from the Rome Statute of the International Criminal Court: South Africa, Burundi and The Gambia," *Criminal Law Forum* 29 (2018): 63–119, 68–103.
24 Ssenyonjo, "State."
25 AU, *The Protocol on Amendments to the Protocol on the Statute of the African Court of Justice and Human Rights* [the "Malabo Protocol"]. The Protocol also grants the Court jurisdiction over a larger list of crimes, besides the core

international crimes of genocide, war crimes, and crimes against humanity. For the Protocol to come into effect, it must be ratified by 15 States. As of the time of this writing, this has not happened. Sascha-Dominik Dov Bachmann and Naa A. Sowatey-Adjei, "The African Union-ICC Controversy Before the ICJ: A Way Forward to Strengthen International Criminal Justice?" *Washington International Law Journal Association* 29 (2020): 247–301, 250–251.

26 Specifically, the AU's complaint dealt with the incompatibility of Articles 27 and 98 of the Rome Statute, the latter of which states that "the Court many not proceed with a request for surrender or assistance which would require the requested State to act inconsistently with its obligations under international law with respect to the State or diplomatic immunity of a person or property of a third State, unless the Court can first obtain the cooperation of that third State for the waiver of immunity." The argument is that Article 98 of the Statute applies to non-States parties through Security Council Resolution 1593 (March 31, 2005) referring Sudan's case to the ICC (which then applies to all member states of the UN). The request for the decision (through the UN General Assembly), was denied. Eki Yemisis Omorogbe, "The Crisis of International Criminal Law in Africa," 66 *Netherlands International Law Review* 287 (2019), 291.

27 Cayley Clifford, "Justice Beyond the International Criminal Court: Towards a Regional Framework in Africa," *South African Institute of Legal Affairs* (2019): 1–22, 13.

28 The Extraordinary African Chambers (EAC) was created via an agreement between the Senegalese Government and the AU. The EAC tried and convicted Hissène Habré for torture, war crimes, and crimes against humanity in 2016. EAC, "Hybrid Justice, Extraordinary African Chambers," at Chambres Africaines Extraordinaires/Extraordinary African Chambers – Hybrid Justice.

29 Other organizations that touch on international human rights laws include the Community of Sahel-Saharan States, the Arab Maghreb Union, the Commonwealth of Nations, the International Organization of the Francophonie, and the Community of Portuguese Speaking Countries. These organizations are not considered in this chapter due to issues of space. For a good discussion of their role, see Frans Viljoen, *International Human Rights Law in Africa*, 2nd ed. (Oxford, 2012; online ed., Oxford Academic, April 20, 2015), https://doi.org/10.1093/acprof:osobl/9780199645589.001.0001 (accessed May 29, 2024), 17–19. The AU has recognized each of the regional economic communities. African Union, "Regional Economic Communities," at Regional Economic Communities (RECs) | African Union (au.int) (accessed July 3, 2024).

30 Oliver C. Ruppel, "Regional Economic Communities and Human Rights in East and Southern Africa" (2009), 279.

31 Ruppel, "Regional Economic," 282.

32 ECOWAS, *Revised Treaty of the Economic Community of West African States* (1993), at Revised-treaty-1.pdf (ecowas.int), accessed September 7, 2023.

33 Soloman T. Ebobrah, "Critical Issues in the Human Rights Mandate of the ECOWAS Court of Justice," *Journal of African Law* 54(1) (2010): 1–25, 4. Ebobrah makes the point that neither the 1975 Treaty nor its 1993 replacement "enumerates the promotion and protection of human rights as a purpose or function of the organization [ECOWAS]. Both treaties aim at promoting action to 'raise the living standards' of ECOWAS citizens. However, neither treaty lists the promotion and protection of human rights as means to achieve that aim." Ebobrah, "Critical," 5. The fact that the Court was intended to address disputes associated with economic integration makes its handling of human rights issues problematic, especially given the ECCJ's reliance on the ECOWAS Parliament for any changes to its competence.

34 This is an expanded mandate for the Court. Originally, per Protocol (A/P.I/7/91) the Court could only hear cases between States and issue advisory opinions when requested by a State. ECOWAS, *Protocol on the Community Court of Justice* (A/P.I/7/91), at Protocol A/P.I/7/91 on the Community Court of Justice, African Human Rights CLA 2.0 (uwazi.io); also Supplemental Protocol A/SP.I/01/05 Amending the Preamble and Articles 1,2,9 and 30 Relating to the Community Court of Justice and Article 4 Paragraph 1 of the English Version of the Said Protocol (2005), at supplementary protocol (courtecowas.org). Both accessed September 7, 2023.

35 The Authority is the supreme institution of the ECOWAS and consists of the Heads of State and Government of all members of ECOWAS. The Authority is analogous to the European Council of the European Union. See European Union, European Council - Consilium (europa.eu). The ECOWAS Council of Ministers consists of "the Minister in charge of ECOWAS Affairs and any other Minister of each Member State."

36 Ebobrah, "Critical Issues," 9.

37 Ebobrah, "Critical Issues," 9–10.

38 Ebobrah, "Critical Issues," 16–19.

39 The ECCJ has issued some significant decisions, including cases addressing slavery. See *Hadijatou Mani Koraou V. The Republic Of Niger*, Suit N°: ECW/CCJ/APP/08/08 JUDGMENT N: ECW/CCJ/JUD/06/08, Community Court of Justice, Law Report (2004–2009), 217–244, at Final Handbook Law Report English Corrected Rev 1Sep.pmd (courtecowas.org) (accessed September 8, 2023).

40 Karen J. Alter, Laurence R. Helfer and Jacqueline R. McAllister, "A New International Human Rights Court For West Africa: The ECOWAS Community Court Of Justice," *The American Journal of International Law* 107(4) (October 2013): 737–779, 778. Moreover, the fact that the Court enjoys substantial support from the ECOWAS Commission means that the ECCJ's "mandate stands on politically and legally firmer footing" than other courts on the continent (Ibid. 777).

41 East African Community, *Treaty for the Establishment of the East African Community* (1999), at Treaty for the Establishment of the East African Community - East African Court of Justice (eacj.org) (accessed September 8, 2023). The current Members of the EAC are Uganda, Burundi, Rwanda, Tanzania, the DRC, Kenya, and South Sudan.

42 This came about because of the actions taken by Kenya in response to a ruling by the EACJ (see below). EAC, *The Treaty for the Establishment of the East African Community* (Amended on 14th December 2006 and on 20th August, 2007), at The_Treaty_for_the_Establishment_of_the_East_Africa_Community_2006_1999.pdf (eala.org) (accessed September 8, 2023).

43 For example, the case *Katabazi and Others v. Secretary-General of the East African Community and the Attorney General of the Republic of Uganda*, Reference No. 1 of 2007 addressed the wrongful reincarceration of defendants after bail had been granted. James Thuo Gathii, "Mission Creep or A Search For Relevance: The East African Court Of Justice's Human Rights Strategy," *Duke Journal Of Comparative & International Law* 24 (2013): 249–296, 254–259. In a freedom of the press case—*Burundian Journalists' Union v. Attorney General of Burundi*—the EACJ found in favor of the journalists, holding the country's restrictive press law (No. 1/2011) to be in violation of the EAC Treaty. The Court's decision induced the legislature to revise the press law in question, but shortly thereafter, violence ensued and the clamp-down on the press increased. V. Lando, "The Domestic Impact of the Decisions of the East African Court of Justice" (2018) 18 *African Human Rights Law Journal* 46. A few cases have

been brought by individuals or organizations against Rwanda in the EACJ, none having to do with violations of prohibitions on torture or extrajudicial killings. However, *Plaxeda Rugumba v. Secretary General of the EAC and Attorney General of Rwanda*, involved accusations of arbitrary arrest and detention made by Rugumba, the sister of a former Lt. Col. Seveline Rugigana Ngabo. The EACJ found for the plaintiff and its decision was upheld on appeal. As a result of this case the Military Court in Rwanda declared the detention unlawful and issued a separate detention order more in line with Rwanda's penal code.

44 *Anyang Nyong'o v. Attorney General of Kenya*, Reference No. 1 of 2006 (Nov. 27, 2006).

45 Laurence Hefler, "Backlash Against International Courts in West, East, and Southern Africa," *Proceedings of the Annual Meeting* (American Society of International Law) 109, Adapting to a Rapidly Changing World (2015): 27–30, 29.

46 SADC, *Protocol of the Tribunal in the Southern African Development Community* (2000), at Protocol_on_the_Tribunal_and_Rules_thereof2000.pdf (sadc.int) (accessed September 8, 2023). Article 16 of the SADC Treaty left the mandate of the Tribunal to be determined by later Protocols (which it has been). However, human rights are mentioned in the SADC Treaty as one of the foundational principles of SADC (Article 4) and the various areas of cooperation listed in Article 21 include issues which fall under the rubric of human rights, including social welfare. See SADC, *Declaration and Treaty of SADC* (1992), at Declaration & Treaty of SADC (1992) | SADC (accessed July 1, 2024).

47 This refers to the revision to Article 20 A in the 2007 Protocol to the Tribunal. See SADC, *Amendment to the Protocol of the Tribunal of the Southern African Development Community* (2007), at Agreement_Amending_the_Protocol_on_the_Tribunal_-_2007_-_French.pdf (sadc.int) (accessed September 8, 2023).

48 Ruppel, "Regional Economic," 294–295.

49 Ruppel, "Regional Economic," 294.

50 COMESA, *Treaty Establishing the Common Market for Eastern and Southern Africa* (2009) Comesa_treaty_revised_2009.pdf (comesacourt.org) (accessed July 2, 2024).

51 Ruppel, "Regional Economic," 285–288.

52 International Resource Justice Center, *The Common Market for Eastern and Southern Africa Court of Justice*, at Common Market for Eastern and Southern Africa Court of Justice – International Justice Resource Center (ijrcenter.org); also COMESA, *Treaty Establishing the Common Market for Eastern and Southern Africa* (2009), at Comesa_treaty_revised_2009.pdf (comesacourt.org) and COMESA, *COMESA Court of Justice, Rules of Procedure* (2016), at RULES-of-the-Court_final.pdf (comesacourt.org). All accessed September 13, 2024.

53 AU, RECs, at Regional Economic Communities (RECs) | African Union (au.int) (accessed July 3, 2024).

54 Taylor Nchako, "Climate Change, Corruption, And Colonialism: Solving the Conundrum with Regional Courts" (2023) 118 *NorthwLRev* 817, 840, citing Traité Révisé Instituant La Communauté Économique Des Etats De L'Afrique Centrale art. 29, Dec. 18, 2019, Loi No. 32 2020 autorisant la ratification du traité révisé instituant la communauté économique des Etats de l'Afrique centrale (Congo).

55 Gathii, "Mission."

56 Gathii, "Mission,"252.

57 Helfler, "Backlash."

58 Helfler, "Backlash," 29.

59 On this point, see Gathii, "Mission," 268–287. See also fn. 165 above. Although the EACJ disagreed on the legality of the process under which these amendments were made, in the end, it upheld the amendments based on unlikeliness of a

similar process repeating itself and the fact that some of the amendments were not incompatible with the EAC Treaty. Gathii, "Mission," 270.

60 The categorization scheme Gathii relies on is that created by Karen J. Alter, Laurence R. Hefler and Mikael R. Madsen, "How Context Shapes the Authority of International Courts," 79 *Law and Contemporary Problems* 1 (2016): at: https://scholarship.law.duke.edu/lcp/vol79/iss1/1 (accessed September 11, 2023).

61 James Thuo Gathii, "Variation in the Use of Subregional Integration Courts Between Business and Human Rights Actors: The Case of The East African Court Of Justice," 79 *Law and Contemporary Problems* 37 (2016). In his analysis he finds that private business actors, by comparison, avoid the use of the EACJ altogether as they perceive it as a means of polarizing relations with governments.

62 *Campbell and Others v. Zimbabwe* (Merits), Case No. SADC (T) 2/2007 (Nov. 28, 2008).

63 These States banded together in 2010 and deprived the Tribunal of the quorum needed to function by blocking the choice of the Tribunal's judges. Sebastian Bates, "Law Society of South Africa and Others v. President of the Republic of South Africa and Others," 114 *American Journal of International Law* 275 (2020).

64 Hefler, "Backlash," 30. For further analysis of Zimbabwe's reaction, see Frederick Cowell, "The Death of the Southern African Development Community Tribunal's Human Rights Jurisdiction, 13 *HUM. RTS. L. REV.* 153 (2013); Erika de Wet, "The Rise and Fall of the Tribunal of the Southern African Development Community: Implications for Dispute Settlement in Southern Africa," 28 *ICSID REV.* 45 (2013).

65 Bates, "Law Society," 276–277. The Constitutional Court also ruled that Zuma's action in signing the Protocol was irrational and violated the customary norm of *pacta sunt servanda* codified in Article 26 of the Vienna Convention. Bates, "Law Society," 277.

66 In this instance, the Tanzanian High Court found that Tanzania's action in obstructing the choice of Judges for the SADC Tribunal violated rule of law provisions in the SADC Treaty.

67 Bates refers to the recent decision of the Tanzanian government to withdraw direct access to the ACtHPR for individuals and NGOs. "Law Society," 278 at fn. 11. For an especially in-depth analysis of the 2014 Protocol, see Tapiwa Shumba, "Rising from its ruins? The Southern African Development Community (SADC) Tribunal," *Law, Democracy and Development* (2022): 287–310.

68 Alter, Hefler, and McAllister, "A New International Human Rights Court," 778. On this point, see also Solomon Tamarabrakemi Ebobrah and Victor Lando, "Africa's Sub-Regional Courts as Back-Up Custodians of Constitutional Justice." In *The Performance of Africa's International Courts: Using Litigation for Political, Legal, and Social Change, International Courts and Tribunals Series*, ed. James Thuo Gathii (Oxford: Oxford Univ. Press, 2020).

69 Viljoen, *International*, 10.

70 Anne-Marie Slaughter, "Judicial Globalization," 40 *Virginia Journal of International Law* 1103 (Summer 2000).

71 There are several terms for this process, aside from "transjudicial," there is also "inter-judicial coordination," and "international judicial dialogue." Moreover, there is an abundance of literature on this topic (by whatever label used). See Amrei Müller and Hege Elisabeth Kjos "Introduction." In *Judicial Dialogue and Human Rights. Studies on International Courts and Tribunals*, eds. Amrei Müller and Hege Elisabeth Kjos, 1–24. (New York: Cambridge University Press, 2017), 2–3, at fns. 8–18. There is disagreement among scholars as to whether this "conversation" is beneficial and to whom. For example, Slaughter advocates for greater dialogue between courts regarding human rights as contributing to a stronger global human rights regime (see Anne Marie Slaughter, "A Typology of

Transjudicial Communication," 29 U. Rich, L. Rev 99 [1995]; "Judicial Globalization"; and *A New World Order* (Princeton University Press, 2004), particularly, chapter 2 [65–103]). Others such as D. Long and W.C. Chang voice concern about the "selective use" by domestic judges of the decisions of other courts. For their more complete review of extant literature on this issue, see Müller and Kjos, "Introduction," 7–10. Judicial dialogue can be vertical or horizontal. By "vertical" it is meant lower courts referencing the rulings of higher external courts, like the Inter-American Court for Human Rights or the ACtHPR. "Horizontal" dialogue exists between the domestic courts of countries, or it could also mean between international courts. Michael Freitas Mohallem, "Horizontal Judicial Dialogue in Human Rights: The Practice of the Constitutional Courts in South America." In Müller and Kjos, *Judicial Dialogue*, 67–113.

72 They do, however, make an exception for those instances in which a domestic court is bound by an international court to enforce a decision. Müller and Kjos, "Introduction," 14.

73 Izabella Skomerska-Muchowska, "Judicial Dialogue on International Human Rights Law in Poland and Eastern Europe." In Müller and Kjos, *Judicial Dialogue*, 31–32. In her assessment of the use of external courts' decisions by the Polish and other Eastern European domestic courts, she found that the decisions issued by courts such as the European Court of Human Rights and the EU Court of Justice tended to be used by domestic courts to "increase the authority of their own judgments." Skomerska-Muchowska, "Judicial," 66.

74 One of the landmark rulings for human rights in South Africa in which the Constitutional Court relied on a great many sources of international law, including the soft law decisions of the HRC, is the *State v. Makwanyee and Another* (1995 [3] SALR 391 [CC]) which involved the constitutionality of the death penalty. Adjami, "African," 150–152; see also Slaughter, "Judicial Globalization," 1110.

75 Adjami, "African."

76 The European Convention had a large impact on the constitutions of many African States because of the specificity of the rights included and the "colonial clause" of the Convention which applied the Convention to former colonies per the choice of the former colonies. Adjami, "African," 116–117.

77 Adjami, "African," 130–131.

78 1993 (l) ZLR 242 (S.Ct.).

79 The case concerned the argument that being placed on death row was a form of inhuman and degrading treatment in violation of the Zimbabwean Constitution and international law. However, Adjami points out that the Supreme Court of Zimbabwe's decision did not suggest that the ICCPR or the decisions of the CCPR are in any way superior to or should have greater influence over the Court's decisions than the rulings of any of the other courts cited, including the European Court of Human Rights. This is problematic because the Superior Court of Zimbabwe "viewed its role primarily as one of elevating its national human rights jurisprudence to the international or civilized standard rather than acting as a locus of judicial review of Zimbabwe's compliance with its obligations under international law." Adjami, "African," 147. Still, the Supreme Court ruled that the death penalty for the applicants in this case *was* unconstitutional and changed their sentences to life imprisonment. The opinion by the Chief Justice of the Court, Anthony Gubbay, is insightful for its reliance on several sources of comparative law. For her full assessment of the opinion, see Adjami, "African," 146–148. A host of other similar examples of judicial dialogue between domestic courts in Africa and between African domestic courts, regional and international bodies, and the domestic courts of non-African States, in more recent times, can be gathered from the latest issues of the *Journal of African Law*, *African Yearbook of International Law*, and the *Eastern Africa Law Review* for starters.

5 The UN Charter-Based Processes and Evaluations of Africa's Conflicts and Human Rights Protections

Henry F. (Chip) Carey

Introduction

This chapter seeks to understand what the United Nations (UN) might reveal about Africa's human rights protection, conflict management, and other aspects of human development, and, just as significant, how the UN treats Africa compared to other regions. When we speak of the UN, this chapter focuses on UN Charter bodies, whose legal and political authority comes from the human rights and general provisions of the UN Charter. The UN Charter-based mechanisms include especially the Secretariat, the UN General Assembly (UNGA), the UN Security Council (UNSC), the UN High Commissioner for Refugees (UNHCR) and the Office of the High Commissioner for Human Rights (OHCHR), as well as the Human Rights Council (HRC) and its Special Procedures. These are the *political* bodies of the UN, which are theoretically, though not always practically, subject to the more overt political control of the UN member states.

Research about how the UN treats Africa would naturally focus on UN activities, on the one hand, and the nature of the conflicts and conditions in Africa itself, on the other. This chapter examines what the UN reveals about Africa and what the UN does to support or undermine Africa. It might follow that a continent with low human development (according to several UN indices) or a high number of armed conflicts would naturally absorb more attention from the UN. While this activity might be appropriate to an institution devoted to raising human development and reducing the number and intensity of armed conflicts, it might also reflect biases or double standards toward that country or region. Of course, the interaction of the UN could easily be inadequate, complex, and interactive in various levels of governance within and beyond the UN itself. But this interaction effect determines how much UN monitoring pressure, along with jawboning, positive and negative sanctions, and other coercive sanctions, may improve human rights practices.

The UN Treaty-based institutions are often strong in their critique of human rights violations, but weak in the powers of mediation or other forms of peace management and human rights protection. Special representatives of the Secretary-General have the most power to mediate, for example, but

DOI: 10.4324/9781003471677-7

often remain dependent on strong states with interests in a conflict and consent. Such generalizations can be temporal. For example, in the early 1990s, because of a US desire to create a norm of democracy protection in the Americas, Haiti was arguably the most important issue on the UN agenda (and of newspapers and the US administration of that time). Right now, in 2024, the UN's rhetorical focus is on the Gaza and Ukrainian wars, but decisive action is not possible with a veto-deadlocked UNSC. However, it would not be correct to say that the wars in Sudan, Yemen, Ethiopia, and Libya get no attention from the UNSC or the UNGA. There is limited attention to sending peacekeeping troops to these countries, making way instead for mediation efforts that include the "good offices" of the Secretary General, as well as talks hosted by various states such as Qatar.

In attempting to understand whether there are biases and other forms of different interactions with Africa at the UN, it would be necessary to compare Africa with how the UN organs treat that region with other regions to see if double standards exist. However, such comparisons are beyond the scope of this chapter and would require a book-length treatment. This chapter instead examines the root causes of Africa's lack of political development and its difficulties in legalizing human rights laws. This chapter then focuses on the work that the UNSC, the OHCHR, the HRC and relevant special procedures mechanisms are conducting in Africa. These activities reveal a great deal about the success of UN attempts at embedding internationally accepted human rights practices in these African States. Of course, it goes without saying that the UN is inherently a political body made up of sovereign states, each with their own agendas and interests. This chapter concludes with a discussion about the limitations of UN Charter-based bodies in Africa.

The Root Causes of Human Rights Violations in Africa

Several African countries face critical human rights violations, notably their failure to deliver services or direct actions on the part of their governments that amount to violations. Violations of positive rights, meaning the inability of most African nations to provide relevant programs and services necessary for their people's well-being, are very serious. A clear example can be drawn from Mozambique, where less than 60 percent of the population is able to access healthcare services. This is because of inadequate health infrastructure, insufficient medical supplies, and few trained health professionals. There are similar situations in Nigeria, especially in the north, where access to education is still very low due to the ongoing insurgencies, many of which directly target children.[1] Situations like these demand multidimensional efforts that dedicate investments in education, healthcare, and security as three principles toward a better future for all.

Negative rights violations are direct actions taken by governments against their citizenry. In Eritrea, arbitrary detentions, torture, and disappearances of political dissidents occur absent due process.[2] As discussed in Chapter 12 of this volume, Zimbabwe is experiencing extrajudicial killings and heavy political repression against political opponents and activists.[3] The justice systems of these and other African countries lack transparency and accountability and have been the recipient of condemnation from the international community at large. It is only when the rule of law and respect for the rights of the citizens are upheld that these countries will be able to experience the tenure of true justice and stability.

Despite numerous challenges, African countries have improved health and life expectancy remarkably. During the past three decades, due to enhanced vaccinations, better nutrition, and access to health services, the population of the continent gained 15 years in life expectancy. However, on a global scale, these successes are often overlooked. The world focuses instead on what's not going well, which is discouraging for health workers and the public who have made great efforts to bring these improvements about. Global recognition of successes in health is very important, however small they may appear to be.[4]

Many of the human rights violations in Africa have been attributed by the UN Charter-based bodies to the legacies of colonial rule.[5] Borders drawn regardless of local populations and the colonial exploitation of resources influenced the policy trajectories of most African states in the postcolonial era.[6] Legislation and institutions were inherited from colonial times. To cultivate long-lasting peace and justice in Africa as elsewhere in the postcolonial world, the causes of the problems need to be unraveled.

Additionally, weak governance structures which foment instability and corruption in these states as well as economic turmoil play a large role in their inability to legalize international human rights protections.[7] Strong institutions are necessary for an effective system of administration of justice to function. Their competences must be clearly defined, their powers delimitated from and balanced against each other, and the independence of the judiciary guaranteed. A legal framework must be in place that makes these institutions accessible and their functioning transparent. To this end, the state also must provide appropriate financial means.[8] An absence of accountability and transparency within many governments only continues the impunity that fosters a culture of abuse and violence. Due to the need for robust governance structures, it is hard to make any change to the very foundations of human rights violations.

Acute state failure massively degrades a state's capacity to address a myriad of crisis situations ranging from a stricken economy, disaster events, to political turmoil. Where governance is weak, such crises are usually *not* followed with appropriate and timely strategies to address these challenges. This ineffectiveness increases focus and enhances the effects of contemporary crises in the background and leads to human rights abuses. When institutions and mechanisms are weak, the governments fail to protect the citizens and offer them support and assistance. Due to economic losses, for instance, weak governance might result in impaired social protection and support mechanisms; hence, vulnerable persons and groups are exposed to abuse and suffering. Likewise, natural disasters can seriously threaten people's well-being because, often, an ineffective or corrupt centralized government leads to inadequate disaster response and aid distribution, which affects the marginalized to the greatest extent. Different authors have indicated that poor governance is characterized by weak institutions and political instability, meaning that human rights are likely to be violated since those in authority can act in an arbitrary manner. Summing up, the inactivity of the state for the time of crisis undermines the citizens' protection a lot and aggravates the chances to become a target of human rights violation or be used for that purpose.

Moreover, autocratic influence over the human rights mechanisms is one of the critical factors that compromise their operations. Most African states face tremendous political pressure concerning their judiciary systems as well as human rights commissions and other supervisory structures. This control can be exerted by manipulative appointments and restricted funding or, in extreme cases, direct intimidation of these institutions' capacity to work objectively. Creativity also fades away, and decisions that are made are influenced by the authoritarian state and may not be fair to others. This interference is very grave for human rights protection. Thus, when the institutions endowed with safeguarding rights are weakened, citizens become defenseless against exploitation and abuse. Where the judiciary is not independent, there is probability of bias in the rulings in favor of the ruling party so that those who have been denied their rights, including those who are persecuted, do not get justice. This erosion undermines democratic institutions, decreases public trust in the governance, and maintains the orbits of injustice and instability.

With respect to economic instability, a report by the United Nations Economic Commission for Africa connects economic crises and suppression of human rights to the fact that poverty and economic hardships lead to the vulnerable circumstances. In miserable conditions people are ready to engage in criminal behaviors, like robbery or trafficking in human beings. Inability to obtain funds limits human beings' rights of education, health, and shelter. Poverty exacerbates social issues and struggles for resources; hence, human rights infringements.[9] One can conclude that any human rights difficulties can be alleviated by addressing economic vulnerability.

To use Sudan as an example, the transitional government has a mountainous task dealing with a legacy of abuses of human rights in an atmosphere of persisting violence and political instability. The Darfur region remains a major zone of conflict, with unabated fighting between the government forces, militias, and rebels killing and displacing civilians.[10] Powerful political and military actors and structural flaws further hinder the attempt to bring criminals of the past to justice. This transition is further complicated by arbitrary arrests, detentions, and crackdowns on dissent. Efforts to build a democratic and inclusive political atmosphere are undermined. All these challenges are worsened both by economic difficulties and by the need for comprehensive reforms to dismantle the systems that have allowed past abuses to occur. While some positive developments have taken place, long-lasting peace and justice in Sudan will still be very difficult to achieve, with enormous challenges lying ahead, which will need the sustained support of the international community and a strong commitment to human rights and democratic values internally.

The OHCHR has highlighted the need for comprehensive strategies on the development challenges created by displacement and social cohesion. It also calls for comprehensive approaches toward development, including reconciliation of conflicts, security, and humanitarian crises. According to the report, climate change alone causes over 30 million people (about the population of Texas) to be displaced annually. There is a call for collaborative actions toward establishing strong communities through incorporating human rights into development and humanitarian activities. These strategies focus more on long-term solutions and work for the well-being of affected populations with an eye toward reaching inclusive progress toward the UN's Sustainable Development Goals. They also prioritize human rights in their attempt to reduce the worst consequences of displacement and encourage social cohesion.[11]

The next section of this chapter assesses the Charter-based bodies' explanations as to why the progress African states make in their implementation and compliance with international human rights protections has been uneven and incomplete.

The Unevenness and Lack of Comprehension in the Legalization of Interlinked Human Rights in Africa?

The HRC has written, "[w]hile some areas [in Africa] have seen improvements, many other sectors remain problematic, resulting in partial recognition of progress."[12] The paper describes how in some countries, advances in specific areas like health and education go hand in hand with deterioration of political and civil liberties. Sometimes, advancement in the health and education sectors may be noticed while political leadership or judicial systems may remain poor. This means a human rights record is an institution progressing at unequal paces, leading to a mixed bag of improvements and continued deterioration of human rights. For instance, a country that may have reasonably low instances of child mortality at the same time could be experiencing political repression and corruption. Overall assessments are still negative because of troubles in other areas, which contribute to only partial acknowledgment of improvements.

In Africa, the rights of a human are well intertwined, which is to say that advancement in one area cannot make up for a lack of advancement in others. For example, better health and education are needed; however, they should be paired with enhancement of political, economic, and social justice that are all under the human rights banner. Peace is focused on the topic of political repression, economic injustice, and other similar questions to establish the conditions necessary for the realization of the rights. For example, citizens may be unable to realize such gains due to lack of political liberty and a good governance system, though education and health have improved. Likewise, lack of economic stability and social justice causes human rights programs to yield minimal progress. To embrace the totality of human rights political, economic, social as well as cultural rights are essential in order to guarantee the delivery of the tenets of human rights as a way of promoting and transforming the lives of people for the better in Africa and establish the substance and essence of the political, economic, social, and cultural rights that are essential for human dignity and the acceleration of human rights for positive change on the continent and the globe. The next section of this chapter examines the specific activities of the UN Charter-based bodies in Africa.

The Charter-Based Bodies of the UN

On human rights issues, the distinction between UN Charter-based and multilateral Treaty-Based institutions was developed by Flood, who argues that Charter-based bodies, despite the paradox that human rights and other legal issues are supposed to be apolitical and legally neutral, are more potent in addressing human rights issues of concern to the UN.[13] Why and where "states of importance" choose to make their influence felt would naturally show the extent of UN institutional effectiveness in its more political, Charter-based bodies, especially through the medium of the UNSC and UNGA on a multilateral basis, in addition to what they might do on a unilateral or bilateral basis.

As far as internal UN practices are concerned, the UN remains an environment of mutual dependence that might lead to continued effectiveness when and if the political will can be mustered, especially if there is interdependence on some issues of common interest and the expectation of some reciprocity. When there is coherence in the political UN Charter-based bodies, more pressure can be brought to bear. Where and when there is division or polarization, as occurred during the Cold War, these institutions are going to be less influential. In the late Cold War, there were various openings between the Soviet Union and the United States, and the UN human rights bodies (Treaty- and Charter-based) gained more autonomy. Since the return of divisions in international politics with the rise of multipolarity, especially in the 21st century, however, we see a breakdown in the political influence of the more political Charter-based bodies within the UN compared to the UN Treaty-based bodies as well as other treaty-based bodies (e.g. the International Criminal Court, the European Union). Of course, the divisions in world politics have also led to less cooperation with Treaty-based bodies than may have existed before. And we see this most prominently in the failure of the

International Criminal Court to become consistently proactive toward non-African states.

The UN Security Council

Africa, both sub-Saharan and its largely ethnic Arab northern region, has absorbed a disproportionate share of attention from institutions created by the UN Charter as a share of the world's population. Most of the scholarship and political activism regarding the UNSC has been focused on both the veto authority of the five permanent members and the lack of representation of Africa. Of course, there were few independent states in Africa prior to the wave of decolonization that began mostly in the early 1960s, other than in Egypt, South Africa, and Ethiopia. In March 2005, the AU adopted the "Ezulwini Consensus" for Africa and African countries to be "fully represented in all decision-making organs of the UN, particularly the Security Council."[14]

The role of the African three plus members of the UNSC (A3+) is a mechanism for projecting Africa's influence in UNSC decision-making. The A3+ are *not* permanent members of the UNSC but are three of the ten members that serve on a rotating basis. Nearly two decades later, the AU has used its A3+ representation on the UNSC, three from Africa, plus, currently Guyana, which caucuses with the AU member states on the UNSC (currently Sierra Leone, Somalia, and Algeria), to advance Africa's interests. Pending major reform of the UNSC, the A3+ will continue as the instrument on which African countries use for consolidating Africa's agency in peace and security decision-making in the UN system. The operation of the A3+ as a unified body representing a collective voice of Africa as expressed through the AU Peace and Security Council (PSC) has far exceeded the initial motivation of avoiding the pursuit of divergent positions by the PSC and the A3+. It has since transformed into an instrument for negotiating power and projecting influence in UNSC decision-making.[15]

However, it has not always been this way. According to Forti:

> Despite much time having been spent on African issues, many UNSC members have treated Africa as marginal or less strategic compared to Syria, North Korea or the Middle East. African files (including many UN peacekeeping operations) have therefore, often not been very contentious in the council. The council's five permanent members—China, France, Russia, the United Kingdom, the US—are mired by impasses and conflicting strategic interests, including among once-strong allies. Clashes in other parts of the world are now affecting the UNSC's engagements with Africa.[16]

A3+ members can show unity through various approaches. They can issue joint statements to the council, define joint negotiating positions for outcome documents, and convene joint public press stakeouts. The role played by the AU permanent observer mission to the UN is particularly important. It helps coordinate A3+ and AU engagements, facilitate regular interactions with diplomats and officials in Addis Ababa, and retain AU and UN institutional memory. A3+ members alone have limited influence on the UNSC. But a unified position on African files, especially when informed by AU Peace and Security Council decisions, provides legitimacy, credibility, and leverage in A3+ engagements with other Security Council members and can influence outcomes. In a sign of such unity, the A3+ in 2019 delivered 16 joint statements in the UNSC during both country-specific and thematic debates.

According to Allen,

> The rise and persistence of African-led peace operations represent a trend toward localized ownership over conflict management. African-led peace operations have been vital tools for managing Africa's complex array of security challenges, though continued reform is needed to intervene more decisively in the continent's most devastating conflicts. Due to a divided UNSC and what has been perceived to be the limited success of large, multidimensional, UN-sponsored missions, the deployment of UN forces in Africa has waned. No new UN mission has been authorized in Africa in close to a decade. With the drawdown of MINUSMA, the UN mission in Mali in December 2023, the UN has only five remaining active missions on the continent. Meanwhile, the AU, Regional Economic Communities ("RECs"), and regional actors have authorized 16 new peace operations over the past decade, 10 of which are active.[17]

In September 2024, the US government proposed that two *permanent* UNSC seats for Africa (as it has also proposed for India, Japan, and Germany but *not* for Brazil).[18] None of these additional regional permanent seats would have veto authority under the US proposal.

The HRC, Special Procedures Mechanisms, and the Activities of the OHCHR

The amount of work accomplished by the OHCHR and the HRC cannot be included in its entirety in this chapter. To conserve word space this chapter limits its analysis to the HRC's special procedures and the OHCHR's treaty-building capacity, its efforts to promote good practices and due diligence and compliance among states, its efforts to address more current issues, such as AI and climate change, and its efforts to promote judicial independence, civil society and governmental accountability in African states.

The composition of the Human Rights Council at its 56th session included Algeria (2025); Benin (2024); Burundi (2026); Cameroon (2024); Côte d'Ivoire (2026); Eritrea (2024); Gambia (2024); Ghana (2026); Malawi (2026); Somalia (2024); South Africa (2025); and Sudan (2025).[19]

The HRC's special procedures system currently includes 83 mandate holder positions, with 81 active mandate holders. The HRC appointed 16 mandate holders in 2023. The gender balance is 59 percent women and 41 percent men. The total number of Special Procedures mandates is currently 60, of which 46 are thematic and 14 are country specific.[20] As of December 31, 2023, 25 percent of mandate holders came from African States. At its 54th session, the Human Rights Council created a Working Group on the rights of peasants and other people working in rural areas (resolution 54/9). The Coordination Committee most recently held its 29th annual meeting of special rapporteurs, independent experts, and chairs of working groups.[21]

Mandate holders conducted 82 on-site visits to 56 States and territories and 3 institutions.[22] A total of 128 States and 1 non-member Observer State had extended standing invitations as of the end of 2023.[23] At the same time, 172 States had been visited by at least 1 mandate holder, while 21 States had not yet received any visits. Among the latter, four had not received requests, sixteen had not accepted requests and one had accepted requests for visits that had yet to take place.[24] In 2023, mandate holders transmitted 723 communications (inquiries about human rights violations, 621 of which were sent jointly to 126 States and 163 non-State actors). The communications covered 1,128 individuals, 298 of whom were identified as female. A total of 433 replies (399 substantive replies) were received in 2023, which includes replies to communications sent before 2023. A total of 341 replies to communications sent in 2023 were received, of which 312 (43.15 percent reply rate)[25] were substantive replies. Some communications received more than one reply.[26]

Communications sent and replies received are available on a dedicated website,[27] through which users can access the database of all communications sent and replies received since the eighteenth session of the Human Rights Council. Communications and associated replies from governments and others can be searched by mandate, country, geographical region, time, and/or by the communications reports submitted to the Council since 2011. All communications are made public after 60 days, and other letters, which are related to draft or existing legislation, policy, or practice not deemed to be in compliance with international human rights norms and standards, after 48 hours. Responses received are also released publicly.[28]

During the three 2023 sessions of the HRC, 56 country reports were presented by thematic mandate holders Eleven reports concerned States in Africa, including Angola (Special Rapporteur on the elimination of discrimination against persons affected by leprosy (Hansen's disease) and their family members); Botswana (Working Group on Arbitrary Detention); Ghana (Special Rapporteur on the implications for human rights of the environmentally sound management and disposal of hazardous substances and wastes); and Liberia (Working Group on the issue of human rights and transnational corporations and other business enterprises).[29] At the 54th session of the Human Rights Council, the Working Group of Experts on People of African

Descent, which typically focuses on ethnic African minorities *not* in Africa, presented its annual report, as well as several specific reports.[30] The Independent Expert on the Enjoyment of Human Rights by Persons with Albinism provided three reports, including a country visit to Madagascar.[31] This form of discrimination is prevalent, but it certainly is not restricted to Africa.

The country-specific mandate holders submitted reports that included the Special Rapporteur on the situation of human rights in Burundi; the Independent Expert on the situation of human rights in the Central African Republic (CAR); the Special Rapporteur on the situation of human rights in Eritrea; the Independent Expert on the situation of human rights in Mali; and the Independent Expert on the situation of human rights in Somalia.

The concept of norm diffusion, in its positive sense, usually describes the process whereby States learn from others' best practices in developing and strengthening their own human rights norms. A negative pattern of norm diffusion is discernible when States emulate discriminatory and restrictive legislation curtailing freedoms of expression, peaceful assembly, and association based on sexual orientation and gender identity.

The Independent Expert on protection against violence and discrimination based on sexual orientation and gender identity, Graeme Reid, concluded that one of the arguments used by those seeking to restrict LGBT rights—both those who do so on ideological grounds and those seeking political capital—is that transnational advocacy for equality is evidence of "foreign" interference by Western actors seeking to impose their values to the detriment of national sovereignty and cultural integrity. Echoes of such rhetoric and framing are evident in Africa and the Caribbean.[32]

Through its treaty body capacity-building program, OHCHR supported engagement with the human rights treaty bodies of parties to the human rights treaties, including representatives of Burundi, the CAR, the Democratic Republic of Congo (DRC), Guinea-Bissau, Senegal, Sierra Leone, Tunisia, and the United Republic of Tanzania. The OHCHR also supported exchanges of good practices relating to national mechanisms for implementation, reporting, and follow-up. This included a regional event in the Middle East and North Africa. OHCHR supported States in the establishment or strengthening of national mechanisms for implementation, reporting, and follow-up in Burundi, the CAR, Chad, Ethiopia, Lesotho, and Mozambique. OHCHR organized webinars on Sustainable Development Goal 16 indicators in the Middle East and North Africa, in conjunction with the United Nations Office on Drugs and Crime (UNODC), UNDP, the United Nations Educational, Scientific and Cultural Organization (UNESCO), and United Nations regional economic commissions. In September 2023, OHCHR, UNODC, and UNDP released the first Global Progress Report on Sustainable Development Goal 16 indicators.[33]

Today as part of the B-Tech Project, OHCHR developed resources for preventing and addressing human rights risks relating to generative artificial intelligence.[34] For example, OHCHR enhanced knowledge and capacity on business and human rights and the implementation of the Guiding Principles on Business and Human Rights at the regional and national levels, including through the Business and Human Rights Africa Project[35] and the Joint Project on Responsible Business Conduct in Latin America and the Caribbean.[36] Among other activities, OHCHR supported multi-stakeholder dialogues in Chile, Honduras, Mexico, and Rwanda. In October 2023, OHCHR also organized the Eighth Regional Forum for Latin America and the Caribbean on Business and Human Rights. OHCHR participated in field monitoring visits to industrial sites, including in Liberia, as part of its work on human rights due diligence. OHCHR engaged in support of the development of the European Union Corporate Sustainability Due Diligence Directive.[37] A guidance note on business and human rights in challenging contexts[38] was published in August 2023 and formed the basis for a multi-stakeholder session during the 12th annual meeting of the Forum on Business and Human Rights.

OHCHR also jointly organized forums on environmental human rights defenders in East Africa.[39] OHCHR supported legal developments relating to the right to a clean, healthy, and sustainable environment, including ongoing judicial cases. The Office supported the African Union to integrate human rights into its early warning system. In Ethiopia, OHCHR started the process of establishing early warning mechanisms at the community level. The Office designed and delivered training modules on integrating human rights into early warning and conflict prevention, and deployed surge teams to Gabon, Liberia, Senegal, and Tunisia, as well as to the Occupied Palestinian Territory. The Office strengthened the integration of a gender perspective in documenting, analyzing, and reporting on the human rights situation by OHCHR and mandated bodies, including in Afghanistan, Belarus, the CAR, DRC, Mali, and the Sudan.

OHCHR supported human rights components in United Nations peacekeeping operations and special political missions, including in United Nations transition contexts and in integrating human rights into relevant policies and guidance. OHCHR also conducted 18 specialized courses benefiting more than 240 military, police, and civilian peacekeepers, with a focus on training of trainers and senior mission leaders, and the piloting and roll-out of new programs. Through strategic engagement, OHCHR sought to strengthen or preserve the inclusion of human rights in UNSC resolutions on the mandates of peace operations in the CAR, the DRC, Libya, Somalia, South Sudan, and the Sudan, as well as in Abyei.[40]

With respect to human rights due diligence and compliance networks, OHCHR headquarters provide support in implementing the United Nations human rights due diligence policy to its field presences, United Nations peace missions and United Nations country teams in Burkina Faso, the CAR, Chad, the DRC, Libya, Madagascar, Mali, Mozambique, Nigeria, Somalia, South Sudan, the Sudan, the Syrian Arab Republic, and Yemen, as well as in Abyei. OHCHR also supported United Nations entities in developing internal due diligence procedures and processes, and the European Union in developing a human rights due diligence policy for its support to the security sector.

OHCHR supported implementation of the African Union Compliance and Accountability Framework, in partnership with the AU and the EU. OHCHR also advocated inclusion of human rights provisions in Security Council resolution 2719 (2023), establishing the foundation for a new generation of AU peace support operations authorized by the Security Council and financed on a case-by-case basis through United Nations assessed contributions.[41] The Office ended its support for the Joint Force of the Group of Five for the Sahel.

OHCHR continues to provide technical assistance to States and other stakeholders on transitional justice processes, including in the CAR, Chad, the DRC, Ethiopia, the Gambia, Guinea, Libya, and South Sudan.[42] This included, for example, support for the development of the transitional justice policy and accountability for violations in Ethiopia.

OHCHR continues to monitor, train, and advise state institutions and other actors to strengthen the administration of justice and the rule of law, including in the CAR, Ethiopia, the Gambia, Kenya, Libya, Madagascar, Mozambique, and South Sudan. Examples of such work include the delivery of technical assistance to the Police Department of Belize. OHCHR advised authorities and monitored conditions of detention, including in Chad, Liberia, South Sudan, and Tunisia. In the DRC, an OHCHR judicial protection scheme was instrumental in the success of joint investigation teams and mobile courts.[43]

OHCHR supports efforts to facilitate effective, inclusive, and safe civil society participation in UN processes and forums, including in the context of concerns regarding the absence of hybrid modalities in the work of United Nations human rights mechanisms and other processes. The Office reinforced its monitoring capacity on civic space–related issues, including through in-house artificial intelligence models and digital tools, building on efforts made in 2022 to track attacks against human rights defenders.[44] The Office convened protection networks to promote the sharing of good practices in protecting civil society actors, including human rights defenders, and improve coordination. OHCHR continued to engage with States and support the efforts of the United Nations system to prevent and address intimidation and reprisals against those who cooperate with the United Nations, including through the Secretary-General's report on reprisals.[45]

In total, the OHCHR helped establish or strengthen national human rights institutions in 55 countries.[46] OHCHR organized a fellowship program for staff of national human rights institutions that had been accredited with A status with the participation of the institutions of Cameroon and Kenya.

OHCHR headquarters provided support in implementing the United Nations human rights due diligence policy to its field presences, United Nations peace missions, and United Nations country teams in Burkina Faso, the CAR, Chad, the DRC, Kenya, Lebanon, Libya, Madagascar, Mali,

Mozambique, Nigeria, Somalia, South Sudan, the Sudan, the Syrian Arab Republic, and Yemen, as well as in Abyei. OHCHR also supported United Nations entities in developing internal due diligence procedures and processes, and the European Union in developing a human rights due diligence policy for its support to the security sector.[47]

Conclusions: The Relative Ineffectiveness of International Responses

Despite the voluminous work that the Charter-based institutions have done in Africa, much work remains. The UNDP has stated that "Many international human rights initiatives in Africa lack sufficient funding and resources to be effective."[48] The UNDP report considers issues that are financial and material where human rights programs are in question. These include inadequate funding and resources to enable states to support the implementation and sustainment of international human rights. A lack of funds, human resources, and structures diminish the ability to deal with human rights problems efficiently. To increase the efficiency of human rights programs, funding and resources which are available for human rights programs should be raised.

Moreover, hindrances like accessibility, terrain, insecurity, and access restrict the supply of assistance and help to conflicted regions. To overcome the challenges, better coordination, infrastructure, and securing of aid delivery must be attained. [49] Adding insult to injury, "[i]nternational interventions often suffer from a lack of coordination, leading to fragmented and ineffective responses."[50] Money, people, and materials might be wasted, resources may be duplicated or misallocated, and because of that, initiatives might not have the synergies required to create a tangible change. The problem requires a coherent and synchronized strategy to achieve the highest level of efficiency in international actions in the sphere of human rights, especially in situations in which human rights abuses are rampant.[51]

Lastly, and as discussed in Chapters 7 and 13 of this volume, there is always the matter of geopolitics and political will. Political and diplomatic processes affect the human rights intervention mechanisms. Organization politics, which include concepts like state authority, balance of power, and diplomacy, curtail the extent of human rights interventions. Coordination of all these constraints with the imperatives of human rights actions is always a delicate issue of lobbying. Certain reactions by countries and with reference to geopolitical situations may also worsen the situation since human rights are not of much importance as political power. However, when international responses focus on geopolitical concerns rather than human rights, the position tends to be worse. Maneuvers imposed by strategic or political interests are likely to disregard the best interest of the people who are affected within society at large, resulting in unproductive and unconstructive activities.[52]

Notes

1 OHCHR, "Report of the Independent Fact-Finding Mission on Libya," (August 18, 2022), (A/HRC/49/4).
2 OHCHR, A/HRC/49/4.
3 OHCHR, "Report of the Independent Fact-Finding Mission on Libya," (June, 2022), (A/HRC/50/63).
4 OHCHR, "Report of the Working Group on the Universal Periodic Review," (Jan. 6, 2022) and "Annual report of the United Nations High Commissioner for Human Rights," (June 14, 2022), (A/HRC/50/4).
5 OHCHR, "Report of the Working Group on the Universal Periodic Review," (January 7, 2022), A/HRC/49/14.
6 African Commission on Human and Peoples' Rights, *"Human Rights Situation in Africa"*, (2019), UN ACHPR/RES/2019; HRC, *"Report on Post-Colonial Conflicts in Africa"*, (2021), (UNHRC/2021/45); United Nations Development Programme (UNDP), *"The Impact of Colonial Borders in Africa,"* (2018), (UNDP/2018/30); Yakin Ertürk, *"Promotion and Protection of all Human Rights UNHRC"* (2008), (A/HRC/7/6/Add.4.); also, World Bank. *"Colonial Economic Impacts in Africa,"* (2020), (WB/2020/22).
7 OHCHR, "Report of the Working Group on the Universal Periodic Review," (April 5, 2022), A/HRC/50/9; also, OHCHR, A/HRC/49/4. Transparency International, *"Corruption and Human Rights Abuses in Africa"*, (2020), TI/2020/10; African Court on Human and Peoples' Rights, *"Strengthening the Judicial System for Human Rights Protection"*, (2017), ACHPR/2017/15; International Crisis Group. *"Governance in Africa: Challenges and Solutions,"* (2020), ICG/2020/25; Amnesty International, *"Political Influence in African Institutions,"* (2021), (AI/2021/12).
8 HRC, *"Promotion and Protection of all Human Rights,"* (2008), (A/HRC/7/4/Add.4), 73.
9 UNECA, *"Economic Crises and Their Impact on Human Rights,"* (2019), (UNECA/2019/40), 40.
10 OHCHR, "Situation of human rights in Belarus in the run-up to the 2020 presidential election and in its aftermath," (March 4, 2022), (A/HRC/49/71).
11 OHCHR, "Report of the Special Rapporteur on the promotion and protection of human rights in the context of climate change, Ian Fry," (June 22, 2022), (A/HRC/50/39).
12 HRC, "Human Rights Progress in Africa," (2023), (UNHRC/2023/14), 14.
13 Patrick James Flood, *The Effectiveness of UN Human Rights Institutions* (Westport, CT: Praeger 1998). Flood does not examine the UNGA and UNSC, even though he acknowledges that both expanded their human rights activities under Chapter VI and VII of the UN Charter during the late Cold War. To the extent that space permits, this chapter does look at these two institutions not only because of their direct human rights monitoring and actions, but also because the very existence of armed conflict is correlated with and arguably causes human rights and international humanitarian law violations to occur with much greater frequency and intensity.
14 The Common African Position On The Proposed Reform Of The United Nations: *"The Ezulwini Consensus", Executive Council, African Union, 7th Extraordinary Session, Addis Adaba* (March, 2005), https://old.centerforunreform.org/sites/default/files/Ezulwini%20Consensus.pdf, (accessed August 1, 2024).
15 Solomon Ayele Dersso. "How Africa is using the A3 as a de facto permanent power block in global peace and security decision-making," (Amani Africa, December 21, 2023), https://amaniafrica-et.org/how-africa-is-using-the-a3-as-a-

de-facto-permanent-power-block-in-global-peace-and-security-decision-making/, (accessed August 1, 2024).

16 Daniel Forti. "Africa Can Become More Influential In The UN Security Council: What Will It Take For The A3 To Shape Debates, Break Geo-Political Deadlocks, And Guide Collective Action?" Institute for Security Studies. March 12, 2023, https://issafrica.org/iss-today/africa-can-become-more-influential-in-the-un-security-council.

17 Nate D.F. Allen. *African-Led Peace Operations: A Crucial Tool for Peace and Security*. Africa Center for Strategic Studies. (August 9, 2023).

18 Michelle Nicholls, "*US Supports two UN Security Council seats for Africa*," *Reuters*, September 12, 2024, https://www.reuters.com/world/us-supports-two-permanent-un-security-council-seats-africa-2024-09-12/. (accessed September 15, 2024).

19 See OHCHR | 56th session of the Human Rights Council (18 June to 12 July 2024).

20 HRC, "Facts and figures with regard to the special procedures in 2023," (March 21, 2024), (A/HRC/55/69/Add.1), sect. XV.

21 HRC, "Activities of Special Rapporteurs, Independent Experts and Working Groups Of The Human Rights Council Undertaken in 2023," (March 27, 2024), (A/HRC/55/69).

22 A/HRC/55/69/Add.1, sect. VI.

23 A/HRC/55/69/Add.1, sects. III and IV.

24 A/HRC/55/69/Add.1, sect. VII. Information on the status of all country visits requested by mandate holders and on forthcoming visits is available at https://spinternet.ohchr.org/Home.aspx?lang=en.

25 As of 2018, the response rate includes only substantive replies.

26 A/HRC/55/69/Add.1, sects. IX and X.

27 See https://spcommreports.ohchr.org.

28 See Communications Sent (ohchr.org), (accessed September 10, 2024).

29 Details of the five United Nations regional groups of Member States are available here: www.un.org/dgacm/en/content/regional-groups.

30 HRC, "Economic empowerment of people of African descent," (July 21, 2023), (A/HRC/54/67 and A/HRC/54/67/Corr.1); HRC, "Visit to the United Kingdom of Great Britain and Northern Ireland," (October 5, 2023), (A/HRC/54/67/Add.1); HRC, "Facilitating the journey from rhetoric to reality," (A/HRC/54/71): and UNGA "Note by the Secretariat referring A/HRC/54/67 and A/HRC/54/71 to the General Assembly," (A/78/277).

31 HRC, "Human Rights Defenders Working on Albinism," (December 27, 2022) (A/HRC/52/36) and HRC, "Visit to Madagascar," (Jan. 26, 2023), (A/HRC/52/36/Add.1); UNGA "Climate Change and Persons with Albinism," (December 21, 2023), (A/78/167).

32 Graeme Reid, "Report of the Independent Expert on protection against violence and discrimination based on sexual orientation and gender identity. Human Rights Council. 18 June–12 July 2024" A/HRC/56/49 (un.org).

33 See https://www.ohchr.org/sites/default/files/documents/issues/sdgs/2023/20230919-global-progress-report-on-sdg-16-indicators.pdf.

34 See https://www.ohchr.org/en/business-and-human-rights/b-tech-project.

35 See https://www.ohchr.org/en/business/bhr-africa.

36 See https://www.ohchr.org/en/business/joint-project-responsible-business-conduct-latin-america-and-caribbean.

37 See https://www.ohchr.org/en/business-and-human-rights/mandatory-human-rights-due-diligence-mhrdd.

38 See https://www.ohchr.org/sites/default/files/documents/issues/business/bhr-in-challenging-contexts.pdf.

39 Annual report of the United Nations High Commissioner for Human Rights. See g2407389.pdf (un.org).
40 HRC, "Human Rights Council Fifty-sixth session 18 June–12 July 2024," at. https://documents.un.org/doc/un.oc/gen/g24/073/89/pdf/g2407389.pdf.
41 Security Council Opens Door to UN Funding for African-led Peace Missions, Unanimously Adopting Resolution 2719 (2023) | Meetings Coverage and Press Releases, (accessed September).
42 References to Kosovo shall be understood to be in the context of Security Council resolution 1244 (1999).
43 HRC, "Human Rights Council Fifty-sixth session."
44 Civil Society Space Resolution 53-13 of 6 July 2023.pdf (ecnl.org) (July 6, 2023), (accessed September 15, 2024).
45 OHCHR, OHCHR and intimidation and reprisals for cooperation with the United Nations in the field of human rights | OHCHR. (January 30, 2024), (accessed September).
46 See https://www.ohchr.org/sites/default/files/documents/countries/nhri/StatusAccreditationChartNHRIs.pdf.
47 UN Human Rights Chief urges EU leaders to approve key business and human rights legislation | OHCHR. (February 13, 2024), (accessed September 15, 2024).
48 UNDP, "Lack of Economic Opportunities and Social Unrest in Africa," (2020), (UNDP/2020/64), 64.
49 UNDP, "Governance for Sustainable Development: Lessons from Weak Institutions in Africa," (2022) (UNDP/2022/43), 43.
50 International Crisis Group. (2020). "*Governance in Africa: Challenges and Solutions,*" (ICG/2022/67), 67.
51 World Bank, "Economic Inequalities and Their Relationship to Human Rights in Africa". (2021), (WB/2021/37), 37.
52 UNDP, "Lack of Economic Opportunities and Social Unrest in Africa," (2020), (UNDP/2020/55), 55.

Part II

Continent-Wide Progress in the Legalization of Prohibitions against Torture, Disappearances, and Killings in African Countries

6 Taking the Broad View

Stacey M. Mitchell, Veraline Nchotu, and Lem Lilian Atanga

Introduction

This chapter approaches the legalization of human rights prohibiting the official use of violence in African countries from a quantitative perspective. The choice to rely on the use of quantitative methodology is intended to permit a large-scale test of each of the hypotheses referenced in Chapter 2 of this volume, including this study's primary hypothesis which is as follows:

> The more inclusive the communities of practice involved in the legalization process—the greater their ability to freely operate and litigate for the creation and implementation of human rights laws prohibiting torture, disappearances, and extrajudicial killings—the more likely that these laws will become embedded in the governing system.

We also hypothesize that the degree of inclusiveness in the communities of practice involved in policymaking processes in African states is impacted in various ways by a number of endogenous and exogenous factors which include a country's *economic health*, its *internal stability*, political stability of the geographical region in which it exists, the presence of international actors within a country, and *female representation* in government at the national level.

This chapter proceeds as follows. First, the authors introduce the model used in this analysis. Focus is placed on the choice to make the dependent variable of this study *congruence* a composite variable as well as how this variable is constructed. Then the measures of each of the five categories of independent variables being tested are explained. Attention is also given in this section to the sources of data used for these variables. The results of a multivariate regression for the period 2012 to 2021 are then provided and assessed.[1] This analysis demonstrates that greater international involvement and regional stability, and large populations of refugees and internally displaced persons (IDPs), have significant impacts on the legalization of human rights laws prohibiting violence in a country. This study concludes with some observations about the broader contributions this study makes to the legalization literature (including compliance studies),[2] and the risk assessment

DOI: 10.4324/9781003471677-9

studies that look at the potential for mass violence in Africa and other parts of the world.[3]

Methodology

Dependent Variable[4]

The dependent variable *congruence* is an amalgam of six different components: *societal engagement*, *local authority*, *independent judiciary*, *access to justice*, *corruption*, and *information access*. The choice to use a composite score stems from this study's argument that *congruence* comprises a multitude of factors that are interactive. Focusing just on civil society or judicial independence, for example, would be insufficient, as they each constitute one aspect of *congruence*. The use of a composite score also avoids the obvious issues of multicollinearity that would arise if each of these indicators were to be included in the model separately. Apart from *information access*,[5] data for *societal engagement*,[6] *local authority*, *independent judiciary*,[7] *access to justice*, and *corruption* were gathered from the Institute for Democracy and Electoral Assistance's (IDEA) Global State of Democracy (GSoD) database.

Because not all the components of *congruence* are measured the same, this study relies on the use of their z scores to create a composite index (Figure 6.1):

In this case, z is the number of standard deviation units, χ the score to be standardized, μ the indicator's mean for the period in question, and σ, the standard deviation. Koo, Kong, and Chung used this method in their analysis to assess the progress of the implementation of positive and negative human rights in Korea from 1990 to 2007.[8] The z-score value indicates the difference between a specific observation and the mean in terms of standard deviation units, which for this study translates into the progress (or not) a country has made on each of the measures of *congruence* relative to the mean of all other scores of that measure across cases.

To create the composite index, the z-scores of each individual measure of *congruence* are combined and that sum is divided by the six individual indicators of the variable. The use of z-scores combined into a single index assumes that each individual indicator exerts a similar impact as the other measures included in the combined index. This study ran a *Cronbach's alpha* test to determine reliability of the combination of the individual items within the composite variable, and the results indicate a high level of internal consistency (.860). As suspected, there is a great deal of collinearity between the six individual measures of *congruence*, and the squared multiple correlation—the extent to which each item within *congruence* explains variation in

$$C = z_1 + z_2 + z_3 + \ldots, \text{ where } z = \frac{\chi - \mu}{\sigma}$$

Figure 6.1 Congruence as a composite variable.

the each of the other measures—ranges from .398 (*local authority*) to .857 (*access to justice*).

Independent Variables and Hypotheses

The current chapter tests each of the five hypotheses made about the endogenous and exogenous factors that weaken or strengthen the communities of practice involved in the legalization of human rights laws prohibiting torture, disappearances, and extrajudicial killings in African states.

Hypothesis 1 argues that economic health of a country has a positive impact on the inclusiveness of the communities of practice involved in the process of legalizing international human rights laws prohibiting torture, political killings, and disappearances. We rely on the log of aggregate GDP (*log GDP*) to measure *economic health*.

Of course, one thing to be wary of when assessing a country's wealth status is the distribution of wealth within that country. Just because a country like South Africa or Egypt has a higher aggregate GDP relative to other countries on the continent does not mean that the population within these countries is flourishing economically. Many commonly used measures for economic well-being, such as GDP growth, trade imbalances, not to mention GDP per capita, tell us little about how well the average citizen of a country is faring.

Some studies have shown a correlation between income inequality and terrorism within a country,[9] as well as with political instability,[10] and/or political violence.[11] Others, including the study by Østby, Nordås, and Rød, find that regional income inequalities increase the potential for conflict.[12] The present study seeks to further examine this relationship. *Economic inequality* is measured by the Gini Index or Coefficient. Data are gathered from the United Nations Development Programme for each year. As a secondary hypothesis to hypothesis 1, this study suggests that greater income disparity within a country leads to less inclusive lawmaking communities of practice in that state.

Hypothesis 2 contends that conditions of internal stability in a country have a positive impact on the legalization of human rights laws prohibiting political violence. The authors of this chapter chose to focus on the presence of refugee and IDP populations and the number of terrorist attacks in a country each year (of the given time frame) to test this hypothesis, the idea being that terrorist attacks and refugee populations are detrimental to a country's degree of stability and hence law as practice in that country.

The inclusion of refugees and IDPs is important as large refugee populations and populations of IDPs remain particularly vulnerable to abuse during periods of internal crisis. At the time of this writing, according to the UN High Commissioner for Refugees (UNHCR), 117.3 million people are currently displaced around the world, the bulk of these persons in countries in the Global South.[13] Whether fleeing conflict, starvation, conditions of climate change, and/or persecution, refugees and IDPs experience conditions of structural violence in their host country, including poor living conditions, no access to social services, sexual abuse, kidnapping, and death.[14] Data for *refugees* and *IDPs* were gathered from the UNHCR database; data for terrorist attacks were obtained from the Global Terrorism Database.[15]

Hypothesis 3 addresses regional stability, specifically the human rights practices of states within a region. The authors of this chapter choose to rely on the Personal Integrity and Security Index (PISI) from the CIRI dataset, which is used by Bell, Clay, and Murdie and others to measure regional human rights practices.[16] The variable *region* measures the occurrence of tortures, disappearances, and killings within a region for a given year. To calculate the regional index, the average of the PISI scores for all states within 50 kilometers of the border of a country is used.[17] This is an additive index, where the higher the score, the better the human rights practices within a region. Hypothesis 3 suggests that better regional human rights practices positively impact the legalization of human rights laws within each state of that region.

Hypothesis 4 contends that the relationship between a substantial international presence in a country and the legalization of human rights is a positive one. Because few countries in Africa have an ongoing UN, AU, or regional peace keeping mission within their borders at the time of this writing, the authors of this chapter focus instead on the use of sanctions against a state and a greater presence of international nongovernmental organizations (INGOs) and embassies within each country to assess whether these elements of international involvement truly do make a difference on human rights legalization. Data for *sanctions* were obtained from the Global Sanctions Database.[18] Countries are coded "1" for sanctions, "0" for no sanctions.

To measure INGO involvement, this study relies on the de facto political globalization score from the KOF database, which measures the absolute number of embassies in a country and the number of INGOs with members in that country or territory. *Poliglobal* scores each country on a 100-point scale, with higher numbers indicating greater international presence in a country.[19]

The final hypothesis concerns female representation and suggests that the more female representation at the national level, the greater the legalization of human rights. *Fem LH* measures the percentage of female legislators in a country's lower house of parliament. Data on female representation were gathered from IPU Parline.[20]

Controls

The present study controls for other factors that may exert an influence on the process of legalization of international human rights laws in a state. These variables include urbanization and population density,[21] and literacy of the adult population.[22] These measures tap into Fuller's second and fourth criteria for legality; in other words a body of law that is made public, and is clear and understandable, respectively.[92] This study assumes that the more urbanized and dense the population, the greater the access to the law. Additionally, the more literate the population, the greater the likelihood that the population has some degree of comprehension of the law.

Congruence in Africa 2012–2021

Table 6.1 provides the results of the regression. The overall model is significant at the <.001 level.[23]

As expected, a greater presence of embassies, INGOs and other similar organizations has a positive *and* highly significant impact on the legalization process (<.001). It is *not* surprising that sanctions have a negative impact on the process of legalization that is almost significant at the .10 level. This fits with the work by Drezner, Nosratabadi, and Spaggiari which suggests that sanctions tend to do more harm than good to a population.[24]

The presence of large refugee populations in a country has a very significant negative impact on the extent to which legalization is an open and inclusive process at <.001. Refugees exacerbate conditions of internal stability, particularly in conflict or post-conflict countries, like Sudan, South Sudan, Nigeria, Kenya, and Ethiopia, to name just a few, all of which are also under sanction by foreign countries. IDPs are significant at the .05 level (.02). This is also not surprising. For both variables, large populations of refugees and/or IDPs are likely to cause governments to clamp down on who is or is not permitted certain human rights protections. Efforts of civil society or the public, even the courts, to combat these derogations, are likely to be

Table 6.1 Model 1

	Unstandardized Coefficients		*Standardized Coefficients*		
	B	*Std. Error*	*Beta*	*t*	*Sig.*
Constant	-10.939	.995		-10.997	<.001
refugees	-3.350E-6	.000	-.163	-3.888	<.001
IDPs	-5.628E-7	.000	-.097	-2.265	.024
terrorist	-.001	.002	-.023	-.534	.594
region	.529	.200	.101	2.643	.009
gini	.068	.009	.211	5.732	<.001
literacy	0.31	.031	.130	3.335	<.001
pop. density	-.003	.002	-.060	-1.520	.129
urbanz.	-.003	.012	-.012	-.268	.789
fem LH	-.032	.014	-.085	-2.282	.023
log gdp	-.620	.412	-.082	-1.505	.133
sanctions	-.650	.345	-.069	-1.882	.060
poliglobal	.131	.012	.579	11.011	<.001

unsuccessful. These findings reinforce the findings of several studies about the problems refugee communities encounter in host countries and their impact on the environment of these countries.[25] As Wright and Moorthy contend, a large influx of refugees can lead a state to repress these refugees if that state also has far fewer economic resources.[26]

Terrorist attacks (*terror*) have a negative insignificant impact on the process of legalization; whereas *Fem LH*, which was hypothesized to have a positive impact on legalization, has a negative one. The additional fact that the score for this latter variable is significant at the .05 level (.02) is not expected. At the same time, this finding does make sense when the *type* of government is taken into consideration. Just because a government like Rwanda's or Zimbabwe's has fairly large percentages of female representatives at the national level does not automatically translate into a greater protection of human rights, particularly when it comes to rights prohibiting torture, disappearances, and lethal use of force.

Region has a positive and significant impact at the .01 level, indicating that greater regional stability has a significant impact on the legalization of human rights laws within each state within that region. This reinforces the arguments of Simmons, Affa'a-Mindzie, and Strydom, particularly as these findings apply to the Sahel region, but not exclusively so.[27] Conflicts can spill over borders and become intertwined, with leaders in neighboring states engaging in partisan intervention to prop up or aid one side or the other for various reasons.[28]

On the measures for *economic health*, a higher aggregate GDP has a negative impact on the legalization process, while a higher GINI Coefficient has the opposite effect and is highly significant at the <.001 level. What this may indicate is that rather than the overall wealth of a country being significant, it's the distribution of this wealth in this country that may be what really counts. The more equal the distribution of income, the more equal society, perhaps the more inclusive the lawmaking communities of practice. This is a finding that deserves further study.

Lastly, the controls—*literacy, pop density, urbanz*—vary in their significance and provide some support for Fuller's argument about access to the law. Our findings indicate that literacy is very significant at the <.001 level. The more literate the population, the greater the legalization of human rights in a country. This could be taken to mean that the more literate the society, the more likely they are to engage in dissent against government misrule, whether through participation in civil society, through their use of social media sources, such as X (formerly Twitter) or TikTok or their use of the courts to challenge the law and become more engaged in the political process. Literacy is essential for democratic intentionality. As Morais suggests, "The people must be fully informed and participate collectively in debate, decision and, finally, control. [...] [I]t is crucial that all the people intervene, and to this end, they all must be argumentative literates."[29]

Table 6.2 Model 2, including FDI

	Unstandardized Coefficients		*Standardized Coefficients*		
	B	*Std. Error*	*Beta*	*t*	*Sig.*
Constant	-10.888	1.007		-10.808	<.001
refugees	-3.337E-6	.000	-.163	-3.866	<.001
IDPs	-5.636E-7	.000	-.097	-2.265	.024
terrorist	-.001	.002	-.023	-.552	.581
region	.533	.201	.102	2.654	.008
gini	.068	.012	.211	5.691	<.001
literacy	0.31	.009	.130	3.310	.001
pop. density	-.003	.002	-.059	-1.464	.136
urbanz.	-.003	.012	-.012	-.266	.790
fem LH	-.032	.014	-.086	-2.298	.022
FDI	2.280E-11	.000	.012	.336	.737
log gdp	-.640	.417	-.084	-1.536	.125
sanctions	-.657	.346	-.070	-1.897	0.58
poliglobal	.131	.012	-576	10.836	.107

Interestingly, however, population density and urbanization both have a negative impact on the lawmaking communities of practice, although neither is significant and their impact minor.

This study ran an additional model including net incoming foreign direct investment (FDI) for each country for the time period in question. FDI is included as another form of international intervention. The results are provided in Table 6.2. This model was also significant at the <.001 level.

The results are fairly consistent with Model 1. The overall model is significant at the <.001 level. Interestingly, net FDI in a country does not have a significant impact on the process of legalization. However, its impact is in a *positive* direction. Of course, this study does not consider FDI by type or sector. Chapter 8 by Yue Lin fleshes this argument out further, focusing on the impact that type of investment has on conflict and, by extension, *congruence*.

Conclusions

Congruence is impacted by many factors, both internal and external to a country. The purpose of this chapter was to test these suggested relationships. As indicated in Table 6.3, two of the five hypotheses were confirmed. With respect to internal stability, we believe that the fact that *IDPs* and *refugees* were both negative and significant is enough to confirm that a deterioration of conditions of internal stability does not bode well for *congruence* with or without the simultaneous occurrence of terrorist attacks. However,

Table 6.3 Results for Both Models

Hypotheses	*Expected outcome*	*Actual outcome*
H1: Economic health	**Positive**	**Partially confirmed**
H2: Internal stability	**Positive**	**Confirmed**
H3: Regional stability	**Positive**	**Confirmed**
H4: International presence	**Positive**	**Partially confirmed**
H5: Women in government	**Positive**	**Not confirmed**

terrorist attacks, albeit insignificant in these models, do have a negative impact on the stability of a country.

For the two hypotheses that were partially confirmed, the expected relationships between *log GDP* and *congruence* and *sanctions* and *congruence* were in the opposite direction than hypothesized. Moreover, and as discussed above, more female representation at the national level has a negative and significant relationship to *congruence*.

Obviously, more work is needed to determine *how* exactly these various exogenous and endogenous variables have the influence they do on the practice of legalization in a state. With regard to the role of women in government, for example, this study does not consider provincial or municipal governments. Consequently, the findings of this study should not be taken as a sign that female involvement in government makes things worse. Likely this finding is an artifact. Moreover, absent from this analysis is the influence that institutional legacies have on policymaking.[30] This is only a first crack at a larger ongoing effort to quantitatively assess those factors that create the variation in the process of legalization across countries.

The analysis conducted in this chapter adds to the work of Brunnée and Toope, Finnemore and Toope, and Adler and Pouliot, by (1) demonstrating that *congruence* can be quantified as composite index; and (2) that a quantitative model can be used to test the impact that an array of domestic and international factors have on *congruence*.[31] What is particularly important is that the model used in this study is replicable to other regions of the world, permitting a broader assessment of legalization as *congruence*. Moreover, this study adds on to the Fullerian concept of *congruence* with the inclusion of local institutions, societal engagement, and public access to information sources, all of which update the notion of who is involved in the lawmaking and accountability communities of practice in a country.

These findings also contribute to a set of studies within the legalization literature that focus on the compliance gap; "*the disconnect between the legal protections promised and the subsequent actions supporting these promised protections*" (italics in original).[32] The studies by Bueno de Mesquita, Downs and Smith,[33] Cingranelli, Mark and Sadykova-DuMond,[34] Lebovic and Voeten,[35] Bell, Clay and Murdie,[36] and Murdie and Davis[37] argue that whether or not state leaders comply with their treaty obligations is a consequence of certain exogenous and endogenous factors. We suggest that compliance is an outcome of *congruence*. A greater understanding of how exogenous and endogenous factors impact *congruence* will shed greater light on why state leaders choose to comply with their treaty obligations or not.

Finally, the study performed contributes to the risk assessment studies, such as those by Nzitatira and Valentino, which examine the types of factors that increase the odds of mass violence in a state.[38] The process of maintaining the rule of law is an essential safeguard against a state's use of mass violence and genocide. When the rule of law deteriorates in a country, as it has in Burundi, Niger, and Uganda, for instance, the greater the likelihood the government of that country will engage in violent misrule.

Notes

1 The period examined by the authors of this chapter begins in 2012 to include South Sudan, which gained independence from Sudan via a 2011 referendum.

2 See, for example, Jutta Brunnée and Stephen J. Toope, "International Law and the Practice of Legality: Stability and Change," 49 *Virginia Univ. of Wellington Law Review* 429 at 431 (2018); Martha Finnemore and Stephen J. Toope, "Alternatives to 'Legalization': Richer Views of Law and Politics," *International Organization* 55(3) (2001); Emmanuel Adler and Vincent Pouliot, "International Practices," *International Theory*, 3(1) (2011): 1–36 and Emanuel Adler and Vincent Pouliot (eds.) *International Practices* (Cambridge: Cambridge Univ. Press, 2011).

3 Hollie Nyseth-Brehm (Nzitatira), "Re-Examining Risk Factors of Genocide," *Journal of Genocide Studies* 19(1) (2017): 61–87; Benjamin Valentino, "Triggers of Mass Killing," Report on a Research Project for the Political Instability Task Force (Hanover: Dartmouth College, February 2016).

4 Although we are not testing the relationship between our independent variables and the actual commission of torture, disappearances, and killings, it is worth noting that the correlation between *congruence* and each of these crimes is highly significant at the .001 level.

5 For *information access* this study relies on the KOF index for "Informational Globalization," which is a composite score that combines internet users (per 100 people), television use (per 100 people), press freedom, and capacity of international internet bandwidth in bits per second per capita. See Savina Gygli, Florian Haelg and Jan-Egbert Sturm. *KOF Working Papers, No. 439* (Zurich: KOF Swiss Economic Institute, February 2018). Data are available from KOF Globalisation Index – KOF Swiss Economic Institute | ETH Zurich (accessed March 22, 2022).

6 *Societal engagement* combines IDEA's measure "Civic Engagement" with "Civil Society" into one interactive variable. Both are sub-attributes of the "Participation" variable from IDEA's seventh version of the GSoD. The GSoD defines "participation" as follows: "Democratic institutions tend to be hollow if not filled by active citizens in connection with and between different kinds of elections. In other words, politically involved citizens are considered an important part of democracy. The more citizens are allowed to participate at all levels of government and make actual use of these opportunities, through participation in dynamic civil society organizations and elections, the more popular control and responsiveness can be achieved." Claudiu D. Tufis, Alexander Hudson, *The Global State of Democracy Indices, Version 7* (Stockholm, Institute for Democracy and Electoral Assistance, 2023), 185. However, IDEA's "Participation" also includes "Electoral Participation." We excluded this latter attribute from our analysis because we

chose to specifically focus on the work of social organizations, including interest groups, and trade unions in the policymaking process. Whereas "Civil Society" measures constraints on civil society, "Civic Engagement" includes data on participation in independent nonpolitical organizations as well as civil society traditions.

7 We elected to tease out "Independent Judiciary" from IDEA's larger "Judicial Independence" variable because the larger index includes measures that the authors of this chapter feel are redundant and/or reflective components of the variable. Examples of this include the sub-attributes of "Judicial Independence," "High Court Independence" and "Lower Court Independence," as well as "Compliance with the High Court." Separating "Independent Judiciary" from the larger "Judicial Independence" variable permits the authors of this study to more closely zero-in on those features most associated with an independent court system. Tufis and Hudson, *Global*, 63.

8 Jeong-Woo Koo, Suk-Ki Kong, and Chinsung Chung, "Measuring national Human Rights: A Reflection on Korean Experiences," *Human Rights Quarterly* 34(4) (2012): 986–1020.

9 Awatif Yunu, Moses Isdory Mgunda, and Purbayu Budi Santosa, "The Root Causes of Terrorism in Southern Thailand are Socio-Economic Problems as the Root Cause of Terrorism in Southern Thailand?" *SSRN Electronic Journal* (2021). Others including Bandyopadhyay and Ijaz find this correlation to be less than conclusive. See S. Bandyopadhyay and Abdullah Ijaz. "Is There a Relationship Between Inequality And Terrorism? Evidence from a Semi-Parametric Approach." *Applied Economics Letters* 29 (2021): 855–860.

10 See Marzia Ippolito and Lorenzo Cicatiello. "Political instability, Economic Inequality and Social Conflict: The Case In Italy." *Panoeconomicus* (2019): 365–383; Anjan K. Saha, "Early Development, Income Inequality and Political Instability." *Social Science Research Network* (2014): 1–39; and Alberto F. Alesina, and Roberto Perotti. "Income Distribution, Political Instability, and Investment," *Political Economy - Development: Political Institutions eJournal* (1993): 1–33.

11 One of the best-known studies of this phenomena is Edward Nicholas Muller's "Income Inequality, Regime Repressiveness, and Political Violence," *American Sociological Review* 50 (1985): 47–61; see also Ayodele Odusola, Amarakoon Bandara, Rogers Dhilwayo and Becaye Diarra, "Inequalities and Conflict in Africa: An Empirical Investigation," *ERN: Africa (Development) (Topic)* (2017): 220–242. The latter authors find that the correlation is not as straightforward.

12 Gudrun Østby, Ragnhild Nordås and Jan Ketil Rød, "Regional Inequalities and Civil Conflict in Sub-Saharan Africa," *International Studies Quarterly* 53(2) (2009): 301–324.

13 UNHCR estimates that 75% of refugees are hosted by low- and middle-income countries, 69% in neighboring countries. UN High Commissioner for Refugees, *Global Trends: Forced Displacement in 2023*, at Global Trends report 2023 | UNHCR (accessed July 4, 2024).

14 See, for example, UNCHR Press Release, "After 28 Refugee Deaths in Khartoum, UNCHR Urges Sudan's Warring Parties to Allow Safe Passage for Civilians," (July 4, 2023), at After 28 refugee deaths in Khartoum, UNHCR urges Sudan's warring parties to allow safe passage for civilians | UNHCR (accessed July 5, 2023).

15 Global Terrorism Database, University of Maryland National Consortium for the Study of Terrorism and Responses to Terrorism, 2009–2022), at GTD | Global Terrorism Database (umd.edu); also UNCHR, Refugee Data Finder at unhcr.org/refugee-statistics/ (accessed July 5, 2023).

16 Sam R. Bell, K. Chad Clay, and Amanda Murdie, "Neighborhood Watch: Spatial Effects of Human Rights INGOs." Journal of Politics 74(2) (2012): 354–368. The difference between the regional score used by this study and the one used by Bell, Clay, and Murdie is that political imprisonment is not included in the score. The way in which regional human rights practices are used by this study differs from the Clay, Bell, and Murdie study. The latter study focused on the impact that regional human rights practices have on the shaming practices of INGOs, such that the shaming of the activities of a rule-breaking state is refocused by INGOs on the region in which it is located if that state is surrounded by other rule-breaking states.

17 Because of the distance, island states, like Cabo Verde, Mauritius, Seychelles, São Tomé, and Príncipe and Madagascar were excluded, leaving the author of this study with $n = 480$.

18 The Global Sanctions Database is a product of the Drexel University School of Economics, Hochschule Konstanz, University of Applied Sciences and Kiel Institute for the World Economy and is available from Global Sanctions Database – GSDB (accessed March 26, 2022).

19 This index was accessed at KOF Globalisation Index – KOF Swiss Economic Institute | ETH Zurich (accessed March 26, 2022).

20 PU Parline, Global Data on National Parliaments, at Parline: the IPU's Open Data Platform | Your one-stop-shop for information about national parliaments (accessed July 4, 2024).

21 Data for both variables are obtainable from World Bank, World Development Indicators (2013–2019) at World Development Indicators | Data Catalog (worldbank.org) (accessed March 1, 2022).

22 Data for literacy were obtained from the CIA World Factbook (Washington, DC: Central Intelligence Agency, 2012–2019).

23 For this regression, the adjusted R^2 is 0.517. The ANOVA test indicates that the chances that the null hypothesis is true are less than 0.001.

24 Daniel W. Drezner, "The United States of Sanctions: The Use and Abuse of Economic Coercion," *Foreign Affairs* 100(5) (2021): 142–154; Javad Nosratabadi, "The Impact of Trade Sanctions on the Relative Demand for Skilled Labor and Wages: Evidence from Iran," *Journal of International Trade & Economic Development* 32(2) (March 2023): 219–239; Giulia Spaggiari, "Sanctioning Corruption? An Analysis of the Relationship between Economic Sanctions and Anti-Corruption Efforts," *UCLA Journal of International Law & Foreign Affairs* 27(2) (Spring 2024): 185–202 and "Consequences of Economic Sanctions on Minority Groups in the Sanctioned States," *DOMES: Digest of Middle East Studies* 31(3) (Summer 2022): 201–227.

25 See, for example, Jecinta Anomat Ali, David Kamar Imana and Witchayanee Ocha, "The Refugee Crisis in Kenya: Exploring Refugee-Host Community Causes of Tensions and Conflicts in Kakuma Refugee Camp," *Journal of International Relations* 5 (2017): 39–51; also, Md. Saiful Islam and Ali Şahin, "Impact of Forcibly Displaced People's Identity Crisis on Host State's Security: The Case of Rohingya Refugees in Bangladesh," *Saudi Journal of Humanities and Social Sciences* 8(4) (2023): 80–91; Thorin M. Wright and Shweta Moorthy, "Refugees, Economic Capacity, and Host State Repression," *International Interactions* 44 (2018): 132–155.

26 Wright and Moorthy, "Refugees."

27 Beth A. Simmons, *Mobilizing for Human Rights: International Law in Domestic Politics* (Cambridge, UK: Cambridge Univ. Press, 2009); Mireille Affa'a-Mindzie, "Strengthening the Rule of Law and Human Rights in the Sahel," *Stability: International Journal of Security and Development* 2(2) (2013): 1–12; Hennie

Strydom, "Mali and the Sahel: Making Peace in Another Rough Neighbourhood," 66 *Netherlands International Law Review* 75 (2019).

28 The civil war in Sierra Leone is an excellent example of partisan intervention. In exchange for diamonds, President Charles Taylor of Liberia sold weapons to the Revolutionary United Front. Nancy Annan, "Violent Conflicts and Civil Strife in West Africa: Causes, Challenges and Prospects," *Stability: International Journal of Security & Development*, 3(1) (2014): 1–16. 4.

29 José Morais, "Literacy and Democracy," *Language, Cognition and Neuroscience* 33 (2018): 351–372, 362.

30 One possible way to do this is by including a variable measuring colonial legacy. Minkler and Sweeney, for example, include colonial rule in their analysis to examine the theory that a "country's legal origins affect things like its judicial independence, investor protection, regulation, corporate law, labor law, and government ownership." Lance Minkler and Shawna Sweeney, "On the Indivisibility and Interdependence of Basic Rights in Developing Countries," *Human Rights Quarterly* 33(2) (May 2011): 351–396, 359. This translates into the suggestion that the legal legacies associated with British colonial rule are more conducive to promoting and protecting civil liberties; French rule, with its greater reliance on the government for economic intervention, is more conducive (perhaps) to economic, social, and cultural rights. Minkler and Sweeney, "Indivisibility," 358–359. In their study, they find some evidence to confirm that the legal origin of a country impacts the ability of a state to ensure greater human rights compliance.

31 Brunnée and Toope, "Practice of Legality"; Finnemore and Toope, "Alternatives"; Adler and Pouliot, "International Practices"; Adler and Pouliot (eds.) *International Practices*.

32 Dane R. Mataic, and Robert Finke, "Compliance Gaps and The Failed Promises Of Religious Freedoms. Religion," *State and Society*, 47(1) (2019): 124–150, 125. DOI: 10.1080/09637494.2018.1528788.

33 Bruce Bueno de Mesquita, George W. Downs and Alastair Smith, "Thinking Inside the Box: A Closer Look at Democracy and Human Rights," *International Studies Quarterly* 49(3) (2005): 439–457.

34 David L. Cingranelli, Skip Mark and Almira Sadykova-DuMond, "Democracy, Capacity, And The Implementation Of Laws Protecting Human Rights," *Laws* 2(1) (2023): 1–19. https://doi.org/10.3390/laws12010006.

35 James H. Lebovic and Erik Voeten, "The Cost of Shame: International Organizations and Foreign Aid in the Punishing of Human Rights Violators," *Journal of Peace Research* 46(1) (2009): 79–97.

36 Bell, Sam R., K. Chad Clay, and Amanda Murdie, "Join the Chorus, Avoid the Spotlight: The Effect of Neighborhood and Social Dynamics on Human Rights Organization Shaming," *The Journal of Conflict Resolution* 63(1) (2019): 167-193.

37 Amanda M. Murdie, David R. Davis, "Shaming and Blaming: Using Events Data to Assess the Impact of Human Rights INGOs," *International Studies Quarterly*, 56(1) (March 2012): 1–6.

38 Nzitatira, "Re-Examining"; Benjamin Valentino, "Triggers of Mass Killing."

7 Do Peace Missions in Africa Matter?

Miao-ling Lin Hasenkamp and Stacey M. Mitchell

Introduction

Several empirical peacebuilding studies in Africa have shown that tensions, limitations, and contradictions over ideas and the prioritization of and impact of various components of peace agendas prevent peace missions from meeting their expectations and objectives.[1] This chapter addresses the puzzle of why peace missions fail to consistently achieve sustainable peace.

Peace missions are defined as those that cover peacekeeping and peacebuilding missions, including the work of fact-finding missions, political missions, and, in some cases, special rapporteurs. For this study, a condition for long term peace is assumed to include the domestic legalization of human rights prohibitions against political violence, including prohibitions against torture. Peace missions are now the subjects of much criticism, including for their "tone-deaf" attitude to the needs of local communities, and a multitude of allegations of sexual misconduct perpetrated by peacekeepers. Moreover, the long-time presence of peace missions in countries like Mali and Sudan did not prevent these countries from collapsing into humanitarian disasters.[2]

This chapter first addresses the concept of the peace mission, what it is and what it is intended to achieve. The discussion of peace missions largely addresses UN missions although regional missions are also assessed. Following a discussion of the UN's *Rule of Law Indicators*,[3] the theoretical framework used by this study is explained. Emphasis is placed on the "Local/Comparative" peace paradigm and the ways in which it improves on other International Relations (IR) paradigms as a means of testing this volume's fourth hypothesis:

> H4: The greater the international presence in a country, the more inclusive the communities of practice involved in the policymaking and implementation processes, the more likely international human rights laws prohibiting torture, political killings, and disappearances will be legalized.

DOI: 10.4324/9781003471677-10

The Local/Comparative paradigm shares with constructivism an emphasis on the notion of peace processes as multidirectional and multilayered. This perspective also neatly aligns with the legalization theory on which the authors of this volume rely. This chapter then turns its focus to the examples of peace missions conducted in Mali and Burundi and assesses the impact these missions have had strengthening the domestic communities of practice involved in the domestication of laws prohibiting domestic political violence.

The authors find some evidence that suggests that the more closely peace missions incorporate local interests and agendas, the greater the likelihood that the development of civil society and the other necessary components of *congruence* will occur, although the extent to which these components effectively impact a state's implementation of and compliance with international human rights prohibitions against torture, extrajudicial killings, and disappearances remains uncertain. This is an observation that applies equally to regional missions, including those conducted by the African Union (AU) and the Economic Community of West African States (ECOWAS). As implied, the results achieved by this study are tentative. Peacebuilding is a long-term project whose successes are neither immediate nor necessarily permanent and are most frequently contingent on the "good will" of the international community as well as the interests of the target (recipient) states.

Peace Missions in Africa

Peace missions encompass several different actions, including peacekeeping, peace enforcing, and peacebuilding activities along with the work of special rapporteurs, aid missions, and various fact-finding investigative missions, including those conducted at the request of the United Nations Human Rights Council (HRC) and the Security Council (UNSC).[4] The UN's Department of Political and Peacekeeping Affairs is also engaged in several political missions in Africa. The Special Envoy for the Great Lakes Region, the Special Envoy for the Horn of Africa, the UN Support Mission in Libya, and others work tirelessly to improve political inclusiveness, help consolidate institutional reforms, and other tasks.[5]

Peace missions are intended to help conflict and post-conflict countries build and consolidate institutions that resolve and prevent conflicts and ensure stability and development. These institutions include legal and political institutions, economic institutions, and social justice mechanisms, including truth and reconciliation commissions.[6] Additionally, peace missions now have a greater focus on gender equality, including gender participation and gender sensitivity.[7]

In recent years, the UN has focused more directly on the rule of law in transitional countries. The UN's *Rule of Law Indicators* is not intended to assess states' compliance with international laws and standards; rather, it provides guidance for states on how to monitor and improve performance on a number of rule of law indicators, two of which are similar to the components of *congruence* examined by this study: judicial independence and access to justice.[8] The focus of the *Rule of Law Indicators* rests with the justice system—courts, police, prisons. Specifically,

> [f]or each institution, the instrument includes a number of indicators to measure how the system treats minorities, victims, children in need of protection or in conflict with the law, internally displaced persons, asylum-seekers, refugees, returnees, and stateless and mentally ill individuals.[9]

In his quantitative assessment of UN peace operations and the rule of law in Africa, Blair finds that these missions have a positive impact on rule of law in post-conflict countries over a short period of time, specifically the three-year period after the signing of a peace treaty, having mostly to do with UN personnel rather than the presence of troops, and tend to work better when the UN engages with local populations.[10]

While his study adds strength to the argument that the involvement of local communities in a peace process is essential for its sustainability, as well as the important role the UN has in the establishment of rule of law in post-conflict countries, it says little about *why* rule of law falters over time. Certainly, a UN presence is better than no presence for many of these countries, but even with a UN presence, why have so many governments in recent years collapsed into violent civil war and authoritarian rule? Some of this discrepancy may be attributable to the relative absence of nongovernmental organizations (NGOs) in the rule of law process. As the authors of this volume contend, NGOs and other local associations are integral to explaining human rights laws in practice. Shutting out civil society and societal engagement weakens rule of law *regardless* of a UN presence or for that matter, the presence of a regional peace mission.[11] Moreover, what does the presence of mercenary groups, like the Wagner group, and participants from authoritarian governments in peace missions have on rule of law in African countries? The trajectories of rule of law are clearly a consequence of a complex set of actors and institutions.

Although the UN has taken a lead role in conducting peace missions, regional organizations in Africa have become more involved in peace processes over the past few decades. It has been suggested that peace and security initiatives launched by the ECOWAS and the AU in Mali, Côte d'Ivoire, and Libya were effective and demonstrated the role of African agency in the application of Responsibility to Protect on the continent, including the Responsibilities to Prevent, to React, and to Rebuild.[12]

Arthur attributes the relative successes of ECOWAS peace missions in Côte d'Ivoire and Togo in the early 2000s to lessons learned from the peace missions ECOWAS conducted in the 1990s. A lack of consensus among leaders of ECOWAS states about the legality of the use of ECOMOG (the

ECOWAS Ceasefire Monitoring Group) in conflict situations and the need for UN approval,[13] problems with the financing and logistics of missions, and allegations of impropriety on the part of ECOMOG made early ECOMOG efforts in Liberia and Sierra Leone only partially successful.[14] Since that time, Arthur argues that ECOWAS has come into its own with respect to maintaining neutrality in its missions and has a working knowledge of what is required to conduct a successful and sustainable peace mission, including the support of all parties to the conflict for a peaceful solution and greater efforts toward disarmament.[15]

As of the time of this writing, however, efforts by ECOWAS, the AU, and other regional organizations to effectively respond to the wave of coups d'état in Western Africa over the past few years have proven less-than-successful. The involvement of the Wagner group as a spoiler in these conflicts makes intervention even more problematic. Adding insult to injury is the defense pact reached between the military governments of Niger, Mali, and Burkina Faso—all members of ECOWAS—to respond to any attempt to remove them from power with force.[16] To date, the AU has suspended all States party involved in recent coups, including Niger, Sudan, and Mali.[17]

The Model Used by This Study

Many approaches to understanding and explaining peace missions seldom focus on the importance of local "buy in" in the process. This omission is problematic given that these theories also have a prescriptive function for policymakers.[18]

Realism with its focus on state security and its preference for short-term peace is ill-suited as a vehicle for understanding what is necessary for a peace mission to succeed. The chief emphasis is placed on maintaining internal security and stability of the state at the expense of longer-term issues of reconciliation or conditions of structural violence.[19] As the authors of this volume make clear, achieving stability without the creation of rule of law merely kicks the can down the road and avoids the tougher decisions about the kinds of institutional development that would most benefit that country.

At the same time, realism can explain the shifting collectives of actors—states/organizations—who participate in these missions and why. With Mali, for example, the policymaking behavior of powerful states like the United States or France amid a resurgence of terrorist activities and political coups in the Sahel illustrates the significance that national security continues to have in starting or ending peace missions. For Burundi, it is the national interests of the leadership of Burundi that have come to dominate peace processes, which is to say the government's resistance to a regional or international peace mission, observer mission, etc. The choice of this government is geared toward a selective and strategic peace process, one which involves a *national commission vérité et réconciliation* that only addresses violence perpetrated by Tutsi-led regimes of the distant past.[20]

The liberalist approach to peacebuilding has been the dominant model. And while it focuses on internal dynamics within a state, it largely assumes a more Western perspective in which the intent of the international community is to rebuild and remake the post-conflict state. The idea of a one-size-fits-all model is problematic for obvious reasons. Institutional legacies of political, economic, and social development are unique in each country. To assume that the majoritarian system of government, for example, will work just as well in Uganda as it does in the United States is preposterous.

As Jeng argues, the liberal peace project is ethnocentric and mirrors the "very society that determines its content, praxis and operational hierarchy."[21] In particular, the relationship between international law and its postcolonial application in former colonies

> creates a strong basis for alternative thinking – that considers and engages propositions from Third World perspectives on international law and their relevance to the need for conceptual recasting of approaches to violence and conflicts. This is particularly compelling given that a significant part of postcolonial African statehood has been characterized by the eruption [...] of violence and conflicts.[22]

Resentment, and the ineptitude and inefficacy of many liberal peace missions, plus the common perception of international law as universal, leave many African states few options and very little agency.

Constructivism, with its focus on objective and subjective qualities of policymaking, gets closer to understanding why peace missions so often fail to achieve their objectives. McCandless and Donais contend that what is necessary is a multi-level dialogue between actors engaged in the peace process. Absent a continuing interaction between international, state, and non-state actors, peace missions will fall flat. As they suggest,

> in a globalised setting norms—far from being simply 'transmitted'—emerge and evolve through complex systems of interaction and channels of influence that run not only top-down and bottom-up, but also horizontally across borders, types of actors and networks.[23]

The local/comparative approach to peace missions is based on the idea that a bottom-up approach toward peace missions is essential to achieve local ownership of the peacebuilding process.[24] Like constructivist approaches to peace building, the assumption that prevails in this subset of IR peace literature is that not all societies are alike; each has its own patterns of political, economic, and social development that require acknowledgment and understanding. Peace missions in all their many forms serve as critical junctures in the institutional development of a country. Kurtenbach, Hoven, Paris, Mac Ginty, and Jabri suggest that the incorporation of domestic perspectives and background knowledge in a peace project is necessary for its success in the creation of rule of law and the other outcomes that are expected to ensue from a mission.[25] As van Leeuwen et al. state, "Localized peacebuilding is expected to gear intervention towards everyday experiences of violence and local understanding of how to deal with these, and would make peacebuilding more sustainable as a result of local ownership and legitimacy."[26]

Moreover, van Leeuwen et al. argue that the concept of "local" is ambiguous. Whether we're talking about civil society, traditional institutions, or indigenous leaders, there is no one local authority per se, but a mixture of groups across a country with competing interests and agendas.[27] Rather than "essentialize" the local, peacebuilding requires an understanding of the complex nature of local institutions, and how their interaction with national and international institutions impacts, and is impacted by, these institutions; "the local community is made and remade, making it hard to identify and generalize about the local's actual nature."[28] Rather than focus merely on national leaders, peace missions would be more successful in encouraging and supporting local actors and non-state institutions in their processes of negotiation and competitions for legitimacy.[29]

Conceiving of the local community in this way aligns the Local/Comparative paradigm well with this study's theory of legalization. Aside from the fact that the local perspective acknowledges institutional change and development as a process that mandates input from the public, not merely political elites, or outside interests, it also posits local community as something that is not static, but subject to constant change in relation to the environment in which local institutions operate and people live.

When it comes to the legalization of civil and political liberties in post-conflict states, several factors impair the work of local institutions as an important aspect of the fledgling communities of practice which impact law-making in that state. Institutional legacies of division and exclusion (colonial and postcolonial), regional politics, conditions of internal instability, and how peace missions are conducted impact legalization processes. International and regional intervention—in whatever form it takes—is itself a product of global politics. The authors of this chapter delve into the work of peace missions in Mali and Burundi and examine how these missions have been conducted as well as the intersectionality of these missions with local and regional politics, and global and regional policy trends and agendas.

Mali

Between 2013 and 2024, international and regional peace missions aimed to support Mali in restoring peace, combatting terrorism, monitoring human rights, creating conditions for the provision of humanitarian assistance, and preparing for free, inclusive, and peaceful elections. These missions took place against the backdrop of a significant global change in security strategy, priorities, and Great Power engagements.[30] Because the concurring intervention and engagement efforts failed to consider regional complexities, these missions enhanced the authoritarian rule of the Malian government and left the prospect of human rights promotion at best unfulfilled.[31]

In January 2012, a Tuareg Movement known as the *Mouvement national pour la libération de l'Azawad* (MNLA), along with Islamic armed groups such as *Ansar Dine* (Defenders of the Faith), Al-Qaida in the Islamic Maghreb (AQIM), the *Mouvement pour l'unicité et le jihad en Afrique de l'Ouest* (MUJAO), and Malian deserters from the armed forces initiated a series of attacks against government forces in the north. After the 2012 coup, the Heads of State and Government of ECOWAS appointed the President of Burkina Faso, Blaise Compaoré, to mediate in the crisis. ECOWAS organized an African-led International Support Mission to Mali (AFISMA) with German and French forces in February 2013.

Concurrently, Mali interim authorities asked for UN assistance to build their capacity in the areas of political negotiation, elections, governance, security sector reform, and humanitarian assistance. The UN Multidimensional Integrated Stabilization Mission in Mali (MINUSMA), authorized by UNSC Resolution 2065 (December 20, 2012), was established in July 2013. MINUSMA's mandate was to provide coordinated and coherent support to the ongoing political and security processes, including support for the planning, deployment, and operations of the AFISMA Mission. Following MINUSMA's road map, the essential tasks for Mali's Transitional Government consisted of restoring territorial integrity and organizing free and fair elections. Despite improved security situations following the re-hatting of peace operations from the French and African military operations alongside the Malian army to the UN-led MINUSMA in northern areas, serious challenges remained, including those stemming from terrorist activities and ongoing military operations in some areas.[32]

As a consequence of the high losses sustained by MINUSMA, and with French support, Mali and its regional neighbors formed the Group of Five Sahel Joint Force (FC-G5S) in 2014 to fight terrorist organizations in the Sahel. As part of the military pillar of European Union (EU) action in Mali the EU deployed its training mission (EUTM Mali) to strengthen the capabilities of the Malian Armed Forces.[33] FC-G5S became a favorite partner with whom Western allies and EUTM Mali liked to work to provide financial support and capacity-building, all of which was considered as part of the global "burden-sharing" of security challenges between the United States and its allies.

In November 2019, the AU's Peace and Security Council conducted a mission in Mali, together with the EU's Political and Security Committee, to assess the situation and identify the support needed for promoting peace and security in Mali and for stabilizing the Sahel region.[34] The EUTM's Fifth Mandate in March 2020 upheld its strategic objectives in supporting FC-G5S to improve its military education system and to strengthen regional cooperation.

The efforts of international and regional ad hoc coalitions to restore and stabilize Mali marked a return of Europe to peacekeeping in Africa as well as greater Chinese involvement in African peace missions. Whereas Chinese and African personnel were mostly involved in MINUSMA operations on the ground, Europeans were deployed predominantly in coordinating activities and in strategic roles guided by a limited approach to avoid further overseas casualties. Unequal burden-sharing as well as an unstable political context shaped by competing, even incompatible agendas among diverse government and nongovernment armed factions, limited the effectiveness of MINUSMA. The 2015 *Algiers Accord* was disrupted several times among its signatories by fighting on the ground. External observers and most of Mali's population regarded the *Accord* as an elite affair being enforced by international partners.[35]

A series of global crises since 2019 exposed the harsh reality of existing unequal relations between the developed world and the Global South and the recurring anti-Western resentment dating back to colonial times for many African societies. For Mali, two coups took place during this time: the first in 2020, a second in May 2021. In the second coup the military replaced the transitional interim government set up after the 2020 coup. Since then, Mali's relationship with the West has sharply deteriorated. The presence of international peace missions is increasingly put under scrutiny.[36] MINUSMA ended its mission in December 2023. The military junta regime officially invited Russia's Wagner group to fight against Islamist groups. The brutal operations conducted by the Wagner group have provoked international concern.[37]

At the end of the day, the data from the Institute for Democracy and Electoral Assistance (IDEA) indicate that between 2015 and 2022, the components of *congruence* improved only slightly for a few of the indicators, with little to no change for the rest.[38] Can this purely be attributed to the failure of peace missions in Mali? Likely not, but the fact that few of Mali's missions focused on granting agency to local institutions and actors means that the work to establish rule of law in Mali remains an unfinished product (Table 7.1).

Table 7.1 Congruence in Mali[39]

	Societal engagement	*Local authority*	*Access to information*	*Independence of judiciary*	*Access to justice*	*Absence of corruption*
2015	0.567852	0.37661	56.1	0.463778	56.1	0.330179
2016	0.574882	0.37661	50.1	0.490102	50.1	0.336539
2017	0.562069	0.340881	52.97	0.48852	52.97	0.312488
2018	0.545292	0.340881	54.59	0.483434	54.59	0.312488
2019	0.561515	0.340881	55.74	0.502557	55.74	0.338739
2020	0.52893	0.3844	55.98	0.486856	55.98	0.338739
2021	0.514427	0.3844	55.25	0.4647	55.25	0.332386
2022	0.535911	0.3844	55.61	0.458139	55.61	0.332386

Burundi

The 2000 Arusha Peace and Reconciliation Agreement ended the civil war and called for the implementation of a new consociational system of government.[40] Accompanying these changes was the instillation of the UN Operations Mission in Burundi (ONUB) which began in 2004.[41] ONUB's mandate included demobilization and disarmament of rebel forces, promoting cease-fire agreements between fighting forces and the government, and enabling these and other conditions for the Arusha Agreement to be implemented, as well as providing advice and assistance for the Transitional Government. ONUB was succeeded by the United Nations Integrated Office in Burundi (BINUB) which worked to strengthen conditions for long-term peace in Burundi, including (but not limited to) helping re-establish rule of law, strengthening democracy, helping the government coordinate democracy initiatives with donor countries, and demobilizing rebel forces and reforming the security sector.[42] BINUB remained in Burundi until December 2014, at which time it handed off its authority to a UN country team, consisting of a host of actors and based on the UN Development Assistance Framework (UNDAF).[43]

For a time, Burundi made progress.[44] A separate UN mission to oversee the 2015 elections in Burundi—the UN Electoral Observation Mission in Burundi (MENUB)—began its work in the country in January 2015 and ended its mission in December that same year. Conditions deteriorated in 2015 after former *Conseil National pour la Défense de la Démocratie-Forces pour la Défense of Démocratie* (CNDD-FDD) rebel leader and President Pierre Nkurunziza declared his intent to run for another term. Opponents, civil society, and even members of the CNDD-FDD ruling party challenged his plan on the grounds that it violated the terms of the Arusha Agreement, which limited presidential terms to two. Backed by the Constitutional Court, however, Nkurunziza successfully ran and was re-elected. Whether these results are attributable to flaws in the consociational design or to the fact that Nkurunziza is a former rebel leader, they quickly prompted an increase in political violence, threats to individual physical integrity and security, and reduced Burundi's status from a hybrid democracy to an authoritarian state. MENUB declared that the July 2015 elections proceeded in a peaceful manner, although the environment in which the elections took place "was not conducive for an inclusive, free and credible electoral process."[45]

The 2015 elections and all activities that have occurred since exemplify rule *by* law of the CNDD-FDD regime. Burundi's constitution has been changed three times since 2005; the latest version permits the president to serve more than two terms of seven years each, so long as these additional terms are not consecutive to the first two. The constitution also increases the legislative power of the CNDD-FDD relative to the opposition.[46] Critics of these changes at the time noted that they permitted then-President Nkurunziza to potentially stay in power until 2034, and that the referendum itself was illegitimately conducted.[47] Changes to the Penal Code and Code of Criminal Procedure in 2013 and 2018, respectively, reflect the government's rule by law tendencies and their response to the sharp deterioration of stability in Burundi.[48]

These changes transpired *despite* the presence of various UN missions after 2015, including the UN Office of the Special Envoy for Burundi (OSEB) which ended in 2021 at the request of the Government of Burundi.[49] Additionally, a UN fact-finding mission—the UN Commission for Inquiry (COI)—was created in 2016 to examine the violence that followed the 2015 election. Regarding the use of torture, the COI found that "Such violence was aimed at intimidating, controlling, repressing, or punishing women and men for their supposed or actual political opinions, their refusal to join the ruling party or their links with an armed movement."[50] Despite its urgent need in the country, the COI was ended in 2020. A UN Independent Investigation in Burundi (UNIIB) was established in 2015 pursuant to HRC Resolution S-24/1 to investigate the situation on the ground. Their final report contains strikingly similar findings to reports of the COI, including their conclusion that the violations of human rights "are 'patterned'."[51]

Looking at the six components of *congruence* examined by this study, the data show some improvement for the authority of local institutions, independence of the judiciary, control of corruption, and public access to information and institutions of justice, but overall, these numbers indicate very weak communities of practice in Burundi (Table 7.2).

Although civic engagement has declined, several qualitative studies indicate that the work of civil society in Burundi and other types of local organizations (or "local peace committees" to use the term relied on by van Leeuwen et al.) paints a different picture, which demonstrates progress on the creation of dialogue and cooperation between communities as well as the complexity of the involvement of local actors in the peacebuilding process.[52] Féron writes about the valuable contributions that women's groups in Burundi make through their networks of groups and civil society organizations that focus on conflict

Table 7.2 Congruence in Burundi

	Societal engagement	*Local authority*	*Access to information*	*Independence of judiciary*	*Access to justice*	*Absence of corruption*
2015	0.247772	0.124288	36.45	0.272134	0.199565	0.171044
2016	0.219348	0.009234	36.54	0.251987	0.16993	0.124779
2017	0.222396	0.009234	36.19	0.251987	0.196677	0.124779
2018	0.222396	0.009234	36.72	0.220669	0.174162	0.124779
2019	0.222396	0.15417	39.16	0.241153	0.198253	0.135038
2020	0.211437	0.037469	38.9	0.213961	0.191214	0.181896
2021	0.163385	0.037469	31.76	0.27359	0.244604	0.306678
2022	0.146636	0.037469	35.33	0.274049	0.262903	0.377012

mediation and prevention.[53] They serve as a "rich source of new ideas and creative approaches, that also have the advantage of being rooted in local context."[54]

The work of the *bashingantahe* traditional conflict resolution institutions, and a variety of other institutions at the local level, such as the *Commissions Justice e Paix*, and *MiParec* work on programs meant to resolve disputes, reintegrate ex combatants, raise awareness about human rights, and/or foster dialogue and forgiveness between individuals.[55] Many "peace clubs" were created by national and international organizations to increase reconciliation and avoidance of conflict. The competition between these institutions for greater authority at the local levels has diminished the legitimacy of traditional institutions like the *bashingantahe*.[56]

The work of local peace communities (and their support by national/international peacebuilding NGOs and institutions) is essential to grounding the peace and reconciliation processes in Burundi. These local actors in Burundi operate below and, in a manner, distinct from the governing apparatus. Although they cannot directly deal with macro-level inequities resulting from long-term conditions of structural violence,[57] they approach disputes over land, marriage, theft, and violence against women in a pragmatic manner and with an understanding of the larger constraints imposed on them by the state. Their ability to investigate violent state misbehavior, for example, or address political issues of representation between groups is limited. At the same time, these local peace committees and (inter)national NGOs have "worked on strengthening local capacities for advocacy, training in democracy, good governance, the rule of law, and citizen participation in policy decisions, notably women and youth."[58]

Discussions and Preliminary Conclusions

Peacekeeping efforts in Mali demonstrate how the interests of external powers and neighboring states and a general lack of consideration of competing heterogeneous local perspectives in peace processes hinder constructive legalization practices at both national and local levels.[59]

The ongoing crisis in Burundi remains the subject of international and regional concern. No regional or international peacekeepers are presently in Burundi, although the African Commission on Human and People's Rights conducted a fact-finding mission to Burundi in December 2015. Their report verified the allegations made by the COI that acts of torture, political violence, and murders were taking place in the country.[60] The fact that the government repudiated these findings[61] and has not changed its policies may be reflective of the AU's lack of influence.[62]

The interplay of changing regional dynamics and international interests, and the lack of appreciation for local and regional contexts, have been mutually reinforcing in shaping the outcomes of UN/regional missions in Mali and, to a lesser extent, Burundi. In the case of the latter, the impact that the

UN, outside donors, and NGOs had on improving the work of local peace communities has *not* translated into larger changes in the governing system or stemmed the tide of serious human rights abuses.

Even though peace and conflict studies indicate the limitations and inadequacies of realist approaches to understanding and tackling the multifaceted challenges peace missions face, realism remains a legitimate framework for understanding how and why some states chose to engage in these missions as well as the scope and strategy of their engagements. Mali showcases how international and regional actors, particularly under French leadership, have been efficient in mobilizing resources to reshape the scope and agendas of MINUSMA and AU's involvement in countering the actions of diverse Islamist groups. Moreover, the intervention experience in Mali impacted the AU's policies on peace and security, including its creation of an African Standby Force to enhance the African capacity for immediate response to crises.[63]

Analysts have highlighted serious negative consequences of implementing multidimensional integrated peace missions. These include the deterioration of UN legitimacy, the subordination of the protection of civilians, and, for Mali, increases in human rights violations.[64] Karlsrud notes that under such circumstances, the emphasis on the human rights due diligence framework in MINUSMA's work demonstrates lingering concerns about the increasingly close cooperation between UN peace operations and ad hoc counterterrorism actors in countering violent extremism action.[65] Moreover, the participation of Chinese peacekeepers in MINUSMA as well as Russia's increasing influence in Mali, Niger, and elsewhere on the continent increases the likelihood of the spread of illiberal conflict management and peacebuilding practices in the region.[66]

The increasing entanglement of peace missions and counterterrorism operations has changed the UN's peacebuilding paradigm, both in discourse and in practice. The shift from a primary focus on institution building to the immediate protection of civilians led to the adoption of a more reactive approach to security incidents with limited goals in accordance with the United States and its Western allies' counterterrorism doctrine. This shift has been to the detriment of elaborating a long-term people-centric strategy.[67] It is under such an international environment that international and regional ad hoc coalition peace efforts in Mali took place. It is not surprising that the outcome of the UN peace missions in Mali fell prey to the vicious circle of foreign counterterrorism strategies with a perverse result: the higher the US aid levels to personalist regimes with weak institutional capacities, the higher the recurring cases of terrorist attacks. Not only have the UN and the West suffered a loss of credibility and reputation, but the vacuum they left in the region created fertile soil for the spread of illiberal peacebuilding activities.[68]

For Burundi, the UN missions were geared toward implementing the Arusha Peace Agreement and maintaining stability. Underlying these missions was an appreciation for efforts to maintain the multiparty government.

Although attempts have been made to enhance local institutions, including civil society and mediation groups, there is a disconnect between the work of these organizations and the national government. Although the data reflect stronger public components of *congruence*, studies suggest that these components are constrained and unable to effectively impact the policymaking and accountability processes.

The adoption of a local/comparative approach might well support liberal actors to find a balanced match in addressing both immediate security challenges and the root causes of the conflicts in Africa. Bottom-up and space-sensible historical comparative accounts can help illuminate the root causes of a deep domestic crisis fueled by long-standing ethnic grievances and the increasing disenfranchisement of segments of the population. The issues of geography/spatial perceptions and framings in shaping the interactions among different actors, chronic corruption, religious extremism, and the colonial legacy of Mali all deserve a careful reading in the Malian context.[69]

The dynamics of emerging trans-local peace communities involved in diverse conflict resolution and transitional justice initiatives in Burundi as well as the growing attention to women's potential contributions as security actors in preventing and countering violent extremism in the private sphere in Mali offer evidence of the merits of adopting a bottom-up peacebuilding perspective sensitive to local/comparative approaches (e.g. the inclusion of diverse and competing discursive practices of representation and local knowledge of conflict resolution methods).[70]

Notes

1 Burundi has experienced contradictions of international peacebuilding efforts despite its successful political transition to a multi-ethnic power-sharing system (such as it is). See Devon Curtis, "The international peacebuilding paradox: Power sharing and post-conflict governance in Burundi." *African Affairs* 112(446) (2013): 72–91; also, Devon Curtis and Albert G. Dzinesa, *Peacebuilding, Power, and Politics in Africa* (Ohio University Press, 2012); Séverine Autesserre, *The Trouble with the Congo: Local Violence and the Failure of International Peacekeeping* (New York: Cambridge Univ. Press, 2020) and *The Frontlines of Peace: An Insider's Guide to Changing the World* (Oxford: Oxford Univ. Press, 2021).

2 Amnesty International (AI), "Human Rights in Mali, 2022," at Human rights in Mali Amnesty International, accessed March 2, 2023 (accessed May 5, 2023). In Mali, a military junta runs the government and is suspected of several egregious human rights violations, including tortures, disappearances, and scores of civilian deaths. In Sudan, the State of Emergency proclaimed by the military government under Lieutenant General Abdel Fattah al-Burhan, commander of the Sudanese Armed Forces, led to mass protests, killings, and the resignation of Prime Minister Abdalla Hamdock in January 2022. The current battle has created a mass exodus of millions of people to neighboring countries. Amnesty International is just one of many organizations that have written numerous reports about the violence. See AI, "Sudan: UN Human Rights Council's Special Session on Sudan Should Establish an Investigative Mechanism" (New York: Amnesty International, May 2023) at Sudan: UN Human Rights Council's special session on Sudan should

establish an investigative mechanism - Amnesty International (accessed July 4, 2024); also, Enrica Picco, "The Fallout in Chad from the Fighting in Darfur," International Crisis Group (August 10, 2023) at The Fallout in Chad from the Fighting in Darfur|Crisis Group (accessed September 28, 2023).

3 The United Nations Department of Peacekeeping Operations (UN Peacekeeping), *The United Nations Rule of Law Indicators: Implementation Guide and Project Tools*, 1st ed. (New York: United Nations Publications, 2011).

4 Peacekeeping, peacemaking, peace enforcing, and peacebuilding missions all differ with respect to their purpose, their targets, as well as their ability to use force. For an excellent explanation of these differences, see Raymond Taras and Rajat Ganguly, *Understanding Ethnic Conflict*, 4th ed. (Abingdon: UK; New York: Routledge, 2010), chapter 4.

5 United Nations Peacekeeping Operations, Special Political Missions, and Other Political Presences | (unmissions.org) (accessed September 29, 2023).

6 For an excellent assessment of the complexities surrounding security sector reforms and peace missions in Africa, see the volume *Africa Security Review* 26(2) (2017).

7 These reforms have come from the highest level and include a zero-tolerance approach to gender violence and exploitation. See, for example, UNSC Resolutions 1325 (2000) and 1820 (2008); also, Sara E. Davies and Sarah Teitt, "Engendering the Responsibility to Protect: Women and the Prevention of Mass Atrocities," *Global Responsibility to Protect* 4(2) (2012): 198–222. For further information about the UN's zero-tolerance policy, see UN General Assembly, *Special Measures for Protection from Sexual Exploitation and Abuse Report Of The Secretary-General*, A/75/754 (February 15, 2021).

8 UN Peacekeeping, *Rule of Law*, v.

9 UN Peacekeeping, *Rule of Law*, 4.

10 Robert A. Blair, *Peacekeeping, Policing, and the Rule of Law after Civil War* (Cambridge, UK: Cambridge Univ. Press, 2020), 90–121.

11 IDEA data indicate that civil society engagement dropped substantially in several African countries over the past two years, including in Sudan, South Sudan, Burundi, Eswatini, Central African Republic, and Zimbabwe. IDEA, *Global State of Democracy Indicators*, 2019–2021, at Global State of Democracy Indices | International IDEA (accessed September 4, 2023).

12 Kwesi Aning and Fiifi Edu-Afful, "African Agency in R2P: Interventions by African Union and ECOWAS in Mali, Cote D'ivoire, and Libya," *International Studies Review* 18 (2016): 120–133.

13 Peter Arthur, "ECOWAS and Regional Peacekeeping Integration in West Africa: Lessons for the Future," *Africa Today* 57(2) (Winter, 2010): 2–24. The ECOWAS Charter, its Protocol on Non-Aggression as well as the Charter of the Organization of African Unity (Article 3), address the importance of state sovereignty, and the peaceful resolution on disputes. See Arthur, "ECOWAS," 10.

14 Arthur, "ECOWAS," 14–16.

15 Arthur, "ECOWAS," 17–19.

16 *Reuters*, "Mali, Niger and Burkina Faso sign Sahel Security Pact," September 16, 2023, at Mali, Niger and Burkina Faso sign Sahel security pact | Reuters (accessed September 29, 2023).

17 Political Geography Now, Map Update: Record Number of African Union Members Suspended (Sep. 2023) – Political Geography Now (polgeonow.com) (accessed September 29, 2023).

18 For an excellent assessment of the different International Relations perspectives on peace missions, see Henry F. Carey and Onur Sen, "Introduction: Bridging the Conceptual and Theoretical Divides on Peace and Peacebuilding." In Henry

F. Carey ed., *Peacebuilding Paradigms: The Impact of Theoretical Diversity on Implementing Sustainable Peace* (Cambridge: Cambridge Univ. Press, 2020), 1–28.

19 For studies on peacemaking that adopt a realist stance, see Naazneed H. Barma, *The Peacebuilding Failure: Political Order in Post-Conflict States* (Cambridge: Cambridge Univ. Press, 2017); also the work of Norrin M. Rippsman, "Two Stages of Transition From a Region of War to a Region of Peace: Realist Transition and Liberal Endurance," *International Studies Quarterly*, 49(4) (December 2005): 669–693 and Rippsman, "Realism, Rationalism, and Peace: A Top-Down and a Staged Perspective." In Carey, *Peacebuilding Paradigms*, 47–58.

20 The *Commission vérité et réconciliation*, or CVR was created by the Nkurunziza regime in 2014. Its purpose is to address the partial genocide perpetrated by the Tutsi-led Micombero regime in 1972–1973.

21 Abou Jeng, *Peacebuilding in the African Union: Law, Philosophy, and Practice* (Cambridge University Press, 2012), 4.

22 Jeng, *Peacebuilding*. Jeng examines whether an alternative approach to peacebuilding can be generated under the Constitutive Act of the African Union. Using a pluralist constructivist approach that challenges the dominance of international law on peacebuilding in postcolonial Africa, he contends that the AU's more integrative approach, which combines peace and security, may have more success.

23 Timothy Donais and Erin McCandless, "International Peace Building and the Emergence of the Inclusivity Norm," *Third World Quarterly* 38(2) (2017): 291–310, 305; see also, Erin McCandless and Timothy Donais, "Generations of Constructing Peace: The Constructivism Paradigm and Peacebuilding." In Carey, *Peacebuilding Paradigms*, 126–144.

24 The idea of placing greater focus on local dynamics in peace processes is inspired by the writings of Johan Galthung (for example, *Peace by Peaceful Means: Peace and Conflict, Development and Civilization* [International Peace Research Institute Oslo; Sage Publications, Inc., 1996] and Galtung and Paul D. Scott, *Democracy, Peace, Development*, [Transcend Univ. Press, 2008]) and Séverine Autesserre (for example, *Peaceland: Conflict Resolution and the Everyday Politics of International Intervention* [Cambridge: Cambridge University Press, 2014] and *The Trouble with the Congo*).

25 John Hoven, "Paradigm Partners." In Henry F. Carey ed., *Peacebuilding Paradigms: The Impact of Theoretical Diversity on Implementing Sustainable Peace* (Cambridge: Cambridge Univ. Press, 2020), 255-270; Sabine Kurtenbach, "Why is Liberal Peacebuilding so Difficult? Some Lessons from Central America," *European Review of Latin American and Caribbean Studies* 88 (April 2010): 95–110; Roland Paris, "Saving Liberal Peacebuilding," *Review of International Studies* 36 (2012): 337–365; Roger Mac Ginty, "Where is the Local? Critical Localism and Peacebuilding," *Third World Quarterly* 36(5) (2015): 840–856; Vivienne Jabri, "Peacebuilding, the Local and the International: A Colonial or a Postcolonial Reality?" *Peacebuilding* 1(1) (2013): 3–16; Roger Mac Ginty and Olivier P. Richmond, "The Local Turn in Peace Building: A Critical Agenda for Peace," *Third World Quarterly* 34(5) (2013): 763–783; Thania Paffenholz, "Unpacking the Local Turn In Peacebuilding: A Critical Assessment Towards An Agenda For Future Research," *Third World Quarterly* 36(5) (2015): 857–874.

26 Mathijs Van Leeuwen, Joseph Nindorera, Jean-Louis Kambale Nzweve, and Corita Corbijn, "The 'Local Turn' and Notions of Conflict and Peacebuilding – Reflections On Local Peace Committees in Burundi and Eastern DR Congo," *Peacebuilding* 8(3) (2020): 279–299, 280. The value of considering a local perspective in peacebuilding is not in and of itself always a good idea. The authors point to literature that raises issues about who determines which local communities should have a voice in peace processes and how their participation is to

proceed. See Van Leeuwen et al. "'Local'," 281 and the studies by Oliver P. Richmond, including "The Romanticisation of The Local: Welfare, Culture and Peacebuilding," *The International Spectator* 44(1) (2009): 149–169; see also Birgit Bräuchler and Philipp Naucke, "Peacebuilding and Conceptualisations of the Local," *Social Anthropology* 25(4) (2017): 422–436.

27 Van Leeuwen et al., "'Local'," 282–283.

28 Van Leeuwen et al., "'Local'," 283. They suggest that the concept of "local" needs to be deconstructed by outside actors to understand who among these local actors speaks for whom and why, who is claiming legitimacy and why, and so on.

29 Van Leeuwen et al., "'Local'," 282–284.

30 John Karlsrud, "From Liberal Peacebuilding to Stabilization and Counterterrorism," *International Peacekeeping*, 26(1) (2019): 1–21.

31 Karlsrud, "From Liberal"; Marc Lanteigne, "China's UN Peacekeeping in Mali and Comprehensive Diplomacy," *The China Quarterly* 239 (2019): 635–655. Harold Cheung, "The Rise of Illiberal Peacebuilding and Authoritarian Modes of Conflict Management," *The Cornell International Affairs Review*, XIII (Fall 2019): 4–41.

32 See UN MINUSMA *History*.

33 See EUTM https://eutmmali.eu/eutm-mali-mission/ (accessed on March 1, 2024).

34 See UNGA, HRC, *Report of the Independent Expert on The Situation of Human Rights in Mali*, A/HRC/43/76, 24 Feb.–20 March 2020, Agenda item 10.

35 International Crisis Group, "Mali: An Imposed Peace?" Report 226 (May 22, 2015); Yvan Guichaoua, "A Northern Kno: Untangling Local Peacebuilding Politics," *Insight on Conflict* (Aug. 31, 2016).

36 Bernd Dörries, "Alienation" *Süddeutsche Zeitung* (June 22, 2022), 4.

37 Human Rights Watch, *World Report 2024. Mali. Events of 2023*, 2024, https://www.hrw.org/world-report/2024/country-chapters/mali (accessed on March 12, 2024).

38 For all measures of these components of *congruence*, the data remain in the poor category (0 to .399).

39 For information on how these variables are measured, see Chapter 2 of this volume.

40 The civil war between the Tutsi military and several Hutu rebel groups in Burundi began in 1993 after the assassination of Hutu president-elect Melchoir Ndadaye. The agreement was signed in 2000 and went into effect in 2004 after the last rebel groups signed on. Stef Vandenginste, "Legal Loopholes and the Politics of Executive Term Limits: Insights from Burundi," *African Spectrum* 51(2) (2016): 39–63.

41 An AU peacekeeping mission operated in Burundi from 2003 to 2004 and was replaced by ONUB. The AU offered to send troops to address the violence in 2015, but the plan was rejected by President Nkurunziza. Mark Cauldwell, "AU Proposes Peacekeepers for Burundi," *Reuters* (December 18, 2015).

42 UNSC, Resolution 1719 (2006).

43 United Nations Office in Burundi, "Closure of BINUB," at Closure of BNUB | BNUB (unmissions.org). (accessed March 12, 2024).

44 Stacey M. Mitchell, *Institutional Legacies, Decision Frames and Political Violence in Rwanda and Burundi* (London: Routledge, 2018), 213–214.

45 MENUB, Preliminary Statement at unmissions.org (accessed March 12, 2024).

46 Human Rights Watch *Burundi: Events of 2018* (2019), available at: <https://www.hrw.org/world-report/2019/country-chapters/burundi> (last accessed February 28, 2021). The 2005 constitution requires two-thirds of the National Assembly and three-fifths of the Senate to pass a law. Articles 180 and 191 of the 2018 constitution make it so that now three-fifths of each body of the legislature is needed to pass a law. Constitution of Burundi (2018), available at:

<https://www.constituteproject.org/constitution/Burundi_2018.pdf?lang=en> (last accessed February 4, 2021); also, *Constitution of Burundi* (2005), available at: <https://www.constituteproject.org/constitution/Burundi_2005> (last accessed February 4, 2021).

47 *Al Jazeera*, "Burundi Backs New Constitution Extending Presidential Term Limits," (May 22, 2018).

48 The 2018 revisions grant police wider latitude in how they conduct searches, monitor, and surveil suspects. Law No. 1/09 (2018) includes several provisions that violate rights enshrined in the constitution, including article 25 prohibiting torture. HRC, A/ HRC/39/CRP.1, 564–565.

49 The OSEB was asked to leave in 2019 by Nkurunziza, who then passed away in 2020. His successor, General Évariste Ndayishimiye, followed through with his request. Julia Steers, "Why Burundi's Ongoing Political Tensions Risk Devolving into Ethnic Violence," *World Politics Review* (2019): 1–5.

50 HRC, *Report of the Special Commission of Inquiry on Burundi*, A/HRC/45/32 (13 August 2020) 11, available at: <https://undocs.org/en/A/HRC/45/32> (last accessed January 3, 2021).

51 UNIIB, *Report of the United Nations Independent Investigation on Burundi (UNIIB) established pursuant to Human Rights Council Resolution S-24/1*, A/ HRC/33/3,7 Section 132 (September 20, 2016).

52 On this point, see also Popplewell's discussion about civil society associations in Burundi. Rowan Popplewell, "Civil Society, Hybridity and Peacebuilding in Burundi," *Third World Quarterly* 40(1) (2019): 129–146.

53 Élise Féron, "Reinventing Conflict Prevention? Women and the Prevention of the Reemergence of Conflict in Burundi," *Conflict Resolution Quarterly* 27 (2019): 239–252.

54 Féron, "Reinventing," 250.

55 Van Leeuwen et al., "'Local'," 287–288.

56 Van Leeuwen et al., "'Local'." Attempts to make the traditional *bashingantahe* more inclusive contributed to its loss of legitimacy in the rural areas of the country. Popperwell, "Civil Society," 136–138.

57 One type of policy that has caused more harm than good are the government's villagization policies. In their present iteration they are referred to as "peace villages." The goal is reconciliation, assimilation, and development. However, these villages understandably created conflict and mistrust among populations given Burundi's past histories of conflict and current and past government misrule. Andrea Purdekova, "Respacing for Peace? Resistance to Integration and the Ontopolitics of Rural Planning in Post-War Burundi," *Development and Change* 48(3): 534–566.

58 Van Leeuwen et al. "'Local'," 291. Kasherwa, contends that greater involvement of the youth in the peace process in Burundi is especially necessary as they constitute a vast majority of the population (66% under the age of 25). Amani C. Ksherwa, "The Role of Youth Organizations in Peacebuilding in the African Great Lakes Region: A Rough Transition from Local and Non-Governmental to the National and Governmental Peacebuilding Efforts in Burundi and Eastern DRC," *Journal of Peace Education* 17(2) (2020): 123–160.

59 Karlsrud, "From Liberal"; Peter Albrecht and Signe Cold-Ravnkilde, "National Interests as Friction: Peacekeeping in Somalia and Mali," *Journal of Intervention and Statebuilding*, 14(2) (2020): 204–220.

60 African Commission, *Final Communiqué Fact-Finding Mission of The African Commission on Human and Peoples' Rights to Burundi 7–13 December 2015*, available at: <achpr-com-fact-finding-mission-burundi-13-12-2015.pdf (peaceau.org)> (last accessed November 13, 2020).

61 African Commission, *40TH Activity Report of The African Commission on Human and Peoples' Rights* (2016), 10, available at: <file:///C:/Users/smitchell64/Downloads/actrep40_2016_eng.pdf> (last accessed November 13, 2020).

62 A similar claim can be made about the East African Court of Justice (EACJ). A case was filed with the EACJ challenging the 2015 ruling of the Constitutional Court allowing Nkurunziza's bid for a third term. The case was dismissed by the EACJ on the grounds that the EACJ did not have the authority to overrule the Constitutional Court's decision. East African Community, "Press Release: First Instance Division Dismisses Case Challenging Decision of The Constitutional Court of Burundi On Presidential Term Limits," available at: <https://www.eac.int/press-releases/561-980-119-first-instance-division-dismisses-case-challenging-decision-of-the-constitutional-court-of-burundi-on-presidential-term-limits> (accessed November 2, 2020).

63 See Katharina P.W. Döring, "The Changing ASF Geography: From the Intervention Experience in Mali to the African Capacity for Immediate Response to Crises and the Nouakchott Process," *African Security*, 11(1) (2018): 32–58.

64 In his 2020 report, the UN's Independent Expert notes arbitrary arrest cases by MINUSMA's peacekeepers, summary executions, enforced disappearances, torture, ill-treatment, and arbitrary arrests by the Malian defense and security forces. Terror acts committed by armed groups vis-à-vis local populations are documented, too. See UNSC/HRC 2020, FN 33; also, Louise W. Moe, "The Dark Side of Institutional Collaboration: How Peacekeeping-Counterterrorism Convergences Weak the Protection of Civilians in Mali," *International Peacekeeping*, 28(1) (2021): 1–29 and Karlsrud, "From Liberal."

65 Karlsrud, "From Liberal," 9.

66 See for example Cheung, "The Rise."

67 Karlsrud, "From Liberal," 3–4.

68 Cheung, "The Rise."

69 See Matthieu N. Guerrero, *Understanding Mali: Lessons for Policymakers* (Maxwell Airforce Base, Alabama: School of Advanced Air and Space Studies, June 2014); Katharina P.W. Döring and Jens Herpolsheimer, "The Spaces of Intervention for Mali and Guinea-Bissau," *South African Journal of International Affairs*, 25(1) (2018): 61–82.

70 See Jenny Lorentzen, "Women as 'New Security Actors' in Preventing and Countering Violent Extremism in Mali," *International Affairs*, 97(3) (2021): 721–738.

8 How Foreign Investment Fuels Social Conflicts in Africa

Yue Lin

Introduction

The pros and cons associated with foreign direct investment (FDI) in Africa have triggered heated discussions. Africa has received new capital, opened and expanded emerging industries, and even developed renewable energy that could potentially fulfill sustainable economic recovery, thanks to outside investors.[1] Meanwhile, when local citizens in investment-recipient countries fear that future economic returns will be expropriated, they might seek violent and nonviolent tools to express dissatisfaction. Though scholars have long worked to quantify how FDI might or might not fuel social unrest in Africa, each sector's disaggregated impacts from foreign investment remain obscure. This chapter seeks to examine the following unexplored research questions: How do different sectoral investments from foreign countries fuel social conflicts in Africa? How do divergent weights of investment in each sector contribute to the likelihood of inciting new conflicts in host countries?

Implicit in these questions is the idea that greater social conflict spurs on greater government response. Testing for the impact FDI has on social conflict in recipient countries is also a test of the degree to which prohibitions against torture, disappearances, and extrajudicial killings have become institutionalized in these countries.

This chapter starts with an examination of extant investment and conflict literature which demonstrates that most studies focus on how conflicts impact investment, whereas few examine the reversed relationship. What's more, scholars mainly explore the problem of information asymmetry and the audience costs associated with it. Some draw from information asymmetry and commitment problems to approach how specific investment projects like mining lead to a spike in social conflicts.[2] Others rely on the bargaining theory of conflict to study the role of international actors as third parties in punishing states' policy choices, such as entering into internal violence.[3] However, none tests for the effects of different foreign sectoral investment on domestic conflicts in host countries.

In this chapter, I argue that foreign investment in "extractive" sectors, such as mining and oil industries, is more likely to trigger social conflicts in

DOI: 10.4324/9781003471677-11

recipient countries than in more "inclusive" sectors, like construction and infrastructure. The proposed causal mechanism is that the more extractive an investment project becomes, the more likely citizens in investment-recipient countries behave aggressively against growing inequality and rampant corruption.

I then lay out the mixed methods to test these arguments. First, a difference-in-difference (DID) method is used to examine the relationship between foreign investment and the likelihood of social conflicts in Africa. I also offer two case studies: on the one hand, I focus on Chinese oil investment in Sudan; on the other hand, I examine Chinese construction and manufacturing investments in Ethiopia. Both case studies demonstrate that the sectors targeted by foreign investors *do* impact somewhat the propensity for conflict for the time-period covered. The prevalence of social conflict can be seen as a partial proxy for the strength of the legalization of human rights laws prohibiting a government's use of excessive force. Moreover, FDI either exacerbates an already unfavorable situation in which *congruence*—rule of law—is extremely weak (Sudan), or it has no salient impact on the strength of rule of law at all (Ethiopia). This chapter concludes with some observations about FDI's role in human rights legalization.

The Relationship between FDI and Conflict

How Do Intrastate Conflicts Affect Foreign Investment?

The state of the art in disentangling the relationship between conflict and FDI is primarily centered on how domestic conflict affects FDI, rather than the other way round. Specifically, scholars have debated two contradictory streams of mechanisms. Some argue that conflict deters investors from proceeding with existing investment projects or prevents them from embarking on new ones, while others believe that conflict represents unique opportunities in chaos, where foreign investors can enjoy unexpected benefits and opt to cooperate further.

In the globalization era, it is widely believed that many developing countries deem FDI as a crucial source of capital. However, in foreign investors' eyes, if their future economic returns become risky, they will be disincentivized to invest. In line with this logic, some scholars claim that a government's domestic political instability significantly lowers FDI. They attribute the negative conditional correlation to institutional weakness, political risk, and firms' cost-benefit analyses.

Institutional vulnerability and political risk are widely considered to discourage foreign investment in wartime societies. Underdeveloped institutional conditions in investment-host countries, such as government instability, low quality of bureaucracy, internal conflict and ethnic tensions, violation of human rights, insufficient law and order, and corruption, are found to attract less inward FDI.[4] Moreover, environmental factors like degrees of development and competitive industrial atmosphere entail varying moderation effects on the significance of the relationship.[5] Others confirm that negative influences of poorly performing institutions may create a risky investment environment, and thus present adverse consequences for investors.[6] By contrast, post-conflict countries are more prone to and more successfully appeal to FDI, largely due to the different socioeconomic environment a post-conflict society presents from a wartime society.[7] Comprehensive peace agreements and their subsequent implementation play a crucial role in overseeing conflict actors' commitments to peace and stability, which signal credibility to foreign investors and attracts more FDI.[8]

Investment companies' cost-benefit calculation is another critical factor when formulating corporate strategies. Empirically, Klapper, Richmond, and Tran claim that unrest in Côte d'Ivoire beginning in 2000 led to an average decline of 16–23 percent in total firm factor productivity, presenting high operating costs for foreign investors to continue doing business.[9] Thus, internal uncertainty during conflicts can lead to production disruption, weak state protection of foreign properties, and inefficient provision of public services, which deters multinational corporations (MNCs) from further investing capital and human resources.[10]

Rather than inhibiting FDI, other scholars believe that conflict does not necessarily deter investment. For instance, in the eyes of diamond mining firms, Angola's civil war in 2002 generated some "counterbalancing benefits" that outweighed the costs.[11] Civil war violence also offered conditions that facilitated FDI inflows, so FDI entered conflict zones despite the outbreak of civil war in Colombia.[12] There are multiple mechanisms at play in a null or positive relationship between conflict and FDI, including unique institutional features during turbulence, such as reduced governance capability and political instability. They also explore different sources of variations among different dependent variables, samples, and models.

First, instability may reduce expropriation risk by discouraging the state from leaving away assets from technologically superior firms.[13] Counterintuitively, in this case, foreign firms may exploit governance oversight opportunities, such as government incapacity, instability, and resource non-lootability, and thus identify growth options for their investment as well as expand resource extraction.[14]

Second, political stability may or may not influence FDI flows. Though theoretically, during conflicts, political instability creates an unpredictable environment to discourage FDI by disrupting economic processes, the results are mixed when empirically testing their relationship.[15] Some studies acknowledge that MNCs favor credible, stable, and honest political institutions, whereas others argue that political instability does *not* affect FDI flows.[16] The noninterference effect holds especially in some Latin American countries and within technology-intensive industries.[17]

What's more, there is no consistency in measuring political (in)stability. Woodward and Rolfe and Loree and Guisinger adopt a composite variable to measure political risk from the International Country Risk Guide.[18] Others like Barro and Lee, Campos and Nugent, and Korbin measure political instability by the number of assassinations and revolutions per year.[19] Additionally, Trevino et al. borrow the Policy Constraints Index from the Wharton Political Risk Lab to indicate political uncertainty. The Index measures the likelihood of major political or policy change in an investment-recipient country in a given year.[20] Sethi et al. utilize a 100-point scale from the Association for Investment Management and Research and describe a lower score as representing less political stability.[21] However, inconsistent measurements of political instability can yield varied results. For instance, the disparate statistical outcomes between the Campos and Nugent and Kobrin studies could be the result of different longitudinal periods covered in the datasets, 1960–90 and 1964–67, respectively.[22] Though there are abundant existing studies investigating *how* conflict may or may not affect foreign investment, a very limited number of articles explore the opposite way in a systematic manner.[23]

How Do Foreign Investments Affect Intrastate Conflicts?

One-sided information asymmetry and commitment problems have proven to be valid mechanisms through which FDI generates social unrest. Christensen refers to informational asymmetry as a situation where workers' lack of knowledge about the levels of salaries and compensation foreign investors (the employer) can afford prompts them to strike for wage demands.[24] When lacking policies to promote transparency, correct the informational asymmetry issue, mitigate the potential commitment problem due to mismatched expectations, and facilitate effective conversations between two parties, FDI in a mining sector can lead to an upsurge of social protests surrounding mining cells.[25]

External economic forces may also decrease the occurrence of domestic conflicts thanks to the constraints of the global marketplace as an "audience." As Fearon points out, third parties or audiences may improve the exchange of costly information via imposing audience costs or penalties upon players who repeatedly engage in cheap talk.[26] Extending this argument, the international marketplace can also serve as a third party that monitors government policies, and the market audience can become stronger as states get more integrated into the world economy, since the polity bears higher audience costs if it acts *against* the interest of the marketplace.[27] Meanwhile, considering that the multifaceted risks attached to a violent civil conflict may hamper investment projects, domestic unrest is prone to incur punishment by the global marketplace. Thus, under the audience cost theory, FDI could lower both the probability and the intensity of conflict.[28]

To explain why FDI could affect social conflicts in different directions, I focus on the relatively underdeveloped field of sectoral investment and evaluate whether FDI's influence on conflict is invariant to subcategories of FDI. Existing research, like Christensen, only focuses on the impact of one large set of FDI projects (i.e., mining), rather than foreign investment in general.[29] Borrowing from Li, Murshed, and Tanna, I investigate the disaggregated effects of subcategories of FDI in developing African economies.[30]

Generally, investment can be disaggregated into three categories: investment in the primary, secondary, and tertiary sectors. Such a classification focuses on the destination of foreign investment and is most used when evaluating disaggregated effects of FDI due to the convenience in real-world statistics. However, this categorization fails to capture the potential influence of different types of investment. FDI in various sectors may cause heterogeneous effects, and investors in different industries seize different proportions of overall investment benefits. Therefore, to capture the differences in the investment's effect and investors' motivation, this chapter categorizes foreign sectoral investment into two subcategories: "extractive" and "inclusive" investment.[31]

Historically, highly extractive institutions prevent most of a population from participating in political or economic affairs (e.g., the slave age). Consequently, these economic and political institutions do not create an inclusive society. Likewise, extractive institutions also traditionally favor elites, allowing them to disproportionately benefit from wealth and other opportunities compared to the rest of society. In the case of investment, extractive investment indicates that investors (and sometimes the elites involved) gain a vast proportion of the benefits generated by the FDI. The host countries' residents tend to be exploited by the investors since they receive incomes disproportionate to their labor and outputs.

It is practically challenging to categorize investment as inclusive and extractive because it is difficult to identify the motivation and evaluate the effects of each investment. However, the categorization of FDI into categories of primary, secondary, and tertiary works well with the definition of inclusive and extractive investment used by this study. First, FDI toward the primary sector, which broadly refers to the mining and agricultural industries, may function as an "extractive" investment and trigger social conflicts. Developing resource-abundant sectors could benefit the domestic economy via export gains and increased employment in the short run, but it may also incur in increased inequality and corruption in the long term, and chain the country to a resource curse trap.[32] Severe wealth disparities can trigger anger and violence toward the wealthy, including firm members and political elites. Moreover, corruption will further fuel a population's dissatisfaction and distrust about FDI.

FDI in the secondary sector (especially the construction and manufacturing industries) tends to be inclusive investment and may alleviate social conflicts. Construction and infrastructure projects can generate short-term economic advantages and contribute to public welfare improvement in the long term. Railway construction can facilitate communication convenience, encourage migration to big cities for better jobs, promote cross-border trading, and have positive spillover effects on surrounding residents' business activities. Additionally, the training of employed local workers strengthens their competitiveness in the job market and their long-term income growth. Investors could also contribute to public services that serve as a playing field where people can exchange and contract, providing a platform to collect information and adjust policies accordingly. All these benefits explain why inclusive investment in the secondary sector may pacify social conflicts.

Finally, investment in the tertiary sector (i.e., the service sector) should also help reduce conflicts in host countries. Like those in the secondary sector, investments in the tertiary sector can help promote a short-term income increase. This FDI can also improve employees' competency through education and training provided by investors. Therefore, this study suggests that such investment can be treated as an "inclusive" one that helps alleviate potential social conflicts.

This study makes the following hypotheses:

> H1: Foreign investment has heterogeneous effects across sectors on social conflicts in Africa.
>
> > H1a: Foreign investment in "extractive" sectors, like the mining and oil sectors, is more prone to trigger social conflicts in recipient countries than in other more "inclusive" sectors, like construction and infrastructure.

Empirical Strategy

To measure the independent variable, *foreign sectoral investment*, data are extracted from fDi Markets, which captures project-based greenfield investment from MNCs across 191 countries and 39 industries.[33] To capture the dependent variable, *social conflicts*, I draw on data from the Armed Conflict, Location, and Event Project (ACLED) in Africa (2013–2019).[34] The change of probability of riots and protests after the receipt of different sectoral investment projects is compared to areas that do not host new projects. A DID method is used to examine the relationship between foreign investment and the likelihood of inciting social conflicts in Africa.

The idea of DID design comes from Christensen, who evaluates the impact of mining on conflicts in African countries.[35] Notably, the DID strategy is a quasi-experimental design where the treatment is seen as (mostly) exogenous, which is theoretically sound: the sectoral investment from foreign countries is decided by investors outside the host country. They are thus not caused by the conflict situation *after* investment occurs. Therefore, this study can use the DID design to test the effect of sectoral foreign investment on domestic conflicts.

Arguably, the conditions of host countries before any investment takes place may impact both investment decisions and conflicts after investment. For example, many African countries suffer from civil wars, which prevent investors from entering the market. It may also lead to long-term domestic instability that influences the measure of local conflicts. Therefore, to control for the prior impacts of domestic conditions, this chapter includes both time and country fixed effects into the DID design. Such fixed effects will incorporate the across-country and across-year differences except for those explained by the sectoral investment. It thus enables the investment to resemble quasi-experimental shocks to the African countries.

The effect of sectoral foreign investment may not be immediate. FDI may trigger conflicts in the short term. However, it can also affect the behavior of citizens of the host country in the long run, for the investment activities take some time, even years, to implement on-site. Therefore, in addition to the short-term effects, this study also estimates the long-run impacts of sectoral investment on social conflicts by lagging the investment in time. The paper thus adopts the DID design with the following panel model (Figure 8.1):

In this model, α_i and δ_t denote country and year fixed effects, respectively; y_{it} refers to conflicts in the host country i at year t. D_{iT} is a binary indicator reflecting whether there is a sectoral foreign investment in year T. The coefficient β is the variable of interest, capturing the DID effect estimation. Since the paper evaluates both the immediate and long-term effects of sectoral FDI, the value of T can range from t to t-3. In this case, the panel model (1) can estimate the effects of D_{iT} in a time range of 0 to 3 years after the investment occurs.

Datasets from two sources (fDi Markets and ACLED) are combined to measure the variables in the model (1). To measure the dependent variable, ACLED captures social conflicts, including riots and protests in Africa from 2013 to 2019 on the event-based record.[36] Both types of events correspond to the concept of social conflict with a different level of violence involved.

Social conflicts in a specific country are measured i at year t as a sum of protests and riots in that country-year. For the dependent variable y_{it}, the first set of measurements focuses on the *probability* of conflicts, riots, and protests in each country. The variable y_{it} is measured by whether there is any conflict/riot/protest in each country i at year t. It thus generates three binary variables indicating the existence of conflicts, riots, and protests in the host country. The coefficient β, in this case, estimates the effect of sectoral FDI on the probability of domestic conflicts.

The second set of measurements captures the *intensity* of conflicts in African countries. I measure y_{it} by the number of riots, protests, and overall conflicts in each country i at year t. The coefficient β will thus capture the

$$y_{it} = \alpha_i + \delta_t + \beta D_{iT} + \varepsilon_{it}\ (T = t, t-1, t-2, t-3)\#(1)$$

Figure 8.1 Panel model.

DID effect of sectoral foreign investment on the frequency of domestic conflicts.

For the independent variable, *foreign sectoral investment*, I use data from *Financial Times*' fDi Markets, which contains information about investment flows by sector, and it is by far the most comprehensive and widely used database about sectoral FDI.[37] To better categorize sectors, this study emulates Li, Murshed, and Tanna to split FDI flows into the primary, secondary, and tertiary industries for African host countries, based on the original data from fDi Markets.[38] Note that in the dataset, Li, Murshed, and Tanna measure the secondary sectoral investment by the investment in the *manufacturing* industry. Although it does not capture all the foreign investment into the secondary sector, it distinguishes the manufacturing investment (an "inclusive" type of FDI) from other types of investments. The coefficient of the secondary sector foreign investment, thus, will capture the effect of foreign investment in the manufacturing industry on social conflicts. Table 8.1 includes the summary statistics of all variables.

Results

Figures 8.2–8.4 demonstrate how foreign investments in the primary, secondary, and tertiary sector impact the *probability* of social conflicts across years. In each figure are three panels, each reflecting the effect of *foreign sectoral investment* on the chance of conflicts, protests, and riots, respectively. The x-axis indicates the year since the *foreign sectoral investment* is made, ranging from 0 to 3. The y-axis reflects the magnitude of the coefficients. Each coefficient comes with a 95 percent confidence interval, illustrated by the vertical line around the coefficients. Finally, the horizontal line indicates a non-effect of sectoral investments.

The primary sector FDI has a weak and insignificant impact on *social conflicts*. In Figure 8.2, its immediate effects tend to be positive, and the long-run effects turn out to be negative, considering the probability of overall conflicts, protests, and riots as the outcome variables. However, none of these effects are significant at the 95 percent level, which indicates a weak impact of primary sector investment on the chance of social conflicts.

Regarding the secondary and tertiary sector foreign investments, although they have insignificant effects on the *conflicts* and *protests*, they significantly reduce the chance of *riots* two years after the investment takes place. Notably, in Figures 8.3 and 8.4, the secondary and tertiary sector investments have no significant impact on the possibility of both overall conflicts and protests in host countries. However, in the third panel of both figures, both panels reveal that the secondary and tertiary sector foreign investment (1) has an insignificant immediate effect on the possibility of riots, and (2) has a negative long-run impact on the chance of riots. Note that the secondary sector investment is measured by manufacturing industry investment in the dataset, and both the manufacturing industry and tertiary sector are considered "inclusive" in this study. Therefore, such a negative effect echoes the prediction made by

Table 8.1 Summary Statistics for Conflicts and Sectoral Investments

	n	*mean*	*sd*	*median*	*min*	*max*	*skew*	*kurtosis*	*se*
Year	126	2016.00	2.01	2016	2013	2019	0.00	-1.28	0.18
Riots	126	36.76	81.29	15	0	678	5.31	33.86	7.24
Protests	126	80.45	231.54	15	0	2080	6.23	45.63	20.63
Conflicts	126	117.21	277.88	34	0	2099	5.08	29.59	24.76
Riot Binary	126	0.81	0.39	1	0	1	-1.56	0.43	0.04
Protest Binary	126	0.83	0.37	1	0	1	-1.77	1.13	0.03
Conflict Binary	126	0.86	0.35	1	0	1	-2.02	2.08	0.03
1st Sector Invest	90	534.00	1489.51	0	-74	7832	3.47	12.12	157.01
1st Sector Invest (lag 1yr)	108	574.44	1563.43	0	-74	7832	3.30	10.52	150.44
1st Sector Invest (lag 2yr)	126	584.78	1579.00	0	-74	7832	3.31	10.49	140.67
1st Sector Invest (lag 3yr)	126	670.92	1681.67	3	-74	7832	3.05	8.58	149.82
2nd Sector Invest	90	87.32	214.68	0	-144	1502	4.10	20.85	22.63
2nd Sector Invest (lag 1yr)	108	574.97	1563.25	0	-74	7832	3.30	10.52	150.42
2nd Sector Invest (lag 2yr)	126	106.84	223.76	2	-144	1502	3.28	13.33	19.93
2nd Sector Invest (lag 3yr)	126	121.69	235.84	11	-144	1502	2.89	10.21	21.01
3rd Sector Invest	90	313.89	562.77	76	0	2641	2.52	6.04	59.32
3rd Sector Invest (lag 1yr)	108	322.38	574.78	85	0	2714	2.60	6.60	55.31
3rd Sector Invest (lag 2yr)	126	339.97	599.80	101	0	2714	2.51	5.82	53.43
3rd Sector Invest (lag 3yr)	126	384.78	664.55	153	0	3571	2.57	6.57	59.20
1st Sector Binary	90	0.41	0.49	0	0	1	0.36	-1.89	0.05
1st Sector Binary (lag 1yr)	108	0.44	0.50	0	0	1	0.26	-1.95	0.05
1st Sector Binary (lag 2yr)	126	0.46	0.50	0	0	1	0.16	-1.99	0.04
1st Sector Binary (lag 3yr)	126	0.52	0.50	1	0	1	-0.06	-2.01	0.04
2nd Sector Binary	90	0.49	0.50	0	0	1	0.04	-2.02	0.05
2nd Sector Binary (lag 1yr)	108	0.44	0.50	0	0	1	0.26	-1.95	0.05
2nd Sector Binary (lag 2yr)	126	0.54	0.50	1	0	1	-0.16	-1.99	0.04
2nd Sector Binary (lag 3yr)	126	0.59	0.49	1	0	1	-0.35	-1.89	0.04
3rd Sector Binary	90	0.56	0.50	1	0	1	-0.22	-1.97	0.05
3rd Sector Binary (lag 1yr)	108	0.57	0.50	1	0	1	-0.30	-1.93	0.05
3rd Sector Binary (lag 2yr)	126	0.60	0.49	1	0	1	-0.38	-1.87	0.04
3rd Sector Binary (lag 3yr)	126	0.65	0.48	1	0	1	-0.63	-1.62	0.04

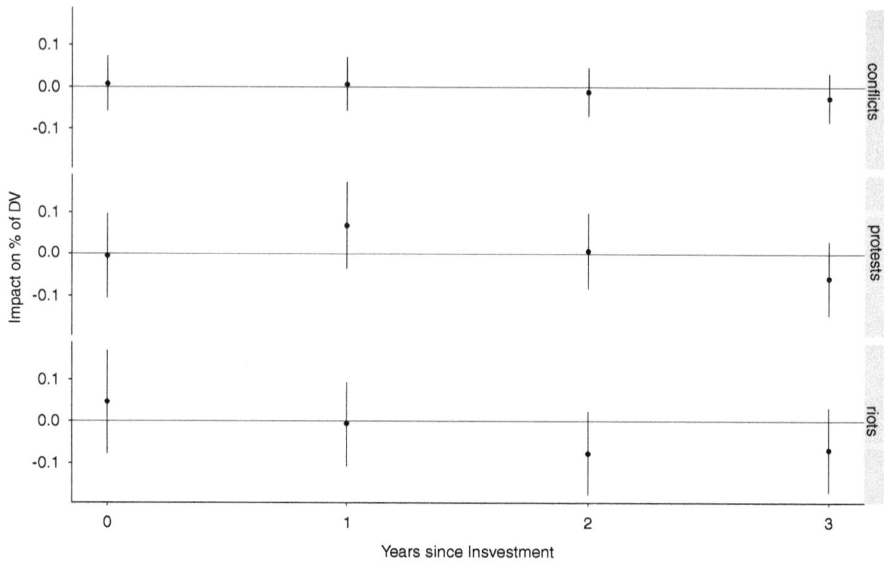

Figure 8.2 Primary Sector Investments on Probability of Conflicts, Riots, and Protests.

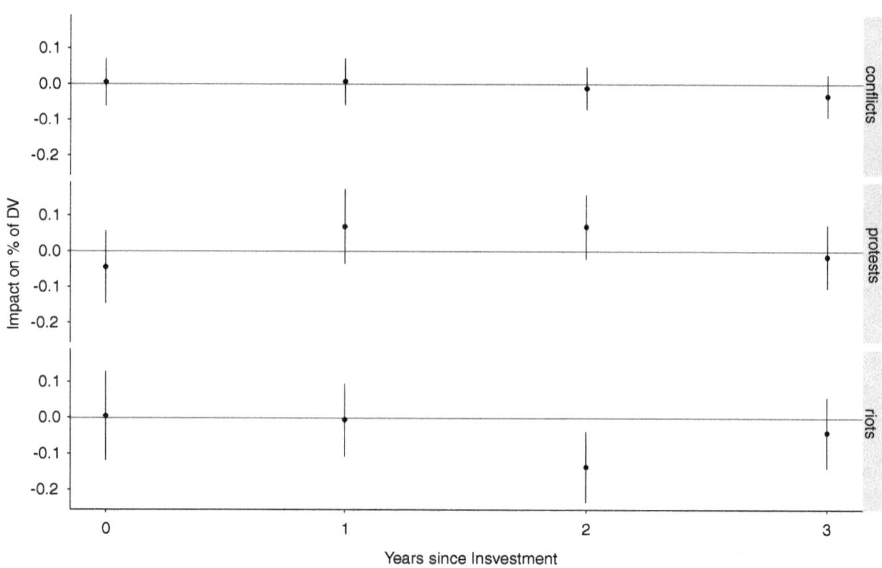

Figure 8.3 Secondary Sector Investment on Probability of Conflicts, Riots, and Protests.

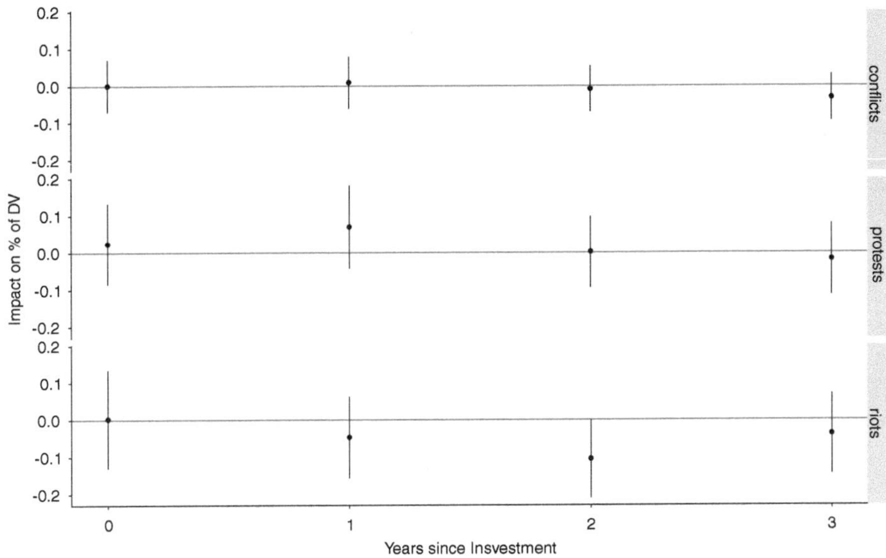

Figure 8.4 Tertiary Sector Investments on Probability of Conflicts, Riots, and Protests.

this study that investment in inclusive industries and sectors can help reduce *social conflicts*. It also points out that this effect is more likely to be observed in the long run rather than in the short term.

Third, the effects of *foreign sector investment* on the possibility of *social conflicts* are limited in scale and time horizons. Most of the coefficients in the three figures are insignificant. And while secondary and tertiary sector investment negatively impacts the chances of riots in host countries for the second year after an investment is made, such an effect disappears in the third year after the investment occurs. Therefore, all these results show that the effect of *foreign sectoral investment* on *social conflicts* may be weak and may "phase out" with an increasing time horizon.

I also focus on how *sectoral foreign investment* affects the *intensity* of *social conflicts* across time based on results from Figures 8.5 to 8.7, which present the impacts of primary, secondary, and tertiary sector foreign investment respectively. In each figure, the three panels reflect how sectoral investment influences the frequency of conflicts, protests, and riots.

On the one hand, foreign investment into the host country's primary sector has a positive short-term effect on the frequency of riots, while such an effect is weak and inconsistent across time. In the third panel of Figure 8.5, primary sectoral investment increases the intensity of riots in the host country at year 0 (or the same year when such investment is made). It shows that although primary sector investment may not improve the possibility of conflicts (as is shown in Figure 8.2), it can add to the magnitude of riots in host countries. Since primary sector investment usually involves the

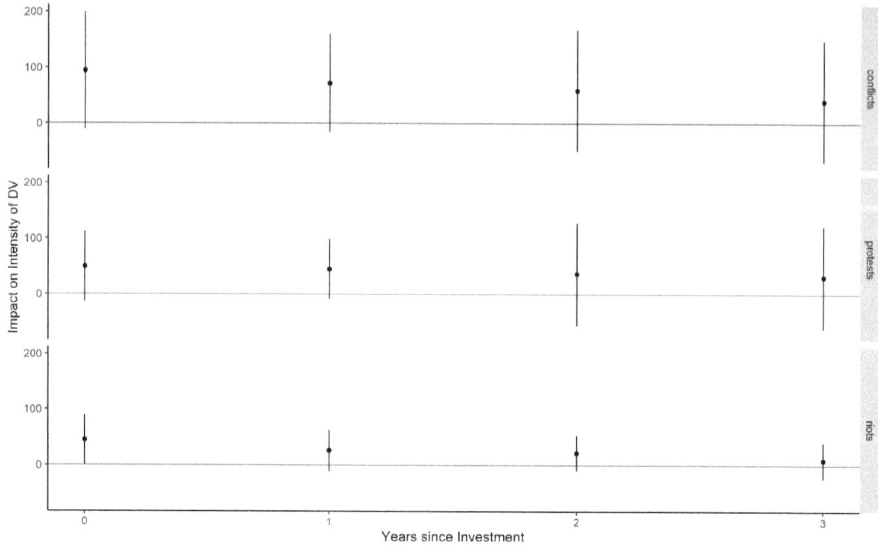

Figure 8.5 Primary Sector Investment on Intensity of Conflicts, Riots, and Protests.

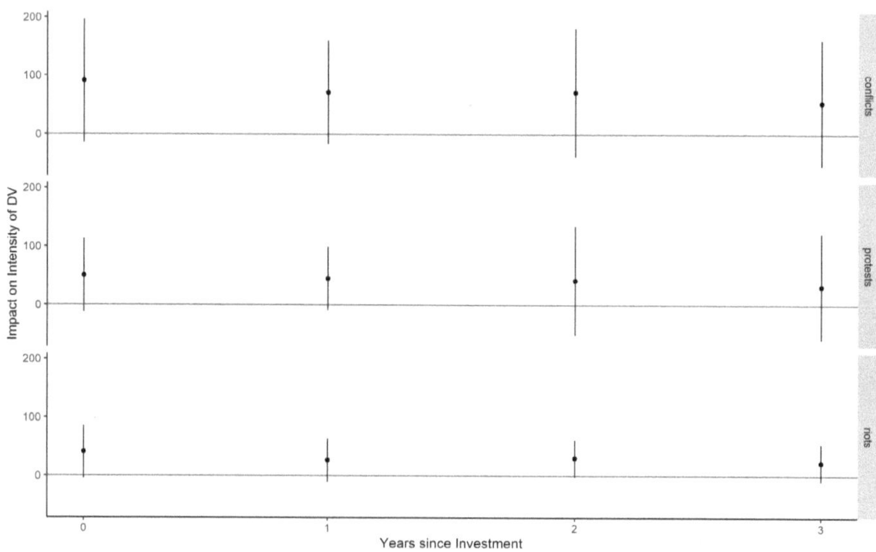

Figure 8.6 Secondary Sector Investments on Intensity of Conflicts, Riots, and Protests.

extraction of resources in African countries, such results correspond to this study's theoretical predictions that investment in the extractive sectors may trigger more conflicts. However, the positive effect turns insignificant as time goes on. It illustrates that the primary sector investment's impact is weak across time.

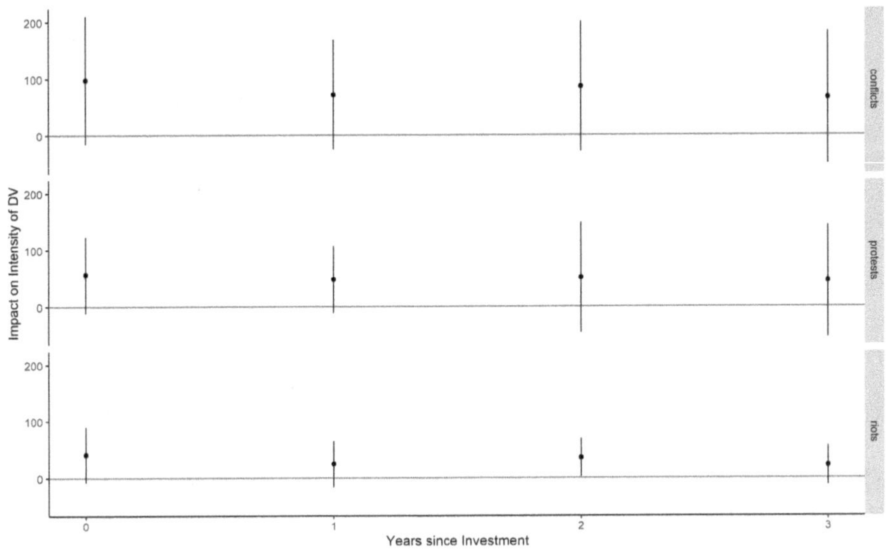

Figure 8.7 Tertiary Sector Investment on Intensity of Conflicts, Riots, and Protests.

Meanwhile, the effects of *foreign sectoral investment* on the intensity of social conflicts are overall limited. Based on Figures 8.5 to 8.7, all types of *foreign sectoral investment* have relatively weak and insignificant effects on the frequency of conflicts, which shows that sectoral foreign investment exerts a more substantial impact on not the magnitude but the possibility of conflicts.

What does this quantitative evidence mean for the legalization of international prohibitions on torture, political killings, and disappearances? The measure of legalization used by this study frames legalization as a process incorporating the communities of practice that are involved in the policymaking process. The quantitative results suggest that foreign investment in extractive sectors may lead to conflicts because exclusive policymaking in host countries triggers public protests to address wage and wealth disparities.

Looking at the data gathered from the Institute for Democracy and Electoral Assistance (IDEA) for this same time period, all six components of *congruence—local authority, societal engagement, independent judiciary, access to justice, corruption, access to information*—indicate very little change over time for any of these countries, regardless of democratic development or economic wealth.[39] At the same time, I contend that the *type* of FDI does impact the likelihood of social conflicts. Whether a government subsequently relies on torture or other forms of political violence to address riots, protests, and conflicts mirrors the strength of rule of law in that country. The cases of Sudan/South Sudan and Ethiopia demonstrate this.

Case Studies

In this section, I compare two cases of Chinese investment in Ethiopia, as well as Sudan and South Sudan to evaluate the impact of foreign sectoral investment on local conflict outcomes. China concentrates on two distinguished types of sectoral investment: the oil industry (extractive investment) in Sudan, as well as the construction and manufacturing industries in Ethiopia (inclusive investment). Readers might doubt if the two cases are cherry-*picked, given that Chinese investment may not represent the whole picture of "foreign investment." Indeed, China as an investor is not equal to a generalized symbol of *all* investment home countries; however, after 2003, China overtook the United States as the largest equity investor in FDI in Africa, given the economic complementarities between China and Africa, as well as Africa's potent economic growth ability.[40] What's more, the dataset in the previous section ranges from 2013 to 2019, when *Chinese* investment in Africa dominated, so it is reasonable to use the cases of "China-Sudan" and "China-Ethiopia" investment as representatives to contextualize the statistical results.

Sudan and South Sudan

Due to the rapid development of the oil sector in Sudan, FDI by Chinese state-owned companies and private Chinese entrepreneurs has grown substantially, especially in the mining sector. Since the 1990s, China has put a considerable amount of investment into the oil industry of Sudan. Trade with China has grown, with oil representing the largest portion, as well as the importation of manufactured goods, capital, and transport goods related to oil. In fact, China accounted for 75 percent and 21 percent of Sudan's exports and imports in 2006, compared with 0.1 percent and 13.8 percent in 1998, respectively.[41] As for inflows of FDI into Sudan, from 2000 to 2007, the inward investment in the mining sector took up 72 percent, with the services sector coming in at around 24 percent of total investment.[42] Investment in the industrial sector amounted to about $200 million, less than 3 percent of the total.[43] Chinese investment in Sudan concentrates on the extractive mining sector. Notably, the investment in the oil sector presented an opportunity for China to meet its demands for energy due to its growing economy. At the same time, Chinese sectoral investment sustained the al Bashir regime in Sudan, which was squeezed for foreign capital due to the boycotts by foreign donors and sanctions.[44] Sudan was politically isolated both regionally and internationally due to its long-term conflicts with South Sudan and was declared uncooperative by multilateral financial institutions like the World Bank and the International Monetary Fund. As such, Chinese investment contributed to a solid economic linkage between Sudan and China.

However, the economic interests of China in Sudan brought the risk of conflict to Sudanese society. China became the major trading partner of

Sudan, with its massive investment in the oil industry and importation of Sudanese oil. However, China's role is seen as consolidating the al Bashir government's power because Chinese oil investment fostered the growth of the Sudanese economy and facilitated local governments' provision of goods. In this case, Chinese oil investment became a legitimate target by anti-government groups, including the movements fighting the government in Darfur and the Sudan People's Liberation Movement/Army (SPLM/A) before South Sudan obtained independence in 2011. The bonds between China and Sudan led to attacks on the oil installations invested by China, which indicates a higher level of local conflicts.

The role of Chinese oil in consolidating the government's position also raised public dissatisfaction with the corruption and wealth involved in such investment activities. For one thing, many Chinese businesses, including government-linked and government-owned companies, routinely use corrupt practices to gain an advantage in Africa. It can be seen as another form of extraction where Chinese firms extract local benefits illegally. In a 2017 report, McKinsey cited corruption as the largest point to be addressed to make the China–Africa trade partnership sustainable in the long term.[45] The report indicates that 60 percent to 87 percent of Chinese firms admitted that they had paid a "tip" or bribe to obtain a license related to business transactions in Africa.[46] Moreover, the corruption problem is "a vicious cycle in these countries—one fed by perceptions on both the African and the Chinese sides," which harms the African people's perception of Chinese investment.[47]

For another, wealth inequality between the Chinese investors and local residents may give rise to the local dissatisfaction toward Chinese merchants and firms. This problem is especially severe in Sudan, where nearly half of the population lived in poverty in 2009.[48] The huge wealth disparity between Chinese investors and local citizens could lead to attacks, robberies, and even deaths. Additionally, during mining and oil infrastructure construction in Sudan, Chinese companies exploited workers and brought the pressure of competition to local companies, which triggered the hostility of Sudan's residents toward Chinese companies and employees.

Although Chinese oil investment can trigger *social conflicts*, it is still possible for China to pacify Sudan's conflicts through its influence on Sudan through oil investments. In fact, China has been working to resolve Sudan's conflicts, especially its rivalry with South Sudan. For example, the conflict in Darfur in Sudan, with a huge displacement of population and loss of lives, attracted the attention of international and humanitarian organizations and nongovernmental organizations who called for an active role by China toward a resolution of the conflict. These forces have pushed China to balance its pursuit of its economic interests against its complicity in maintaining current political conditions in Sudan.[49] Therefore, China has gained the capacity to reduce the potential of conflicts in Sudan through oil industry investment, but international pressure may be further needed to push China on the way to maintaining Sudan's peace.

Ethiopia

In recent years, Chinese investors have played a leading role in the construction sector in Ethiopia. In the past two decades, China provided Addis Ababa, the capital city of Ethiopia, with an 86 million USD ring road, an 800 million USD six-lane highway, and the famous Ethio-Djibouti Railway line that cost 4 billion USD.[50] Moreover, China Civil Engineering Construction Corporation (CCECC), a Chinese construction company, launched the Modjo dry port expansion project valued at 110 million USD in June 2021. It aims to modernize landlocked Ethiopia's logistics sector, according to the Minister of Transport Dagmawit Moges.[51] All these investment projects differ from Chinese investment in Sudan, where China's presence in the mining industry is most outstanding.

China's heavy investment in Ethiopia's manufacturing sector (an "inclusive" sector as defined before) contributes to the consistent and inclusive development of the local economy. The constant economic growth benefits local citizens and alleviates the possible conflicts raised by poverty and inequality. One example of such sectoral investment is the Addis Ababa-Djibouti (AAD) railway project.[52] The AAD railway is the first modern cross-border, electrified railway in Africa. Also, it is the first modern overseas railway constructed by Chinese enterprises with complete adoption of China's railway standards and equipment.

Such a project is believed to contribute greatly to the Ethiopian economy. It shortens the transportation time between Djibouti and Addis Ababa from seven days to ten hours, facilitating cross-border trade between countries. Also, during the construction, hundreds of Ethiopian workers were employed and trained. This increased the employment competitiveness of local workers, benefiting their long-term income growth. In addition, residents in the surrounding villages can transport agricultural products to bigger cities, while villagers may migrate to urban areas for better job and education opportunities, all of which reflect the positive spillover effect of the AAD railway. Therefore, Chinese construction and manufacturing investment in Ethiopia contributes to inclusive economic growth, by which people gain access to long-run well-being. It thus reduces the potential of social conflicts caused by economic failure.

Chinese investment in Ethiopia will continue to accumulate in the manufacturing and construction industries, even after the shock of COVID-19. From January 2020 to April 2020, at least 30 Chinese-invested projects were approved for registration in Ethiopia, with a total registered capital of over $1.1 billion.[53] These newly established companies cover various fields, including textiles, plastics, metal, clothing, medical services, railway and real estate engineering, and data center services. Most of them fall into the secondary and tertiary sectors, focusing on "inclusive" manufacturing and construction by Chinese investors. These projects are expected to provide around 30,000 jobs for Ethiopians by 2022, and the related economic benefits will facilitate local economy growth and consequently pacify social conflicts due to the long-term issues of poverty and inequality.[54]

In all, Chinese investment in Ethiopia has long been concentrated in the manufacturing sector, and such a trend is still predominant. Such investment has a pacifying effect in Ethiopia. As a result of the development of such inclusive industries, Ethiopia has been increasingly seen as an emerging destination for light industries such as textile, apparel, and footwear. It has attracted transnational suppliers from middle-income economies, such as China and India, as well as developed countries in the Global North.

Conclusions: FDI and Its Implications for the Legalization of Human Rights

Globalization has triggered both positive and negative reactions in the targeted countries, and generated spillover effects in multiple areas of domestic politics. Among the waves of globalization, FDI in Africa has not only brought observable economic gains and opportunities but also triggered both peaceful and restless reactions. By splitting foreign investment into extractive and inclusive attributes, I demonstrate how different sectoral investments might fuel or alleviate social conflict in Africa. Investment toward "inclusive" sectors, including the manufacturing, construction, and service sectors, is more likely to pacify host countries' social conflicts: such investment brings about positive spillover effects for surrounding areas and provides long-term public welfare like training and migration chances for local workers. The positive economic gains, in the long run, improve people's compliance with social orders. On the other hand, investment in "extractive" sectors, including the oil and mining sectors, tends to intensify host countries' social conflicts. This investment has short-term economic gains but may increase social dissatisfaction due to growing inequality and rampant corruption in investment projects. These problems will add to the risk of social conflicts.

Both quantitative and qualitative evidence lend support for my theories. Foreign investment toward the secondary and tertiary sectors can reduce the possibility of riots, but such an effect only takes place two years after the investment is made and will become insignificant over time. Investment toward the primary sector increases the frequency of riots in host countries immediately after the investment, but this effect diminishes over time. The case studies of Chinese investment in Sudan and Ethiopia corroborate these findings to some extent. Chinese investment in the oil industry in Sudan has exacerbated government corruption and the disparity of wealth between investors and local citizens. These problems trigger social dissatisfaction and thus lead to attacks, robberies, even the killing of Chinese workers. On the contrary, Chinese investment in Ethiopia is mainly located in the manufacturing and construction sectors. The accomplished projects have a positive spillover effect on their surrounding villages. Local citizens have a higher chance of migrating to big cities and receiving training and education that benefit their long-run competence in the job market. These projects thus provide local people with long-term economic benefits and help alleviate their willingness to protest and riot.

This chapter's argument has some policy implications for investors. First, it may suggest proper timing for market entry, readjustment, and even withdrawal for MNCs. If, at a particular stage, specific sectoral investments trigger observable increases in violent activities, it is in the best interest of companies to re-evaluate their market strategies and take countermeasures to avoid further sabotage. I take the position that the relationship between *foreign sectoral investment* and *social conflict* engenders a need for greater evaluation of the dynamics of corporate market strategies as well as the changing socio-strategic environment.

Second, investment managers should learn about how resource allocation across sectors could affect local security performance. Companies engaging primarily in backward vertical FDI—bringing raw materials or finished products, such as oil, gas, and auto, back to home countries from the investment recipient countries—tend to invest in production or plant facilities overseas and concentrate in the primary and secondary sectors. By contrast, firms with horizontal FDI start new markets and sell products there. In this case, investment in the secondary and the tertiary sectors prevails. Gaining more understanding of the security implications of different sectoral investments can contribute to better distribution and reallocation of capital, goods, and human resources.

For African countries where social conflicts pertinent to FDI have been pervasive, I also shine light on the need for greater investor conflict management, such as making and implementing targeted policies to alleviate wealth disparities and offering complementary measures to offset the sacrificed economic benefits in extractive industries.

However, it is important to recognize that Sudan/South Sudan and Ethiopia have histories of conflict and government over-responses to riots, protests, rebel groups, and suspected terrorist activities. The use of torture, murder, and disappearances is rampant and persists in these countries. Moreover, these countries have large populations of internally displaced persons, have seen a great many terrorist attacks, and have been embroiled in civil wars.[55] Over the 2013–2019 period, Ethiopia and Sudan experienced an average of 13 and 101 terrorist attacks, respectively. Did FDI contribute to these conditions? The most this study can say is that FDI *may* affect the likelihood of social unrest over the short term, depending on the type of investment. Future scholars should investigate whether FDI could alter political institutions and influence the structural violence that persists in many countries throughout Africa.

Notes

1 Sosten Gwengwe and Ratnakar Adhikari, "Why Foreign Direct Investment Is Key To Africa's Sustainable Recovery," *World Economic Forum* (2021), available at

https://www.weforum.org/agenda/2021/08/foreign-direct-investment-key-africa-sustainable-recovery/ (accessed March 22, 2022).

2 Darin Christensen, "Concession Stands: How Mining Investments Incite Protest in Africa," *International Organization* 73(1) (2019): 65–101.

3 Robert G. Blanton and Clair Apodaca, "Economic globalization and violent civil conflict: Is openness a pathway to peace?" *The Social Science Journal* 44(4) (2007): 599–619, available at https://doi.org/10.1016/j.soscij.2007.10.001 (accessed April 26, 2022).

4 Matthias Busse and Carsten Hefeker, "Political Risk, Institutions And Foreign Direct Investment," *European Journal of Political Economy* 23(2) (2007): 397–415, available at https://linkinghub.elsevier.com/retrieve/pii/S0176268006000267 (accessed March 21, 2022); Bo Bernhard Nielsen, Christian Geisler Asmussen, and Cecilie Dohlmann Weatherall, "The Location Choice Of Foreign Direct Investments: Empirical Evidence And Methodological Challenges," *Journal of World Business* 52(1) (2017): 62–82, available at https://ideas.repec.org/a/eee/worbus/v52y2017i1p62-82.html (accessed April 28, 2022); and Mujtaba Ahsan and Martina Musteen, "Multinational enterprises' Entry Mode Strategies and Uncertainty: A Review and Extension," *International Journal of Management Reviews* 13(4) (2011): 376–392, available at <https://onlinelibrary.wiley.com/doi/abs/10.1111/j.1468-2370.2010.00296.x> (accessed April 28, 2022).

5 Nicholas Bailey, "Exploring the Relationship Between Institutional Factors and FDI Attractiveness: A Meta-Analytic Review," *International Business Review* 27(1) (2018): 139–148, available at <https://ideas.repec.org/a/eee/iburev/v27y2018i1p139-148.html> (accessed April 28, 2022).

6 Rodion Skovoroda, Shaun Goldfinch, Karl DeRouen, and Trevor Buck, "The Attraction of FDI to Conflicted States: The Counter-Intuitive Case of US Oil and Gas," *Management International Review* 59(2) (2019): 229–251, available at <https://doi.org/10.1007/s11575-018-0374-y> (accessed March 21, 2022).

7 Madhav Joshi and Jason Michael Quinn, "Civil War Termination and Foreign Direct Investment, 1989–2012," *Conflict Management and Peace Science* 37(4) (2020): 451–470, available at <http://journals.sagepub.com/doi/10.1177/0738894218778260> (accessed March 22, 2022).

8 Joshi and Quinn, "Civil."

9 Leora Klapper, Christine Richmond, and Trang Tran, "Civil Conflict and Firm Performance: Evidence from Cote d'Ivoire 6640," *Policy Research Working Paper* (World Bank, Washington, DC, 2013) .

10 Agnieszka Paczynska, "Liberia rising? Foreign Direct Investment, Persistent Inequalities and Political Tensions," *Peacebuilding* 4(3) (2016): 297–316, available at <https://www.tandfonline.com/doi/full/10.1080/21647259.2016.1193938> (accessed March 22, 2022).

11 Massimo Guidolin and Eliana La Ferrara, "Diamonds Are Forever, Wars Are Not: Is Conflict Bad for Private Firms?" *American Economic Review* 97(5) (2007): 1978–1993, available at <https://www.aeaweb.org/articles?id=10.1257/aer.97.5.1978> (accessed March 21, 2022).

12 David Maher, "The Fatal Attraction of Civil War Economies: Foreign Direct Investment and Political Violence, A Case Study of Colombia," *International Studies Review* 17(2) (2015): 217–248, available at <https://academic.oup.com/isr/article-lookup/doi/10.1111/misr.12218> (accessed March 21, 2022).

13 Skovoroda et al. "Attraction."

14 Skovoroda et al. "Attraction."

15 Bailey, "Exploring"; Tim Büthe and Helen V. Milner, "The Politics of Foreign Direct Investment into Developing Countries: Increasing FDI through International Trade Agreements?" *American Journal of Political Science*

52(4) (2008): 741–762, available at <http://www.jstor.org/stable/25193847> (accessed May 3, 2022); David W. Loree and Stephen E. Guisinger, "Policy and Non-Policy Determinants of U.S. Equity Foreign Direct Investment," *Journal of International Business Studies* 26(2) (1995): 281–299, available at <https://doi.org/10.1057/palgrave.jibs.8490174>, accessed May 3, 2022; Friedrich Schneider and Bruno S. Frey, "Economic and Political Determinants Of Foreign Direct Investment," *World Development* 13(2) (1985): 161–175, available at <https://www.sciencedirect.com/science/article/pii/0305750X85900026> (accessed May 3, 2022).

16 Steven Globerman and Daniel Shapiro, "Governance Infrastructure and US Foreign Direct Investment," *Journal of International Business Studies* 34(1) (2003): 19–39; Steven J. Kobrin, "The Environmental Determinants of Foreign Direct Manufacturing Investment: An Ex Post Empirical Analysis," *Journal of International Business Studies* 7(2) (1976): 29–42.

17 Len J. Trevino, Douglas E. Thomas, and John Cullen, "The Three Pillars Of Institutional Theory And FDI In Latin America: An Institutionalization Process," *International Business Review* 17(1) (2008): 118–133; Globerman and Shapiro, "Governance."

18 Dougls P. Woodward and Robert J. Rolfe, "The Location of Export-Oriented Foreign Direct Investment in the Caribbean Basin," *Journal of International Business Studies* 24(1) (1993): 121–144; Loree and Guisinger, "Policy."

19 Robert J. Barro and Jong-Wha Lee, "Losers and Winners in Economic Growth," *The World Bank Economic Review* 7 (suppl_1) (1993): 267–298; Nauro F. Campos and Jeffrey B. Nugent, "Aggregate Investment And Political Instability: An Econometric Investigation," *Economica* 70(279) (2003): 533–549; Kobrin, "Environmental."

20 Trevino and Cullen, "Three Pillars"; see also The Political Constraint Index Dataset. *Management Department*, available at https://mgmt.wharton.upenn.edu/faculty/heniszpolcon/polcondataset/ (accessed May 3, 2022).

21 Deepak Sethi, S.E. Guisinger, S.E. Phelan, and D.M. Berg, "Trends in Foreign Direct Investment Flows: A Theoretical and Empirical Analysis," *Journal of International Business Studies* 34(4) (2003): 315–326.

22 Campos and Nugent, "Aggregate"; Kobrin, "Environmental."

23 Christensen, "Concession."

24 Christensen, "Concession."

25 Christensen, "Concession."

26 James D. Fearon, "Domestic Political Audiences and the Escalation of International Disputes," *The American Political Science Review* 88(3) (1994): 577–592.

27 Blanton and Apodaca, "Economic."

28 Blanton and Apodaca, "Economic."

29 Christensen "Concession."

30 Li, Murshed, and Tanna (2017) split FDI into the primary, secondary, and tertiary sectors and examined the impact of civil war on each investment sector. Chengchun Li, Syed Mansoob Murshed, and Sailesh Tanna, "The Impact of Civil War on Foreign Direct Investment Flows to Developing Countries," *The Journal of International Trade & Economic Development* 26(4) (2017): 488–507.

31 Acemoglu and Robinson (2012) define extractive and inclusive institutions as institutions that permit elites to rule over and extract wealth from others, and the institutions that encourage nondiscriminatory access to resources and services, respectively. Similarly, this study defines inclusive investment as foreign investment that not only promotes the interest of investors but also benefits the economies in host countries, with these two benefits distributed nondiscriminately across investors and recipients, and across recipient countries' residents. Daron

Acemoglu and James A. Robinson, *Why Nations Fail: The Origins of Power, Prosperity, and Poverty* (New York: Random House, 2012).

32 Michael Ross, "What Have We Learned about the Resource Curse?" *Annual Review of Political Science* 18(1) (2015): 239–259.

33 Financial Times. "fDi Markets: the in-depth crossborder investment monitor from the Financial Times," (various years). Available at <https://www.fdimarkets.com/> (accessed March 23, 2022).

34 The Armed Conflict, Location, and Event Project (ACLED) (various years), available at <https://acleddata.com/> (accessed March 21, 2022).

35 Christensen, "Concession."

36 As the ACLED codebook mentions, protests refer to peaceful public demonstration, and riots are a violent form of protests. ACLED, *Armed Conflict Location & Event Data Project Version 8 Codebook* (2017), available at <chrome-extension://efaidnbmnnnibpcajpcglclefindmkaj/viewer.html?pdfurl=https%3A%2F%2Freliefweb.int%2Fsites%2Freliefweb.int%2Ffiles%2Fresources%2FACLED_Codebook_2017FINAL%2520%25281%2529.pdf&clen=656767&chunk=true> (accessed June 4, 2024).

37 Li, Murshed, and Tanna, "Impact."

38 Li, Murshed, and Tanna, "Impact." Special thanks go to Li, Murshed, and Tanna for their generous sharing of replication files on disaggregated FDI by sector, where they accessed data from fDi Markets.

39 The author of this chapter refers to the Global State of Democracy Indices at Global State of Democracy Indices | International IDEA.

40 Shirley Ze Yu, "Why substantial Chinese FDI is flowing into Africa" (2021), available at <https://blogs.lse.ac.uk/africaatlse/2021/04/02/why-substantial-chinese-fdi-is-flowing-into-africa-foreign-direct-investment/> (accessed May 1, 2024).

41 Nour Eldin A. Maglad, *Scoping study on Chinese relations with Sudan.* Working Paper. AERC Scoping Studies on China-Africa Economic Relations (2008).

42 Maglad, *Scoping.*

43 Maglad, *Scoping.*

44 Between 2013 and 2019, Sudan was sanctioned by at least 13 different parties, including European countries and the US. Global Sanctions Database (various years). Available at Global Sanctions Database—GSDB, accessed May 1, 2024. Sudan is still under foreign sanction today.

45 Irene Yuan Sun, Kartik Jayaram, and Omid Kassiri, *Dance of the Lions and Dragons: How are Africa and China Engaging, and how Will the Partnership Evolve?* (McKinsey Global Institute, 2017).

46 Sun, Jayaram, and Kassiri, *Dance.*

47 Sun, Jayaram, and Kassiri, *Dance.*

48 James Copnall, "Sudan: A Country Ensnared by Poverty, Inequality and Underdevelopment," *The Guardian* (Mar. 6, 2014), available at <https://www.theguardian.com/global-development/poverty-matters/2014/mar/06/sudan-poverty-inequality-underdevelopment> (accessed May 5, 2022).

49 Maglad, *Scoping.*

50 Jenni Marsh, "Skyscrapers, Trains and Roads: How Addis Ababa came to look like a Chinese City," *CNN* (Sept. 3, 2018), available at <https://www.cnn.com/style/article/addis-ababa-china-construction-style/index.html> (accessed March 22, 2022).

51 Xinhua, "Chinese Firm Launches 110-mln-USD Expansion Project of Ethiopian Dry Port," (June 17, 2021). Available at <http://www.xinhuanet.com/english/africa/2021-06/17/c_1310014014.htm> accessed March 22, 2022.

52 Addis Ababa-Djibouti Railway, Ethiopia. Available at <http://www.crecg.com/english/10059090/10059186/10060566/index.html> (accessed May 5, 2022).

53 *Ethiopian Herald*, "Ethiopia: Chinese Companies Invests Over U.S.$1.1 Billion in Ethiopia" (October 17, 2020). Available at <https://allafrica.com/stories/202010170083.html> (accessed May 5, 2022).
54 Elissa Jobson, "Chinese Firm Steps up Investment in Ethiopia with 'Shoe City'." *The Guardian* (April 30, 2013). Available at <https://www.theguardian.com/global-development/2013/apr/30/chinese-investment-ethiopia-shoe-city> (accessed May 5, 2022).
55 Data on IDPs are provided by the UN High Commissioner for Refugees, unhcr.org/refugee-statistics/. Data for torture, killings and disappearances are provided by David L. Cingranelli; David L. Richards, K. Chad Clay, "The CIRI Human Rights Dataset, Version 2014.04.14." (2021), https://doi.org/10.7910/DVN/UKCPXT, Harvard Dataverse, V1, UNF:6:+N2W6SCqRsXxIn6+qCBSyg== [fileUNF] (accessed May 5, 2024). Data for terrorist attacks were obtained from the Global Terrorism Database at START (National Consortium for the Study of Terrorism and Responses to Terrorism). (2022). Global Terrorism Database 1970–2020 [data file]. https://www.start.umd.edu/gtd (accessed June 9, 2024).

Part III

Case Studies and Conclusions

9 Cameroon and Human Rights at a Time of National Crisis

Roland Djieufack

Introduction

Cameroon has ratified many UN human rights conventions and thus has made binding international commitments to adhere to the standards laid down in these universal human right documents. Cameroon is a State party to the International Covenant on Civil and Political Rights (ICCPR), the International Covenant on Economic Social and Cultural Rights (ICESCR), the Convention Against Torture (CAT), the International Convention on the Elimination of All forms of Racial Discrimination (ICERD), the Convention on the Elimination of Discrimination Against Women (CEDAW), and the Convention on the Rights of a Child (CRC).[1] Cameroon is a party to the African Charter on Human and People's Rights or the Banjul Charter.[2]

In principle, the government in Cameroon is bent on respecting the fundamental human rights of citizens by offering the opportunity to live dignified lives. In line with this objective, the government has promoted several policies aimed at attracting foreign investment which is believed to boost economic development by aligning to the strict respect of human rights. The government is making efforts to create a healthy environment for business.[3] At the regional level, Cameroon is leaving no stone unturned. It is a Member of the Central African Economic and Monetary Community (CEMAC), whose aim is to eliminate barriers to trade in the subregion.[4] Cameroon is equally a Member of the Organization for the Harmonization of Business Laws in Africa (better known by its French acronym, OHADA)[5] which was created by the Port Louis Treaty.[6]

After ratification of international human right treaties, the next most important phase is the realization of the rights enshrined in those instruments. A good faith reading of these international human rights instruments requires that States employ appropriate legislative, administrative, and judicial mechanisms to ensure the effective implementation and application of these instruments. The question this study addresses is whether Cameroon effectively complies with its international treaty obligations. From a global human rights perspective, it has not. As the data in Table 9.1 demonstrate, acts torture, disappearances, and killings remain rampant in the country

DOI: 10.4324/9781003471677-13

Table 9.1 Human Rights as Practice in Cameroon 2012–2020

Year	*Tortures*	*Disappearances*	*Killings*
2012	0	2	1
2013	0	2	1
2014	0	2	1
2015	0	2	1
2016	0	1	0
2017	0	0	0
2018	0	1	0
2019	0	1	0
2020	0	1	0

The above data are from the CIRI dataset, which measures torture, disappearances, and killings by their frequency. A "0" indicates that an action is widespread, a "1" means that an action frequently occurs, and a "2" indicates that the occurrence of an action is infrequent.[7]

The primary obligation for the protection, promotion, and fulfillment of international human rights prohibitions against torture and violence rests with the state. However, in Cameroon, just as in Mali and elsewhere in the Western region of Africa, non-state actors like separatist or insurgency groups are also responsible for widespread human rights violations and like the state are obligated under international treaty law to refrain from the same. In Cameroon, the government in its efforts to halt the activities of separatist gangs and restore social order has a huge responsibility to ensure the strict respect of human rights. Despite Cameroon's ratification of these treaties and its codification of these international laws into its domestic system, the question remains, why is there such a mismatch between the system of legal control and the reality on the ground? If human rights are crucial to Cameroon's development, stability, and so forth, why do the practices of torture and the use of lethal violence continue to prevail? What makes these practices legitimate in the eyes of the government?

Against this background, this chapter makes a critical interpretative analysis of the human rights situation on the ground in Cameroon by contextualizing the problem at stake. Following a discussion of the current twofold political crises in Cameroon, an assessment of the actions taken by the government toward the legalization of human rights demonstrates that in practice the extent to which these rights are well institutionalized is doubtful. Focus is placed on the role of the judiciary as an essential component of the policymaking process in Cameroon and the extent to which it is limited in its ability to effectively challenge the use of force by the government. The study concludes with some thoughts about the future of human rights in Cameroon.

Contextualizing the Problem

Human rights violations are rife in Cameroon, although the government has made some effort to promote and protect human rights. Cameroon is very dedicated to ratifying international instruments. However, when it comes to the implementation of the rights, especially through judicial mechanisms, the government demonstrates reluctance, particularly when it comes to the application of these international human right laws in Cameroonian courts.

At present, Cameroon is facing threats on two fronts. The first is the anglophone movement or the Ambazonian cause. "Ambazonia" refers to a separate Anglophone Cameroon, which includes the north and southwestern regions of the country.[8] The crisis began with strikes by anglophone lawyers and teachers in October 2016 in protest of perceived government-backed attempts to marginalize traditional practices within anglophone courts and schools. Schools closed and cities became "ghost towns."[9] In response to the unrest, the Biya government relied on the use of coercion and force, which fueled an escalation of tensions and demands. Since 2016, the conflict has become increasingly violent, with crimes committed by multiple parties. Identification with the Ambazonian cause is wide-reaching. At the same time, not all who identify with the cause support the actions of more extremist groups like the "Amba boys," who are responsible for several especially violent acts.[10] Those fighting for a free Ambazonia were likened by President Paul Biya to "terrorists."[11]

All parties to the conflict have shown a consistent disregard for human rights laws and the government has repeatedly refused to implement and engage with international human rights judgments. Such historic disregard of the rule of law makes the conditions of the current conflict especially volatile. Cameroonian authorities continuously rely on practices of arbitrary arrests, detentions incommunicado, the use of excessive of lethal force, and torture in detention facilities in Yaoundé, Cameroon's capital, and elsewhere outside of the State Defense Secretariat.

Likewise, the war lessons dished out to most of the Amba separatist fighters camped in far-off interiors and difficult-to-access zones in Ambazonia run counter to their prime objective of securing an independent Ambazonia. They are taught and encouraged by protagonists in the Diaspora to shoot and kill everyone linked to French-speaking Cameroon and to vandalize and destroy every person of agency that stands in support any structure associated with French colonial rule.[12] Violations perpetrated by the Amba across regions of Cameroon have been documented in various Concluding Observations issued by the Committee against Torture (CAT), the Committee on Civil and Political Rights (CCPR), and the UN Human Rights Council (HRC).[13]

It remains an open legal question whether this crisis can be classified as a non-international armed conflict between government forces and separatist armed groups in Ambazonia in line with Article 1 of the 1977 Additional Protocol I of the Geneva Conventions.[14] The government claims that the situation is not serious enough to merit the description of a war.[15] Perhaps, the rationale behind this decision is the avoidance of the application of international humanitarian law to the crisis. At the same time, and regardless of its classification as an internal war or not, international human rights instruments apply to *all* parties involved in the Ambazonia crisis.

Cameroon has also been engaged in a regional insurgency conflict with the Boko Haram who operate in the far northern regions of the country along Cameroon's borders with Nigeria and Chad. Other groups include the Islamic State of Iraq and Syria-West Africa (ISIS-WA) as well as criminal gangs.[16] The human rights violations arising from these conflicts are many, including deaths from suicide bombings, the use of sexual assault as a weapon of war, and the use of torture.[17] Like its response to the Ambazonian cause, the government has relied on arbitrary arrests and detentions of those suspected of being affiliated with Boko Haram (and other groups), disappearances, and the use of excessive force, often lethal. Although Cameroon is not a State party to the Disappearances Convention, it is obligated to refrain from disappearing people per the ICCPR.[18]

Evidence of human rights abuses committed by Cameroonian forces and by separatist groups both within and outside of the Anglophone regions prevails, including extrajudicial killings, torture, destruction of property, due process violations, and inhumane and degrading conditions of detention.[19] These violations breach both Cameroonian national law and the international human rights laws that bind Cameroon.

Moreover, social media has in many ways worsened these crises as it enables the spread of misinformation and fear among the population. Initially used as a tool by anglophone lawyers to inform the population (and the world) of the crisis, over time, the use of social media morphed into a tool to enforce compliance with the *insurgency* and not as a tool to engender constructive dialogue with the government.[20] Social media stokes and exploits the anxieties and fears of individuals and is utilized by aggressors to illegally appropriate money with threats of physical aggression.[21] Social media platforms were used by unknown gunmen and bandits to threaten and/or terrorize citizens with death, bodily harm or destruction of their property should these targeted persons fail to comply with their dictates.[22] Social media outlets were also used by some in the Anglophone Diaspora to encourage recruits into the armed militias, and to place their confidence in mystic practices with the main goal that the traditional Fons and their palaces would serve as a hiding ground to conduct the business of war.[23]

Such threats cause emotional distress, displacements of multitudes of people, and even psychological harm to those against whom they are directed. Government workers, especially university and secondary teachers, students and pupils, and political leaders, became targets under the guise that these persons are traitors (or "black legs").[24] Such threats became xenophobic when these faceless men of the underworld started targeting French-speaking inhabitants living in the north and southwest regions of Cameroon. These threats forced many to either flee the region or dole out huge sums of money to their social media attackers. As Amin writes, many in the anglophone areas (both English-speaking and French-speaking)

> were [...] critical of what they called the hypocrisy and deceitful ways of the diaspora population. They accused pro-Ambazonian Cameroonians in the diaspora of "manipulation" and of using the crisis "to seek asylum for friends and relatives." A recurring criticism was how Cameroonians living in the diaspora could oppose the reopening of schools in the country but celebrate graduations of their friends and family on Facebook. Others challenged diaspora Cameroonians, saying that one way to show support was for them to quit their jobs and withdraw their children from school, as was occurring in the region. In fact, by the end of the second year of the protest, locals had increasingly become critical of self-proclaimed leaders in the diaspora.[25]

Moreover, many of the outbursts of violence and various forms of protest by radicalized and aggrieved contingents of the population of Anglophone Cameroon have little or nothing to do with the desecration of traditional authorities or their offices.[26] Rather, these actions were inspired by violent propaganda released by radicalized groups which encouraged all traditional authorities in anglophone Cameroon to defend their offices against the threat of the ever-encroaching French-speaking state. Armed groups count on the support of local populations to fight and win the war against the Cameroonian military. Any pressures that can be exerted on local populations by their traditional authorities (Fons, Chiefs, Lamidos, and other notables) to fight for the cause is encouraged.

The Legal Landscape of Human Rights in Cameroon

International human rights must be domesticated into a State's legal framework. In its *General Comment No, 9* addressing domestic implementation of the ICESCR, for instance, the Committee on Economic, Social and Cultural Rights states,

> Although the precise method by which Covenant rights are given effect in national law is a matter for each State party to decide, the means used should be appropriate in the sense of producing results which are consistent with the full discharge of its obligations by the State party.[27]

The members of the Committee proposed firstly to use means which guarantee the fulfillment of the obligations under the Covenant. The second principle is to choose the most effective means which suit a particular State; the third is to use direct incorporation.

There exist various methods of incorporation, for example, in a dualist legal system like the United Kingdom, legislation can be passed which refers to a treaty but implements it only in part. There can also be a statute which refers to a treaty but enacts its terms independently. Codification can also consist of an independent enactment with the treaty referred to and included as a schedule. The most common practice of incorporation of a treaty is to translate the entire international instrument into national law.[28]

According to Article 43 of the Constitution of Cameroon,

> The President of the Republic shall negotiate and ratify treaties and international agreements [...]. Treaties and international agreements falling within the area of competence of the Legislative Power as defined in Article 26 shall be submitted to Parliament for authorization to ratify.[29]

A purely textual reading of Article 43 may lead to the conclusion that the role of the legislature in the process of treaty making in Cameroon is small and passive. According to Article 44, however, if the Constitutional Council finds a provision of a treaty unconstitutional, the ratification of said treaty is deferred by the legislature until the constitution is amended.[30] The active role of the legislature can also be inferred from the attribution the Constitution assigns to the Senate and the National Assembly in Article 26(1) and (2) (a)-(b) of the constitution.[31]

Human rights are addressed in the preamble of the constitution, which affirms their attachment to the fundamental freedoms enshrined in the Universal Declaration of Human Rights (UDHR) as well as the Banjul Charter. The current constitution also refers to international law by mentioning the authority conferred on the executive to negotiate, sign, and ratify international treaties.[32] The preamble to the Cameroonian Constitution contains traditional fundamental rights, freedoms, and protections.[33] These include the right to life, liberty, and security of persons; the prohibition of torture or cruel, inhumane or degrading treatment or punishment; fair trial protections; equal protection before the law and nondiscrimination; and the prohibition of arbitrary arrest, detention or exile.[34]

The constitution is an important tool for the protection and promotion of human rights. It explicitly commits Cameroon to respecting international law and human rights and it enables Cameroon to translate these international agreements into domestic law. Even though Cameroon does not faithfully reproduce the provisions of the UDHR, they are at least inspired.

Implementation of International Human Rights Instruments on Torture and Political Violence in Cameroon

The constitution does not contain any provision which provides, in clear terms, that international human rights are enforceable. However, the author of this chapter is of the opinion that the human rights provided in the Preamble are those enshrined in the international human rights instruments which are part of the national legal order of Cameroon from the date they were duly ratified. Cameroonian courts are competent to apply these instruments as duly ratified international treaties override the constitution.[35]

Cameroonian law prohibits the use of torture, and detainees have the right to be free from inhuman and degrading treatment. Cameroon adopted Law No. 2017/012 of July 2017 to lay down the Code of Military Justice, which gives competence to military courts to try cases of serious war crimes, crimes against humanity, and genocide.[36] Cameroon also set up a commission for compensation as part of the Supreme Court in 2016 and established the Ad Hoc Interministerial Committee for the Management of Urgent Refugee Situations in Cameroon in 2014.[37]

The Constitution, Penal Code,[38] the Code of Criminal Procedure,[39] and the Anti-terrorism Law adopted by Cameroon on December 23, 2014,[40] prohibit and criminalize the use of torture and other similar treatments by any individual or entity. However, a definition of torture that complies with the Torture Convention (ratified in 1986) has *not* been incorporated into the criminal code. Similarly, a national policy or concrete strategy prohibiting the use of torture and other types of ill-treatment does not exist.[41] At the national level, Cameroon amended the Penal Code in 2016 to reinforce the criminalization of certain serious violations, such as female genital mutilation, breast ironing, rape, trafficking in persons, and forced labor and torture.[42]

Under Article 9(2) of the Constitution, the executive is empowered in given circumstances to protect the security of the Nation and its citizens. It reads:

> In the event of a serious threat to the Nation's territorial integrity or to its existence, its independence or institutions, the President of the Republic may declare a state of siege by decree and take any measures as he may deem necessary. He shall inform the Nation of his decision by message.[43]

Notwithstanding the different meanings emerging from the reading of the English and French versions of this constitutional provision, the bottom-line rests with the fact the executive arrogates certain powers to restore public order and security of persons and property in Cameroon.[44] This denotes that a state of siege confers control of administrative and judicial institutions from civilian authorities to the military. In fact, this emergency regime affords the president enormous power to the extent that he can unilaterally revise the Constitution. However, there exist checks and balances instituted by the Constitution as seen in Article 16 which provides that;

> [...] after thirty days of the exercise of such emergency powers, the matter may be referred to the Constitutional Council by the President of the National Assembly, the President of the Senate, sixty Members of the National Assembly or sixty Senators [...] to rule on whether the state of exception be carried on.[45]

On the strength of the above provisions, the use of de facto emergency powers of the executive was demonstrated in Cameroon throughout the northern regions and western regions of Ambazonia. Though a state of siege has not been officially declared for these areas, the persistent military interventions by the government and its application of harsh sanctions against the civilian populations of these areas demonstrate that the primary goal is to restore order. Tortures, arrests, and detentions of separatist suspects are seen by the government as a valid exercises of the law. Cameroonian security forces, in particular the Rapid Intervention Battalion (BIR), have engaged in a systematic campaign of terror against anglophone communities. Security forces have reportedly burned down hundreds of structures such as homes, businesses, and local government buildings.[46]

With respect to the judiciary as an essential safeguard against the overuse of power by the executive, a crucial determinant of *access to justice* is the presence of an independent judiciary, having equal status with the other arms of government. Despite efforts to protect the judiciary, the issue of its independence is a matter of dispute. Previous Constitutions never recognized the judiciary as a power equal to the other branches of government. In fact, the 1960 Constitution of Cameroon referred to the legislature and executive as "governmental powers," while it considered the judiciary to only be an authority.[47] However, the latest constitution recognizes the Judiciary as a power by referring to it unequivocally as "Judicial Power."[48] At the same time, Article 37(3) gives the president the authority to guarantee the independence of the courts.[49]

While the judiciary does demonstrate impartiality and independence at times, it is more often subject to political influences. As indicated in Table 9.2, absence of corruption, access to justice mechanisms, and the judiciary's independence remain at very low levels.[50]

Corruption in the judiciary has made it difficult for the administration of justice in Cameroon to be fair. The 2019 Global Corruption Barometer showed that 54% of Cameroonians think the judiciary is corrupt compared to 51% in 2015.[51] The overall percentage of citizens who had to bribe

Table 9.2 The Judiciary in Cameroon

Year	*Access to Justice*	*Independent judiciary*	*Absence of corruption*
2015	0.342522	0.301115	0.213952
2016	0.341175	0.282667	0.213952
2017	0.325348	0.282667	0.221917
2018	0.325348	0.267897	0.206282
2019	0.325348	0.267897	0.19569
2020	0.312682	0.260553	0.19569
2021	0.312682	0.260553	0.212248
2022	0.314779	0.308655	0.175626

officials to get services in Cameroon is 48%. Similarly, the 2015 Afrobarometer survey showed that 50.6% of respondents believed that most or all judges and magistrates were corrupt, and 6.4% claimed they had bribed, given gifts or done favors to get assistance from the courts.[52] This systemic corruption makes it an uphill task to access fair justice.

An anticorruption campaign called Opération Epervier (Operation Sparrow Hawk) was put in place in 2006, but critics say it has only been used to remove potential political opponents. Former minister and presidential hopeful Marafa Hamidou Yaya, for example, was sentenced in 2012 to 25 years in prison for embezzlement. Cameroon's former Ambassador to the United States, Jérôme Mendouga, died in 2014 after spending five years awaiting trial in Yaoundé's notorious Kondengui prison on embezzlement charges. In October 2013, former Prime Minister Inoni Ephraim and former Minister of State Atangana Mebarawere were sentenced to 20 years in prison for corruption and embezzlement.[53]

Lengthy pretrial detentions are commonplace, and there are reports of arbitrary detention and judicial harassment of activists. For example, local NGO leader Bensingi has been arrested multiple times for his environmental activism and his trial postponed nearly a dozen times. Célestin Yandal, the leader of an Adamaoua-based youth advocacy NGO, has likewise been subject to arbitrary detention and judicial harassment.[54] The security forces act with impunity for human rights violations perpetrated against journalists, activists, and others critical of the government, including excessive use of force, torture, and extrajudicial executions. Moreover, prisons are overcrowded, and conditions are frequently life threatening. Potable water is scarce, and cholera and other illnesses are frequent.[55] Torture and abuse of detainees are widespread.[56]

The constitution designates the president as "first magistrate," thus, "chief" of the judiciary, making him the legal arbiter of *any* sanctions against the judiciary, although he has not played this role publicly. The constitution specifies the president is the guarantor of the legal system's independence. He appoints all judges, on the advice of the Higher Judicial Council.[57] While judges hearing a case should be governed only by the law and their conscience as provided for by the constitution, in some matters, they are subordinate to the Ministry of Justice. For example, the Special Criminal Court must have approval from the Minister of Justice before it may drop charges against a defendant who offers to pay back the money he/she is accused of having embezzled.[58] The fact that the president appoints all members of the bench and legal department of the judicial branch, including the president of the Supreme Court, and may dismiss them at will is concerning and permits the use of the judiciary as a tool for the legitimation of illegal practices by the government.

With regard to proceedings before the military courts, executive hegemony over the judicial process is once more evident. Section 13(4) of the Code of Military Justice states that, "The Minister in charge of military justice may, at the instance of the President of the Republic, enter a nolle prosequi at any stage of the proceedings before judgment is passed by the military tribunal."[59] This was demonstrated when Biya interfered with the judicial process and ordered an end to proceedings against some anglophone persons, notably Agbor Balla and Fontem Neba in 2017. Executive deference is also evident from the fact that the Military Code requires the State Prosecutor to seek the authorization of the Minister in charge of military justice before requesting a *nolle prosequi* if it is in the interest of maintaining public order.[60]

More generally, the laws in Cameroon permit terrorist suspects to be detained indefinitely.[61] Moreover, trials of Boko Haram and other terrorist suspects are frequently not made public. Under the law, defendants have the right to be informed promptly and in detail of the charges, with free interpretation as necessary from the moment they are charged through all appeals. They have the right to a presumption of innocence, but the government often does not respect that right, resulting in many pretrial suspects being treated as if they were convicted. Defendants also have the right to be present and to consult with an attorney of their choice or have one provided at public expense, and the government should respect this right, especially in criminal matters. However, the government regularly violates these rights in practice, whether we're talking about terrorist suspects, separatists, or members of the general population more broadly.[62]

Nonetheless, the government must be appreciated for putting in place laws with provisions that deal with human right abuses. In 2004, for example, the government set up a National Commission for Human Rights and Freedoms (NCHRF) with Law No. 2004/016 of 22 July 2004 and the enabling instrument No. 2005-254 of 7 July 2005.[63] However, it is worth noting that members of this committee are appointed by the government and the work of the NCHRF remains hampered by a shortage of funds. In 2009 the NCHRF conducted some investigations into human rights abuses, visited prisons, and organized several human rights seminars for judicial officials, security personnel, and other government officials. Although the commission rarely criticized the government's human rights abuses publicly, its staff intervened with government officials in specific cases of human rights abuses by security forces. Government officials also attended several seminars organized by the commission.

Conclusions

Cameroon is a country that continues to face many challenges. Its efforts to implement human rights prohibitions against political violence have been selective. In the face on continuing national security threats in the western and northern regions of the country, the government has had to rely on the use of force to quell separatist movements and continued attacks from terrorist groups. As the chapter by Mali in this volume indicates, national security and the need to protect law and order are also the primary driving forces behind the use of violence by political elites and security forces in Cameroon.

However, the government tends to cast a wide berth with respect to who is and who is not a threat to the state. Activists, members of the press, and political opponents also come under fire. According to the Institute for Democracy and Electoral Assistance, the application of the law by the executive and the judiciary demonstrates a large gap between what the government has promised its population and what the law is in practice.[64]

The recent round of *Afrobarometer* surveys, however, indicate that most French-speaking citizens of Cameroon approve of the administration of long-time President Paul Biya.[65] As Ratsimbaharison and Bongang write, Cameroonians approved of the president and his ruling party despite the corruption and the handling of the ongoing conflicts in the country: "the durability of the Paul Biya regime [is] based not only on what the regime is doing to repress the opposition, but also on the personal connection or affinity between the Cameroonians and their president and members of the Parliament."[66]

This chapter demonstrates that legalization is about more than just treaty ratification and codification of treaty provisions into law. Instead, legalization requires a vibrant and inclusive policymaking community that is free to express its opinions and take part in the policymaking process. I add that it also depends on the opinions of the public. The wider Cameroonian public may perceive the government's actions to suppress the opposition and its use of force against those connected to the Ambazonian cause or to terrorist groups in the north as legitimate acts to maintain national security. Efforts by the Biya regime to breach the divide between French and English-speaking Cameroon, such as the passage of legislation to recognize both French and English as languages as well as the holding of a 2019 National Dialogue, have not had their desired effects.[67] The country remains divided, with the institutionalization of human rights prohibitions of political violence held hostage.

Notes

1 UN General Assembly, *International Covenant on Civil and Political Rights*, United Nations, Treaty Series, vol. 999, December 16, 1966, https://www.refworld.org/legal/agreements/unga/1966/en/17703; UN General Assembly, *International Covenant on Economic, Social and Cultural Rights*, United Nations, Treaty Series, vol. 993, December 16, 1966, https://www.refworld.org/legal/agreements/unga/1966/en/33423; UN General Assembly, *Convention Against Torture and Other Cruel, Inhuman or Degrading Treatment or Punishment*, United Nations, Treaty Series, vol. 1465, December 10, 1984, https://www.refworld.org/legal/agreements/unga/1984/en/13941; UN General Assembly, *International Convention on the Elimination of All Forms of Racial Discrimination*, A/RES/59/176, UN General Assembly, March 2, 2005, https://www.refworld.org/legal/resolution/unga/2005/en/30346; UN General Assembly (33rd sess.:

1978–1979), *Draft Convention on the Elimination of Discrimination against Women*, A/RES/33/177, UN General Assembly, December 20, 1978, https://www.refworld.org/legal/resolution/unga/1978/en/5602; and UN Commission on Human Rights (46th sess.: 1990, Geneva), *Convention on the Rights of the Child.*, E/CN.4/RES/1990/74, UN Commission on Human Rights, March 7, 1990, https://www.refworld.org/legal/resolution/unchr/1990/en/47325. All documents accessed June 9, 2024.

2 Organization of African Unity (OAU), *African Charter on Human and Peoples' Rights (Banjul Charter)*, CAB/LEG/67/3 rev. 5, 21 I.L.M. 58 (1982), June 27, 1981, https://www.refworld.org/legal/agreements/oau/1981/en/17306 (accessed June 9, 2024).

3 Law no. 2002/004 of 19th April 2002 Instituting The Investment Charter Of Cameroon. This law contains incentives to foreign investors who wish to invest in Cameroon.

4 Regulation No. 17/99/CEMAC – 020-CM-03 Relating to the CEMAC investment Charter. See precisely the Preamble ("The Investment Charter shall be a general framework involving all the measures aimed at ameliorating the institutional, fiscal and financial environment of enterprises so as to promote growth and diversify the economies of member States, on the basis of a better definition of the role of the State and of a harmonious development of the private sector through investments from within and outside the country").

5 Organisation pour L'Harmonisation en Afrique du Droit des Affaires.

6 The Treaty was signed in October 1993 and ratified in 1997. In Article 1, the primary objective of this treaty was to provide a secured legal and judicial environment for companies to operate in.

7 David L. Cingranelli, David L. Richards and Chad K. Clay, "The CIRI Human Rights Dataset, Version 2014.04.14." (2021), at https://doi.org/10.7910/DVN/UKCPXT, Harvard Dataverse, V1, UNF:6:+N2W6SCqRsXxIn6+qCBSyg== [fileUNF] (accessed June 9, 2024).

8 Confidence Ngam Chia, "War for and War against Secession of Anglophone Cameroon: A Tragedy of Miscalculation," *Revue Africaine de Droit et de Science Politique-RDSP*, xi (31) (2023): 509–550, 522–525. The areas of German Kamerun were made a part of Nigeria by the British upon acquisition of these areas in 1916. After independence from France in 1960, the citizens of British Cameroon voted to unify with French Cameroon. The Foumban Agreement of 1961 called for a federal system of government, although anglophones (who made up 20% of Cameroon's population) had little power. Julius A. Amin, "President Paul Biya and Cameroon's Anglophone Crisis: A Catalog of Miscalculations," *Africa Today* 68(1) (2021): 95–122. For further information on the rise of the anglophone movement, see Amin, "President Paul Biya," 97–104.

9 Amin, "Paul Biya,"108.

10 International Crisis Group, "Cameroon's Anglophone Crisis: Dialogue Remains the Only Viable Solution," December 21, 2017, at https://www.refworld.org/reference/countryrep/icg/2017/en/119612 (accessed June 9, 2024).

11 Amin, "Paul Biya," 107.

12 Confidence Ngam Chia, "Their Spirits are High and Willing but That is Not Enough: Profiling the Cameroon Separatist Anglophone Radical Militia (Amba Boys)," *Youth and Globalization* 2 (2020): 210–231. The establishments that fall squarely within the Amba targets include government offices, schools, and other national emblems like the Cameroon flags, effigies, and matriculated vehicles from the French-speaking regions. Cases have been known of Amba groups forcing retired and active workers from the Cameroon government and politicians to declare their allegiance to Amba or face what they called "the amba law," which dabbled between, ransom, extensive torture, and seizure and destruction of

property. This information is based from personal observation by the author who is living in this part of the region for the past eight years as corroborated by Chia, "Their Spirits are High."

13 See Office of the High Commissioner for Human Rights, *Reporting Status: Cameroon*, at tbinternet.ohchr.org/_layouts/15/TreatyBodyExternal/countries.aspx?CountryCode=CMR&Lang=EN.

14 International Committee of the Red Cross (ICRC), *Protocol Additional to the Geneva Conventions of 12 August 1949, and relating to the Protection of Victims of International Armed Conflicts (Protocol I)*, 1125 UNTS 3, June 8, 1977, https://www.refworld.org/legal/agreements/icrc/1977/en/104942 (accessed June 9, 2024).

15 Chia, "War," 531.

16 United States Department of State (SOS), *Cameroon Human Rights Report 2023*, at CAMEROON 2023 HUMAN RIGHTS REPORT (state.gov) (accessed June 8, 2024).

17 Amnesty International, *Human Rights Under Fire: Attacks and Violations In Cameroon's Struggle With Boko Haram*, AFR 17/1991/2015.

18 Amnesty International, AFR 17/1991/2015, 15.

19 This is evident by photographic and videographic media material received via the messaging service *WhatsApp* from August 2018 till date. Estimates can only be made from the social media footages that were often flaunted by leaders of different factions constituted the Amba boys though some arguments have been raised that they often inflated numbers to attract foreign sponsorship and to play on the morals of their war enemy. This information is culled from Richard Holt, "Scars of Torture from Cameroon," *The Telegraph* May 28, 2010, available at: http://www.telegraph.co.uk/news/worldnews/africaindianocean/cameroon/7766554 (accessed December 5, 2023).

20 The Biya regime did not simply stand by and take this. Rather, internet services were interrupted in the anglophone areas of the country. Amin, "Paul Biya," 110.

21 S.A. Nkongho, ICT4D, "Social Media and Small Media Use During The Anglophone Crisis In Cameroon," Master's thesis, Malmo University, Greater Stockholm (Sweden, 2018), available at http://muep.mau.se (accessed July); J. Nfi, "The Anglophone Cultural Identity in Cameroon 50 Years After Re-Unifcation," 2 *Int. J. of Adv. Res.* 2 (Feb. 2014), at https://www.journalijar.com (accessed July 5, 2024); Paul N. Nkwi and Francis B. Nyamnjoh, eds. *Regional Balance of National Integration in Cameroon: Lessons Learned And The Uncertain Future* (Bamenda, Cameroon: Langaa RPCIG, 2011).

22 Irene Sama-lang and Roland Djieufack, "Social Media Threats and the Anglophone Crisis: An Interpretation of the Cameroonian Criminal Law Response." In *Democracy and Africanness Contemporary Issues in Africa's Democratization and Governance*. eds. Hannah Muzee, Tata Emmanuel Sunjo, and Andrew Osehi Enaifoghe. 111–125. (Switzerland: Springer Nature, 2022), 113.

23 The membership of these groups consists of young boys and girls who have attained the age of majority. Most of them are less educated and jobless and abandoned their family circles with the expectation of having financial benefits through extortion of huge sums of money from people through torture, kidnapping, confiscation of property and brutal killings. The generic label of "Amba Boys" includes assorted factions exerting hegemony over their geographical locations and includes the Ambazonian Defence Force (ADF), the Red Dragons of Libialem, the Unity Warriors of Bui, and the Marine forces of Babalang.

24 Tanda Theophilus, "Dialogue is Essential to Unite Cameroon's Disparate Voices," International Crisis Group, July 27, 2018, at https://www.crisisgroup.org (accessed April 21, 2020).

25 Amin, "Paul Biya," 111.
26 Confidence Ngam Chia, "Armed Violence and the Desecration of Traditional Authorities and Emblems in Anglophone Cameroon," *IIARD Journal of Humanities and Social Policy*, 9(1) (2023): 78–97, 90.
27 UN Committee on Economic, Social and Cultural Rights (CESCR), *General Comment No. 9: The Domestic application of the Covenant*, E/C.12/1998/24, December 3, 1998, https://www.refworld.org/legal/general/cescr/1998/en/53238 (accessed June 6, 2024), para. 5.
28 UN Doc E/C./12/1998/24.
29 Constitute Project, Constitution of Cameroon 1972 (rev. 2008), art. 43, at Cameroon 1972 (rev. 2008) Constitution - Constitute (constituteproject.org) (accessed June 1, 2024).
30 Constitute Project, Constitution, art. 44.
31 Constitute Project, Constitution, art. 26 (1) and (2) a–b.
32 Constitute Project, Constitution, art. 43.
33 Hurst Hannum, "The Status of the Universal Declaration of Human Rights in National and International Law," 25 *GA. J. INT'L & COMP. L.* 287 (1996), 296.
34 Constitute Project, Constitution, Preamble; also, Judgment of May 19, 1975, *Attorney-General v. Antigua Times, Ltd.*, Jud. Comm. P.C., reprinted in 60 *I.L.R.* 135, 137.
35 Constitute Project, Constitution, art. 45.
36 Law No. 2017/012 of July 2017, Section 8(a–c).
37 Presidential Order No. 269 of 13th March 2014 setting -up an Inter-ministerial Committee to handle Issues concerning Refugees in Cameroon.
38 Law No. 2016/007 of 12 July 2016, relating to the Penal Code.
39 Law No. 2005 of 27 July 2005 on the CRIMINAL PROCEDURE CODE.
40 Law No. 2014/28 of 23 December 2014 of the suppression of Acts of Terrorism.
41 Maeva Réné-Barry et al., *Cameroon: Torture, Detention, and the Fight against Terrorism* (April 5, 2023) Submission Joint submission to the 4th Cycle of the UN Human Rights Council's Universal Periodic Review – Stakeholder report, 1–2.
42 Law No. 2016/007, Sections 277-1, 277-2, 296, 293, 292, and 277-3, respectively.
43 Constitute Project, Constitution, art. 9(2). The French version reads: "[l]e Président de la République peut, en cas de péril grave menaçant l'intégrité du territoire, la vie, l'indépendance ou les institutions de la République, proclamer, par décret, l'état d'exception et prendre toutes mesures qu'il juge nécessaires. Il en informe la Nation par voie de message."
44 Bobuin Jr Valery Gemandze Oben, "The Rule of Law in Cameroon's Constitutionalism," Master's Dissertation, Department of Public Law and Public Administration, Faculty of Law and Political Science, University of Buea (2020), 110.
45 Constitute Project, Constitution, art. 16.
46 David Ebenezer Ngahna M., "La Légalité de Crise en Droit Public Camerounais," Ph.D. Thesis, Department of Public Law, Faculty of Law and Political Science, University of Dschang, Cameroon (2020), 149–150.
47 Inferring that the other arms of government were equally placed as opposed to the judiciary which was referred to as an authority; Also see Cameroun Constitution 1960, art. 41, which is a copy of French ideals enshrined in its constitution. To this day, the Judiciary in France today is still referred to as an authority. Constitute Project, Constitution, art. 64.
48 Constitute Project, Constitution, art. 37(2).
49 Constitute Project, Constitution, art. 37(3).

50 The data in Table 9.2 were compiled from the Institute for Democracy and Electoral Assistance's Global Democracy Database (GSoD). For information about the measurement of these variables, please see Chapter 2 of this volume.
51 Transparency International, *Global Corruption Barometer* (2019) available at www.transparecny.org/cpi (accessed April 22, 2020). *Global Barometer* (2023) informs that Cameroon occupies the 23rd position to be indicating the perceived level of corruption at the public sector, at www.transparecny.org/cpi (accessed June 12, 2024).
52 Afrobarometer, *Afrobarometer Survey Round 6, Cameroon* (2015), available at Cameroon – Afrobarometer (accessed April 22, 2024).
53 CCPR, "A Strategic Approach to Public Relations, including Relations with the Media," 23 October 2008//UN Doc CCPR/C/94/CRP.3/Rev.1. para. 8.
54 CCPR, "Strategic."
55 SOS, *Cameroon Human Rights*, 6.
56 As of June 2022, the World Prison Brief reports that prison capacity is at 164.8%. At least 50% are pre-trial detainees. *World Prison Brief, Cameroon*, at Cameroon | World Prison Brief (prisonstudies.org), accessed June 9, 2024.
57 Constitute Project, Constitution, arts. 10 and 37(3).
58 Created by Law No. 2011/028 of 114 December 2011, as amended by Law No. 2012/011 of 16 July 2012 setting up the Special Criminal Court.
59 Law No. 2017/012 of 12 July 2017 Laying down the Code of Military Justice.
60 Law No. 2017/012 of 12 July 2017, section 14(1).
61 SOS, *Cameroon Human Rights*, 7–8.
62 SOS, *Cameroon Human Rights*, 9–12.
63 Commonwealth Forum for National Human Rights Institutions, *Cameroon: National Commission for Human Rights and Freedoms*, at Cameroon – CFNHRI (accessed June 8, 2024).
64 According to the Global State of Democracy database, Cameroon has averaged a .257 between 2019 and 2022, meaning that laws are predictably enforced roughly a little over quarter of the time. See IDEA, "Predictable Enforcement, Cameroon," at Cameroon | The Global State of Democracy (idea.int) (accessed June 10, 2024).
65 Paul Biya and his Cameroon Democratic People's Movement have been in power in Cameroon since 1982. He has withstood attempts to oust him from power as well as the country's move to multiparty elections in 1992. Adrien M. Ratsimbaharison and Benn L. Bongang, "Understanding the Durability of the Paul Biya Regime in Cameroon: A Micro-Level Approach Using Afrobarometer's Round 7 National Survey," *Current Research Journal of Social Sciences and Humanities* (CRJSSH) 5(2) (2022): 83–95.
66 Ratsimbaharison and Bongang, "Understanding the Durability," 91. Of course these numbers do not reflect the opinions of citizens in the western regions of the country (north and south). Ratsimbaharison and Bongang, "Understanding the Durability," 88.
67 Amin, "Paul Biya," 115.

10 The Struggle for Human Rights in Guinea

Jean Francois Koly Onivogui

Introduction

This chapter focuses on the status of the application of Human Rights Treaties (HRT) in Guinea and seeks to answer the following question: To what extent have successive waves of state-sponsored violence shattered social capital in Guinea? Tracing the roots of this state-sponsored violence to 1958, the chapter points to the use of political violence as a continuum that links all Guinean governments. Drawing from narratives from human rights organizations and scholars and data from *Afrobarometer*, the study uses a rational choice theoretical framework and a quantitative approach to show the negative implications of cyclical political violence on social capital in Guinea.

The first section of this chapter presents Guinea's international human rights commitments and its constitutional and legal frameworks purported to protect and reinforce its treaty commitments. The second section reviews the state of knowledge on social capital and provides a conceptual refinement. Section three presents the central argument of the chapter. In section four, the model is presented as well as the hypotheses. Section five discusses the results of a logistical analysis and closes the project with concluding thoughts about what judicial weakness and an absence of societal engagement mean for the prospects of the legalization of human rights laws prohibiting political violence in Guinea.

The Human Rights Commitments of the Guinean State

Guinea has ratified and codified 12 of the 18 UN HRTs. Since independence Guinea has had five constitutions. These constitutions indicate the same process of domestication of international treaties, and all present an identical normative hierarchy which ranks the constitution first, followed by ratified treaties, then organic laws, statutes, decrees, administrative regulations, and ordinances. All five constitutions have included language from the Universal Declaration of Human Rights (UDHR) and the African Charter on Human and People's Rights (Banjul Charter). Moreover, each constitution after 1990

DOI: 10.4324/9781003471677-14

Table 10.1 Human Treaties to Which Guinea Is a State Party[2]

Dates	*Official Names of the Treaties*
1966	International Convention on the Elimination of All Forms of Racial Discrimination
1967	International Covenant on Civil and Political Rights
1967	International Covenant on Economic, Social, and Cultural Rights
1975	Optional Protocol to the International Covenant on Civil and Political Rights
1980	Convention on the Elimination of All forms of Discrimination against Women
1989	Convention Against Torture and Other Cruel, Inhuman or Degrading Treatment
1990	Convention on the Rights of the Child
2000	International Convention on the Protection of the Rights of All Migrants Workers
2005	Optional Protocol to the Convention Against Torture and Cruel, Inhuman or Degrading Treatments
2008	Convention on the Rights of Persons with Disability
2011	Optional Protocol to the Convention on the Rights of the Child
2016	Optional Protocol to the Convention on the Rights of the Child Involvement in Armed Conflicts

gives a super legislative status to HRT in Guinea which can be invoked before every court in Guinea (Table 10.1).[1]

Guinea's Constitutional and Legal Frameworks Purported to Protect HRT

Except for the 2024 Constitution, all past constitutions were revamped multiple times to fit the political whims of sitting presidents. For simplicity and based on their ideological underpinnings, the five constitutions can be divided into two cycles: the first, covers the period from independence in 1958 to 1984 when a bloodless military coup overthrew the First Republic after President Sekou Touré's death. The second constitutional cycle started in 1990 and continues to this day.

The First Constitutional Cycle: The Socialist-Communist Constitutions

Guinea's independence from France marked a critical juncture that set the path for constitutional dictatorship, unbalanced separation of powers, hyper-presidentialism, and subsequent egregious human rights violations. It took only ten days for a 15-member committee to draft Guinea's first constitution. The highest law of the land was adopted after only two hours of debate on November 10, 1958.[3] The new constitution was neither a product of political compromise nor the consequence of an inclusive process.

When given the choice to join *La Communaute Française* or be independent from France, Guinea's Pan-Africanist elites under the leadership of the *Parti démocratique de Guinée-rassemblement démocratique Africain* (PDG) overwhelmingly voted for independence on September 28, 1958. Dramé writes that the French considered this an insult and vowed to punish the new African nation by severing all contacts and emptying Guinea's coffer.[4] France's reactions boldened the new Guinean leaders in their revolutionary radicalization. Undaunted but massively unprepared, the new leadership devoted itself to building state institutions, starting with the first constitution.[5]

The 1958 Constitution consists of 53 articles with a word count culminating in 1829 words. It adhered to the UDHR, expressively claiming to uphold civil and political rights (articles 10 and 11), freedom of expression (article 40), and freedom of conscience (article 41).[6] Because it was based on the Soviet model with the party's supremacy over constitutional institutions, the government was unapologetically intrusive and limitless. Kane observes that this reform marked the second critical juncture during which Guinean political development took a turn for the worse.[7] The legislature and judiciary became subordinate to the executive and a politically motivated 15-member committee that effectively ran the country.[8]

While the 1958 Constitution maintained some semblance of adherence to the UDHR, the 1982 Constitution unscrupulously purged any liberal vestiges in its language.[9] Its lengthy preamble rechristened Guinea the *Revolutionary Popular Republic of Guinea* and delineated the constitution's purposes: "to construct a strong, prosperous nation, [and] a socialist society."[10] Behind the Soviet-like verbose lay an unparalleled government intrusion in all aspects of citizens' lives. Article 64 granted lawmakers the power to define and interpret nearly all civil liberties and political rights. Rights of association were banned in favor of the PDG party (article 66). Presidential powers and prerogatives overwhelmed the constitution; the head of state's emergency powers were almost limitless and uncheckable.

The Second Constitutional Cycle: The Era of Sham Liberal Constitutions

In 1984 a loosely tied junta overthrew what had become an ethno-regional dominance of all the public spheres in Guinea and vowed to adopt a democratic regime. Embracing a democratic system entailed not only drafting a constitution that upheld liberal and democratic values but which also gave preeminence to international HRT to which Guinea was a party. However, these inclusions and acknowledgments merely pay lip service to these treaties. Guinea's human rights track record has not improved; each new power structure is no different from its predecessors in terms of human rights progress. This recurring situation begs the question about the status of Guinea's legal framework, which is supposed to protect citizens' human rights.

What about the Judicial System in Guinea?

The evolution of the Guinean judicial system mirrors the country's political development. It can be divided into three stages: the colonial period, the socialist revolutionary period (the first constitutional cycle), and the era of sham constitutions. The common thread linking these periods is the failure of the judicial system to stand up for human rights due to political motivations, widespread corruption, and genuine lack of resources. Kane suggests that the Guinean judicial branch fails its people because legal recognitions and remedies were never its priorities.[11]

During colonial rule two judicial systems existed: one for the French citizenry and one of the natives. French citizens were protected by the French constitution and laws, and the natives, customary laws. Not only was the purview of these customary laws strictly limited to civil matters, but their main goal was reconciliation, not punishment.[12]

At independence Guinea combined these two legal systems, claiming to correct colonialism's misdeeds and guarantee universal access to justice. However, this period was marked by a profound degradation of the judicial system. Scholars point to four characteristics which continue to have damaging effects: de-professionalization of legal occupations, extreme politicization of justice, the banning of the private practice of law (legal representations, notaries, and bailiffs), and a series of improvised, chaotic, and unending judicial reforms.[13]

The era of sham constitutions ushered in a new period wherein the judicial system readopted the standard three-layer judicial structure with the restoration of the private practice of law. However, the change of constitutions and political authorities did not end executive meddling, lack of judicial independence, the weaponization of the courts against political opponents, rule *by* law, and widespread corruption. Today, the court system is still discredited and lacks legitimacy. More than two-thirds of Guineans resolve their conflicts through customary law even though Guinean constitutions have never acknowledged this route.[14] Corruption and insufficient personnel and resources compound the difficulties of the system. Even the 400 percent increase in the salaries of judicial personnel by the now-ousted President Alpha Condé did not stymie the deeply rooted and pervasive corruption.[15]

Afrobarometer survey rounds 5 to 9 report that 84 percent of Guineans believe their judges and magistrates are corrupt. Moreover, the country's discretionary spending scheme is not helpful either. According to the *Minister de la Justice*, less than 1 percent of the national budget is allocated to the judicial branch. Furthermore, the insufficiency of personnel worsens the matter. A recent personnel survey reports that Guinea has 334 magistrates (judges and prosecutors), 280 lawyers, 29 notaries, and 17 Bailiffs for a population of nearly 14 million.[16] Local human rights nongovernmental organizations (NGOs) like *la Federation Guineenne des Droits de l'Homme* (FGDH) lament citizens' limited access to lawyers in Guinea. At present, only 10 percent of criminal cases are tried with legal representation for defendants.[17] Moreover, the hallmark of Guinean law enforcement is a permanent confusion of competencies and usurpation of powers between the various law enforcement bodies, including the *Gendarmerie nationale*, its agencies, and the regular police.[18]

The constitutional and legal frameworks consistently fail to uphold the HRTs which obligate Guinea. This study now turns to the role social capital (*social engagement*) plays as a core component of the lawmaking and implementation communities of practice in Guinea.

Extant Explanations of Social Capital: A Need for Conceptual Clarity

To harness the explanatory power and establish empirical causal links of the social capital construct, a clear conceptual definition is required.[19] Social capital is intuitive and complex at the same time. It is intuitive because it reveals an innate disposition for mutual assistance, gratitude, and reciprocity. People express these dispositions through a web of social relations. Social capital is also considered to be the glue that binds every social unit and lubricates social interactions among its members. It is thus a reservoir of goodwill that underpins every societal change because it reduces transaction costs, resolves collective action dilemmas, and fosters thriving coexistence. In sum, social capital is a useful innovative construct that helps grasp a range of social phenomena, but it is elusive and complex.[20]

Factors that contribute to complexifying social capital include multidisciplinary approaches, analytical confusion, and a plethora of definitions. Because social capital deals with social interactions and their outcomes, the concept finds itself at the confluence of several academic disciplines. This interdisciplinarity renders social capital inherently elusive.[21] The multitude of independent theoretical buildings in each discipline confers multiple meanings to the construct, making it difficult to pin down. Moreover, social capital is multidimensional. It operates at numerous levels, with myriads of factors influencing its sources, components, types, and outcomes.[22] Consequently, several authors amalgamate the analytical elements of social capital, such as its sources, dimensions, types, forms, causes, and effects. This analytical confusion results in logical circularity. *Trust* is a notable variable that is a victim of this confusion.[23] Different authors attribute to *trust* different analytical roles. For instance, while Coleman sees *trust* as the cause of social capital, others equate social capital with *trust*.[24]

Furthermore, a multitude of definitions reduces the possibility of a clear and distinct meaning of social capital. Not only does each author give her specific definition, but these definitions also come with the author's chosen dimensions of social capital. For instance, while some definitions highlight the structural elements of society,[25] others focus on the relational components of social capital, trust, and trustworthiness.[26] Still others shed light on cognitive aspects of social capital, such as shared norms.[27]

Critics of social capital theory target the very metaphor of capital in describing social relations, the weak analogy of social capital with other types of capital (e.g., financial, human, and physical), and measurement issues. Most economists complain that the term "capital" depicts human relations poorly because it is too broad for some and restrictive for others. On the one hand, many economists believe that the word "capital" is too pervasive in that it obfuscates its meaning by blurring the distinctive nature of human relations.[28] On the other hand, Inkeles contends that the use of vocable capital narrows the meaning of social interactions, trust, and norms of reciprocity. Consequently, it fails miserably to capture their positive outcomes. He proposes the term "communal," which better encapsulates social realities than just what people own.[29] Others challenge the weak analogy of social capital with other types of capital. Arrow contends that physical capital has three characteristics, of which social capital shares only one, the temporal dimension (it takes time to build trust and reputation).[30]

This article relies on Bhandari and Yasunobu's definition of social capital because it captures all three agreed-upon dimensions: structural, relational, and cognitive.[31] They define *social capital* as "a collective asset in the form of shared norms, trust, beliefs, and values, networks of social relations, institutions that facilitate cooperation and collective action for mutual benefits."[32] This definition accounts for the structural, cognitive, and relational dimensions.

Structural social capital relates to the pattern of societal stratification and organization. It refers to the social context within which social interactions and networks are built.[33] While structural social capital generates the parameters of interactions among social units, the shared meaning of social norms, code of conduct, acceptable behavior, and expectations among the members is known as cognitive social capital. It is the mental makeup of value internalization, shared representations, and subjective interpretations. Mostly intangible, this dimension of social capital is usually captured by standard linguistic codes of communication and shared paradigms. Another intangible dimension of social capital is relational social capital, which pertains to the content and the quality of social interactions. Relational social capital is measured by societal levels of trust and trustworthiness, namely institutional or political trust.[34]

Social capital is a good that can be both individual and collective. Bourdieu views social capital as a private good.[35] Bourdieu defines social capital as the actual or potential resources that individuals or social groups gain from being members of some institutionalized relationships.[36] One of the main contributions of Bourdieu is distinguishing social capital from other types of capital and showing the fungibility of social capital into other forms of capital. He also emphasizes the individual deliberate decision to get involved or not. For him, building a social network is highly rational.[37]

Like Bourdieu, Coleman also saw people's involvement in social networks as purely instrumental.[38] Coleman applies rational choice theory to social interactions to decipher the incentive structures and contextual factors that prompt agents into cooperating.[39] Like Bourdieu, Coleman admits that social structures are critical determinants for achieving cooperation and conceives social capital as norms of reciprocity, effective sanctions, and obligations in each social setting. However, unlike Bourdieu, Coleman considers social capital to be a collective good. He writes that social capital is comparable to an informal "I owe you" credit slip made enforceable within a trustworthy society.[40] Furthermore, Coleman prefers to underscore the collaborative feature of social groups, ignoring the often-embedded social inequalities.[41]

Another prominent scholar who considers social capital to be a public good is Putnam.[42] In his book *Bowling Alone*, Putnam defines social capital as the collective efficacy drawn from everyone's involvement for the betterment of a social group. He maintains that building this collective efficacy entails networks of social interactions characterized by norms of trust and reciprocity.[43] Putnam's concern lies in the plummeting of associational life in the US.

Critics have questioned whether civic engagement has changed forms. Lemann denounces Putnam's elitist stance in putting squarely the responsibility of the decline of associational life on the hoy polloi's recreational activities rather than on the underpinning economic and societal transformations exserted by both the private and public sectors.[44] Skocpol reports the irony in Putnam's argument.[45] How could the elite accuse the working class of the erosion of local civic engagements when they are the ones who blaze the trail in a constant search for profit? Putnam's work has been criticized widely for its methodological issues. Portes contends that although these criticisms are relevant, they leave out the most glaring flaws of Putnam's argument: its circularity.[46]

Based on the radius of trust, scholars distinguish three social capital functions: bonding, bridging, and linking. Bonding social capital is generated within a group or community through close-knit connections. It is often referred to as exclusive, inward looking, non-progressive, and is marked by strong ties among people who are alike.[47] It is produced by a thick trust or network closure.[48] Bridging social capital by comparison stems from connections between communities that are different in many aspects. It is often called the inclusive, open, outward looking, progressive linkages, and is marked by weaker ties, thinner trust, and networks with structural holes.[49] While bonding social capital is produced *within* a group or community, bridging social capital is *between* social groups, classes, races, religions, or other inherent characteristics. The third function of social capital is linking different spheres of a given community. Linking social capital describes vertical relationships among people or institutions at different levels of societal power hierarchy.[50] The distinction between bonding, bridging, and linking builds on Granovetter's seminal work.[51]

While there is agreement on the three functions of social capital, scholars disagree on the sources or causes of social capital. Some believe that social capital stems from the cultural features of certain societies;[52] others contend that social capital is a universal social phenomenon.[53] Equally, there is a lack of consensus on what causes social capital. On the one hand, some scholars maintain that memberships in voluntary associations lead to the production of social capital.[54] On the other hand, a strand of the literature maintains that the causal direction is the reverse.[55]

While the debate on the specific effects of social capital continues, many authors agree that social capital can have positive and negative outcomes. Its positive impacts include improving social interactions at both individual and aggregate levels. It enables information sharing among members, which expands insurance against risk among members. It achieves this by reducing transaction costs, discouraging opportunistic behaviors, and resolving collective action dilemmas.[56] At the national level, social capital promotes democracy, good governance, and a thriving economy.[57]

Portes contends that social control can have obverse effects, however. It can restrict inclusivity, repress individual freedoms, promote group thinking, and exert excessive pressure on group members. Such adverse effects of social capital happen when social cohesion is done through bonding.[58] Here, too, scholars disagree on whether bonding social capital is entirely detrimental. For instance, Kuenzi disputes the assumption that thick trust (bonding social capital) is a vicious form of social capital and that thin trust (bridging social capital) is the virtuous form of social capital. According to her, both resolve collective action dilemmas and free-rider issues.[59] Several studies demonstrate that a sense of "*weeness*" helps to overcome social maladies. In-group solidarity among members is not necessarily mutually exclusive with openness to out-group members. Bhavnani and Backer challenge this stance by claiming that overlapping interethnic groups favor political conflicts.[60]

Admittedly, a vibrant scholarly debate on the analytical components of social capital will continue. Equally, pointed criticisms of the concept have helped drive better conceptual refinement. Still, there is a gaping void in the literature: the absence of an investigation into the impacts political violence has on social capital's ability to foster social change. Probing the implications of political violence on social capital at individual and aggregate levels in Guinea helps decipher why the legalization of human rights has thus far failed.

The Theory: Social Capital and Political Violence

The author of this chapter contends that all three dimensions of social capital have been decimated by six decades of political violence, debilitating any impetus for social inclusiveness that generates collective efficacy. This argument builds on Ostrom's contention that all aspects must be integrated for social capital to be productive.[61] All three dimensions—cognitive, relational, and structural—must synergically interact at the individual and institutional (informal, formal) levels. This has not occurred in Guinea. Successive political administrations, Sekou Touré, and successive military dictatorships have ruined social capital in Guinea.

Touré's 26-year reign of terror destroyed cognitive and structural social capital in Guinea. Touré's presidency represents the period of Guinea's most atrocious human rights violations. Pierret and Correau argue that Touré's long brutal grip on Guinea left lasting impressions on the psyche of the Guinean people.[62] The waves of violence started with three interrelated events constituting the second critical juncture in Guinea's political development. For the first time after achieving independence, Touré's leadership came under dispute from those colleagues who felt he was not crypto-Marxist enough. Secondly, Touré got rid of any possible contenders for the presidency ahead of the 1961 election by transforming the newly built Camp Boiro into a venue for torture and death for scores of Guineans. Thirdly, the failed 1960 French attempt to depose Touré (*Operation Persil*) gave Touré the opportunity to expand his definition of "existential threat" and execute all opposition.[63]

Throughout his reign, Touré adopted colonial lexicon and vicious practices. Over-used phrasings like *permanent plots* and *fifth columns* became integral to Touré's killing strategies.[64] Ideologically, he imitated the Soviet system and installed a one-party state. To cap this ominous critical juncture, the cult of Touré's personality and fabulating historical narratives became an essential part of public policy.[65] Later, in the 1960s and 1970s, Guineans were forced to adopt new beliefs and value systems that erased their cultural traditions in the name of "modernization."[66] Although the 1960s dashed all hopes born out of the independence era, political violence was largely limited to political elites, not the hoi polloi. This would change with another attempted coup in 1970.

Pierret describes the events of 1970 as the year that witnessed the most egregious human rights violations in Guinea.[67] He writes that Touré's killing clique exterminated their own people using the pretext of an ill-prepared external invasion. Following a failed coup associated with an attempt by the Portuguese *Mare Verde Operation* to free Portuguese POWs in Conakry in November 1970, Touré's regime unleashed a wave of never-before violence, including arbitrary mass arrests and detentions, Kangaroo trials by popular tribunals, group sentencing, and public hangings. Overnight, more than 100 people were lynched in public plazas across the country.[68] Adama Camara, a 17-year-old boy in 1971, remembers that not only were school children mandated to attend these traumatizing spectacles, but they were encouraged to insult and stone the victims even if they were relatives.[69]

The wave of unlawful killings and arbitrary mass detentions that occurred in Guinea in 1976 were more regional. Mohamed Saliou Camara maintains that this time the paranoia among the Touré's clique made them target a specific region and severely punish ethnic groups originating from these regions.[70] Everyone was suspicious. It was a Gestapo-like existence. Everyone saved their lives by distrusting everyone else, including parents, friends, and public institutions.[71] Touré died on March 26, 1984, without a clear line of succession. Infighting broke out among his immediate family members for a power grab, leading to the first of many military coups d'état in Guinea.

Successive military dictatorships sanctioned by sham constitutions have broken relational social capital in Guinea. Relational social capital conveys diffuse support and institutional trust on which the political authorities anchor their legitimacy. That support has consistently been eroded since the first military coup led by Colonel Lansana Conté on April 3, 1984. All military coup leaders or civilian presidents in Guinea since that time are no different from Touré. The only difference is that these later presidents faced more media exposure and public outcry.[72]

The very iconic November 8 Bridge on which Touré hung five innocent senior civil servants was the theater of Conté's bloody repressions.[73] More than 275 people were killed by the presidential guards led by Conté's elder son, Moussa Dadis Camara, who succeeded Conté in yet another unconstitutional takeover. Camara is accused of ordering the massacre of more than 150 unarmed demonstrators in 2009. He is facing his responsibility in an unprecedented trial of these massive human rights violations committed under his watch.[74] Even Alpha Condé, the so-called civilian, and first democratically elected President of Guinea, did not hesitate to revamp the constitution to stand for a constitutionally banned third presidential term. During his ten years of presidency, he condoned perpetrations of massive human rights violations wherein more than 300 unarmed demonstrators lost their lives.[75]

The era of sham constitutions is also marked by a massive organizational failure that exacerbates the destruction of relational social capital. *Organizational failure* is a society where agencies are irresponsive to the citizenry's demands.[76] Irresponsiveness and the brutality of the political system have pushed individuals to insulate themselves from the public arena; genuine grassroots movements that could have articulated their demands are shut down. There is no organic linking mechanism that could articulate the needs of the polity to policymakers, leaving a gap that segments the Guinean polity. This gap is often filled by antidemocratic structures run by formal nomenklatura officials or state mafia organizations.[77] Organizational failure has fostered predatory and marginal political institutions in Guinea.

A tell-tale example is the Guinean law enforcement agencies. The system is semi-transparent, whereby rule by law *is* a pretext for rent-seeking behavior rather than a guide to promote accountability. Law enforcement corruption is endemic; the judicial process is privatized because plaintiffs bear the costs of any investigation conducted by public law enforcement agents.[78] For instance, in the case of embezzlement, plaintiffs must agree to pay 20 percent of any amount recovered.[79] Bratton's description of African predatory states captures the Guinean state and its political institutions. They are also entirely marginal to society, having lost any capacity to connect meaningfully with ordinary citizens. What outsiders see is a display of outward, ceremonial, and formal attributes of statehood, but these institutions are lifeless and emptied shells because they are devoid of ordinary citizen inputs.

Methodology and Hypotheses

The argument made by this study is demonstrated in Figure 10.1.

Hypotheses

This study hypothesizes the following:

Hypothesis I
State-sponsored violence negatively impacts institutional trust (relational social capital)

Hypothesis II
State-sponsored violence negatively impacts generalized trust (structural social capital)

Model Design and Data

The dependent variable in this study is *social capital*. To capture two of the three dimensions of social capital—structural, relational[80]—it is divided into two outcome variables: dependent variable one is *political/institutional trust* (relational social capital) and dependent variable two is *social trust* (structural social capital). Due to limited space, this chapter does not focus on cognitive social capital. However, this study's findings have implications for understanding the relationship between violence and cognitive social capital.

In assessing any causal relations involving social capital, conventional wisdom requires that the researcher indicates upfront analytical elements about the concept.[81] These include the approach and instrument of measurement,

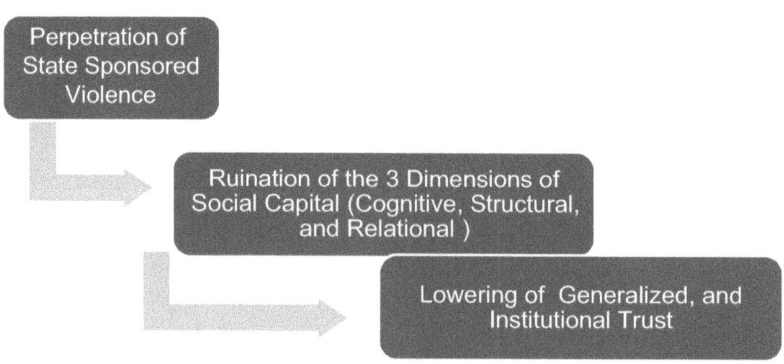

Figure 10.1 The Causal Mechanism of the Destruction of Social Capital in Guinea.

the level of analysis, and the type of good used in the research. In extant literature, scholars distinguish two approaches to investigating social capital: the social structure and network perspectives. The network perspective focuses on social capital functions; it evaluates the strength of bonding, bridging, and linking social capital. Structural social capital depicts the social context that nurtures or inhibits the realization of social interactions which produce cooperation and mutual benefits.[82] This study relies on the social structure approach.

Social trust measures structural social capital. Structural social capital demonstrates the interlocking parts of society and different social groups and how they behave toward each other. The structural dimension of social capital describes how various elements of society exchange information, access resources, and share knowledge.

The relational aspect of social capital (*political/institutional trust*) seizes upon the quality and features of social relationships, such as trust and trustworthiness of institutions.[83] It also entails the legal venues available to individuals, grassroots, and policy entrepreneurs.

The explanatory variables are attitudinal expressions of state-sponsored violence ordinary Guineans report in *Afrobarometer* round 6. These independent variables include *violent repressions* (*VR*),[84] *fear of political competition* (*FPC*), *membership in a political party* (*MPP*), *impunity of public officials* (*IPO*), and *corruption of courts* (*CC*) and *law enforcement* (*CLE*).

Controls include *education* (*Ed*), *employment* (*Emp*), *residence area* (*Ur*), and *party identification* (*ID*). These latter variables are considered to increase the level of social capital and civic engagement in a society (Figure 10.2).

Results, Discussions, and Conclusions

As shown in Table 10.2, the statistical analyses of the quantitative data substantiate the central theory of this investigation: the broken relationship between ordinary Guineans and their political authorities hampers a meaningful collective efficacy. Included below are the results for those factors that obtained statistical significance.

The causes of this disconnect are rooted in state-sponsored violence variables, including a permanent state of violent repressions, citizens' fear of political competition, and pathologies of organizational failure (pervasive corruption of the court system, corruption of law enforcement, and impunity

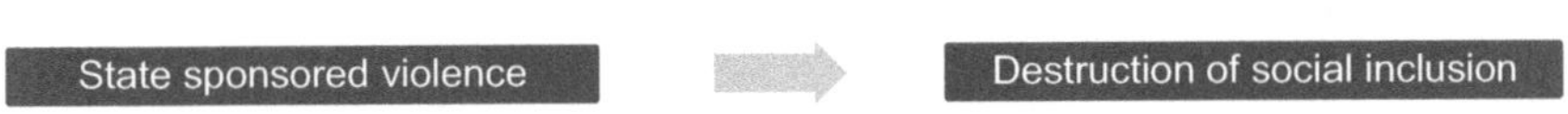

$$SC = \beta_1 R + \beta_2 VR + \beta_3 CC + \beta_4 FPC + \beta_5 IPO + \beta_6 Ed + \beta_7 CLE + \beta_8 Ur + \beta_9 Emp + \beta_{10} ID + \beta_{11} MPP\ ai + ut + eit$$

Figure 10.2 Model Specifications.

Table 10.2 Logistical Regression Results

Independent Variables	*Dependent Variable: Social Capital*			
	Political Trust/Institutional Trust			*Social Trust*
	Parliament	President	Courts	
Suffered violence or intimidation	–0.97***	–0.94***		
Corrupt courts	–0.75***	–0.51***	–0.72***	
Fear from political competition	–0.45***	–0.97***	–0.50***	–0.52***
Impunity of public servants	–0.14*	–0.23**		–0.19*
Education		–0.20**	–0.047**	
Corrupt law enforcement				–0.26***
Urban dwellers				–0.84**

N = 12,000 Log likelihood = –1782; LR Chi2 = 30; Log likelihood = –1815; LR Chi2 = 30; Log likelihood = –1525; LR Chi2 = 48 Prob > chi^2 = 0.0000. Pseudo R^2 = 0.6769 (***) = P-value = (000).

of public servants). These findings are informative and corroborate the qualitative assessments of political development in Guinea.

The high values and statistical significance of the variable *VR* indicate that Guineans live in a permanent state of abuse of their political rights and civil liberties. This, in turn, negatively impacts their trust in both the executive (–0.94***) and legislative (–0.97***) branches. These figures reveal that ordinary Guineans who have suffered from or live in a perpetual state of fear of repression differentiate the planners from the perpetrators of political violence.

An equally worrisome finding is the impact of fear from *FPC* on institutional trust. This variable depresses the two dimensions of social capital: relational (*political/institutional trust*: trust in the parliament [–0.45***], trust in the President [–0.97***]), and *social trust* (generalized trust [–0.52***]). While the negative impact is more pronounced for the executive branch, its values for the legislative branch and generalized trust are sizable enough to raise concerns. More importantly, the indicator of fear from political competition translates both the Guineans' lassitude of an untrustworthy political process and their genuine fear for their lives.

As this analysis and human rights watchdog organizations report, fundamental human rights are violated by the state year around and these violations scale up during political contests, resulting in mass extrajudicial killings and disappearances at the hands of Guinean security forces.[85] Not only does fear from political competition impact *political/institutional trust*, *FPC* also impacts *social trust*. This finding suggests that electoral violence is perpetrated by the state directly and indirectly. Direct violence occurs when security forces quash demonstrations of opposition parties. Indirect violence occurs when political leaders stoke interethnic conflicts by pitting ethnic group(s) against one another.[86] This is a common occurrence in urban areas.

City dwellers bear the harshest brunt of political violence that has far-reaching and lasting negative consequences on the social fabric of communities (−0.84**). These results are alarming because *political/institutional trust* is the fulcrum of political legitimacy and the political system's support.[87] Additionally, *political/institutional trust* is the contextual motivating factor that induces everyone to behave constructively. When the political context makes it possible, citizens can find ways of creating mutually reinforcing beneficial expectations and trust to overcome the perverse short-run temptation they face.[88]

The results on pathologies of organizational failure (pervasive corruption of the courts [−0.72***] and law enforcement [−0.26***], and impunity of public servants [−19*]) cripple structural and relational social capital in Guinea. Widespread law-breaking behaviors, arbitrary decision-making, and bribery are the norms in the public sphere with incalculable adverse effects.[89] For instance, corruption in the courts and law enforcement agents undermines Guineans' political efficacy by cultivating a pervasive sense of powerlessness and fatalism among the population.[90] Consequently, many Guineans turn their backs on the judicial system altogether due to corruption.

What does this mean for the hopes of legalizing prohibitions against torture and other forms of political violence in Guinea? Social capital is generated from societal engagement but like societal engagement it is heavily impacted by conditions of stability in a country. Decades of abuses and impunity for elites has a path-dependent quality to it in that it has generated a set of rules woven into norms, codes of conduct, and conventions that continue to destroy social interactions. This study also demonstrates the strong link between the components of *congruence*, particularly *independent judiciary, access to justice, corruption*, and *societal engagement*. Another finding symptomatic of the missing middle is the lack of connection between membership in communal or civic associations and any type of trust. This is not unique to Guinea. Similar observations were made in African and Western countries.[91]

Notes

1 Ibrahima Kane, "Chapter 4. Guinea Building the Rule of Law for Social Development." In *Human Rights Under African Constitutions: Realizing the Promise for Ourselves*, ed. Abdullahi Ahmed An-Naʿim. 97–151 (University of Pennsylvania Press, 2003), 103.

2 Office of the High Commissioner for Human Rights, Human Rights Dashboard, at - OHCHR Dashboard (accessed July 16, 2024).

3 Kane, "Guinea Building," 99.

4 Patrick Dramé, "Indépendence et dépendance: les intérêts économiques français en Afrique de l'Ouest (1960–1980)." In Maurice Demers and Patrick Dramé, *Le Tiers-Monde postcolonial: espoirs et désenchantements* (Montréal, Presses de l'Université de Montréal, 2014), 100.

5 Kane, "Guinea Building," 100.

6 Guinea, The Constitution of the Republic of Guinea: November 10, 1958, at The Constitution of the Republic of Guinea: (berkeley.edu) (accessed June 1, 2024).
7 Kane, "Guinea Building," 105–115.
8 Kane, "Guinea Building," 105–115.
9 Guinea, The Constitution of May 14, 1982, at La constitution du 14 mai 1982. (berkeley.edu) (accessed June 1, 2024).
10 Guinea, 1982 Constitution, preamble.
11 Kane, "Guinea Building."
12 Kane, "Guinea Building," 109.
13 Kane, "Guinea Building," 111.
14 K. Konde, C. Kuyu and E. Le Roy, "Demandes de justice et accès au droit en Guinée," *Droit et Société*, (51/52) (2002): 383–393, 385.
15 BTI.2022. *Country Report 2022: Guinea*, page 26. https://www.ecoi.net/en/document/2069804.html (accessed May 30, 2023).
16 Ministere de la Justice de la Republique de Guinee, *Annuaire Statistique de la Justice* (2018): 3–30, 5.
17 RefWorld, "Guinea: La Police et le System Judiciaire," at https://www.refworld.org/reference/countryrep/landinfo/2011/fr/109019 (accessed July 17, 2024).
18 Human Rights Watch, *World Report 2011: Guinea*, at World Report 2011: World Report 2011: Guinea | Human Rights Watch (hrw.org), (accessed June 2, 2024).
19 Tristan Claridge, "Introduction to the Theory of Social Capital" (2018), at https://www.socialcapitalresearch.com/wp-content/uploads/edd/2018/08/Introduction-to-Social-Capital-Theory.pdf (accessed June 1, 2023); Kenneth Arrow, "Observations on Social Capital." In eds. Partha Dasgupta and Ismail Serageldin, *Social Capital: A Multifaceted Perspective*. 3–5 (Washington, D.C.: The World Bank, 2000).
20 Robert D. Putnam, *Making Democracy Work: Civic Traditions in Modern Italy*, (Princeton, NJ: Princeton University Press, 1993); Elinor Ostrom, *Governing the Commons: The Evolution of Institutions for Collective Action* (Cambridge: Cambridge University Press, 1990) and "Institutions and Common-Pool Resources," *Journal of Theoretical Politics*, 4(3) (1992): 243–245; and James S. Coleman, "Social Capital in the Creation of Human Capital," *American Journal of Sociology* 94 (1988a): S95–120.
21 Claridge, "Introduction," 7.
22 Hunneth Bhandari and Kumi Yasunobu, "What Is Social Capital: A Comprehensive Review of the Concept," *Asian Journal of Social Science* (37)3 (2009): 480–510.
23 Claridge, "Introduction."
24 Robert D. Putnam *Democracies in Flux: The Evolution of Social Capital in Contemporary Democracies* (Oxford: Oxford Univ. Press, 2002) and *Making Democracy*; Francis Fukuyama, *Trust: The Social Virtues and the Creation of Prosperity* (New York: Free Press, 1995); Coleman, "Social Capital"; and Michelle Kuenzi, "Social Capital, Political Trust, and Ethnicity in West Africa," *Afrobarometer Working Paper No. 96*. (2008) at https://www.afrobarometer.org/publication/wp96-social-capital-and-political-trust-west-africa/ (accessed July 17, 2024).
25 Pierre Bourdieu, "The Forms of Capital." In *Handbook of Theory and Research for the Sociology of Education*. ed. J.G. Richardson. 241–258 (New York: Greenwood, 1985); Coleman, "Social Capital"; and Alejandro Portes, "Social Capital: Its Origin and Applications in Modern Sociology," *Annual Review of Sociology* 24 (1998): 1–24.
26 Putnam, *Making Democracy*; Fukuyama, *Trust*; Anirudh Krishna, "Creating and Harnessing Social Capital." In Dasgupta and Serageldin, *Social Capital*, 71–93; and Kuenzi, "Social Capital."

27 James S. Coleman, *Foundations of Social Theory* (Cambridge: Harvard University Press, 1998); Richard Rose, "Getting Things Done." In Dasgupta and Serageldin, *Social Capital*, 146–172; and Elinor Ostrom, "Social Capital." In Dasgupta, and Serageldin, *Social Capital*, 172–215.
28 S.S. Smith and J. Kulynych (2002) "It May Be Social but Why Is It Capital? The Social Construction of Social Capital And The Politics Of Language," *Politics and Society* 30 (2002): 149–186, 150.
29 A. Inkeles, "Measuring Social Capital and is Consequences," *Policy Sciences* 33 (2000): 245–268, 249.
30 Arrow, "Observations," 1–5.
31 Bhandari and Yasunobu, "What is."
32 Bhandari and Yasunobu, "What is," abstract.
33 Janine Nahapiet and Sumantra Ghoshal. "Social Capital, Intellectual Capital, and the Organizational Advantage," *The Academy of Management Review* 23(2) (1998): 242–266, 242.
34 Claridge, "Introduction."
35 Bourdieu, "The Forms."
36 Bourdieu, "The Forms," 241–258.
37 Bourdieu, "The Forms," 241–258.
38 Coleman, "Social Capital" and *Foundations.*
39 Coleman, *Foundations*, 94–121.
40 Coleman, *Foundations*, 20.
41 Coleman, *Foundations*, 13–19.
42 Putnam, *Making Democracy*; and *Democracies in Flux.*
43 Robert D. Putnam, *Bowling Alone: The Collapse and Revival of American Community* (New York: Simon & Schuster, 2000), 35.
44 N. Lemann, "Kicking in Groups," *The Atlantic.* 277(4) (April 1996): 22–26.
45 Theda Skocpol, "Unraveling from above," *American Prospect* 25 (1996): 20–25.
46 Portes, "Social Capital," 7.
47 Kuenzi, "Social Capital," 5.
48 Claridge, "Introduction"; Kuenzi, "Social Capital"; and M. Woolcock, "Social Capital and Economic Development: Toward a Theoretical Synthesis and Policy Framework," *Theory and Society* 27(2) (1998): 151–208.
49 Mark Granovetter, "The Strength of Weak Ties," *American Journal of Sociology* 78 (1973): 1360–1380; and Ronald S. Burt, *Structural Holes: The Social Structure of Competition* (Cambridge, MA: Harvard University Press 1992).
50 M. Woolcock, "The Place of Social Capital in Understanding Social and Economic Outcomes," *Canadian Journal of Policy Research* 2(1) (2001): 1–17.
51 Granovetter, "The Strength,"; also, Mark Granovetter, "Economic Action and Social Structure: The Problem of Embeddedness," *American Journal of Sociology* 91 (1985): 481–510 and Mark Granovetter, "A Theoretical Agenda for Economic Sociology." In eds. Mauro F. Guillen, Randall Collins, Paula England, and Marshall Meyer, *Economic Sociology at the Millenium* (New York: Russell Sage Foundation, 2001).
52 Fukuyama, *Trust*; Putnam, *Making Democracy*; and Yamagishi and Yamagishi, 1988.
53 Krishna, "Creating."
54 Putnam, *Making Democracy*; Ashutosh Varshney, "Ethnic Conflict and Civil Society—India and Beyond," *World Politics* 53(3) (2001): 362–398; Fukuyama, *Trust.*
55 Ronald Inglehart, *Modernization and Postmodernization: Cultural, Economic, and Political Change in 43 Societies* (Princeton University Press, 1997); Rose, "Getting"; Pippa Norris, "Making Democracies Work: Social Capital and Civic

Engagement in 47 Societies." Paper for the European Science Foundation Conference on Social Capital: Interdisciplinary Perspectives at the University of Exeter, 15–20 September 2000; Jennifer Widner and Alexander Mundt. 1998. "Researching Social Capital in Africa," *Africa: Journal of the International African Institute* 68(1) (1998): 1–24.

56 Glenn C. Loury, "A Dynamic Theory Of Racial Income Differences." In ed. P.A. Wallace, A.M. La Mond, *Women, Minorities, and Employment Discrimination*, 153–186. (Lexington, MA: Lexington Books, 1977); Bourdieu, "The Forms"; also, Portes, "Social Capital,"; Varshney, "Ethnic Conflict."

57 R. Bhavnani and David Backer, "Social capital and Political Violence in Africa," *Afrobarometer Working Paper No. 90.* https://www.afrobarometer.org/publication/wp90-social-capital-and-political-violence-sub-saharan-africa/ (2009).

58 Portes, "Social Capital," 15.

59 Kuenzi, "Social Capital," 2.

60 Bhavnani and Backer, "Social Capital," 17.

61 Ostrom, *Governing.*

62 Coralie Pierret, "1971, l'anneé de la grande purge." *Memoire Collective: une histoire plurielle des violences politiques en Guinée* (2018). 156–178; Laurent Correau, "Guinée, Avril–Mai 1960: Le Complot Fondateur," *Memoire Collective.* 110–138 both at https://www.memoire-collective-guinee.org/ (accessed May 1, 2024).

63 Correau, "Guinee."

64 William Laguë, "Position dechirante et paroles coupantes: Sekou Toure, la cinquieme colonne et le neocolonialisme." Candidat à la maîtrise, Université de Sherbrooke, *Commandement colonial resistances et decolonization- Une histoire de l'Afriquecontemporaine.* 189–215. (2018), URI: http://hdl.handle.net/11143/19138, (accessed March 5, 2024), 1.

65 Celine Pauthier, "L'Heritage controverse de Sekou Toure 'heros' de l'independence," *Vingteme Siecle. Revue d'histoire* 118(2) (2018): 31–44.

66 Mike McGovern, *Unmasking the State: Making Guinea Modern* (Chicago: Univ. of Chicago Press, 2012).

67 Pierret, "1971."

68 Monseigneur Raymond Marie Tchidimbo, *Noviciat d'un évêque: hui tans de captivité sous Sékou Touré* (Paris: Fayard, 1987).

69 Tchidimbo, *Noviciat*, 48.

70 Mohamed Saliou Camara, "La malice Populaire entre sécurité nationale et répression politique en Guinée," in *Memoire Collective*, 178–192.

71 Camara, "La malice," 180–194.

72 Human Rights and Watch (HRW), *World Reports: Guinea*, various years, at Previous World Reports | Human Rights Watch (hrw.org), (accessed July 1, 2024).

73 Amnesty International (AI), Guinea Country Profile, at Human rights in Guinea Amnesty International, (accessed July 18, 2024).

74 HRW, Guinea's 2009 Stadium Massacre Trial, (September 25, 2023), at Guinea's 2009 Stadium Massacre Trial | Human Rights Watch (hrw.org), (accessed July 18, 2024).

75 HRW, *World Report: Guinea* (2020).

76 Rose, "Getting," 147.

77 Stefan Hedlund and Niclas Sundstrom, "Does Palermo Represent the Future for Moscow?" *Journal of Public Policy* 16(2) (1996): 113–155.

78 Transparency International, *Annual Report 2021*, at Annual Report 2021 - Publications - Transparency.org; BTI, *Guinea Country Report 2022*, at https://

www.ecoi.net/en/file/local/2069804/country_report_2022_GIN.pdf. Both reports accessed July 18, 2024.

79 Justice Sans Frontières in "La Police et le Systeme Judiciaire en Guinee." Landinfo.org 2011, at Guinée-La-police-et-le-système-judiciaire.pdf (landinfo.no) (accessed July 18, 2024).

80 Nahapiet and Goshal, "Social Capital."

81 Claridge, "Introduction," 12.

82 Claridge, "Introduction," 26–42.

83 Claridge, "Introduction," 18.

84 *VR* measures fear of and actual sustainment of repressions.

85 AI, *Guinea*, various years.

86 HRW, *Guinea*, various years.

87 David Easton, *A Systems Analysis of Political Life* (New York: John Wiley, 1965).

88 Ostrom, "Social Capital," 178. Scores of cases illustrate this point in the literature. See for example, John Brehm and Wendy Rahn, "Individual-Level Evidence for the Causes and Consequences of Social Capital," *American Journal of Political Science* 41(3) (1977): 999–1023.

89 Transparency International, *Reports: Guinea*, various years.

90 Afrobarometer, *Afrobarometer Merged Round 6* (2016), at Merged Round 6 data (36 countries) (2016) – Afrobarometer, (accessed May 1, 2024).

91 Rose, "Getting"; Widner and Mundt, "Researching"; Markus Freitag, "Social Capital in (Dis)Similar Democracies: The Development of Generalized Trust in Japan and Switzerland," *Comparative Political Studies* 36(8) (2003a): 936–966.

11 Civil Society and the Struggle for Human Rights in Tunisia

Khedija Arfaoui

Introduction

This chapter explores Tunisia's progress on civil and political rights, especially women's rights, and the work of civil society institutions in the struggle to protect human rights.

Tunisia's progress in expanding gender rights is perhaps best exemplified by the October 2021 swearing-in of the country's first female Prime Minister, Najla Bouden. For years, women constituted over 30 percent of the seats in the country's Assembly of People's Representatives. Unfortunately, the policymaking and implementation processes of human rights laws in Tunisia have narrowed under the rule of President Kaïs Saïed whose government continues to harm the progress made during the "Arab Spring." Concerns about prison conditions and the devolution of gender equality continue.[1]

Tunisia is a State party to all the human rights treaties that are the subject of this volume. Relative to many African states, Tunisia has complied with the reporting processes of the various treaty-based human rights committees and has permitted visits from the Sub-Committee for the Prevention of Torture (SPT). It has also created a national body—the National Authority for the Prevention of Torture—to monitor compliance with the Optional Protocol to the Convention Against Torture and Other Cruel, Inhuman or Degrading Treatment or Punishment (OPCAT).[2] Tunisia is also a party to the Banjul Charter and is one of only eight African States that accept the jurisdiction of the African Court of Human and People's Rights to hear cases brought by individuals and NGOs under Article 34 of the Charter.[3]

Despite this cooperation, human rights in practice in Tunisia remains a constant struggle. This study suggests that civil society, although hobbled by the Saïed regime, continues to shine a light on the consequences associated with the collapse of public engagement in the policymaking process and continues to hold government leaders accountable. The resilience of civil society stems from its decades-long work in improving human rights conditions in Tunisia regardless of the regime in place. In the current context, marked by a consolidation of power in the executive and a shrinking public space for dissent, groups like the Tunisian League of Human Rights (LTDH)

DOI: 10.4324/9781003471677-15

and others continue to serve as an important source of information about government misrule.

This chapter relies on qualitative analysis and the theory of historical institutionalism to trace the course of the legalization of human rights laws for gender equality, as well as those prohibiting state-sanctioned violence and repression in Tunisia. Civil society played a key role in the dissolution of the Ben Ali regime in 2011 due in large part to the involvement of women as guardians of the human rights project. Their continued struggle for improvements in the government's human rights practices means that the critical juncture of regime change imposed by Saïed in July 2021 has not necessarily destroyed the course of human rights development in Tunisia. Rather, during a time of political instability and government campaigns to silence the opposition, civil society continues to actively campaign for a reversal of these conditions.

This chapter proceeds as follows. First, a discussion is provided about the collapse of Tunisia's Arab Spring with emphasis placed on the deterioration of gender rights and representation and the government's efforts to intimidate the population and control dissent. Next, this chapter elucidates the model used by this study, which relies on qualitative accounts of civil society activists, and applies an autoethnographic approach to account for this author's own personal experiences as a human rights advocate in Tunisia. The primary theory used to assess the human rights struggle in Tunisia is historical institutionalism which suggests that a country's institutional legacies impact the course of its future political development. In this light, we can say that the legacies of authoritarian rule in the colonial and postcolonial eras created a culture of government misrule, but also civil society activism. This chapter addresses the work of Tunisian civil society institutions in paving the way for greater gender equality and civil and political rights, despite the contradictory and inconsistent policymaking positions of the Habib Bourguiba and Ben Ali regimes as well as the deteriorating political space created by the current regime. This chapter concludes with some final thoughts about the importance of civil society as a key protagonist for human rights progress not just in Tunisia, but around the world.

The Collapse of Tunisia's Arab Spring

The Arab Spring, also referred to as the "Jasmine Revolution" in Tunisia, began in Tunisia in December 2010 with the suicide of Mohamed Bouazizi by self-immolation. Over the course of the next few months, demonstrations erupted across the Arab world demanding democratic reforms. For Tunisia, these reforms led to the ousting of longtime president Ben Ali and the first open presidential and parliamentary elections in 2014. For women, the Arab Spring (and afterward) increased debate about women's rights and their participation in government and wider society.[4]

Since that time, conditions in Tunisia have deteriorated. Saïed's move to seize and consolidate power stemmed from a growing disenchantment on the part of many Tunisians over their government's inability to improve the economy and expand government accountability. Rising income inequalities, debt, structural inefficiencies, "rampant inflation, currency depreciation, rising poverty, increasing energy costs and a shrinking middle class," and the global COVID pandemic, created the perfect storm that enabled Saïed to assume power.[5]

Saïed came to power in July 2021, and immediately began to dismantle Tunisia's democratic institutions, including the Assembly of People's Representatives and the Council of Justice. He also imposed house arrests and travel bans and excluded political parties from competition. Aside from dismissing the legislature and suspending the country's constitution, Saïed embarked on a campaign to eliminate the independence of Tunisia's judiciary. The High Judicial Council, an institution responsible for maintaining judicial independence, was dissolved in February 2022. Justified by his "war against corruption," the weakness of the judiciary is one of many newly created obstacles to the protection of human rights in Tunisia.[6]

Despite his appointment of a woman as prime minister, women's rights in Tunisia have been sharply regressing. Indeed, there has been no "concrete achievement" since Bouden's appointment. As researcher Kenza Ben Azouz reports: "There has been absolutely no addition in terms of rights secured for women."[7] Bouden's tenure as prime minister was to be short-lived. She was fired on August 1, 2023, and immediately replaced by Ahmed Hachani who had overseen the Tunisian Central Bank.[8]

The constitution was changed in 2022 in a process that Amnesty International characterizes as "shrouded in secrecy."[9] Although Saïed declared that a national dialogue would take place over the new constitution, he nevertheless informed the public that this "national dialogue would exclude any political parties and any organization or other actors who questioned the process."[10]

The new constitution severely limits the independence of the judiciary and makes it possible for the president to remove judges. Article 96 gives the executive "sweeping emergency powers without the necessary oversight mechanism which could be wielded to curtail human rights and undermine the law."[11]

Saïed has been ruling by decree and allowed for new legislative elections to take place on December 17, 2022, with a run-off on January 29, 2023. The changes adopted resulted in a drastic decline in the number of women parliamentarians, representing "about 16% in the newly elected parliament, against 26%, and 31% between 2014 and 2018."[12] This loss is quite discouraging. Indeed, "Preliminary results show only 25 women candidates won seats in the newly configured 161-seat parliament following the January 29, 2023, election run-off, in which turnout was a mere 11%."[13] UN WOMEN gives a rather pessimistic image of the future for women in Tunisia, declaring that women will need another 130 years to see "gender equality in the highest positions of power."[14]

With respect to conditions of detention and use of the death penalty, on March 15, 2023, two men were sentenced to death for a suicide bombing near the US embassy in Tunis. It killed one policeman, wounded four policemen and one civilian. Two other Tunisians were given a 20-year prison sentence while another was imprisoned for life. Others had lighter sentences. Death sentences are still being pronounced in 2024, although no executions have been carried out since 1990. In 2019, 47 persons received death sentences. There are already 95 people or more on death row, three of them women.[15]

Moreover, there are now 54 legal dispositions allowing the imposition of the death penalty, but some contravene the "most serious crime" definition as enshrined in international standards.[16] The Tunisian Organization against Torture (OCTT) called attention to the great physical, psychological as well as emotional distress endured by death row inmates in Tunisia. Indeed, inmates must bear the brunt of the reduction in public spending on prisons, as well as the lack of follow-up procedure after release. In its section dedicated to the death penalty, the OCTT called for major legislative, health, and humanitarian reforms that would allow for the immediate and definitive abolition of the death penalty and the promotion of human rights in the country.[17]

Historical Institutionalism and an Assessment of Human Rights in Tunisia

The course of the domestication of human rights laws protections, including gender equality, is heavily influenced by Tunisia's colonial past, as well as its pattern of political development in postcolonial times. Throughout the previous century to the present day, the government and a growing and more vocal civil society have been engaged in a contentious debate over issues of government accountability and compliance with international human rights treaty laws.

To explain the course of human rights development in Tunisia, this study relies on historical institutionalism. Scholars including Thelen, Mahoney, Hall, Streeck and others argue that past institutions and policy practices influence the policymaking behavior of political leaders in the future.[18] The same argument applies to societal and/or informal institutions, including those associated with culture. To demonstrate this argument, these scholars rely on the use of process tracing as a tool to explain patterns of institutional development.

Process tracing establishes causality between larger-scale phenomena and their hypothesized outcomes. George and McKeown contend that process tracing enables the researcher

> to uncover what stimuli the actors attend to; the decision process that makes use of these stimuli to arrive at decisions; the actual behavior that then occurs; the effect of various institutional arrangements on attention, processing, and behavior; and the effect of other variables of interest on attention, processing, and behavior.[19]

To explain why and how governments in Tunisia have been reticent to improve many human rights practices in the country, we must first understand Tunisia's institutional past. Through qualitative assessment of documentary evidence, particularly statements made by members of the human rights community in Tunisia, and the use of an autoethnographic approach this chapter traces how Tunisia arrived at the point where it is today. Despite past ruling regimes permitting greater rights for women as well as the development of civil society, there is simultaneously a tradition in Tunisia of clamping down on dissent using arbitrary arrests and detention, and intimidation. Under the Saïed regime, human rights protections have declined as power has consolidated in the executive.

The Growth of the Human Rights Movement in Tunisia

Despite the longtime presence of authoritarian rule in Tunisia, the country simultaneously experienced a growth in human rights activity; some of this occurring at the behest of the government, and some because of grassroots movements in the country; especially notable are women's rights and women's empowerment movements as we examine below.

Women's Empowerment

Tunisia was a protectorate of France from 1881 to 1956, during which time women had few, if any, rights. Access to education and formal employment had long been the exclusive privilege of men. The Code of Personal Status (CPS) offered by Tunisia's first postcolonial President Habib Bourguiba in 1956 was meant to empower women and enable them to participate in the development of their country. Bourguiba could not conceive of any progress or modernization for Tunisia if half of its population were illiterate and held exclusively within the home. Bourguiba said: "there was no feminist movement demanding the promulgation of a Code of Personal Status or the abolition of polygamy."[20] Women did not march in the streets for these important changes to take place. Rather, the initiative was totally governmental. Bourguiba justified his decision as "a choice in favor of progress" and "to encourage the development of a modern nation-state."[21]

After independence, Tunisia sought to protect its liberties, and Bourguiba did not miss the opportunity to free women from a threat that created unbearable suffering for them: *Dar Joued*, a reformatory institution where "rebellious" young girls and wives were sent. Created in the 16th century, *Dar Joued* housed women who dared to ask for a divorce or who refused to marry a man chosen by their parents. They were subjected to ill-treatment until they changed their mind. *Dar Joued* was abolished with the CPS.[22]

The CPS also banned polygamy, and major violence against women; it replaced unilateral divorce with judicial divorce, making divorce a mutual agreement.[23] According to one study, under Article 30 of the CPS: "Divorce may be authorized only by a court," and Article 31 includes "at the request of either spouse."[24]

Bourguiba's legacy of gender equality included a substantial increase (as of 2012) in the percentages of female magistrates (33 percent), lawyers (33 percent), pharmacists (72 percent), medical doctors (42 percent), and university professors (40 percent). Moreover, girls outnumbered boys in secondary schools (57 percent) and in higher education (59 percent).[25]

Thanks to the development of civil society during Bourguiba's rule, women were able to obtain greater rights to the point that Tunisia became the region's exemplar of women's rights. The Ministry of Health undertook a family planning process to lower Tunisia's high fertility rates. Indeed, the average number of children per family was seven, making it difficult to improve living standards and educate women and girls, as well as men and boys. Consequently, family planning products became available in Tunisia in 1961.[26]

Continuing the progress made by Bourguiba, his successor Ben Ali created the Ministry of Women and Family Affairs which became the Ministry of Women, Family, Childhood, and the Elderly. Compulsory education for both boys and girls from ages 6 to 16 allowed the number of girls to exceed that of boys today. The state also created the Center for Studies, Documentation, and Information on Women, a data bank documenting women's achievement.

Like in Morocco and Algeria, women married to non-Muslims could not give their nationality to their children. In 1993, Tunisia changed that with the reform of the Nationality Code. Moreover, since 1993, a Tunisian woman is no longer legally required to obey her husband. Each of these gains is remarkable, even though in practice, women were not always able to defend their cause.

Florence Beaugé, the well-known journalist for *Le Monde*, reported in 2006 that "the situation of Tunisian women remains unique in the Arab world." Not only has Ben Ali endorsed his predecessor's policies, but he has pursued them since coming to power in 1987. It is a fact that both the opposition and the movements defending liberties hate to admit it because of the violence exerted on women who stand up to power. Activist and author Neila Jrad commented,

> [Women] were able to revolt in the face of discrepancies between mentalities and laws that made them reject 'the debt of gratitude' thanks to these gains whose regime considered liable at precisely the same time it was prohibiting citizens' rights and violating human rights.[27]

However, many of these reforms faced cultural backlash, indicating the embeddedness of Tunisian cultural norms regarding women. President Beji Caied Essebsi putting an end to a 1973 decree that forbade Tunisian women from marrying non-Muslims created an uproar among conservative Islamists in Tunisia and elsewhere. After the 2011 revolution, a fierce debate ensued within the Constitutional Assembly over the "complementarity" versus the "equality" of women and men in the draft constitution. The newly empowered Islamists in the Assembly wanted "complementarity," but women and men marched on Habib Bourguiba Avenue in Tunis on Tunisian Women's National Day in 2012 chanting "The Tunisian woman is not Maherzia."[28] The reference to "equality" was eventually adopted in Articles 21 and 46 of the new 2014 Constitution.[29]

Another achievement was the adoption of political parity, mandating women's inclusion on electoral party lists. According to Article 16 of the 2014 Constitution, "Lists shall be established in such a way as to alternate between men and women. Such a success permitted the number of women parliamentarians to reach 26 percent (2014) and 31 percent (2018)."[30] In 2016, there were eight women ministers. Moreover, a woman's candidacy for the presidency was accepted. Kalthoum Kennou, a judge and former president of the Association of Tunisian Magistrates, met the requirements, announcing that "[w]e should combat religious extremism intellectually and socially. When Tunisians elect a woman president, they will tell the world that they care for modernism, progress, and gender equality."[31]

This progress, however, vanished overnight. On July 25, 2021, President Kaïs Saïed suspended Parliament and all political parties' activities, using Article 80 of the 2014 Constitution that allowed changes in the case of imminent danger. The reason given for this declaration of a state of emergency (SOE) was to ensure that "social peace returns to Tunisia and that we save the country."[32]

The fact that Article 96 of the 2022 Constitution removes the requirement for the president to consult with the Constitutional Court to enact an SOE and does not include a time limit for SOEs provides the executive with a great deal of discretionary authority. Additionally, Article 55 permits the executive to derogate various civil liberties and freedoms during SOEs.[33]

The fiercely fought parity law became a thing of the past. Presently, women comprise only 16 percent of the 161 seats in the Assembly and they no longer have an electoral quota.[34] To that, one must add the clear eviction of all political parties that had a significant position during all the preceding elections. Tunisia has many bi-nationals who were particularly hurt by their total exclusion from the elections. Indeed, suddenly, Tunisian politics treated them as outsiders. Sana Ben Achour writes that these changes, including "the eccentricity of individual campaigns, the privatization of financing, [...] has destroyed hope and led straight to seat vacancy and abstention."[35]

Civil Society and the Struggle for Civil Liberties and Gender Rights

Bourguiba was a great politician, but also a dictator and he did not tolerate opposition to his views. He freed women from *Dar Joued*, but simultaneously imprisoned people who did not share his opinions. These prisoners were not well treated. Consequently, people began to organize to defend the right *not* to be tortured. The history of organizations against torture and ill-treatment of imprisoned people in Tunisia begins with the LTDH. Founded in 1976, it was officially recognized by the state in May 1977. The fact that it was the first independent organization in Tunisia gave it enormous prestige.

The founders of the LDTH were respected individuals who included scholars, lawyers, university professors, medical doctors, and journalists. Their goal was to create a democratic political system that would respect and protect the same civil liberties and political rights enshrined in the human rights treaties the state ratified. Less than two weeks after its formal inception, the LTDH started its work in an unexplored area: torture and ill-treatment of political prisoners. LTDH assumed the responsibility of following political trials, intervening whenever they could.

It did not help that the concept of human rights was routinely dismissed by the leftist intelligentsia in Tunisia as "a bourgeois notion and dangerously American."[36] Consequently, members of the LTDH had to look elsewhere for allies, and sought partners among Arab nationalists, Islamists, segments of the left, and liberals from the Movement of Socialist Democrats (MDS), the first recognized political party after Bourguiba's Neo-Destour Party.

Bourguiba despised the divisions that political parties represented.[37] For years, political parties were not welcome. In the early days of independence, people who did not support the ruling Neo-Destour Party became victims of violence. There was no serious opposition under Bourguiba, and the failed 1962 coup attempt put an end to any form of public protest. Several civilians and military officers were jailed and in 1963, ten men were executed for the part they played.[38]

In the aftermath of a violent clash between the General Union of Tunisian Workers (UGTT) and police forces in January 1978, the LTDH was the first of several Tunisian groups to denounce the government's handling of the confrontation and of the many abuses that followed. The LTDH also criticized the bread riots that took place in 1984, stressing the government's ineptitude in handling the crisis, particularly after they fired on the crowds.[39]

When Ben Ali assumed power in 1987, there was a short-lived euphoria as people believed he would live up to his promises of greater democracy. He loosened restrictions on the press and for the first time, the media reported on the opposition. It is worth noting that four LTDH officers were appointed as cabinet ministers under Ben Ali. Soon afterward, however, the parliament adopted a bill that posed a major threat to freedom of expression. "It's rather catastrophic to see Tunisians still denied the right to discuss an important issue," Mokhtar Trifi, President of LTDH, declared.[40]

Over the decades the LTDH launched inquiries into numerous allegations of abuse; it observed all political trials and never failed to intervene on behalf of torture victims. The LTDH conducted studies on a wide range of issues, including incommunicado detention, torture, prison conditions, and rights of association. It also made numerous public statements about press freedoms, special courts, and unconstitutional legislation that infringed on human rights.[41] In 2015, the LDTH and other human rights organizations received the Nobel Peace Prize for their work in the achievement of a pluralistic democracy following the Arab Spring.[42]

The activism of Radhia Nasraoui in the struggle for human rights in Tunisia is also noteworthy. An independent-minded lawyer married to Hamma Hammami, leader of the Communist Party of Workers in Tunisia (POCT), she took a strong stand against torture and defied Ben Ali's repression by denouncing the torture exerted against political opponents.

The UN Committee on the Elimination of Discrimination against Women reported that on February 12, 1998, agents of the government ransacked her office and stole her records. Moreover, "Her house was under constant surveillance, and they cut or regularly tapped her phone line. In addition, her daughters endured constant bullying."[43] Nasraoui was intercepted at the Tunis airport and all her documents were confiscated. Starting in January 2002, the harassment of her and her family increased. A physical attack on her in 2005 left her with serious medical conditions that she still suffers from today. Despite this violence, she continued to express opposition to all injustices against herself and other people after the fall of the Ben Ali regime. Nasraoui reported on severe abuse, ill-treatment, and torture suffered by men and women at police stations throughout the country. Her association received as many as 250 complaints of torture and ill-treatment in 2015. Several victims of these abuses were afraid of complaining for fear of facing harassment and sham trials.[44]

I was also a victim of Ben Ali's police. In 2009, I received a phone call from the judiciary police at El Gorjani police center, asking me to visit their headquarters. I was detained for eight hours, without food or drink, and ordered not to make any phone calls. The police asked questions which I answered before finally asking: "Why am I here?" Their answer was "Facebook! You wrote about organ trafficking." When I informed them that I merely shared information I had received from a young Tunisian woman, they brought me a photocopy of the message. I was shocked and dismayed that they could read our messages. Although they knew of the person who had sent me the message, I was assumed to be *the* culprit. Why? Because I was a member of several autonomous organizations, including Amnesty International. I was to serve as an example to silence the opposition. It was also a signal to autonomous organizations to be careful not to intervene in the upcoming elections. I was accused of disrupting public order by publishing false news under Article 49 of the Tunisian Press Code.

On June 5, 2009, I received an order to appear in court on the following day. I had to appear before the tribunal four times, but the first one was particularly stressful. The police warned me not to ask lawyers belonging to the opposition to defend me. Several lawyers passed by me and expressed their anger at the situation. Nasraoui was one of them and she wanted to attend the trial. But, afraid of what might befall me if she did, I begged her not to. The verdict was an eight-month suspended prison sentence. This is an example of the Ben Ali era's arbitrary "justice." It is also about Nasraoui's courageous stance against injustices of this type.

Secretary General of the Observatory for the Freedom of Press, Publishing, and Creation in Tunisia (OLPEC) Sihem Ben Sedrine reported that "my trial was political" and that "OLPEC considers this verdict to be unjust and out of all proportion with the act of sending a message on Facebook to a very limited number of people."[45]

Other human rights activists and members of civil society faced similar types of harassment. Their families had to bear all sorts of violence, including humiliating searches at airports, defamation campaigns, trials, harassment of relatives, and jail time. For example, Khemais Chamari, former ambassador to UNESCO and founder of the International Federation of Human Rights (IFHR), was jailed several times over several decades in terrible conditions. By 2011, Chamari was considered the enemy of President Ben Ali and his government.

Mokhtar Trifi, former President of the Tunisian Bar Association and the Tunisian Human Rights League, and former Vice-President of the World Organization against Torture, also suffered at the hands of the police. His activities early on led to his arrest in 1973 and his refusal of admission to all Tunisian universities. He was very active in the General Union of Tunisian Students. His main activity was the defense of those whose rights were endangered, including trade unionists and all opponents to the regime, whether they were from the left or from the Islamist movement.

As these testimonies demonstrate, Tunisia suffers from a long history of mistreatment of detainees and unfair trials. The young Tunisian students who in the 1960s and 1970s expressed their opposition to the absolute power of *Mujahid El Akbar* (the Supreme Fighter) suffered the worst abuses.[46] There were unfair trials in 1968, 1972, 1974, and 1975.[47] Zeineb Ben Said-Cherni, one of the students who suffered from the violence and repression, was:

> arrested on 20 November 1974, transferred to the Department of Tunisian Security ("DST"), and, considered one of the leaders of the movement, she was beaten by DST agents and tortured between one questioning and another. Half-naked, she was subjected for hours to the "roast chicken" torture position. Brought before the State Security Court, a special court set up in 1968, she spent several months in jail. Her ordeal did not stop [...] Indeed, she and her husband, also a member of the Perspective Movement, were both banned from the civil service.[48]

During the 1970s and 1990s, all dissident movements suffered repression, in particular Marxist, Perspectivists,[49] and *El Amel Ettounsi* (The Tunisian Worker).

The increasing presence of women and girls wearing the hijab pleased neither Bourguiba nor Ben Ali. Islamists' repression increased between 1992 and 1994 with rapes, tortures, and forced unveilings. In 1994, a 16-year-old schoolgirl wearing the hijab was arrested as she was leaving school. She spent one full year in jail. The hunt for veiled girls and women intensified between 2002 and 2005. Police would arrest veiled girls in public places.[50] Nasraoui would defend all cases, independently of the political or religious creeds of the victims.

In 1993, there were several arrests. Rached Jaidane, a mathematics doctorate student in Paris, visited Tunis to attend his sister's wedding. They arrested him together with 11 other people, accusing him of preparing an attack. Tortured for 38 days within the offices of the Ministry of Interior, they sentenced him to 26 years in jail. He served only half his sentence, but the police kept a constant pressure on him. The 2011 Revolution was a relief to him, and he was one of the first to file a complaint against all his executioners, Ben Ali, and the Ministry of Interior.[51]

After Ben Ali's departure and the launch of the democratic transition, Islamist women were able to form their own association, *Tounissiet*, or Tunisian Women. In 2010, professor and author Mohamed Kerrou wrote "*Hijâb: nouveaux voiles et espaces publics*."[52] But new forms of repression emerged after 2011. The police would arrest and question leftist women and men when they were in the company of foreigners. Women would be imprisoned for adultery if they invited male friends for dinner.[53]

In 2021 Lilia Labidi reported that "[w]hile the mechanisms might be in place for women to bring awareness to abuse, police and judicial institutions do not respond adequately to counter the frequency of violence against women."[54] *Al Jazeera* reports that the police often encouraged women, particularly in rural areas, "to reconcile with their abusers or acquiesce to family mediation rather than pursue criminal complaints."[55] There are countless other examples of incidents in which women and men, including members of the LGBTQ community, are harassed, detained, or worse for violating social and cultural norms in Tunisia despite the legal requirements of equality under the law.

Moreover, persons continue to be detained for posing threats to national security. Tunisia ratified the OPCAT in 2011. However, a visit made by the UN SPT delegation in spring 2022 showed that despite some progress, ill-treatment of prisoners persisted all over the country. In 2004, 8 internet users were sentenced to up to 26 years in prison for consulting Islamist websites and downloading files. Accused of preparing terrorist attacks, they were beaten up, suspended from the ceiling, and subjected to electric shocks.[56] Radio station *Mosaique FM* announced more possible arrests, including activists and politicians Bochra Bel Hadj Hmida[57] and Kamel Jendoubi. The reason: a suspected plot against the security of the state.[58]

Coalition against the Death Penalty

I am a longtime opponent of the death penalty as a matter of policy and personal experience. When an Uzbek terrorist named Abdulrahman shot dead my son and his wife on January 1, 2017, together with 37 other people at the

Reina Club in Istanbul, many people asked for the death penalty. Despite my immense pain, I expressed outright disapproval, to the surprise of many. I am a peace builder and a member of the International Civil Society Action Network and Women's Alliance for Security Leadership (ICAN/WASL). I remained true to my creed: although I was devastated, although I hated the criminal who had destroyed the lives of my beloved children, I did/do not believe he should pay for his crime with his life. Here, I wish to draw attention to the fact that "an eye for an eye" is not my motto. It is my belief that God alone has the power of life and death over people.

There have always been reports of violence used against dissidents by the police. Under the French Protectorate (1881–1956), there were insurgents, known as *fellaghas*, who sought to free their country from colonialism and the French army coldly shot them dead. There were no trials.

Capital punishment is legal in Tunisia. However, Tunisia has been under a moratorium since 1991. The OCTT has been unsuccessfully trying to bring changes and abolish the death penalty, by calling attention to the great physical, psychological, as well as emotional distress endured by death row inmates in Tunisia. Indeed, inmates must bear the brunt of the reduction in public spending on prisons, as well as the lack of follow-up procedures after being released. In its section dedicated to the death penalty, the OCTT called for major legislative, health, and humanitarian reforms that would allow for the immediate and definitive abolition of the death penalty and the promotion of human rights in the country.[59]

Conclusions

Recently, President Saïed visited women in the rural areas of the country and expressed concern over their plight, indicating "I am with you." Simultaneously, he ignores the work of feminists in the country who actively strive to improve conditions for women all throughout Tunisia. Unlike President Ben Ali, Saïed disregards Tunisian Women's National Day and never meets with or congratulates, even recognizes women activists for the positive changes brought about through their work. His visit to the rural areas and his appointment of two women to his cabinet—Saloua Abassi and Samia Briki—are merely symbolic and a strategy to win the female vote in Tunisia's October 6, 2024 presidential election, an election that many feared would be illegitimate.[60]

In the past Tunisia made progress in civil and political rights reforms. The efforts to improve prison conditions, just as with strategies to improve civil liberties and rights for all Tunisians were and continue to be led by civil society. The use of process tracing in this chapter has demonstrated that Tunisia's institutional legacies of human rights violations directed toward opponents and critics of the government, inhumane prison conditions, and longstanding cultural legacies of marginalization of women and the LGBT community continue to inform the policymaking behavior of elites in the country.

That Bourguiba brought important changes for women despite religious taboos while respecting the scriptures of the *Coran* deserves tribute.[61] Soukeina Bouraoui, director of the Center of Arab Women for Training and Research, reported in 2002 that "[w]omen's gains will remain if they are defended not only by the State but by a strong and autonomous grass-roots movement."[62] Moreover,

> male and female citizens need to see their claims to equality succeed and the authorities need to endorse them, but the authorities also need to have male and female citizens claim and react to reforms that they should underwrite, discuss, and even criticize.[63]

There are at present some 150 NGOs working on women's rights. At the same time, inequality between men and women is a fact in Tunisia. This inequality is particularly visible in the violence against women, a matter to which Tunisian feminists have been drawing attention since the 1990s.[64] In 2023, the number of women murdered was three times higher than 2022.[65]

As a test of the fifth hypothesis of this volume, greater female representation would no doubt improve Tunisia's human rights status. During the years *prior* to the Saïed government, women enjoyed greater political freedoms and a far greater impact on policymaking and accountability in Tunisia. Despite the difficulties the country has been facing since 2021, women's activism has not slowed down, but continues its steady, tireless march toward equality. Following the Arab Spring, Tunisia was the only country to codify increased political freedoms and maintain a stable government.

However, the course of policy development since July 25, 2021, remains alarming for both younger and older generations. The experience of civil society in Tunisia demonstrates the significance of civil society as a key protagonist for human rights policymaking. Even with a decline in access to the courts and a lack of judicial independence, civil society keeps the struggle going. Women's organizations, for example, continue to push for greater female participation and inclusion in the political process and to defend the rights of women and men detained for their activity in the public space.[66]

Saïed was re-elected president in October 2024. Tunisia is at a crossroads. It has never been a rich country like its immediate neighbors, Libya and Algeria, but it used to have a large middle class. Today, the middle class has shrunk dramatically while the lower class keeps increasing. Civil society's struggles for equality, justice, and freedom have not come to a halt but need more power, more authority to defend human rights in general, and the advancement of women's rights in particular.

Notes

1 UN Office of the High Commissioner for Human Rights (OHCHR), "Tunisia: Progress Made but Concerns Remain, Says UN Torture Prevention Body," UN

Press Release, April 6, 2022, at Tunisia: Progress made but concerns remain, says UN torture prevention body | OHCHR (accessed June 5, 2022).

2 UN General Assembly, *Optional Protocol to the Convention Against Torture and other Cruel, Inhuman and Degrading Treatment or Punishment*, A/RES/57/199, 9 January 2003, https://www.refworld.org/legal/agreements/unga/2003/en/17704 (accessed July 6, 2024).

3 Organization of African Unity (OAU), *African Charter on Human and Peoples' Rights (Banjul Charter)*, CAB/LEG/67/3 rev. 5, 21 I.L.M. 58 (1982), art. 34, 27 June 1981, https://www.refworld.org/legal/agreements/oau/1981/en/17306 (accessed July 6, 2024).

4 Xenia Sipos, "Women's Role in the Tunisian Process of Democratisation," *Academic and Applied Research in Military and Public Management Science* 2 (November 2022): 69–85. DOI: 10.32565/aarùs.2022.2.5.

5 Dr. Elie Abouaoun, Thomas Mill and Leo Siebert, "Tunisia's New Constitution Expands Presidential Power. What's Next for its Democracy," United States Institute for Peace, July 28, 2022, at Tunisia's new constitution expands presidential power. What's next for its Democracy? | United States Institute of Peace (usip.org), accessed July); Adam Gallagher, "Tunisians Show Support for Democracy, Disillusionment with Ruling Elite," US Institute for Peace, September 23, 2019, at Tunisians Show Support for Democracy, Disillusionment with Ruling Elite | United States Institute of Peace (usip.org) (accessed July 6, 2024).

6 Human Rights Watch, "Tunisia: President Intensifies Attacks on Judicial Independence," February 27, 2023, at Tunisia: President Intensifies Attacks on Judicial Independence | Human Rights Watch (hrw.org) (accessed June 1, 2023).

7 BBC, "Women in Tunisia: Has a Female Prime Minister Changed Tunisia?" July 12, 2022, at https://www.bbc.com/news/world-africa-62053997 (accessed July 13, 2023).

8 AP News, "Tunisia's President Sacks Prime Minister: The First Woman to hold that Job in an Arab League Nation," August 2, 2023, at Tunisia's president sacks prime minister, the first woman to hold that job in an Arab League nation | AP News (accessed September 7, 2023).

9 Amnesty International, "Tunisia: Adoption of New Constitution Must Not Institutionalize Erosion of Human Right," August 19, 2022), at Amnesty Public Statement (accessed September 25, 2023).

10 Amnesty International, "Tunisia."

11 Amnesty International, "Tunisia." See also International Commission of Jurists, *Codifying Autocracy: The Proposed Tunisian Constitution in Light of International Law and Standards* (Geneva: International Commission of Jurist, July 2022).

12 Menna Farouk, "Analysis of Tunisia's Male-Dominated Parliament Deals Blow to Women's Gains" (February 14, 2023).

13 Farouk, "Analysis."

14 UN Women, "In Focus: UN Commission on the Status of Women (CSW65)," 15–26 March 2021, at https://www.unwomen.org/en/news/in-focus/csw65#:~:text=At%20the%20current%20rate%20of,women%20and%20unpaid%20care%20work (accessed June 2, 2023).

15 OCTT, "The Abolition of the Death Penalty in Tunisia," World Coalition Against Torture June 18, 2020, at https://worldcoalition.org/2020/06/18/the-abolition-of-the-death-penalty-in-tunisia-a-fight-against-torture (accessed July 6, 2023).

16 OCTT, "The Abolition."

17 OCTT, "The Abolition."

18 Wolfgang Streeck and Kathleen Thelen eds., *Beyond Continuity: Institutional Change in Advanced Political Economics* (Oxford: Oxford Univ. Press, 2005),

Stephen D. Kranser, "Approaches to the State: Alternative Conceptions and Historical Dynamics," Comparative *Politics* 16(2) (1984): 234; Guy B. Peters, *Institutional Theory in Political Science: The "New Institutionalism,"* (London: Pinter, 1999), Peter Hall and R.C.R. Taylor, "Political Science and the Three New Institutionalisms," *Political Studies* 44(5) (1996): 936–957; James Mahoney, "Strategies of Causal Assessment in Comparative Historical Analysis." In *Comparative Historical Analysis in the Social Sciences* eds. James Mahoney and Dietrich Rueschemeyer, 337–372 (Cambridge: Cambridge Univ. Press, 2003).

19 Alexander L. George and Timothy J. McKeown. "Case Studies and Theories of Organizational Decision-Making," *Advances in Information Processing in Organizations: A Research Annual on Public Organizations* 2 (1985): 1–6.

20 Mounira Charrad, *Women's Rights-The Making of Postcolonial Tunisia, Algeria, and Morocco* (Berkeley; Los Angeles: Univ. of California Press, 2001), 219.

21 Charrad, *Women's*, 220.

22 See Abdelhamid Largueche and Dalenda Largueche, *D'Islam et d'Ailleurs. Marginales en terre d'Islam* (France: Cérès Editions, 2003).

23 Souhayer Belhassen, "L'Islamisme fait-il peur aux Tunisiennes?" *Jeune Afrique* Plus (September–October 1989): 34–45, 37.

24 Ahmad Kazemi Moussavi (ed.), Collectif 95 Maghreb égalité, *Guide to Equality of the Family in the Mahgreb* (Women's Learning Partnership for Rights, Development and Peace, 2005).

25 Hassan Arfaoui, "L'Avenir de la démocratie," *Réalités*. No. 1390 (16–22/8/2012), 4.

26 Rose Vincent, "Les Tunisiennes ont jeté leurs voiles aux cactus," *ELLE Magazine*, No. 1385. (July 3, 1972), 7.

27 Neila Jrad, "A l'orée du féminisme Tunisien: éléments de réflexion," in *100 ans de luttes communistes en Tunisie*. Sous la direction de Habib Kazdaghli. 53–60. Nirvana ed. (December 2021), 56.

28 Maherzia Labidi was elected in 2011 as a representative of Tunisians living abroad. In October 2014, the Constituent Assembly allowed her to become the first deputy speaker.

29 Institute of Democratic and Electoral Assistance (IDEA), *Tunisia Constitution of 2014*, at Tunisia: The Constitution of 2014 | ConstitutionNet (accessed July 6, 2024).

30 Farouk, "Analysis."

31 Asma Ghribi, "Tunisian Presidential Candidate Kennou Takes on the Patriarchy," *Foreign Policy* (October 10, 2014), at Tunisian Presidential Candidate Kennou Takes On the Patriarchy – Foreign Policy (accessed October 13, 2023).

32 Ahmed Maher, "What is Article 80 of Tunisia's Constitution?" (July 26, 2021), at https://www.thenationalnews.com/mena/2021/07/27/what-is-article-80-of-tunisias-constitution/ (accessed June 18, 2023); see also IDEA, *2014 Constitution*, Article 80.

33 Library of Congress, "Tunisia: New Constitution Consolidates Powers in the Hands of the President," August 23, 2022, at Tunisia: New Constitution Consolidates Powers in the Hands of the President | Library of Congress (loc.gov) (accessed July 6, 2024).

34 IPU-Parline, "Tunisia: Assembly of People's Representatives," at Tunisia | Parline: the IPU's Open Data Platform (accessed July 6, 2024).

35 Sana Ben Achour, "Si l'abstention à 91.2 % n'est pas une sanction, de quoi donc est-elle le nom?" Facebook (December 20, 2022).

36 University of California Press, *1982–2004. Human Rights and Reform. Part III. The Tunisian League of Human Rights*, University of California Digital Library. UC Press E-Books Collection, 135. In https://publishing.cdlib.org/

ucpressebooks/view?docId=ft2t1nb1vf&chunk.id=d0e3053&toc.depth=100&brand=ucpress (accessed July 6, 2024).

37 It was for this reason that, until 1983, there was only one political party, the Neo-Destour. To end divisiveness in the country, Ben Ali dissolved the tribes that were found in different regions. Some tribes still exist today. See Rikke Hostrup Haugbolle, "'Together for Tunisia': Tribal Structures and Social Mobilization," Middle East Institute, October 19, 2016, at "Together for Tunisia": Tribal Structures and Social and Political Mobilization | Middle East Institute (mei.edu) (accessed June 6, 2023).

38 Safwan Masri, *Tunisia: An Arab Anomaly* (New York: Columbia Univ. Press, 2017); also, Tunisia (1956-the present), University of Central Arkansas, at https://uca.edu/politicalscience/dadm-project/middle-eastnorth-africapersian-gulf-region/tunisia-1956-present/ (accessed June 6, 2023).

39 Leyla Dakhli, "The Fair Value of Bread: Tunisia, 28 December 1983–6 January 1984," *International Review of Social History* 66(S29) (2021): 41–68. doi:10.1017/S0020859021000110. During these riots, 100 people were killed.

40 Committee to Protect Journalists (CPJ), "Tunisia Moving Forward With Restrictive Bill For Press" (June 17, 2010), at https://cpj.org/2010/06/tunisia-moving-forward-with-restrictive-bill-for-p/ (accessed June 6, 2023).

41 See Tunisian League for the Defense of Human Rights, "Studies," at Home - LTDH.

42 The Nobel Peace Prize 2015. NobelPrize.org. Nobel Prize Outreach AB 2023, at https://www.nobelprize.org/prizes/peace/2015/summary/ (accessed October 14, 2023).

43 Amira Yahyaoui, "Tunisie – Radhia Nasraoui: ' Rien ne justifie la torture, pas même le terrorisme,'" *Jeune Afrique*. (May 13, 2016), at https://www.jeuneafrique.com/324502/politique/radhia-nasraoui-rien-ne-justifie-torture-meme-terrorisme/ (accessed October 14, 2023).

44 Yahyioui, "Tunisie—Radhia Nasraoui."

45 Observatory for the Freedom of Press, Publishing and Creation in Tunisia (OLPEC/IFEX"), "Academic sentenced to eight months in prison for posting message on Facebook" (October 7, 2009), at https://ifex.org/academic-sentenced-to-eight-months-in-prison-for-posting-message-on-facebook.

46 Specifically, the protests "attacked symbols of state authority, including Bourguiba himself, when crowds chanted 'al-shaʿb huwwa al-mujahid al-akbar!' (the people are the supreme combatant), a quip against Bourguiba, known to Tunisians as the 'supreme combatant' for securing independence from France. Such a personal attack against Bourguiba in a public space crossed a red line for the regime." See Idriss Jebari, "'Illegitimate Children': The Tunisian New Left and the Student Question, 1963–1975," *International Journal of Middle East Studies*, 54 (2002): 100–123, 120.

47 Olfa Belhassine, "Tunisia and the Repression of Left-Wing Youth," (Feb. 28, 2020), at https://www.justiceinfo.net/en/43918-tunisia-and-the-repression-of-left-wing-youth.html (accessed June 10, 2023).

48 Zeineb Ben Said-Cherni, "Il était une fois un mouvement de résistance," *La Presse de Tunisie*. (March 4, 2013), at www.lapresse.tn/23102016/65130/il-etait-une-fois-un-mouvement-de-resistance.html (accessed October 30, 2016).

49 The Perspective Movement or El Amel Ettounsi was founded in 1963 in Paris. It is a left and extreme left-wing political party considered as one of the main Tunisian opposition movements in the 1960s and 1970s. See Idriss Jebari, Revolutionary Papers (accessed October 13, 2023).

50 Tounissiet, "Des femmes sous embargo" (January 27, 2004) at http://www.youtube.com/watch?v=I8M1r-MvSA (accessed October 13, 2023).

51 Trial International, "Rached Jaïdane: Victim of Torture," (October 24, 2018), at Rached Jaïdane: victim of torture - TRIAL International (accessed October 13, 2023).

52 Mohamed Kerrou, *Hijâb: nouveaux voiles et espaces publics* (France: Cérès Editions, 2010).

53 Nadia Haddaoui, "Histoire d'un désamour" (January 2, 2016), at http://nawaat.org/portail/2016/01/02/histoire-dun-desamour/ accessed October 10, 2023.

54 Lilia Labidi, "Tunisian Women Denouncing Violence Against Women," October 12, 2021, at https://www.wilsoncenter.org/blog-post/tunisian-women-denouncing-violence-against-women (accessed October 13, 2023).

55 *Aljazeera News Agency*, "Tunisia Law Failing to Protect Women from Domestic Violence" (December 8, 2022) at https://www.aljazeera.com/news/2022/12/8/tunisia-fails-to-protect-women-despite-law-in-place-hrw-says (accessed October 13, 2023).

56 RSP. Apr/6/2004.

57 Bochra Bel Hadj Hmida has since then fled to France to avoid arrest.

58 Souleymane Loum, "Pas de pause dans les arrestations, une autre fournée: ça va secouer en Tunisie et ailleurs," *Tunisie Numérique* (March 30, 2023), at Tunisie numérique.com (accessed October 13, 2023).

59 OCTT (June 18, 2020), at https://worldcoalition.org/2020/06/18/the-abolition-of-the-death-penalty-in-tunisia-a-fight-against-torture (accessed October 13, 2023).

60 Bassam Khawaja, "Tunisia's Electoral Commission Paves the Way for Kais Saied's Second Term" (September 4, 2024), at Tunisia's Electoral Commission Paves the Way for Kais Saied's Second Term | Human Rights Watch (hrw.org) (accessed September 12, 2024).

61 He said: "I never wanted to act against the Coran. I only wanted to show that it could be interpreted differently, Vincent," *Les Tunisiennes*, 4.

62 Soukeina Bouraoui, Gender & Human Rights Issues in Arab Countries – CAWTAR (accessed June 6, 2023), 505.

63 Bouraoui, *Gender*, 509. See also Khedija Arfaoui, "The Development of the Feminist Movement in Tunisia: 1920s–2000s," *International Journal of the Humanities* 4(8) (2007): 53–60.

64 Mohamed Najib Ben Saad writes: "According to a survey conducted by Tunisia's National Institute of Statistics (2015), almost half (48%) of Tunisian women have experienced some form of GBV (gender-based violence) at some point in their lives. [...] Despite government measures to address GBV, enforcement of the laws is often weak." Mohamed Najib Ben Saad, "Tunisians See Gender-Based Violence as a Top Priority, But Domestic Violence as a Private Matter," *Afrobarometer*, February 14, 2023.

65 Olfa Belhassine, "Feminicide, is 'A State Crime' According to Tunisia Feminists" (August 9, 2021), at https://medfeminiswiya.net/2021/09/08/femicide-a-state-crime-according-to-tunisian-feminists/?lang=en; (accessed October 13, 2023); also, David Sadler, "In Tunisia, Failing Authorities in the Face of the Rise in Feminicides," *Globe World News Echo* (May 18, 2023), at https://globeecho.com/news/africa/in-tunisia-failing-authorities-in-the-face-of-the-rise-in-feminicides/ (accessed October 13, 2023).

66 Democratic Women-ATFD, email (July 23, 2024).

12 Zimbabwe and a Reassessment of Institutional Anomie Theory

Shannon M. Gibson

Introduction

In November 2017, Zimbabwe experienced a critical juncture with the military's unconstitutional deposition of longtime president and Zimbabwe African National Union-Patriotic Front (ZANU-PF) leader Robert Mugabe. Any hopes of reforms to Zimbabwe's political system by Mugabe's successor, Emmerson Mnangagwa quickly dissipated. Legislation like the Patriotic Bill which prohibits criticism of the government,[1] Mnangagwa's fraudulent election in 2018 and reelection in 2023, and the government's continued use of force and intimidation (among other things, including outright denial at one point of any non-health crisis in Zimbabwe),[2] demonstrate that the protection of human rights in practice in Zimbabwe remains in peril. Institutional corruption prevails and the independence of the judiciary remains highly questionable. Politics as usual appears to prevail as conditions of economic and social stability in the country worsen.

Zimbabwe presents an interesting case. On some of the factors of *congruence–independent judiciary, corruption, societal engagement* (through civil society), *local authority, access to justice and information access*–there is some decline from 2018, but for others, little change. Data for all but access to information were provided by the Institute for Democracy and Electoral Assistance's (IDEA) Global State of Democracy (GSoD) index (Table 12.1).[3]

However, these data do not accurately reflect the public's reaction to the post-Mugabe regime. The author of this chapter applies a revised version of Institutional Anomie Theory (IAT) to examine whether the public has the will to push forward to progressively impact the policymaking process in Zimbabwe. Since its inception, IAT has been expanded by scholars to explain crime as well as attitudes toward unethical behavior across countries—largely developed democracies. According to IAT, the motive of criminal behavior is assumed to be economic, driven by a market mentality that is either counterbalanced or reinforced by extant non-economic institutions in a country. Individuals living in conditions of income inequality will either perpetrate or not perpetrate economic crimes depending on the strength of these mediating institutions and economic conditions in a country. The author of this chapter

DOI: 10.4324/9781003471677-16

Table 12.1 Congruence in the Post-Mugabe Era

	Local authorities	*Societal engagement*	*Corruption*	*Independent judiciary*	*Access to justice*	*Information access*
2018	0.263147	0.378094	0.28948	0.404648	0.515034	50.01
2019	0.261024	0.369696	0.285027	0.3879	0.513734	50.04
2020	0.277841	0.367468	0.293691	0.385329	0.513578	50.59
2021	0.277841	0.353872	0.284264	0.379282	0.485684	49.24
2022	0.277841	0.288964	0.264723	0.37938	0.488915	50

shifts the focus of IAT to the legacy of violence and misrule by ZANU-PF and the role that widespread corruption and politics as usual have on willingness of the public to constructively engage with the government. Like Chapter 10 about Guinea, the behavior of the public, partially demonstrated by their attitudes toward the former Mugabe regime, as well as ZANU-PF, corruption, and the viability of the political opposition, indicate that a desire to "tune out" the government may be emerging as a type of self-preservation for many in Zimbabwe.[4]

This chapter proceeds as follows. After an assessment of Zimbabwe's political past and present, the author of this chapter introduces IAT, a theory developed by Steven F. Messner and Richard Rosenfield,[5] which attributes the perpetration of crime in the United States to a desire on the part of would-be criminals to achieve the "American Dream." Its assumptions about the role of institutions as a mediating force on human behavior make IAT useful to explain the relationship between public engagement in the public sphere and government. After explaining the theory, a working hypothesis is introduced that explains the response of Zimbabweans to the current state of political affairs in the country as reflecting institutional legacies of misrule. In the section that follows, this hypothesis is assessed using survey data from the *World Values Survey* (*WVS*).[6] The data indicate a growing lack of public trust in political and social institutions and leaders, as well as the absence of a desire to engage in the public space. Public opinions are then addressed against the backdrop of the shrinking public space in Zimbabwe, particularly as this pertains to voicing dissent against the government. Although the data suggest an increase in public dissatisfaction and a desire to disengage to some extent from the public sphere, these results are tentative at best. This chapter concludes with some thoughts about what the combination of a voluntary lack of engagement and a more exclusive space for public dialogue hold for improvements of human rights in Zimbabwe.

Political Crisis in Zimbabwe

The rule of Mugabe as the "father of Zimbabwe" lasted nearly four decades until his ouster in 2017.[7] During his rule, Zimbabwe's economic and political fortunes sharply degraded over time as Mugabe struggled to maintain power amid growing demands for political and economic reforms on the part of political opposition groups and civil society organizations, like the Zimbabwe Congress of Trade Unions (ZCTU) and the National Constitutional Assembly (NCA).[8]

Among Mugabe's most controversial policy choices was his support of the Fast Track Land Reform Programme (FTLRP) which forcefully and often violently redistributed lands from white farmers to indigenous persons.[9] In many respects, the FTLRP was used by the Mugabe regime to increase support during the economic downturn, amid growing opposition and a humiliating defeat in a national constitutional referendum.[10] These lands were not distributed equally but favored Mugabe's allies. Combined with his attempts to placate veterans of the civil war with generous stipends, the economy of Zimbabwe entered a tailspin, with hyper-inflation, a drop in agricultural exports and tourism, famine, and increasing poverty and debt.[11] Once considered the breadbasket of Africa the land reform turned Zimbabwe into a net exporter of grain.

Mugabe's rule is associated with a legacy of violence. The use of torture, lethal force, arbitrary arrests and detention, and disappearances have a long history as a means of controlling dissent within (and outside of) the ruling party as well as the vote in Zimbabwe. From the wars of independence to the present day, violence has been a dependable "strategy" of the ZANU-PF.[12]

One of the most visible examples of this legacy are the massacres of approximately 20,000 citizens in Matabeleland by the Zimbabwe National Army in the early to mid-1980s. Known as "Gakurahundi" the "killings [...] were extensive, indiscriminate and utterly brutal in nature."[13] Mass rapes, torture, disappearances as well as extensive property damage were intended by Mugabe to destroy a rising political opponent, Joseph Nkomo, and his Zimbabwe African People's Union (ZAPU) which enjoyed substantial support in Matabeleland.[14]

In later years, multiparty democracy was enshrined in Zimbabwe's 2013 Constitution, yet opposition parties, like the Movement for Democrtaic Change (MDC), led by the late Morgan Tsvangirai, continuously challenged the results of elections which suspiciously favored the ZANU-PF.[15] The use of violence and tactics of intimidation, including the withholding of food aid, plagued most elections in Zimbabwe particularly from the early 2000s on. In the most recent presidential election held in August 2023, incumbent President Emmerson Mnangagwa quickly took after his defeated opponent, Nelson Chamisa of the Citizen's Coalition for Change and all others who criticized the results of the election.[16]

Mnangagwa has been referred to as a "wooden figure with zero charisma," not to mention an absence of democratic credentials.[17] He has been involved in past instances of excessive force and murder, including the Gakurahundi and the violence conducted against the opposition in 2008.[18] The manner with which protestors of the 2018 election results were treated—many shot and killed—indicated that "Mnangagwa was never going to open and expand the democratic space" as it threatened his hold on power.[19]

Not surprisingly, the Mnangagwa regime continues to rely on the use of coercion, including the use of torture, abduction, and lethal force as a means to control dissent.[20] Although Zimbabwe is not a party to the Convention Against Torture and Other Cruel, Inhuman or Degrading Treatment or Punishment (Torture Convention), or the International Convention for the Protection of All Persons from Enforced Disappearance,[21] it is party to the International Covenant on Civil and Political Rights (ICCPR), which prohibits torture, violation of one's right to life, and disappearances.[22]

The GSoD's variable "Personal Integrity and Security," which measures freedom from torture and political killings, demonstrates that Zimbabweans remain threatened by the government's use of force. Between 2018 and 2022, Zimbabwe has averaged .23, which on a scale from 0 to 1, is quite low, indicating little security for Zimbabwe's population.[23] According to the CIRI Human Rights database torture in Zimbabwe remains widespread and political killings frequent.[24]

The public's access to social media and resources are restricted for a variety of reasons, some of which is a consequence of the Patriot Bill. Restricted access also reflects the country's continued economic distress and lack of internet penetration. According to Freedom House, Zimbabwe is ranked as "partly free" with respect to internet access and free use.[25] Rather than aid democracy, internet use is geared toward state-sponsored campaigns of disinformation. Users who were critical of Mnangagwa were subject to arrest and harassment ahead of the 2023 elections.[26] Moreover, internet blackouts are a tactic the regime continues to rely on as well as efforts to slow down access due to connectivity restrictions.[27] In addition to the harassment of journalists, and the arrests and detentions of opposition leaders like Joe Sikhala, efforts to clamp down on the use of social media reflect a shrinking space for political dissent.[28]

Institutional Anomie Theory (IAT)

IAT was developed by Messner and Rosenfeld.[29] Initially their model was used to explain why the United States has higher crime rates compared to other developed nations.[30] They argue that collective American culture, which lauds the notion of the American Dream, instills in its citizens the values of individual achievement, an entitlement to success through hard work, and a fetishism of money (e.g., money as a benchmark for success).[31] The achievement of the American Dream is mediated through various institutions, which can help or hinder this effort. Economic institutions provide goods and services. Government aids in providing security as well as social control through laws and sanctions for violators. Family, civil society (religious institutions) and educational institutions provide informal social controls such as teaching persons right from wrong and instilling responsibility in citizens.

An institutional imbalance prevails when more emphasis is placed on the economy at the expense of these other institutions.[32] When non-economic institutions are weakened due to economic dominance, *anomie*—a collective sense of normlessness (e.g., panic, fear)—may result leaving citizens with the desire to succeed by "any means necessary."[33] In their analysis Messner and Rosenfeld contend that American citizens generally support strong crime control initiatives such as mass imprisonment and long prison sentences to "protect what they have," but this does not prevent the subtle cultural encouragement of achieving material gains by any means if *legitimate* means are deemed unattractive or unavailable.[34]

Use of IAT to Explain Other Types of Phenomena

In recent years, IAT has been expanded to explain deviant behaviors such as cheating and selling secondhand items without identifying their flaws to potential customers,[35] theft and other types of crime,[36] attitudes toward immigration,[37] voting behaviors,[38] and corruption[39] as potential outcomes of economic domination and weakened non-economic institutions.

Attitudes toward immigration could be considered an indicator of collective anomie, or the idea that immigrants could pose a threat to natural-born citizens' overall well-being in the economy if "market mentality" is strong and non-economic institutions cannot act as a buffer to temper this mentality.

In her 2022 study of 28 European nations, for example, Nickel's demonstrated with the use of the 2018 wave of the *European Social Survey* that market-driven values helped to predict "non-immigrant" attitudes, while successful perceptions of non-economic institutions helped to reduce prejudice against immigrants.[40] Moreover, In his 2023 examination of the Organization for Economic Co-operation and Development (OECD), José Cruz tested to determine whether perceived corruption was a potential outcome of weakened non-economic institutions and stronger economic ones.[41] Relying on fuzzy-set qualitative comparative analysis, he found that lower levels of education, higher divorce rates and lower levels of voter turnout and income equality coincide with a high public perception of corruption.[42] He concluded that weak non-economic institutions and high economic inequality were sufficient conditions to increase perceived corruption.[43]

Other studies suggest that voting patterns could impact perceived corruption, as there may be lower levels of trust in government during various time periods and consequently less chance of support for certain political parties. In their study of 401 voting districts in East (N=77) and West Germany (N=324) circa 2021, Amelie Nickel and Eva Groß focused their examination on the Alternative for Germany (AfD), a populist party with a strong focus on competition and hierarchy based on economic achievement and the exclusion of individuals based on their "non-profitability," or low economic contributions.[44] Ordinary least squares (OLS) regression results suggested that

German districts with strong political institutions had less support for the AfD compared to districts with weak political institutions.[45]

Current cross-national research demonstrates that IAT is useful as a means of explaining a variety of public opinions about the relationship between the economy, institutions, and societal wellbeing. This chapter utilizes IAT to explain the opinions of Zimbabweans toward institutions of the post-Mugabe government as well as a range of nongovernmental institutions and the economy, and their willingness to engage in the political process. The working hypothesis is as follows:

> H1: The strength and effectiveness of political institutions inform the public's willingness to engage as members of the communities of practice involved in the protection and promotion of human rights.

The author of this chapter contends that the survey data outlined below demonstrate that a growing sense of anomie does not bode well for the rule of law in the country. The public space for dissent in Zimbabwe is shrinking due to increasing internal instability and economic decline, and the lack of public willingness to engage only magnifies this problem.

"Politics as Usual" in Zimbabwe?

To examine Zimbabwe's perceptions of the government and other institutions, the *World Values Survey, wave 7* data are examined. On a regular basis, *WVS* asks citizens from various developed and developing nations their opinions on a wide range of subjects, including their views on government corruption, how much they value family, religion, work, etc.[46] *WVS* is especially advantageous as a data source because it provides data for numerous countries over several time periods and is extremely useful as a means of identifying changes and trends over time. This study also relies on data from the GSoD indices to demonstrate the exclusiveness of the communities of practice that surround the legislative process in Zimbabwe.

According to the *WVS* data Zimbabweans' perceptions of economic growth and well-being demonstrate a sense of economic distress. The majority of the 1,215 sample of Zimbabweans surveyed (54.3 percent) feel that their standard of living is worse than their parents.[47] When it comes to satisfaction with the financial status of their household, 77.6 percent of those surveyed rated their satisfaction as adequate (a "5") or lower.[48] Table 12.2 illustrates Zimbabweans' attitudes toward the economy's ability to meet their vital basic needs.

These results reflect erratic fluctuations in Zimbabwe's economic growth and the maintenance of income inequalities. Between 2018 and 2022, economic growth in Zimbabwe fluctuated between a low of –6.14 (2018) to a high of 5.13 (2021).[50] The GINI index indicates that the income distribution between the wealthiest and the poorest in Zimbabwe has stayed the same

Table 12.2 World Values Survey Economic Wellbeing Data for Zimbabwe[49]

	Often	*Sometimes*	*Rarely*	*Never*
Frequency (last 12 months) you/family has gone without cash income	50	24.3	15.1	10.6
Frequency (last 12 months) you/family has gone without enough to eat	22.9	23.6	25.0	28.5
Frequency (last 12 months) you/family has gone without a safe shelter	12.3	6.6	11.6	68.3
Frequency (last 12 months) you/family has gone without medicine/medical treatment	36.2	19.2	15.1	29.1

over this period. Zimbabwe consistently scores a 50, which indicates wide income disparities.[51]

Table 12.3 includes *WVS* data about the level of confidence Zimbabweans have in government and civil society institutions, including the press. Large percentages of Zimbabweans who were surveyed reflect a lack of confidence in the government, the judiciary, civil services, and parliament.[52] Although in some cases the majority of those surveyed indicate confidence in government institutions like the judiciary, these were very slim majorities.[53] Over 51 percent of Zimbabweans express a great deal of confidence and quite a lot of confidence in the government compared to 47.8 percent who have little to no confidence in government.[54] A similar finding occurs with the level of confidence in Zimbabwe's security forces. For the police and the military, the split between confidence/quite a lot of confidence and not very much/no confidence is roughly even.[55]

The data on confidence in elections are rather telling.[56] A majority of those surveyed indicate that they do not have very much or no confidence in the

Table 12.3 World Values Survey Trust of Government and Civil Society Institutions

	A great deal	*Quite a Lot*	*Not very much*	*None at all*	*Don't know*
Confidence in the government	18.4	33.3	24.4	23.4	0.4
Confidence in parliament	12.6	31.4	28.5	26.7	0.8
Confidence in elections	14.3	27.2	26	31.4	0.9
Confidence in the police	20.1	30.3	29.7	19.7	0.2
Confidence in justice system	17.1	34.6	28.1	19.0	0.9
Confidence in civil services	15.7	36.2	29.5	17.7	0.8
Confidence in armed forces	20.9	30.2	29.2	18.6	0.9
Confidence in labor unions	14.9	32.8	32.3	16.9	3.1
Confidence in Churches	39.2	29.1	26.9	4.7	0.1
Confidence in political parties	8.7	19.9	33.7	36	1.5
Confidence in the press	8.4	22.6	38.9	27.8	2.1

electoral process in Zimbabwe. Other data in the survey indicate that over 45 percent of those surveyed indicate that voters are threatened at the polls often to fairly often,[57] and that over 47 percent of the time, elections are seen as unfair.[58]

For civil society associations, churches by far have the greatest share of confidence among those surveyed, with labor unions and especially political parties[59] and the press, substantially lagging.[60] This lack of trust can be seen as reflected in a lack of membership or active membership in voluntary organizations. For instance, over 80 percent of those surveyed are not members of a labor union, and 74.5 percent are not members of a political party.[61]

Table 12.4 includes data on Zimbabweans' perception of corruption in various institutions in the country. Corruption has long been endemic in Zimbabwe's institutional structures. According to the GSoD, over the years since Mugabe left, corruption has remained high. Between 2018 and 2022 GSoD's variable "Absence of Corruption" averages at around .28 for Zimbabwe, with lower numbers indicating greater institutional corruption.[62]

Respondents were asked to estimate how many people within each institution they perceive to be involved in corruption. As indicated by the data in Table 12.4, nearly 60 percent of Zimbabweans feel that national authorities are involved in corruption, over 50 percent of local authorities and most civil service providers. Moreover, over 66 percent of Zimbabweans believe that corruption is pervasive in the country.[63] Over 60 percent of those surveyed indicate that they have had to pay a bribe or make some sort of "gift" to local officials or members of civil service to obtain services.[64]

Considering the prevalence of institutionalized corruption in Zimbabwe as well as doubts about the effectiveness of government, it is not surprising that most of those surveyed indicate no interest in politics (31.8 percent compared to 11.2 percent very interested), and 46.2 percent never discuss politics with friends (compared to 8.6 percent that do).[66] Additionally, very small percentages of those surveyed partake in political activities including joining a boycott (9.7 percent), attending a peaceful/lawful demonstration (8.6 percent), or joining an unofficial strike (3.6 percent).[67]

Despite the pessimism on the part of respondents, 78 percent of them agreed that democracy was the preferred system of governance,[68] and nearly 75 percent agreed that democracy was absolutely important.[69] This is despite the finding that most Zimbabweans feel cautious about trusting their fellow

Table 12.4 Perceptions of Corruption in Institutions in Zimbabwe[65]

	None	*Few*	*Most*	*All*	*Don't know*
National authorities	6.1	30.8	42.5	17.0	3.5
Local authorities	8.3	36.4	41.6	11.3	2.2
Civil service providers	8.8	31.4	43.1	14.9	1.6
Journalists/media	17.9	42.2	25.2	7.9	6.5

Zimbabweans (97.8 percent).[70] This caution extends to trust in government. Over 60 percent of Zimbabweans agree that one must be cautious when dealing with government,[71] and another 54 percent feel that most politicians are not honest.[72]

It appears that a high level of implied economic inequality in Zimbabwe and a low overall confidence in governmental institutions could potentially lead to anomie as IAT proposes. Question 49 of the *World Values Survey* asks respondents to rate how satisfied they are with their life overall (on a scale of one to ten, with ten being completely satisfied).[73] Table 12.5 illustrates respondents' answers to this question. Over 28 percent of Zimbabweans feel completely dissatisfied with their lives, whereas only 18.8 percent feel completely satisfied, lending possible support to the notion of anomie, depending on how "life satisfaction" is defined.

So how do these data on public perceptions translate into public engagement in the political process? The GSoD data in Table 12.6 indicate that public engagement in the political process in Zimbabwe has dropped slightly in the post-Mugabe era on some indicators. "Engagement," which measures the extent to which citizens participate in all levels of government through "participation in dynamic civil society organizations and elections"[74] and civic engagement,"[75] declined from 2018 to 2022. "Civil society," has remained steady since 2018.[76] All measures included in Table 12.6 are measured on a basis of "1" to "0," with 1 being the strongest.

To better gauge the status of public engagement the author of this study unpacked the broader estimates of participation, civil society, civic engagement. "CSO part. enviro." indicates that the environment in which civil society organizations in Zimbabwe operate is largely voluntary, that societal engagement in significant policy changes in Zimbabwe was fairly "wide and independent," and that important civil society organizations were consulted, although likely not as a matter of routine practice.[77] However, participation of society electronically,[78] and in interest groups[79] declined or remains low (respectively), and social capital in Zimbabwe, or trust among citizens and the presence of voluntary institutions of self-organization, remains low.[80]

The question arises whether these numbers indicate a fear of greater involvement in political and/or public spaces in Zimbabwe or whether this data reflect a growing sense of apathy of citizens toward government more generally. The author of this chapter suggests that it is likely a mixture of both. Based on the documentary and survey evidence utilized by this study,

Table 12.5 Overall Life Satisfaction in Zimbabwe

10	*9*	*8*	*7*	*6*	*5*	*4*	*3*	*2*	*0*
18.8	2.7	4.9	5.8	6.6	16.7	7.1	5.2	3.7	28.5

Table 12.6 Participation in Public Spaces in Zimbabwe

Year	*Particip.*	*Civil society*	*Civic engagement*	*CSO part. enviro.*	*Engaged society*	*CSO consult.*	*e-part.*	*Interest groups*	*Social capital*
2017	.5584	.4830	.7796	.7285	.6091	.5002	.2881	.3333	.375
2018	.5839	.4849	.7796	.7390	.5816	.5562	.2753	.2222	.375
2019	.5654	.4741	.7796	.7390	.5736	.5208	.2753	.2222	.375
2020	.5654	.4713	.7796	.7124	.5792	.5001	.4524	.3333	.375
2021	.5556	.4789	.7388	.7175	.6045	.5001	.4524	.3333	.375
2022	.5129	.4890	.5909	.7175	.6045	.5228	.2273	.3333	.375

we can tentatively conclude that many Zimbabweans are indeed unhappy with the current state of political affairs in their country, as well as dissatisfied with economic conditions. Wealth inequality remains rather high and many feel that their prospects for doing better are poor.

This author also suggests that the decline in participation electronically and in interest groups may reflect this dissatisfaction. It may also reflect the closing of public space and the government's use of coercive tactics to prevent dissent. The jailing of journalists and violence against protectors, including torture, likely impacts the larger society's desire to engage in any discourse with the government. However, it is also important to recognize the fact that it was civil society and the public that helped bring down the Mugabe regime. Consequently, it is most likely far too soon to count the public out.

Conclusions and Directions for Further Research

Zimbabweans continue to suffer the ill-effects of ZANU-PF rule and Zimbabwe's Second Republic.[81] This chapter found some evidence to suggest that this dissatisfaction may be reflected in a desire to disengage from public dissent. However, as indicated above, the jury is still out. One observation that the author of this chapter makes is that Zimbabwe's status as a fragile state does not bode well for Zimbabwe's future.[82] With the ever-growing restraints placed on civil society and the political opposition, not to mention the exercise of free speech more broadly, the prospect of Zimbabweans "tuning out" the government and its misrule only heightens the chances of future bloodshed.

Notes

1 Mnangagwa signed the bill into law in June 2023 to stifle public criticism of his administration heading into presidential elections in August 2023. Ray Ndlovu, "Bad-Mouthing the State Is Outlawed Before Election in Zimbabwe," Bloomberg. Com, https://search.ebscohost.com/login.aspx?direct=true&AuthType=ip,shib&db=bth&AN=164091337&site=eds-live&scope=site (accessed August 12, 2023).

2 Kirk Helliker and Gerald Chikhozo Mazarire, "Mnangagwa's Zimbabwe: Crisis? What Crisis?" *Journal of Asian and African Studies*, 56(2) (2021): 171–175.

3 Institute for Democracy and Electoral Assistance (IDEA), Global State of Democracy indices, at Global State of Democracy Indices | The Global State of Democracy (idea.int). Data for "Information Access" were obtained from the KOF database.

4 David Coltart, opposition leader, suggested that the willingness of those Zimbabweans who continue to support ZANU-PF after Mugabe's downfall is analogous to Stockholm Syndrome. David Coltart, "After Mugabe: Mnangagwa's Choice," *Policy* 34(1) (2018): 51–54, 53.

5 Steven F. Messner and Richard Rosenfeld, "An Institutional Anomie Theory of the Social Distribution of Crime." In P. Cordella, L. Siegel, eds., 143–148. *Readings in Contemporary Criminological Theory* (Boston, S. 2013).

6 Robert Inglehart, C. Haerpfer, A. Moreno, C. Welzel, K. Kizilova, J. Diez-Medrano, M. Lagos, P. Norris, E. Ponarin & B. Puranen et al. (eds.). 2021. *World*

Values Survey: Round Seven - Country-Pooled Datafile Version: https://www.worldvaluessurvey.org/WVSDocumentationWV7.jsp. Madrid: JD Systems Institute (accessed August 12, 2023).

7 Zimbabwe, formerly South Rhodesia, was a settler colony. Herbst and other scholars suggest that the legacies of colonial rule continue to impact the manner of political rule in Zimbabwe (with its heavy reliance on one-group rule) as well as its economy, the latter of which remains based in agriculture and mineral production. Jeffrey Herbst, *State Politics in Zimbabwe* (Berkeley, CA: Univ. of California Press, 1990). Agriculture would always serve as a weapon for governments to quell opposition. Fifteen years of international sanctions against Southern Rhodesia for its blatantly racist policies toward non-whites culminated in the rise of a black counter-elite and a civil war. The Lancaster House Agreement of 1979 ended the war, but on the condition that white farmers could keep their land and occupy 20 percent of the seats in the new government (among other provisions). The first elections in the new system brought Mugabe to power in 1980 with ZANU winning overwhelming support. Herbst, *State Politics*, 25–30; see also Sue Onslow and Martin Plaut, *Robert Mugabe* (Athens, OH: Ohio Univ. Press, 2018); Mawere Munyaradzi, Ngonidzashe Marongwe, Fidelis Peter Thomas Duri, eds. *The End of an Era? Robert Mugabe and a Conflicting Legacy* (Bamenda, Cameroon: Langaa RPCIG, 2018); and David Comagnon, *A Predictable Tragedy: Rubert Mugabe and the Collapse of Zimbabwe* (Philadelphia: Univ. of Pennsylvania Press, 2011).

8 Comagnon, *Predictable*, chap. 3.

9 Tenson Muyabo, "The Fast Track Land Reform Programme in Post-colonial Zimbabwe: A Sloganeering Gimmick?" In *The End of an Era? Robert Mugabe and a Conflicting Legacy*, 323–352. Mawere Munyaradzi, Ngonidzashe Marongwe, Fidelis Peter and Thomas Duri, eds. (Bamenda, Cameroon: Langaa RPCIG, 2018). For a very critical view of the FTLRP, see Comagnon, *Predictable*, 166–190.

10 Tendai Chibaya and Phanos Matura, "The Fast Track Land Reform Programme (FTLRP) and Tourism Development in Zimbabwe during Mugabe's Reign." In *The End of an Era? Robert Mugabe and a Conflicting Legacy* eds. Mawere Munyaradzi, Ngonidzashe Marongwe, Fidelis Peter and Thomas Duri, 385–416 (Bamenda, Cameroon: Langaa RPCIG, 2018), 385.

11 Regarding the tourism industry in Zimbabwe, see Chibaya and Matura, "Fast Track," 386–387; for the damage to the wider economy, see Comagnon, *Predictable*, 181–190.

12 Comagnon, *Predictable*, 181–190.

13 Stuart Dornan, "Zimbabwe: What Britain and the West Did—and Didn't—do During the Matabeleland Massacres of 1983–4," *Daily Maverick* (April 24, 2017), at Zimbabwe: What Britain and the West did – and didn't – do during the Matabeleland massacres of 1983–4 (dailymaverick.co.za) (August 12, 2023).

14 Dornan, "Zimbabwe"; also, Comagnon, *Predictable*, 50–52.

15 Comagnon, *Predictable*, 50–52.

16 The 2023 elections were widely criticized by observer groups and others as being poorly run and unconstitutional. Nyasha Chingono, "Emmerson Mnangagwa Wins Second Term as President of Zimbabwe," *The Guardian* (August 26, 2023), at Emmerson Mnangagwa wins second term as president of Zimbabwe | Zimbabwe | The Guardian (accessed October 1, 2023). Chingono writes about brutal attacks on opponents as well as fraudulent charges leveled against them for various crimes, including murder. Nyasha Chingono, "Zimbabwe Opposition Figures Detained in Crackdown After Disputed Election," *The Guardian*

(September 26, 2023), at Zimbabwe opposition figures detained in crackdown after disputed election | Zimbabwe | The Guardian (accessed October 1, 2023).

17 Simukai Tinhu, "Understanding Mnangagwa's Political Doctrine," *The Zimbabwean* (January 10, 2020), at Understanding Mnangagwa's Political Doctrine (thezimbabwean.co) (accessed October 15, 2022).

18 Tinhu, "Understanding." Mnangagwa was State Security Minister at the time the massacres took place in Matabeleland. These massacres were led by the army's Fifth Brigade under the leadership of Perrence Shiri. John Campbell, "The Matabeleland Massacre and Contemporary Zimbabwe," *Council on Foreign Relations*, April 27, 2017, at The Matabeleland Massacre and Contemporary Zimbabwe | Council on Foreign Relations (cfr.org); and Bram Janssen and Andrew Meldrum, "Zimbabwe's Matabeleland Massacre Haunts Monday's Elections," *Reuters* (July 28, 2018), at Zimbabwe's Matabeleland massacre haunts Monday's elections | AP News. Both accessed November 2, 2023.

19 Janssen and Meldrum, "Zimbabwe's."

20 Human Rights Watch is one of many international human rights NGOs that document the state-sanctioned abuse of Zimbabweans on a regular basis. See, for example, Human Rights Watch, *"Crush them Like Lice": Repression of Civil and Political Rights Ahead of Zimbabwe's August 2023 Election* (August 3, 2023), at "Crush Them Like Lice": Repression of Civil and Political Rights Ahead of Zimbabwe's August 2023 Election | HRW (accessed November 2, 2023).

21 UN General Assembly, Convention Against Torture and Other Cruel, Inhuman or Degrading Treatment or Punishment, December 10, 1984, United Nations, Treaty Series, vol. 1465, available at: https://www.refworld.org/docid/3ae6b3a94.html; UN General Assembly, International Convention for the Protection of All Persons from Enforced Disappearance, December 20, 2006, available at: https://www.refworld.org/docid/47fdfaeb0.html. Both documents accessed October 6, 2023.

22 UN Human Rights Committee (CCPR), *CCPR General Comment No. 6: Article 6 (Right to Life)*, 30 April 1982, available at: https://www.refworld.org/docid/45388400a.html (accessed August 6, 2023).

23 Institute for Democracy and Electoral Assistance (IDEA), Global State of Democracy indices, at Global State of Democracy Indices | The Global State of Democracy (idea.int) (October 6, 2023).

24 David L. Cingranelli, David L. Richards, and Chad K. Clay, "The CIRI Human Rights Dataset, Version 2014.04.14.", https://doi.org/10.7910/DVN/UKCPXT, Harvard Dataverse, V1, 2021 UNF:6:+N2W6SCqRsXxIn6+qCBSyg== [fileUNF].

25 Estimates on internet penetration vary depending on the source. One estimate is that almost 35 percent of the country has internet access. This is largely a consequence of a lack of infrastructure, power blockages, and the high cost of internet access due to inflation. Freedom House, *Freedom of the Internet Report, 2023*, "Zimbabwe," at Zimbabwe: Freedom on the Net 2023 Country Report | Freedom House (accessed November 2, 2023).

26 Freedom House, *Freedom*.

27 Freedom House, *Freedom*.

28 Amnesty International, "Zimbabwe: Continued Detention of Joe Silkhala is a Gross Miscarriage of Justice," (October 26, 2023), at Zimbabwe: Continued detention of Job Sikhala is a gross miscarriage of justice—Amnesty Zimbabwe (accessed November 2, 2023). Sikhala is a leader of the opposition movement the Citizens' Coalition for Change (CCC). Started in January 2022, CCC founder Nelson Charisma emerged as a challenger to Mnangagwa in the August 2023 elections (see above).

29 Steven F. Messner and Richard Rosenfeld, *Crime and the American Dream* (Wadsworth, Belmont, 2013).

30 Messner and Rosenfeld, *Crime*, 97–98.
31 Messner and Rosenfeld, *Crime*, 71–73.
32 Messner and Rosenfeld, *Crime*, 79–87.
33 Messner and Rosenfeld, *Crime*, 88–90.
34 Messner and Rosenfeld, *Crime*, 97–98.
35 Stephen W. Baron, "Marketized Mentality and Instrumental Offending: The Overlooked Roles of Noneconomic Institutions and Relative Deprivation in Individual Level Institutional Anomie Theory," *Journal of Crime and Justice*, 46(3) (2023): 331–347; and Helmut Hirtenlehner, Stephen Farrall and Johann Bacher, "Culture, Institutions, and Morally Dubious Behaviors: Testing Some Core Propositions of the Institutional-Anomie Theory," *Deviant Behavior*, 34(4) (2013): 291–320.
36 Shannon M. Gibson, "Every Dream has Its Price: A Cross-National Test of Institutional Anomie Theory," Ph.D. Dissertation, Florida State University, College of Criminology and Criminal Justice (2016).
37 Amelie Nickel, "Institutional Anomie, Market-Based Values and Anti-Immigrant Attitudes in 28 European Countries," *International Journal of Conflict and Violence* 16 (2022): 1–15.
38 Amelie Nickel and Evie Groß, "Assessing Regional Variation in Support for the Radical Right-Wing Party 'Alternative for Germany' (AfD)—A Novel Application of Institutional Anomie Theory Across German Districts," *Social Sciences* 12(412) (2023).
39 José N. Cruz, "A Fuzzy-Set Qualitative Analysis of Corruption and Homicide in Organization for Economic Cooperation and Development Countries through the Lens of the Institutional Anomie Theory," *European Journal of Criminology* 20(4) (2023): 1285–1308.
40 Nickel, "Institutional Anomie," 7–10. To measure market mentality, respondents were asked about their perceptions regarding power and achievement and their perceptions of benevolence and universalism (the idea that everyone should be treated equally as pertains to economic and non-economic institutions). To create the final measure, benevolence and universalism were subtracted from power and achievement.
41 Cruz measured corruption with the use of an index of perceptions of corruption taken from the 110-question Bayesian Corruption index, which measures aggregated levels of citizens' opinions on whether governments, nongovernmental organizations, as well as officials working in these organizations, are corrupt. Cruz, "Fuzzy-Set," 1295.
42 See Ragin for detailed descriptions of this procedure. C.C. Ragin, *Fuzzy-set Social Science* (Chicago: Univ. of Chicago Press, 2000) and *Redesigning Social Inquiry: Fuzzy Sets and Beyond* (Chicago: Univ. of Chicago Press, 2008).
43 Cruz, "Fuzzy-Set," 1297–1300.
44 Nickel and Grob, "Assessing," 6.
45 Nickel and Grob, "Assessing,"10–12. For Eastern German regions, economic dominance strongly impacted AfD voter support in the positive direction ($p<.001$), while it was insignificant in Western regions. This is due to the massive changes in the economic structure in the east in the 1990s as Eastern Germany was transformed into a "neoliberal" region without benefit of strong state protection and anti-corruption initiatives. Nickel and Grob, "Assessing," 13.
46 Inglehart et al. *WVS*.
47 Inglehart et al., *WVS*, 265.
48 Inglehart et al., *WVS*, 253.
49 These data refer to Question 51, 53–55. Inglehart et al., *WVS*, 255, 259–261.

50 World Bank, World Development Indicators, "GDP Growth," 2018–2022, at World Development Indicators | DataBank (worldbank.org). "GDP growth" is measured as the annual percentage rate of change in nominal gross domestic product (Constant Prices). GDP for 2022 for Zimbabwe was 3 percent.
51 World Bank, World Development Indicators, "GINI Index," 2018–2022, at World Development Indicators | DataBank (worldbank.org) (accessed July 1, 2024).
52 Inglehart et al., *WVS*, 295, 293, 299.
53 Inglehart et al., *WVS*, 293.
54 Inglehart et al., *WVS*, 295.
55 Inglehart et al., *WVS*, 283, 291.
56 Inglehart et al., *WVS*, 305.
57 Inglehart et al., *WVS*, 643.
58 Inglehart et al., *WVS*, 639.
59 As a general note: political parties do not belong in the category of civil society associations in that they have a stake in the distribution of power in government. Civil society association may influence policymaking in a government, but they do not control the government. Thomas Carothers, "Civil Society," *Foreign Affairs* 117 (Winter 1999–2000); also, Jan Aart Scholte, "Civil Society and Democracy in Global Governance," *Global Governance* 8(3) (2002): 281–304. Inglehart et al., *WVS*, 281, 285, 289, 297.
60 This may have something to do with the fact that 46.7 percent of the persons surveyed felt that television news in Zimbabwe always favors the governing party. Inglehart et al., *WVS*, 633.
61 Inglehart et al., *WVS*, 357–358.
62 IDEA, GSoD, "Absence of Corruption: Zimbabwe." The findings for "Absence of Corruption" for Zimbabwe over this period never got above 30 percent but remained consistently in the 20th percentile.
63 Inglehart et al., *WVS*, 388.
64 Inglehart et al., *WVS*, 399. This institutionalized corruption also applies to elections. Nearly 40 percent of those surveyed believe that bribery is used to influence votes "very to fairly often." Inglehart et al., *WVS*, 635.
65 Inglehart et al., *WVS*, 389, 390–392.
66 Inglehart et al., *WVS*, 560–562.
67 Inglehart et al., *WVS*, 582–586.
68 Inglehart et al., *WVS*, 658.
69 Inglehart et al., *WVS*, 681.
70 Inglehart et al., *WVS*, 267.
71 Inglehart et al., *WVS*, 887.
72 Inglehart et al., *WVS*, 888. What is particularly interesting is the percentage of those who have absolutely no trust in the head of state (27.8 percent) and those who have a great deal of trust (23.4 percent). The split between no trust and trust is evenly divided, except for those in the middle (13.9 percent). Excluding the 13.9 percent, however, more people distrust (43.8 percent) than trust the head of state, Emmerson Mnangagwa (41 percent).
73 Inglehart et al., *WVS*.
74 Claudiu D. Tufis and Alexander Hudson, *The Global State of Democracy Indices, Version 7* (Stockholm, Institute for Democracy and Electoral Assistance, 2023),, 17–18.
75 "Civic Engagement," measures the "extent to which people engage in political and non-political associations, and trade unions." Tufis and Hudson, *Codebook*, 78–79.

76 "Civil society" is a composite index that measures the "extent to which the legal and political context supports civil society organizations" as well as the strength of "interest groups and social capital." Tufis and Hudson, *Codebook*, 78.

77 IDEA data for each of these three measures come from surveys of relevant groups from various sources, including Michael Coppedge, et al., *V-Dem [Country-Year] Dataset v13* (Gothenburg: Varieties of Democracy Project (V-Dem), 2023), <https://doi.org/10.23696/vdemds23> and are collapsed by IDEA from ordinal measures to interval ones. For further information on these three indicators, see Tufis and Hudson, *Codebook*, 189–191.

78 IDEA's "e-participation index" is derived from the United Nations Department of Economic and Social Affairs (2023) and measures access to "e-information, e-consultation, and e-decision-making." Tufis and Hudson, *Codebook*, 192.

79 IDEA's measure of "interest groups" is derived from a survey data from Bertelsmann Stiftung, *Bertelsmann Transformation Index: Towards Democracy and a Market Economy* (Gütersloh: Bertelsmann Stiftung, 2023), and collapsed into an interval score. Tufis and Hudson, *Codebook*, 193.

80 IDEA's measure of "social capital" is also derived from survey data from Bertelsmann Stiftung, *Bertelsmann Transformation Index: Towards Democracy and a Market Economy* (Gütersloh: Bertelsmann Stiftung, 2023) and collapsed into an interval score. Tufis and Hudson, *Codebook*, 194.

81 This chapter did not include an assessment of the independence of Zimbabwe's judicial system or the ability of citizens to access justice. On these two measures, the GSoD indicates that the judiciary has less independence from government control (39 percent independent) and that societal access to justice is fair (averaging at 50 percent).

82 Maurice Taonezvi Vambe, "Zimbabwe: The Fall from a Jewel Status," *Third World Thematics: A TWQ Journal* 8(4–6) (2023): 181–188.

13 The Power of Regional Peripheries

The Making and Unmaking of Legalization of Human Rights in Mali

Miao-ling Lin Hasenkamp

Introduction

This chapter tests this volume's hypothesis about regional stability as a contributor to the legalization of human rights laws prohibiting torture and political violence. This author focuses on Mali against the backdrop of several overlaps between a dysfunctional state and bad governance, increasing ethnic tensions and the spread of jihadists' violence and protection economies including arms and drug trafficking, and climate degradation.

Mali was once portrayed as the darling of Western donors for its democratic institution-building and civil engagement initiatives including security sector reforms, youth activism, and women empowerment programs to promote human rights and good governance.[1] Several coordinated multidimensional and regional peacekeeping missions and military training measures to halt terror and restore regional stability following the 2012 coup of separatist Tuareg and rebel groups in northern Mali were once hailed as setting up a new model of external security interventions. Paradoxically, behind the façade of multiactors' security and development engagements, Mali remains a weak state trapped in the so-called fragility dilemma, and is not only in critical need of external assistance and military support, but has limited absorption capacity to tackle the multilayered challenges found in the security-development-migration-climate nexuses.[2] Its fragile political, socioeconomic, and legal environments mirror the dynamics of a changing process of several competing regional imaginaries in a "wider Sahel region" in connection with its neighboring countries (notably Algeria, Senegal, Nigeria, Burkina Faso, Niger, and Mauritania) and the Lake Chad region, where cross-border practices of various actors and informal institutions have shaped the region's fuzzy political reality.

The evidence is alarming: Mali has experienced three coups within ten years. The current coup leader Assimi Goïta expelled the former interim government in 2021. By 2023, Goïta's unelected transition government also pushed out France, Mali's closest partner and former colonial ruler, and embraced Russia as a new security partner. Despite some backlashes in fighting against jihadists and rebel groups, the junta has solidified its power and

DOI: 10.4324/9781003471677-17

created a climate of suppression through suspending political activities and arresting critics.[3] Observers and civil society actors note shrinking civic spaces, serious rights violations, and impunity practices committed by non-state militant actors (which are tolerated by the Malian transition authorities), rising hostility toward human rights defenders, international institutions, and civil society organizations.[4]

What kind of specific regional structures and trans-local dynamics and rationales, postcolonial, geopolitical, and socioeconomic elements, and borderland interplays have contributed to perpetuating the Sahelian conflicts surrounding the coordination of regional and international counterinsurgency initiatives, on the one hand, and the Malian government's bad governance, the shock of climate insecurity, and the power dynamics among local tribes and transnational Islamic jihadist groups, on the other?

An emerging interdisciplinary literature seeks to grapple with this complex picture by moving beyond the state-centric security and the human rights framework which so often limits its focus to development-induced or norms-guided governance reforms and regime stability and neglects the micro-regional dynamics of conflicts and local needs.[5] Studies have begun to delve into places and relationships between borderlands and political violence where non-state actors are *actively* constructing transnational regions either in opposition or complicity with state actors.[6] However, despite the rich theoretical inputs and insights these studies offer, we nonetheless know little about the ways in which those trans-local dynamics and actors driven by their own security, economic, and cultural imaginaries at the margin of the political maps have affected democracy, participation, human rights, and justice practices. Following the tumultuous events over the past decade that eroded the hegemony of powerful tribe families,[7] questions arise concerning the challenges and opportunities that the politics of the uprising in Mali has generated and how international actors can learn from Mali's experience.

Through a combined interdisciplinary perspective that covers the fringe regionalism, assemblage-thinking/borderwork, and postcolonial geopolitical economic approaches, this study contributes to identifying alternative expressions, flows, and factors articulated and re-framed by state and non-state actors and agencies whose knowledge systems and positions, strategic and tactic policy practices through categorization and pragmatism have paradoxically exacerbated tensions and governance fragility in conflict-hit northern and central Mali.[8]

This chapter contends that the elusive and displacement nature of the human rights legality model in Mali is the byproduct of competing demarcations of a fuzzy region-making process and security practices rooted in states' peripheries and alternative, overlapping sources of legitimacy and identity. This chapter's analysis of two focus cases underscores that the contingency, limitations, disillusion, and potentials of human rights narratives and promotion resulted from the spatial and social dynamics of collaboration, conflict, and rule-manipulation within a highly fluctuating Sahelian imaginary.

The first of these cases highlights the nexuses of anti-terror/climate insecurity, development, migration, drug, and securitization issue-framing. It focuses on local actors' resistance capacities and their fight for survival against the backdrop of the Tuareg's aspiration for independence and political tactics and communal farmer-herder violence. The second case examines the *mis-congruence* tendency of local actors' justice and humanitarian agendas. It explains how the embracement of Islamic-based justice and consultation methods to address local tribes' grievances and humanitarian needs has helped uncover the racialized inequalities of the crisis and the limits and potential of local norms in proceeding human rights legalization practices.

This chapter uses content-based and case study analysis of primary and secondary sources, including interdisciplinary Africa-related critical security, postcolonial economic sources as well as annual country reports issued by Freedom House and the US, among others. First, the accounts offered by the literature are examined and combined to explain the development of cross-border violence and the fuzzy picture of the legalization practices of human rights in Mali. Next, the two cases this chapter examines are introduced with a focus placed on the evolving policy nexuses and local participation, and accountability practices from the perspectives of all actors involved. This chapter concludes with a discussion of the theoretical and policy implications of the changing landscape of security regionalism and its effects upon human rights.

Unpacking Mali as a Fringe Actor in the African Sahel's Borderlands from a Relational and Multilayered Perspective

The outbreak of the Malian crisis in 2012 brought the Sahel region into the international spotlight. Despite the 1964 Organization of African Unity agreement that recognized the principle of intangibility of borders, Africa's borders reveal the legacies and scars of colonialism.[9] Scholars have noted how these borders function, how they have been re-framed and exploited by various actors who have initiated different regional projects driven by their own cultural and spatial imaginaries, interests, and specific interpretations of (in)security. One of the major characteristics in the Sahel region is that the further away from the center and the closer to the periphery and fringes, the more diluted the sovereign's power. Borders are not fixed and well-defined.[10]

For local populations, particularly pastoralist groups in the periphery, the notion of territorial borders or national identity has been absent, as their cross-border movements (transhumance) for trade and exchanges as part of their livelihood have long been acknowledged as a valuable economic activity. Meanwhile, compounded by climate change and the farmer-herder conflicts, the mobilities of groups such as Hausa-Fulani are increasingly viewed as problematic, even potentially dangerous in the context of political concerns associated with overgrazing, water weaponization on the part of farmers, influxes of violent extremism, human trafficking, and "illegal" migration to the European Union (EU). Borders are often perceived as dangerous and volatile, acting as creative interfaces, in which geopolitical/security and sociocultural imaginaries and informal economic networks interact and conflict with each other along a logic of dominance, appropriation and control of the periphery, and the external frontiers.[11]

There exist at least four visible and illegible imaginaries elaborated by four groups of actors in the Sahel. External security providers are the *first* group. They perceive the Sahel as a region constituted by fluctuating boundaries of networks of organized crime and terrorism which pose threats to regional and global security. The West, international organizations, and powers such as China and Russia have been involved in bilateral or multilateral cooperation with different security priorities (see Chapter 7 of this volume). The *second* group consists of regional government elites of the Sahel who prefer to construct a "shadow regionalism" to enhance their own legitimacy and guarantee each regime's survival. Once coming to power, coup leaders might undertake negotiation efforts with trans-local Islamist insurgents to generate their political legitimacy. The regional imaginary of the Islamic jihadist rebels as the *third* group involves the revival of a system of norms and rules based on a projected Sahara-Sahelian Islamic identity inspired by the current "global jihad" narrative and memories of several pre-colonial prosperous Islamic kingdoms (e.g. Songhai Empire of the 15th–17th centuries). As the *fourth* group, local communities aim to pursue the goal of safeguarding a specific system of spatial and sociocultural organization based on transborder and transnational networks and kinships.[12]

The increasingly displacement tendency of human rights legalization in Mali can be traced to the changing dynamics of the fluid micro-region-building process in the broader Sahara-Sahel region initiated and adapted by these four groups. To explain how the concurring regional imaginaries have interacted and played out in shaping this fuzzy picture, this study introduces a relational and multilayered perspective which draws on theoretical insights from regionalism studies, assemblage thinking, postcolonial, and critical political economy studies to build a methodological framework. Such a relational perspective, as noted by Woods et al., permits a closer look at the interrelated patterns of region-making processes whose boundaries become increasingly elusive and illegible.[13]

The concept of "fringe regionalism," as Matthies, Raineri, and Russo note, offers a lens for understanding how diverse micro-regions "have been framed and governed as buffer areas separating distinct regional organizations and regional security areas," thereby prompting the emergence of competing narratives.[14] Our focus is then to look at formal and informal institutions and exchanges in specific physical sites and portals within Mali's borderlands, detect, and then analyze practices which perform connective functions across the Sahel. In so doing, the emergence of new identities and regional narratives connected to the cross-border networks can be approached in a holistic manner. The discursive, normative, and material struggle among these four groups is having obvious effects on security, conflict, the legalization of human rights in Mali and elsewhere, not to mention regional instability. Baldaro proposes the concept of "bifurcated regionalism" to disentangle the different region-building initiatives at work in the area. It follows that the Sahel appears to be condemned to instability as an unintended result of a competing process of *inter*regionalism and insurmountable regional rivalries that have hindered the functioning of effective regional cooperation initiatives.[15]

Secondly, assemblage thinking with its accounts of the exteriority of relations (e.g. EU-Mali arrangements to control Mali's borders), (de)territorialization, coding, borderwork, and multiplicity helps to identify the norms and mechanics through which individual places and borders endure and change in the context of trans-local region-building processes. Assemblage thinking also permits better understanding of how these elements (re)produce political violence and security responses and impact development and human rights legalization practices. The use of "borderwork," for instance, understood as constitutive of sovereignty in the gray zone, involves new forms of bordering practices and unpacks how they overlap and evolve in Mali and in the broader Sahara-Sahel region, where new forms of security governance emerge and are increasingly interwoven with the agendas of development, migration, and climate insecurity issues.[16]

Lastly, adopting the postcolonial center/periphery model and critical political economic views serve as powerful tools to dismantle reified binaries, to reveal the power of the marginal, to question "the claims of any culture to possess a fixed, pure and homogeneous body of values" and to expose them "as historically constructed, and thus corrigible formations."[17] They also address socioeconomic challenges intertwined with the struggle for power and the region's strategic resources (e.g. water, gold, petroleum, and uranium). Several field research results and observations have urged the need to address the root causes of the perpetuating insecurity which are of a social and economic nature.[18]

While the Tuareg problem in the Sahel can be regarded as one of unresolved territorial questions in postcolonial times, cross-border relations, and flows that were established during the colonial period continued to flourish after independence and dominate social, economic, and political life in the Sahara-Sahel region. Notwithstanding the hardening of international boundaries in offering the populations in the borderlands opportunities for trade, migration and financial transactions, the old and new trends of licit and illicit trade patterns and the erosion of state capacity to exert sovereign control of these borderlands have provided a nurturing environment for non-state players to strengthen their capacity of taking control of state policies.[19]

As this zone of fragility expands and the involved non-state actors increase, observers see the emergence and spread of sophisticated protection economies developing along the high-value trafficking routes. These protection economies crowd out legitimate economies in the region. It follows that these actors often profit from an illicit though lucrative trade based on price differentials and currency fluctuations. As protection becomes a commodity, those involved are enriched by illicit trafficking and can engage with state institutions at different levels in accumulating resources, controlling, and/or protecting regional illicit flows. Consequently, these groups have little incentive to support the consolidation of good governance or state control.[20] As the trafficking of illicit goods traverses the Sahara, including the Sahel region, local tribes and communities are forced either to take sides with competing fractions of insurgents and traffickers for survival or to mobilize themselves for resistance through self-defense militarization.[21] Moreover, state officials easily get involved in this lucrative protection economy, leaving room for the involved rebel groups and traffickers to augment their power in spite of state actors' knee-jerk response to strengthen law enforcement mechanisms.

Supported by this methodological framework, the following section highlights how the legalization practices of human rights in Mali have been disrupted because of the insecure environments found in the new forms of micro-regional security governance interwoven with the extremist and criminal networks and corrupt state behavior.

Human Rights Legalization Practices between Rule-Making and -Unmaking in the Mali-Sahel Periphery: Actors, Politics, and Adaptation

Though the familiar labeling of "ungoverned space" in the Mali-Sahel periphery remains popular in policy circles, academic debates and policy discussions have gradually been aware of the overlapping and competing micro-regional networks of informal governance and the changing patterns of interactions among the big players driven by their different regional projects.[22]

According to the Fragile States Index 2023, major Sahelian countries (notably Chad, Mali, Niger, and Nigeria) are among the top 20 most fragile states in the world.[23] They all share an inability to successfully handle security threats, high degrees of fragmentation of state institutions along ethnic lines, continuing economic decline, weak state legitimacy, and bad governance complete with violations of civil, political, and social rights. However, behind the dominant "violent borderlands" discourse and statements such as "the Mali-Sahel periphery is a 'lawless zone'" and "Mali is a failed state" exists a complex system involving trans-local dynamics of security governance interwoven in global political economy, policy-nexuses with development, migration, and climate variability, and interactions among various actors to tackle justice issues and to carve out adaptative livelihood strategies.

Evolving Policy-Nexuses between Security, (Livelihood) Development, Migration, and Climate Change: Shifts and Discontinuity

The priority of external security providers in the Mali-Sahelian periphery has been to offer military assistance for combatting regional instability, stopping northbound illegal migration, and reducing terrorist threats. Following the refugee crises between 2014 and 2016, the EU, for example, spent more than one billion Euro for military assistance to support the Sahelian states to stop migration flows through Niger or Mali as transit zones to Europe. However, this is not a main priority for local inhabitants. Besides extremist violence, they have been suffering from a serious downturn of local migration-related economies including smuggling-related and accommodation business in transit cities such as Agadez in Niger. Local tribal communities also increasingly confront precarious livelihood situations as consequences of global climate change. The past experiences toward the end of the 1990s showed that frustrated Tuaregs can quickly become militant, although such a tendency contrasts with the Tuareg's traditional tolerance culture.[24] Regional observers and experts suggested adopting a balanced approach to addressing the complex security-migration-development nexus to not only tackle the precarious insecurity situation in the region through an effective functional regional arrangement, but also enhance state capacity to incorporate human security principles into its development agenda by including education, infrastructural development, and healthcare as the keys to reducing non-military and violent threats that affect the well-being of individuals and communities.[25]

The G5 Sahel was created in 2014; its goal being to strengthen regional cooperation on security and development. Supported by France, Germany, and the EU, this regional body was supposed to elaborate common projects focused on infrastructure, food security, agriculture, pastoralism, and physical security. Several commentators suggest that, if molded in the interests of a development agenda, the G5 Sahel together with its Joint Force could mark a shift in the security geography in Africa and bring about positive changes to the disadvantages of extant regional bodies such as African Union (AU) and the Economic Community of West African States (ECOWAS).[26]

The G5 Sahel initiative has been criticized as "yet another excuse to get more 'boots on the ground',"[27] transforming security regionalism in West Africa through "spatialisation of security and securitization of space,"[28] and overriding rational forum shopping logic and leaving traditional partners behind, which are embedded in the African Peace and Security Architecture.[29] The G5 has very little to offer for Africa's development problems, not to mention Africa's human rights and justice issues in the peripheries.[30]

Rising anti-Western hostility in the region has hindered state-level development cooperation talks, leaving room for junta leaders in the Sahelian states to combat extremism themselves and to clear the migration routes free in cooperation with Russia.[31] Russia and China are not newcomers in the region. They have been involved in the industrialization process of the Sahelian states since the 1950s and 1960s.[32] Today Moscow provides security solutions to fragile states without political strings attached, making Russia a preferred security partner. However, Moscow's opportunistic use of private military diplomacy has exposed the limitations of these partnerships in addressing the peace and development challenges African host countries face.[33] Moreover, countries tied to Russia, especially those with ties of a security nature, must confront diplomatic risks of potential political deadlock and economic strife against the backdrop of the intense geopolitical tensions between Russia and its Western counterparts.[34]

Regional national governments have adapted to this new environment of security governance with and without Western support. Despite extant unequal power relationships, the EU-Malian bilateral agreement granted the Malian state actors agency to subtly negotiate and resist European technologies and rationalities of border externalization, thereby enacting new forms of sovereignty.[35] Following its 2020 coup Mali's ruling military optimized its political position, diversifying and expanding strategic partnerships. Shortly after Mali's second coup in June 2021, France threatened to pull out its 5,100 troops if the coup leaders made a deal with the same Islamist insurgents the troops are fighting.[36] As of 2023, the junta's rupture with France was greeted by most of the Malian population with enthusiasm, particularly young people who consider France responsible for propping up corrupt elites for decades.[37]

With Russia's enhanced support, Mali's military junta took an authoritarian turn, domestically and regionally. Under the banner of maintaining public order, it imposed an infinite ban in April 2024 on political parties and associations. These measures indicate that Malian authorities have no interest in a transition to civilian rule. Together with Burkina Faso and Niger, Mali left the ECOWAS and launched a new mutual defense agreement, the Alliance of Sahel States (AES) in September 2023. In so doing, the junta leaders of all three countries freed themselves from their obligation to hold elections in full cooperation with ECOWAS.

The three countries present a vision of integration within a confederation framework in the AES' grounding *Liptako-Gourma Charter*, which is markedly different from their early cooperation schemes involving mutual aid. For the region's observers, such a confederation project could bring the three countries together in an institutional framework that would enable the pooling of resources, facilitate a common perception, and accelerate the march toward a potential or eventual union. Nonetheless, concerns over the political and legal ramifications of this arrangement immediately arose. The current regimes of these states are the product of military coups d'état. They may or may not be legally able to take measures to alter the political status of their regimes. AES further confronts unfavorable internal and external factors ranging from the lack of domestic support of the different communities, weak institutions, weak economies, and foreign interference, to terrorist threats posed by diverse terrorist and insurgent groups including Boko Haram, the *Groupe de Soutien à l'Islam et aux Musulmans* (JNIM), and the Islamic State in the Greater Sahara (ISGS).[38]

As the third layer of security assemblage, Islamic jihadist and rebel groups, notably ISGS and JNIM, have demonstrated their resistance capacity through several cooperation, re-alliance and coordinated actions, posing significant security and financial risks not only to the US and Europe, but also to government forces and civilians in the Sahel-Sahara. Violence and attacks linked to these groups have surged nearly sevenfold since 2017.[39] Compounded by environmental degradation and transnational organized crime, the continuing collapse of international counterterrorism support, and weakening leadership in regional cooperation and fragile state structures have created a vacuum in which violent extremism and armed militancy can expand.[40]

ISGS has maintained a foothold in the region since 2015. Its former movement, namely, the Movement for Oneness and Jihad in West Africa (MUJAO) was a splinter group of *al-Qa'ida* in the Islamic Maghreb (AQIM). For a time, a special relationship between ISGS and JNIM existed. JNIM is the converging result of several AQIM's franchises including its Sahara wing, *Al-Mourabitoun*, *Ansar Dine*, and *Katiba Macina*. These sub-groups are directly or indirectly involved in transnational organized crime networks by way of their providing access to well-established smuggling operations across the regions and taxing the routes that drug traffickers rely on to move their products.[41] As observed by regional experts, the composition of JNIM is noteworthy, as its leaders represent Tuareg, Fulanic, and Arab jihadists from the Sahel and Maghreb. This breadth of ethnic and geographic representation awakened the impression that they can build a united front with expanding influence. However, each fraction within JNIM has its own shifting interests, territorial influence, and motivations.[42] Notwithstanding intra-group diverging interests between JNIM and ISGS and despite the early defection and public disagreements over who joined the Islamic State, this did not hinder the local wings of two global jihadi movements from communicating or even cooperating on the ground in the Sahel.

The historical ties between local clans and tribes facilitated crossovers of personnel and coordinated actions and allowed for a great ease in cooperation by transcending the group labels. For instance, an important JNIM commander, Almansour Ag Alkassoum, who acted as JNIM's *emir* in the Gourma region, played a role in arranging an important meeting with ISGS regarding ISGS' excessive civilian-targeted violence against Imghad Tuareg and Dawsahak communities amid the jihadi groups' conflict with two pro-government Tuareg militias.[43] Besides the amicable personal relations among factions' leaders, ISGS and JNIM commonly undertook several attacks in the areas of In-Delimane in northern Mali and in central Mali between 2017 and 2019, although neither group claimed responsibility. In several other attacks, both groups claimed responsibility signifying their ambition to expand their extremist ideology and working toward the greater cause of establishing an Islamic State.[44]

By 2019 the relationship between JNIM and ISGS began to erode. An internal ISGS weekly *Al Naba* newsletter in May 2020 officially acknowledged violent clashes between JNIM and ISGS. Since then, these conflicts intensified in central and northern Mali and in the borderlands between Mali and Burkina Faso and along the Burkina Faso-Niger border region. To Nsaibia and Weiss, two major factors were responsible for the growing tensions between the two groups. The first was a deep-seated ideological difference between JNIM and ISGS with regard to the implementation of *Shari'a* law.[45] Secondly, the JNIM/ISGS clashes resulted from the restructuring efforts of the Islamic State, as ISGS became more integrated into the Islamic State's overall structure as part of its West Africa Province. ISGS field commanders and the Islamic State's spokesman complained about JNIM's purported willingness to negotiate with the Malian government and about *al-Qa'ida*'s killings of the Islamic State's men while working together with the Malian government in May 2020. Later, the Islamic State called JNIM "guard dogs" for Algeria and accused the group of working with "nationalist and secular groups."[46]

The meta-narratives, logics, and actions undertaken by militant Islamic groups have revealed how micro- and cross-border regionalism functions. For ISGS and JNIM, the border itself is largely meaningless. Their expressions have more to do with reach and expansion than with size and scale. They also relate to material accumulation, cognitive and historical spaces rather than to a clearly demarcated territorial span.[47] Regardless of their internal divergence and conflicts, ISGS and JNIM have made Salafism the fastest growing strand of Islam in Africa through exploiting distinct historical narratives and theological justifications to legitimize their jihads and to expand land where the *Sharī'a* law as part of Islamic jurisprudence can reign.[48]

Finally, local communities in the peripheries (as the fourth layer of security assemblage) suffer from multiple threats and risks posed by Islamic extremists' and other armed groups' attacks, the Malian government's actions supported by external security providers, and varied forms of socioeconomic and climate insecurities. A BBC source shows that one year after the 2015 peace agreement between the Malian government and a coalition of mainly ethnic Tuareg armed groups from northern Mali, the number of deaths caused by armed violence surged between 2016 and 2019.[49] Since the 2013 external intervention in Mali, the situation has deteriorated, with many young Malians joining extremist groups because of a failure of peacekeeping efforts to address the conflict's root causes.[50]

Moreover, Malian security forces have been involved in egregious human rights violations, including extrajudicial killings, tortures, and arrests based on ethnicity. Tuaregs, easily identifiable by their lighter skin, faced harsh conditions under *Shari'a* law between April 2012 and January 2013 during the occupation by Islamic jihadists allied with Tuareg separatists. Despite this, many Tuaregs now reject living under the Malian army and tribal militias like Ganda Koy, whose discriminatory practices have reignited their push for independence. Additionally, there is growing dissatisfaction among Tuaregs with their own leaders, who have enriched themselves instead of serving their people. For local activists like Fatimata Walet Oumar, a priority for the Tuareg people is education for the poorest children to challenge the dominance of powerful Tuareg families.[51]

Local communities are calling for stronger, coordinated leadership between central and local authorities to facilitate meaningful mediation processes. Several local initiatives have emerged to support dialogue and reconciliation efforts in particular communities. However, as field analysis shows, the leaders behind these initiatives have been instrumentalized and are not necessarily the right individuals for the role. In such a volatile environment, opportunities for mediation and dialogue can quickly collapse into deadlock, deepening the conflict and divisions among communities.

Many ethnic groups in the peripheries increasingly face climate-induced security issues, such as farmer-herder violence and the weaponization of water. Islamic water law, derived from the concept of *Shari'a* as "the watering source," states that water, pasture, and fire are *res communes* (common resources). It emphasizes the universal right of humans and their animals to quench their thirst (*shafa*) and the right of irrigation (*shirb*), ensuring all users can water their crops.[52] At the same time and given global climate change, such issues of allocation and precedence of use can no longer be guaranteed. According to the EU's Normandy Index 2021,[53] the Sahel 5 are more likely to feel the effects of climate change, terrorism, and violent conflict than their sub-Saharan African counterparts. As the Sahel region becomes more arid, the volume of water available for grazing declines and the migration of herdsmen, normally belonging to Hausa-Fulani, has come to encroach on farming communities. Hausa-Fulani are attempting to stay longer on the land which challenges the inheritance rights of indigene farmers favored by national and state governments' laws. Reports of sabotage, such as farmers poisoning wells to kill Hausa-Fulani cattle as revenge for encroachment, reveal how the use of water coupled by unjust governmental policies can cause the widespread resentment needed to motivate an escalation to violent and often deadly clashes among farmers and herders.[54] Such local farmer-herdsmen conflict may even become more complex in the context of the Malian army's counterinsurgency measures. As the Malian army has failed to defeat a "jihadist" insurgency dominated by Fulani, it has sponsored and trained an indigene Dogon militia to attack systematically Fulani villages, thereby causing further counterattacks.[55]

The concurring regional imaginaries and complex interactions among the involved actor groups along the security-development and migration-climate insecurity-nexuses demonstrate how the micro-regional dynamics of conflicts and the lack of appropriately addressing local needs and climate-induced insecurity have reinforced the displacement tendency of the legalization practices of human rights by the governments of the Sahelian region more broadly and Mali more specifically. The examination of the multidimensional key issues driving instability in the Sahel underscores the necessity to adopt an interdisciplinary frame that includes the ecological and political economy of danger in which the dialectic of actors, land, and global politics, the heterogeneity of the interests involved, and the ensuing discursive struggles over the definition of threats linking to the mobilization of resources for establishing security mechanisms can be highlighted in a more systematic manner.[56]

Meanwhile, along these different layers of security assemblage, two anecdotes involving justice and humanitarian work might shed some new light on how the Malian crisis and the power of the peripheries driven by non-state actors including transnational humanitarian workers can be explained from a bottom-up perspective.

Pursuing Justice between Cultural Re-imagination, Displacement, and Mis-congruence Practices

Under the banner of the Global War on Terror, the West's focus on counterinsurgency measures and pragmatic alliance and negotiation politics as seen in the West's ransom payments to the terrorist groups to free its hostages and the EU's training support offered to the Sahel 5, for example, have failed to adequately pay attention to regional political rivalries (notably between Algeria and Morocco), local grievances, and needs. Diverse fractions of jihadist groups were offered new playing grounds to accommodate competing localized interests and to recruit frustrated youth. Commentators note how the major Islamic jihadist rebels, despite their traditional discriminatory narratives against each other, have strengthened their resistance and survival capacity through the appropriation of the history of pre-colonial jihad as well as the attempt to assimilate local conflicts moving toward the cause of global jihadism. Some have turned out to be successful game changers as they have supported social and humanitarian projects and introduced justice and consultation mechanisms to address local grievances, crimes, and tribes' disputes.[57] At the same time, questions arise over the strict imposition of *Shari'a* laws introduced by these jihadist groups which apparently violate the rule of law and personal integrity rights as defined by the international human rights regime. The following two vignettes illustrate how human rights legalization practices have been displaced and reframed through the imposition of *Shari'a* and the attempt to free Malians from French colonial legacy in a way that strays from the *congruence* principles detailed throughout this volume. Specifically, the author of this chapter suggests that this deviation should be framed as "mis-congruence," in that it is an alternative to the Fullerian concept of *congruence* that focuses on the relationship between government and the governed.

Despite the failure of the 2012 attempt to install Islamic jurisprudence in an independent state of Azawad, many local communities turned their support to Islamic groups who could provide the judicial, health, and security services the Malian authorities have failed to deliver. Tronc, Grace and Nahakian explain how jihadists have exploited the excesses of law-enforcement officials by offering an alternative of justice, education, the management of natural resources and public goods to communities. Such offers have attracted a significant segment of the population, especially members of the most deprived communities, notably the Peul/Fulani communities.[58] Following the jurists' reasoning of the *Sunna*, God will punish people if they see injustice and do not act to correct it. It is this consensus that the Islamic *umma* in its entire history agreed upon the duty of commanding good and forbidding evil based on the *Shari'a* and of human reason.[59]

Various studies have detected factors that have driven Malians to join or support radical Islamist movements. Besides ideology, concerns about economic and physical security amid deteriorating governance situations have pushed local communities to choose sides to defend their livelihood. The powerful influence of Salafist ideology in Malian society might have efficiently tackled some urgent injustices and crime issues, as observed by a youth activism field worker.[60] However, the proliferation of conservative Islam with its emphasis upon *Quranic* teaching and indoctrination has brought dangers by exerting pressure upon, for example, access to education and the *type* of education that is offered. This led to the closure of hundreds of schools across the central and northern parts in Mali.[61]

The second anecdote involves the release of Sophie Pétronin, the last French hostage detained overseas in the fall of 2020. The 75-year-old humanitarian worker was captured by insurgents in northern Mali four years prior. The terms of the hostage exchange, Pétronin's religious conversion, her rejection to condemn her captors, and particularly her clandestine return back to Mali to continue her work sparked broad media criticism and a wave of outrage and disapproval in French social media. Observers see the Pétronin case as calling into the question "the boundary between self and other," exposing the contra-productive narratives about the nature of "terrorists" and offering a counterpoint to the masculinization of the conflict.[62] It exposed the uncomfortable situations and risks many humanitarian workers confront in their daily work in the peripheries in Mali. Humanitarian workers have been often criticized for "being blind to the political impacts of their activities, leading local resentment toward them to build."[63]

The failure to empower local actors and integrate local communities into project development processes further prompts a sense of resignation and learned helplessness in local communities.[64] The complex figure in the Pétronin case not only brings attention to the masculinized necropolitics of the Sahelian conflict, in which the exercise of the sovereign power has the capacity to decide "who is able to live and who must die."[65] It also demonstrates that, as long as these disconnects exist between the external limited peacebuilding and development actions, on the one hand, and a lack of trust and communication between non-state armed groups, local communities, and the Malian government, on the other, the ability of transnational humanitarian workers to work even in territory controlled by non-state armed groups might stop short of guaranteeing their endeavor to support the needy in a fragile insecure environment.

Conclusions

This chapter sets out to highlight the displacement tendency of human rights legalization in Mali which can be traced back to the changing dynamics of the fluid micro-region-building process in the Sahel-Sahara initiated and adapted by four actor groups moving along different layers of security assemblage at different levels. The results of both case analyses show the power of local actors in the peripheries in making and unmaking human rights rules found in the contingencies, limitations, disillusion, and potentials of mis-congruence practices vis-à-vis international norms. They also enhance our understanding of the interplay of micro-regional dynamics between external interventions, power struggles, crime and coping, and resistance, which in turn is a first step toward creating more sophisticated analytic tools to elaborate proper policy approaches.[66]

Several points are worth mentioning here in terms of future methodological and policy developments. First, this study demonstrates the necessity of contextualizing the puzzle surrounding the Malian crisis through an interdisciplinary prism which can facilitate adopting a holistic systemic approach to addressing the concurring regional imaginaries and the multiple security challenges in the Sahel-Sahara region.[67] Second, the *mis-congruence* practices found in the justice, social, and educational actions pushed forward by the Islamic jihadist groups as part of the proliferation of the Salafist agenda might have efficiently addressed local grievances and needs in a volatile and insecure environment were it not for their authoritarian and exclusionist applications. Moreover, in view of the lack of trust and communication among the key actors in the region, competent visionary political and religious leaders are needed to undertake critical intra-cultural dialogues and legal debates, so that an appropriate water governance following the Islamic water law, for example, can be installed to tackle decade-long disputes and conflicts among herders' and indigene farmers' communities.

Finally, there are several lessons the West can draw from its past security and development interventions. More attention should be paid, first and foremost, to providing know-how knowledge and support for the delivery of public services, infrastructure investment, and governance reforms. In so doing, the youth in Mali as well as in the Sahel region might be able to construct their own future with alternative regional projects which are sustainable and culturally appropriate. Most importantly, local actors should not have to look to other entities to obtain conditions of social order and rule of law. At the end of the day, it is the responsibility of the state to promote and protect human rights by allowing for an open and fair political process and public input. Humanitarian missions must consider the situation in Mali as part of a broader struggle not only against Islamic extremism but also the conditions of structural violence that pervade these countries.

Notes

1 Information retrieved from a discussion forum "The Sahel Summit," organized by the Center for Strategic and International Studies in Sept. 2019.
2 Kari M. Osland and Henriette U. Erstad, "The Fragility Dilemma and Divergent Security Complexes in the Sahel," *The International Spectator* 55(4) (2020): 18–36, DOI:10.1080/03932729.2020.1833474.

3 See African Digital Democracy Observatory (ADDO), "Mali's Junta Solidifies Power by Suspending Political Activities" (April 11, 2024) at <https://disinfo.africa/malis-military-junta-solidifies-power-by-suspending-political-activities-0bd3400f3f3f. Andy Morgan. "Mali's Tuareg People Retain Dream of Independence Amid Persecution", *The Guardian* (April 3, 2013), <https://www.theguardian.com/world/2013/apr/03/mali-tuareg-independence-persecution>. Both accessed August 1, 2024.

4 Marked by the UN independent expert Alioune Tine in his 2022 yearly report on Mali. See also ADDO, "Mali's Junta."

5 Steven M. Radil, Ian Irmischer, and Olivier J. Walther, "Contextualizing the Relationship Between Borderlands and Political Violence: A Dynamic Space-Time Analysis in North and West Africa," *Journal of Borderlands Studies* 37(2) (2022): 253–271.

6 Daniel Bach, "Beyond Parochialism: Cross-Border Regionalism As A Gateway," *Afro-Regions: The Dynamics of Cross-Border Micro-Regionalism in Africa* (2008): 171–180; Mark Shaw, Tuesday Reitano, and Sahara Knowledge Exchange, "The Political Economy Of Trafficking And Trade In The Sahara: Instability and Opportunities," *Sahara Knowledge Exchange Paper* (Washington, DC, World Bank, 2014); Jean-Pierre Cassarino, "Approaching Borders And Frontiers in North Africa," *International Affairs* 93(4) (2017): 883–896; Frank Mattheis, Luca Raineri, and Alessandra Russo, *Fringe Regionalism: When Peripheries Become Regions* (New York: Springer, 2018); Edoardo Baldaro and Elisa Lopez Lucia, "Spaces of (In-) Security And Intervention: Spatial Competition And The Politics Of Regional Organizations In The Sahel," *Territory, Politics, Governance* (2022): 1–19; Emily McGiffin, "Conflicted Colonialisms: Multi-Dimensional Violence in the Western Sahel," *Third World Thematics: A TWQ Journal*, 6(4–6) (2021): 320–336; Bruno Charbonneau, "The Climate of Counterinsurgency and the Future of Security in the Sahel," *Environmental Science & Policy* 138 (2022): 97–104; Radil et al., "Contextualizing."

7 Morgan, "Mali's."

8 Elisa Lopez-Lucia, "A Tale of Regional Transformation: From Political Community to Security Regions The Politics Of Security And Regionalism in West Africa," *Political Geography* 82 (2020): 102256; Mattheis et al. *Fringe*.

9 AU, BORDER DISPUTES AMONG AFRICAN STATES (AHG/Res. 16(I) at www.peaceau.org (accessed September 15, 2024).

10 Abdelhak Bassou, "State, Borders and Territory in the Sahel: The Case of the G5 Sahel" (Morocco: Policy Center for the New South, October 6, 2017).

11 Michel Foucher, "African Borders: Putting Paid to a Myth," *Journal of Borderlands Studies* 35(2) (2020): 287–306; Stefan Ouma, *Assembling Export Markets: The Making and Unmaking of Global Food Connections in West Africa* (Hoboken, NJ: Wiley-Blackwell, 2015).

12 For more details about the interrelated regional imaginaries and the development of less institutionalized security arrangements, see Edoardo Baldaro, "The Sahel as an Unintended Region: Competing Regionalisms and Insecurity Dynamics," *The Unintended Consequences of Interregionalism* (Milton Park, Abingdon, UK: Routledge, 2020), 147–164. Critiques of the pitfalls and inadequacy of the West's "fragile state" and "ungoverned spaces" discourses as well as the perceived rivalry and threat posed by the presence of emerging powers in Africa include A.J. Ayers, "Beyond Myths, Lies and Stereotypes: The Political Economy of a 'New Scramble for Africa'," *New Political Economy* 18(2) (2012): 227–257. https://doi.org/10.1080/13563467.2012.678821; Cassarino, "Approaching."

13 Michael Woods, Francesca Fois, Jessee Heley, Laura Jones, Anthonia Onyeahialam, Samantha Saville, and Marc Welsh, "Assemblage, Place and Globalisation,"

Transactions of the Institute of British Geographers (46) (2021): 284–298. *DOI: 10.1111/tran.12430.*
14 Matthies, Raineri, and Russo, *Fringe.*
15 Baldaro, "The Sahel" and Baldaro "Rashomon in the Sahel: Conflict Dynamics Of Security Regionalism," *Security Dialogue* 52(3) (2021): 266–283; also Wolfram Lacher, "The Malian Crisis And The Challenge Of Regional Security Cooperation," *Stability: International Journal of Security & Development*, 2(2): (2013): 1–5, DOI: http://dx.doi.org/10.5334/sta.bg.
16 Philippe Mamadou Frowd, "Borderwork Assemblages And The Security-Development Nexus in Senegal and Mauritania," (2012), at Microsoft Word - Frowd - ABORNE paper.docx (squarespace.com) (accessed August 1, 2024); Ida Marie Savio Vammen, Signe Cold-Ravnkilde, Hans Lucht (eds.) *The Long Shadow of the Border* (London/NY: Routledge, 2023).
17 Bill Ashcroft, Gareth Griffiths, and Helen Tiffin, *Post-Colonial Studies. The Key Concepts* (London and NY: Routledge, 2000), 37.
18 Adeyemi Saheed Badewa, "Regional Security Complex: The Boko Haram Menace and Socio-Economic Development Crises in the Sahel," *Conflict, Security & Development*, 22(4) (2022): 321–343, DOI: 10.1080/14678802.2022.2120256; Wolfram Lacher, "Actually Existing Security: The Political Economy of the Saharan Threat." *Security Dialogue*, 39 (4) (2008): 383–405.
19 Bach, "Beyond"; J. Andrew Grant, "Informal Cross-Border Micro-Regionalism in West Africa: The Case of the Parrot's Beak," *Afro-Regions: The Dynamics of Cross-Border Micro-Regionalism in Africa* (2008): 105–120.
20 Shaw et al. "The Political Economy."
21 Java Discover, *Terrorism in the Sahel: The Jihadists of Northern Africa.* Investigative Documentary https://www.youtube.com/watch?v=Cu9PqrnXY0M (2023) (accessed June 28, 2024). Java Discover, *Mali's Jihad Crisis: The Looming Threat of Terror.* (2022) African Politics Documentary. https://www.youtube.com/watch?v=ORI8Gl9he44 (retrieved on June 25, 2024).
22 Morten Bøås, "Crime, Coping, and Resistance in the Mali-Sahel Periphery," *African Security*, 8 (4) (2015): 299–319, DOI: 10.1080/19392206.2015.1100506; Wolfram Lacher, "The Malian Crisis and The Challenge of Regional Security Cooperation," *Stability: International Journal of Security & Development*, 2(2) (2013): 1–5, DOI: http://dx.doi.org/10.5334/sta.bg.
23 Fund for Peace, "Fragile States Index, 2023," at Fragile States Index Heat Map | Fragile States Index (accessed September 15, 2024).
24 See Munzinger, "We Clear."
25 Norman Sempijja and Ekeminiabasi Eyita-Okon, "Examining the Effectiveness of The EU Security-Development Strategy in Tackling Instability in the Sahel: The Case for an Alternative Strategy?" *South African Journal of International Affairs*, 29 (2) (2022): 139–160; Morten Bøås, *Rival Priorities in the Sahel – Finding the Balance between Security and Development.* Policy Note No. 3 (2018).
26 Martin Welz, "Institutional Choice, Risk, and Control: The G5 Sahel and Conflict Management in the Sahel," *International Peacekeeping*, 29 (2) (2022): 235–257, at 236. DOI: 10.1080/13533312.2022.2031993; Bøås, *Rival.*
27 Bøås, *Rival.*
28 Lopez-Lucia, "A Tale,"
29 Friedrich Plank, "Interregional Forum Shopping in Africa–EU Relations: Regional Groups and The Evolving Security-Development-Migration Nexus," *South African Journal of International Affairs*, 29(3) (2022): 271–293.
30 Stephen Osaherumwen Idahosa, Denis Andreevich Degterev and Solomon Ijeweimen Ikhidero, "Securitisation Initiatives and The Lingering Security Challenges In Sub-Saharan Sahel Region: An Appraisal," *African Security Review* 30(3) (2021): 338–367, DOI:10.1080/10246029.2021.1970597.

31 Upon the invitation of the German government, a Sahel Alliance summit took place in July 2024 in Berlin without the governmental representatives of the three major Sahelian states: Mali, Burkina Faso, and Niger. The major donor countries and key development cooperation institutions discussed the possibilities of promoting development work at the grass-root level as a solidarity humanitarian action and compensation for the West's unfulfilled mission during the past decade. See Westdeutscher Rundfunk (WDR), Köln. "Sahel Zone: Democracy only in the Paper Form" (July 16, 2024).

32 Commented by Olaf Bernau, a German observer in the Sahel region. See also Issac Mugabi, "Russia Vows to Boost Military Cooperation with Mali," *Deutsche Welle (DW)* (August 2, 2023). https://www.dw.com/en/russia-vows-to-boost-military-cooperation-with-mali/a-64639926 (accessed July 15, 2024).

33 Ovigwe Eguegu, "Russia's Private Military Diplomacy in Africa: High risk, Low Reward, Limited Impact." *South African Journal of International Affairs*, 29(4) (2022): 445–462, DOI: 10.1080/10220461.2022.2142276.

34 Eguegu, *Russia's*."

35 Signe Marie Cold-Ravnkilde, "Borderwork in the grey zone: Everyday resistance within European border control initiatives in Mali." In Ida Marie Savio Vammen, Signe Cold-Ravnkilde, Hans Lucht (eds.) *The Long Shadow of the Border*. 134–153 (London/NY: Routledge, 2023), 2.

36 Frank Gardner, "West Africa's Islamist Insurgency: Fight at a Critical State," *BBC news* (June 4, 2021), at West Africa's Islamist insurgency: Fight at a critical stage (bbc.com) (accessed Aug. 25, 2024).

37 Arne Perras, "They Pretend to be Robin Hood Camouflage," *SZ* (Aug. 31, 2023), at 2. Heiner Hoffmann. "Finally Out of France's Shadow." *Der Spiegel*, Project Global Society (March 7, 2024), at https://www.spiegel.de/ausland/sahelzone-warum-sich-afrikanische-staaten-vom-westen-abwenden-a-aa4bb1c7-bee1-44f8-889a-5900648fc38b (accessed Mar 24, 2024).

38 Abdelhak Bassou, "From the Alliance of Sahel States to the Confederation of Sahel States: The Road is Clear, But Full of Traps," *Policy Center for the New South*. April 24, 2024 (accessed August 25, 2024).

39 Daniel Eizenga and Wendy Williams, "The Puzzle of JNIM and Militant Islamist Groups in the Sahel," *Africa Security Brief*, No. 38 (December 2020).

40 Sempijja and Eyita-Okon 2022; Eizenga and Williams, "The Puzzle."

41 Eizenga and Williams, "The Puzzle," 3–4.

42 Eizenga and Williams, "The Puzzle," 2.

43 Heni Nsaibia and Caleb Weiss, "The End of the Sahelain Anomaly: How the Global Conflict between the Islamic State and al-Qa'ida Finally Came to West Africa,“ *CTCSentinel*, 13(7) (July 2020).

44 Nsaibia and Caleb Weiss, "The End."

45 Nsaibia and Caleb Weiss, "The End"; also Abdulbasit Kassim and Jacob Zenn, "Justifying War: The Salafi-Jihadi Appropriation of Sufi Jihad in the Sahel-Sahara." *Current Trends in Islamist Ideology* 21 (2017): 86–114.

46 Nsaibia and Weiss, "The End."

47 Bach, "Beyond,“ 171–172.

48 Kassim and Zenn, "Justifying,“ 106.

49 The number of deaths from armed violence in Mali in this period rose to more than 1,500. Acleddata.com, cited in Louise Dewast, "How West Africa is Under Threat from Islamist Militants.“ *BBC* (Jan. 13, 2020) at <How West Africa is under threat from Islamist militants (bbc.com)> (accessed Aug. 26, 2024).

50 Paul Munzinger, "Young, Unemployed, and Angry.“ *SZ* (July 12, 2024), 7. Information acquired also through a short interview in August 2024 with a young woman from Ivory Coast who has received her training as a care worker in Germany. Her brother might plan to come to Germany due to a lack of prospects at home.

51 Cited in Morgan, "Mali's."
52 Franscesca De Chatel, "Drops of Faith: Water in Islam." *Water Resources IMPACT* 11(6) (2009): 5.
53 The Normandy Index adopts an approach tailored by and to the EU action. One of its innovative components is to blend geopolitical indicators with socioeconomic data. European Parliament, Normandy Index, 2021. https://www.europarl.europa.eu/thinktank/infographics/peaceandsecurity/#/normandy-index (accessed July 29, 2024).
54 Marcus D. King, *Weaponizing Water. Water Stress & Islamic Extremist Violence in Africa & the Middle East* (Boulder/London: Lynne Rienner, 2023), 139–140.
55 A. Benjaminsen and Boubacar Ba "Fulani-Dogon Killings in Mali: Farmer-Herder Conflicts as Insurgency and Counterinsurgency," *African Security*, 14(1) (2021): 4–26.
56 See Lipschutz 1999, cited in Lacher, "Actually Existing."
57 See Kassim and Zenn, "Justifying"; McGiffin, "Conflicted."
58 Emmanuel Tronc, Rob Grace, and Anaïde Nahikian, "Realities and Myths of the 'Triple Nexus': Local Perspectives on Peacebuilding, Development, and Humanitarian Action in Mali," *Humanitarian Action at the Frontlines: Field Analysis Series* (2019): 11.
59 Rached Ghannouchi, *Public Freedoms in the Islamic State. Al-Hurriyyat al-'Amma fi-l-Dawla al-Islamiyya.* Translated by David L. Johnston (New Haven& London: Yale Univ. Press, 2022), 232–233.
60 Information retrieved from a discussion forum "The Sahel Summit," *supra* note 1.
61 See Tronc, Grace, and Nahikian, "Realities," xxiv–xxv.
62 See McGiffin, "Conflicted," 321–322.
63 See Tronc, Grace, and Nahikian, "Realities."
64 Tronc, Grace, and Nahikian, "Realities," 23–24.
65 Mbembe 2019, at 66, cited in McGiffin "Conflicted," 322.
66 Radil et al. "Contextualising"; Bøås, "Crime, Coping," 300 and Bøås, *Rival*; Ayers, *Beyond Myths*.
67 Stephen Osaherumwen Idahosa, Denis Andreevich Degterev, and Solomon Ijeweimen Ikhidero, "Securitisation Initiatives and the Lingering Security Challenges in Sub-Saharan Sahel Region: An Appraisal," *African Security Review* 30(3) (2021): 338–67. doi:10.1080/10246029.2021.1970597.

14 Human Rights as a Moving Target in Botswana

Kholisani Solo

Introduction

Botswana prides itself as being a beacon of democracy that upholds the tenets of good governance, respect for rule of law, and judicial independence. Since independence in 1966, Botswana has held regular, free, and fair elections. Botswana continues to thrive economically from the diamond, beef, and tourism industries. However, a puzzle exists. There are mounting concerns about political intolerance, the official use of torture, and intrusions into press freedom. At the same time and relative to the majority of countries on the continent, data provided by the Institute for Democracy and Electoral Assistance (IDEA) indicate that on all of the indicators of *congruence* used by the authors in this volume (*societal engagement, access to justice*, etc.), the communities of practice surrounding the legalization of international human rights laws prohibiting political violence should be more successful than they are in practice. One constant in Botswana's post-independence past is the Botswana Democratic Party (BDP). Using historical institutionalism, this chapter explores the influence that traditional ruling institutions have had on the staying power of the BDP, and in turn, the process of the legalization of human rights prohibitions against torture, lethal force, and other forms of violence in Botswana. This chapter demonstrates that the legalization of human rights is never a finished product.

This chapter first addresses the status of *congruence* in Botswana as well as the increase in political violence in the country. This chapter next introduces the primary theory on which this study is based, historical institutionalism. The value of historical institutionalism as a means of explaining current ruling tendencies in Botswana is emphasized. This chapter then explores the dominant BDP and assesses how and why rule *by* law tendencies persisted and what this has meant for human rights progress in Botswana. Botswana demonstrates that tendencies toward rule by law do not occur in a vacuum but are impacted by years of rigid single party dominance. This chapter concludes with some thoughts about the future of the Government of Botswana following the BDP's historic loss of their majority in the October 30, 2024, elections and what this critical juncture means for Botswana's

DOI: 10.4324/9781003471677-18

future. This chapter also concludes with some thoughts about what the absence of female leadership has for the protection of women's rights in Botswana.

Current Conditions in Botswana

Since 1973, Botswana has consistently been ranked by Freedom House as a "free" country.[1] As indicated in Table 14.1, over the past ten years, the country scores appreciably well on the components of *congruence*, including public access to information, societal engagement, and an absence of corruption. The data from IDEA's Global State of Democracy database suggest a relatively healthy and open relationship between government and society in the policymaking, implementation and accountability processes.

For years Botswana held elections that were considered by international observers as free and fair and several institutions, including the Independent Electoral Commission (IEC), the Directorate on Corruption and Economic Crime (DCEC), and the Ombudsman exist to support democracy in the country.[2]

However, the independence of these institutions has come under doubt in recent years, as has the fairness of elections and the ability of the National Assembly to successfully check the executive.[3] Moreover, civil society in Botswana has been characterized as weak, as "many Batswana in and outside of government do not see or want to see these groups as speaking for the people."[4] Consequently, it has been argued that the "government is free to shape policies and allocate funds in its own interests."[5]

According to Professor Kenneth Good, the president of Botswana is empowered to do as he pleases. Good argued that his deportation from Botswana in May 2005 was politically motivated because of his criticism of the closed process of succession to the presidency. He argued that the government was run by a small elite that manipulated state media. Good was

Table 14.1 Congruence in Botswana

Year	*Societal engagement*	*Local authority*	*Justice access*	*Independent judiciary*	*Absence of corruption*	*Information access*
2013	0.465956	0.75436	0.67266	0.66205	0.621803	57.62
2014	0.465956	0.72563	0.687275	0.645724	0.616667	58.84
2015	0.487216	0.72563	0.687275	0.63644	0.616667	60.01
2016	0.46474	0.66735	0.629214	0.640993	0.618035	62.52
2017	0.458392	0.626308	0.629138	0.689428	0.59892	63.12
2018	0.527724	0.531471	0.630855	0.676654	0.597456	62.71
2019	0.513105	0.550445	0.65174	0.652773	0.666492	62.72
2020	0.553246	0.641139	0.653914	0.662127	0.584815	62.57
2021	0.548993	0.622613	0.566468	0.684269	0.555314	62.6
2022	0.511336	0.75436	0.67266	0.66205	0.621803	57.62

deported without offering any reason, but the ostensible reason was his critique of government policy.[6] His deportation lowered Botswana's self-esteem in the eyes of the world, demonstrating that academic freedom in Botswana is limited in practice.[7]

After the presidency of Festus Mogae (1998–2008), conditions in Botswana worsened under his successor Ian Khama, former head of the Botswana Defense Force. As Good states,

> [d]uring his Presidency General Khama has used the techniques and capacities of personal, militaristic rule to an exceptional degree. Such techniques appear to compensate to some degree for the narrowness of his qualifications for political leadership in a democracy. His experience is restricted to three areas alone: the military; chieftaincy and dynastic politics; and state power.[8]

The Directorate of Intelligence and Security Services (DISS) was created in 2006 by Khama to address domestic and foreign "terrorism." The DISS has the power to conduct arrests without a warrant under certain circumstances,[9] an authority that the DISS has used to arrest political opponents and other critics of the regime of Khama's successor, President Mokgweetsi Masisi, including the legal advisor to the DCED.[10] The power of the DISS remains unchecked and the organization is believed to be responsible for several suspicious deaths in the country.[11]

Table 14.2 includes data from the CIRI human rights database measuring tortures, disappearances, and political killings in Botswana between 2015 and 2021.[12] Although the data indicate that disappearances and political killings in Botswana are relatively rare, the use of torture by the state remains fairly common.

Like other countries around the world, Botswana issued a State of Emergency to control the spread of the COVID virus in 2020. And, like many countries around the world during this time, the government cracked down further on freedom of speech and other civil liberties.[13]

Table 14.2 Political violence in Botswana

Year	*Torture*	*Disappearances*	*Killings*
2015	2	2	1
2016	1	2	2
2017	1	2	2
2018	1	2	2
2019	2	2	2
2020	1	2	2
2021	1	2	2

Section 47 of Botswana's Penal Code prohibits publications deemed to be contrary to "the public interest" by the president, who has complete discretion to ban these publications.[14] According to Tutwane, Botswana is like many other African states that endeavor to control unfavorable media.[15] A particular target of presidents past in Botswana is the *Botswana Guardian*.[16] Moreover, the BDP government made it extremely difficult for independent media critical of the government to obtain state-funded advertising. Some of these instances were outright bans on public advertising to newspapers such as the *Botswana Guardian*. As the International Press Institute (IPI) notes, Botswana's High Court ruled that at least two of these bans were unconstitutional; however, the practice of selectively awarding public advertisement remains. [17]

Sedition and seditious practices are very vaguely defined in the law and easily subjected to broad interpretation by the government. For instance, Section 50(1)(a) of the Penal Code defines a "seditious intention," as one that brings "into hatred or contempt or to excite disaffection against the person of the President or the Government of Botswana as established by law."[18] Among the types of offenses listed in this section of the Code is the publication of materials "seditiously" critical of the president or government (Section 50(1)(c)), as well as the mere utterance of words deemed to be suspicious (Section 50(1)(b)).[19] Moreover section 59(1) of the Code addresses "Alarming Publications," which are defined as those which contain a "false statement, rumour or report which is likely to cause fear and alarm to the public or to disturb the public peace."[20]

These laws were used by the Masisi government to harass and intimidate journalists, political opponents, and others who voiced criticism of the regime's practices. Despite the passage of the Media Associations Practitioners' Act in 2022, which was done in consultation between the government and the media in Botswana, obvious concerns remain about the extent of government interference in and intimidation of the media.[21] The (IPI) writes, in reference to Botswana's strict laws on defamation, that the accusations of defamation made by the government against media outlets and journalists is part of a strategy to

> harass the defendant, [...] through the threat of endless litigation, legal fees, disproportionate fines or damages, and the loss of reputation. This harassment can lead to self-censorship and/or resource drain as journalists are forced to devote time and energy to fighting baseless legal claims instead of carrying out reporting.[22]

An umbrella organization of civil society groups—the Botswana Council of Non-Governmental Organisations (BOCONGO)—raised issues with the Masisi regime's closed process of amending the Constitution. Specifically, the BOCONGO highlighted the fact that, even though the amendments promise to protect democracy in Botswana, the process from start to finish was dictated by the president, with very little input from civil society or the public at large.[23] One of the more interesting aspects of the bill is its limitation of the presidency to ten years, which in effect barred Ian Khama from being re-elected.[24]

These practices paint a picture of a government that is concerned more with maintaining control of the ruling system than living up to its promises of protecting the fundamental rights and freedoms contained in the Constitution.

Historical Institutionalism and the Dominance of the BDP

Historical institutionalism is a good fit for explaining rule of law in Botswana as it contends that institutions, which have been defined by Immergut as including a variety of factors such as "formal rules of political arenas, channels of communication, language codes, or the logics of strategic interactions" shape how political elites respond to new information and phenomena like critical junctures.[25] The trajectory of policymaking behavior is enabled by the particular feedback mechanisms in place within the ruling system.

Policymaking in Botswana demonstrates the use of distributional feedback mechanisms which Thelen defines as "policy arrangements and policy feedbacks [that] actively facilitate the organization and empowerment of certain groups" over others in society.[26] As indicated below, institutional structures, including the electoral system, benefitted the BDP and kept them in power. Moreover, changes made to the system in later years, including the creation of the IEC in the executive branch, simply reinforced extant power arrangements by lending an air of credibility to the political process.[27]

British Colonial Rule

Botswana is also influenced by British colonial rule, which shaped the type of institutional structures put into place during the period of independence. On September 30, 1895, the British declared present-day Botswana a Protectorate. The consequences of this status were that the colonial power was to exercise full control over the external affairs of the territory but allow the government of the territory to control its internal affairs. The practical reality turned out differently. Since there was no formal government having effective control of the territory, the British assumed control of both external and internal affairs of the then Bechuanaland Protectorate.[28]

The Bechuanaland Protectorate General Administration Order in Council was proclaimed in 1891 and empowered a High Commissioner to exercise on behalf of her majesty, Queen Victoria of England, all the powers and jurisdiction which Her Majesty had, subject to such instructions as he might from time to time receive from Her Majesty. The High Commissioner was given powers to appoint persons deemed fit (as in the interest of Her Majesty's service) to be judges, magistrates, and other officers and to define the districts within which such officers should discharge their functions.[29] This laid down the foundation of the present legal system in Botswana. Proclamation No. 36 of 1909 provided,

> the laws in force in the colony of the Cape of Good Hope on the 10th day of June 1891 shall mutatis mutandis and so far as not inapplicable be the laws in force and to be observed in the said Protectorate.[30]

This proclamation, among others, imported wholesale the common law and statutes of general application existing on the stipulated date in the Cape into Bechuanaland. Consequently, the Roman Dutch common law operating in the Cape became part of the Botswana Legal System.

The Rise of the BDP

The Botswana Democratic Party was formed in 1962 by Sereste Khama. As Makgala writes:

> Seretse was a hugely popular but uncrowned Kgosi (Chief) of the Bangwato. The veteran opposition politician, Motsamai Mpho, has argued on several occasions that the BDP is the extension of the Bangwato chieftainship masquerading as a political party. The Bangwato themselves have become quite proud of being the "natural leaders" of Botswana, and do not take kindly to attempts by the BDP leadership to "undermine" this order of things. Significantly for the "tribalism" thesis, Kenneth Koma is also said to be a Mongwato of royal background.[31]

The influence of traditional values and institutions of the Tswana rural majority on the first elections held in 1965 laid out a trajectory that favored conservative and authoritarian traditions in the decades that followed, shutting out the more liberal, modern perspectives.[32] The result is Botswana's "ambivalence" toward democracy.

Maundeni attributes some of this to the rules of succession for Chiefs in Botswana that traditionally sought to "to minimise or eliminate competition between the chief and the heir-apparent" through the system of regency, "whereby an important member of the royal family was appointed to act, [filling] the gap between the ageing chief and the heir apparent and [ensuring] that the regent could rule without laying legitimate claims to the chieftainship."[33] The system ensured continuity, albeit in a process devoid of any real choice. The significance of traditional principles of continuity are demonstrated perhaps best by the fact that the president's successor is always the vice president. It's a closed process that does not permit competition, even within the party. As de Jager and Sebudubudu contend

> the influence of traditional values which placed the emphasis on reverence and submissiveness to authority gave way to weak democratic

> institutions, with a strong presidency overshadowing all the other institutions, a feature that has become a hindrance to Botswana's liberal democracy.[34]

Chieftainship played a role when Botswana transitioned from a traditional system of government to a democratic state in 1966. The traditional system was such that the Chief was the leader, the administrator, and the court of appeal. He was an embodiment of the traditional value system where decision-making was done collectively. People gathered together at the "Kgotla" (Assembly) and made decisions affecting the whole community. This was replicated in today's system of government where there is a House of Chiefs (representing the traditional system) and the National Assembly (parliament). The two systems of governance exist side by side with the House of Chiefs performing an advisory role on traditional matters affecting the nation.[35]

Post-independence Botswana and BDP Rule

According to Raphaeli, Roumani, and MacKeller, at the time of independence, Botswana "was suffering from the effects of eighty years of colonial neglect and one of the severest droughts in its history."[36] Subsequently, it is thought that "the drought and poverty which prevailed at the time of independence [continues] to weigh heavily in the minds of the county's leaders and provide a constant incentive and drive for the efficient marshalling of national resources."[37] Much of Botswana's consideration as an "African Miracle" is a result of its economic development and stability, perhaps less because of its "restricted variant of liberal democracy."[38]

Right after independence the BDP quickly assumed "not only the powers of the British administrators but those of the Chiefs."[39] Botswana's post-independence government was modeled on the Westminster system. The constitution provides for a unicameral legislature: the National Assembly. All citizens are eligible to vote from the age of eighteen. Members are directly elected from 57 districts (enlarged from the original 40 due to the 2001 National and Population census) and these members elect six specially elected members and a Speaker.[40] The presidential candidate whose declared supporters from the majority of directly elected members of parliament takes office as president and selects his ministers from among the members of the National Assembly.[41]

Like Great Britain, the electoral system is a single-member district (SMD) voting system. Molomo suggests that the use of SMD voting has contributed to the dominance of BDP rule. He writes,

> the BDP has won all elections by decisive majorities. In 1965 it won 28 of the 32 seats, and in 1969 it won 24 out of 31 seats. In 1974, the BDP increased its margin by winning 27 of the 32 seats. The BDP's electoral fortunes continued to grow in 1979, when it won 29 of the

> 32 seats. These gains were despite the fact that its popular vote was falling. In contrast, the opposition started to make some gains in 1984 by winning 6 of the 34 constituencies, but still leaving the BDP very much in control of the political landscape. In 1989, the BDP recorded yet another decisive win of parliamentary seats, this time sweeping 31 of the 34 constituencies, but with a low popular vote. Perhaps the 1994 election could be seen as a turning point in Botswana's electoral history as, for the first time, the opposition won close to half the seats polled by the BDP – 13 out of 40 seats. During the 1999 election, the BNF poll, which constitutes the main opposition, dropped as a result of the split it experienced in 1997. In that election the opposition parties won 7 seats altogether in comparison to BDP's 33 seats. Eight political parties, and a few independent candidates contested the 2004 election. Of these eight, only three are represented in parliament. In the 2004 election, the opposition increased its poll by winning 13 seats and the BDP 44 seats.[42]

Political fragmentation has until only recently accounted for the weakness of the opposition.[43] In the 2019 elections, the center-left Umbrella for Democratic Change (UDC) gained substantial electoral ground, although the BDP still pulled off a majority victory.[44] The most interesting aspect of these elections, as well as an indicator of a growing rift in the BDP itself, was the fact controversial former president of Botswana, Ian Khama ran in these elections as the head of a breakaway party, the Botswana Patriotic Front (BPF), albeit with little success.

The BDP's share of seats in the National Assembly steadily declined over the decades from a peak of 80 percent in 1965 to 52.6 percent in 2019 to 6 percent in 2024.[45] What accounts for these declines and the emergence of a more competitive system is attributed by Brown to changing demographics which favored parties like the Botswana National Front (BNF) in the 1980s and 1990s which had strong support among younger people in the urban areas.[46] Although the strength of the opposition BNF party faltered over the next few decades, the misrule of the BDP government under Khama and the rise of a more united opposition front, the UDC (which now includes the BNF) demonstrate the appeal and need for a viable alternative to the BDP.[47]

The BDP dominated the political landscape of the country since independence in 1966. However, beginning in 1994 people living in urban areas who were politically conscious came to pose a threat to the BDP, voting in large numbers against the ruling party. Years passed by and in 2014, people again voiced their concern about the BDP government by replicating the voting pattern of 1994. This trend continued in the 2019 elections and on October 30, 2024 the opposition UDC, headed by Duma Boko, ended the BDP's majority in the parliament. The BDP's share of seats in the National Assembly was reduced from 38 to 4 seats.[48]

In later years the institutional changes and policies created by the BDP sought to curtail criticisms about the transparency and fairness of the electoral process and democratic governance as a whole. One of these was the creation of the DISS; also, the IEC. Under Article 65A of the Constitution, the IEC is mandated with overseeing

> (a) the conduct and supervision of elections of the Elected Members of the National Assembly and members of a local authority, and conduct of a referendum; (b) giving instructions and directions to the Secretary of the Commission appointed under section 66 in regard to the exercise of his or her functions under the electoral law prescribed by an Act of Parliament; (c) ensuring that elections are conducted efficiently, properly, freely and fairly; and (d) performing such other functions as may be prescribed by an Act of Parliament.[49]

The IEC was intended by the BDP government to impress upon the public that the electoral process was free and fair. However, even the IEC was not above reproach. As Lekorwe and Tshosa contend, however, the fact that the IEC falls under the jurisdiction of the Minister of Presidential Affairs and Public Administration and that the Secretary of the IEC is appointed by the president casts a shadow on the impartiality of the body.[50] Balule writes further that,

> The Constitution does not expressly guarantee the institutional independence of the IEC, nor give guidance on the attributes that make it independent. It would appear that the drafters of the provision assumed that by referring to the institution as independent, this would guarantee it institutional independence. The failure to guarantee expressly the institutional independence of the IEC is anomalous in that the same Constitution expressly guarantees the independence of other democracy-supporting institutions, such as the Delimitation Commission and Judicial Service Commission.[51]

The opposition in Botswana understandably distrusted the objectivity of the IEC given the lack of constitutional protections provided for its independence.[52] Mogalakwe argues that the IEC doesn't have the ability to ensure that elections are fair due to

> (1) Botswana's EMB [electoral management body] reliance on public officers who are bound by the Public Service Act to be loyal to the government of the day, (2) lack of equal access to public media and the abuse of public officers working for the state/public media as propagandists for the ruling party and (3) the choice of election date which is the prerogative of the President or his minister and therefore advantages the ruling party.[53]

Botswana's Vision 2016, aimed at achieving seven pillars including "An Open, Democratic and Accountable Nation," and "A Safe and Secure Nation."[54] It has since been replaced by Vision 2036 which aims to address areas in need of improvement in a way that aligns with the UN's Sustainable Development Goals.[55] Pillar four of the Vision 2036 goals addresses governance and includes a long list of aspirations, such as effective oversight and creating a meaningful role for the traditional Bogosi chieftaincy and the Kgotla conflict resolution system.[56] However, whether these conservative, traditional institutions hold much favor in Botswana today, especially in the cities, is debatable. What remains to be seen is how these democratic goals are approached by the new UDC government.

Conclusions: Challenges That Remain for Botswana

Botswana has for decades been a success story for Africa. Much of this has been attributed to the stability of the BDP and the positive impact that BDP governance has for the country. The extent to which Botswana is an *illiberal* democracy became more apparent in recent years. Income inequality remains high in Botswana and approximately 23 percent of its total workforce is unemployed as of 2022 and over 39 percent of its working-age youth.[57] Some of this decline is attributable to COVID, but the GINI coefficient has hovered at 53 for Botswana since 2015.[58]

The question as to whether the BDP survives as the only political game in town has now been resolved. Botswana is at a critical juncture. The UDC's victory is easily interpreted as a response by the voters to the illiberal system created by BDP governments. At present, it remains to be seen how much the institutional legacies of BDP rule will impact the new UDC government. How will these legacies influence the new government's ability to address the corruption, unemployment, and poverty that continue to plague the country? Will the DISS be reformed? Will transparency be returned to those governing institutions that were "weakened or compromised under [Masisi's] government through interference"?[59] The UDC Manifesto advocates for several things, including the creation of jobs, a green economy, and constitutional reforms.[60] They have a tough road ahead, although they have begun efforts to improve the ruling system.[61]

A particularly serious problem for Botswana is the lack of female representation in government. Although the findings of the analysis in Chapter 6 of this volume indicate that more female representation actually has a negative impact on *congruence*, the lack of equality of political power in Botswana is clearly reflected in the absence of effective legislation protecting women from domestic violence, as well as legislation guaranteeing them access to property.[62] There is no electoral quota for women and as of the time of this writing, women account for roughly 8.7 percent of the seats in the National Assembly, down from 11 percent in 2021. Legacies of patriarchal traditions have created a ceiling for women in government and society to some extent. Overall, the data for Botswana on gender equality paint a mixed picture. Although they do indicate that women do participate in the civil service, equality of political power is very low.[63]

The political process in Botswana must become more inclusive. Rhoda Sekgororwane of the Botswana Caucus for Women in Politics states,

> The truth is that other countries are practising what is called propositional representation, which works well and addresses what we are seeking as women. I believe it is time the country does what is called Mixed First Past the Post since we are behind when it comes to women's representation.[64]

The UDC government seeks to change the electoral system from mixed-member to proportional representation. Truthfully Botswana's electoral system is only part of the problem. The larger issue is the legacy of BDP dominance. BDP rule and the executive's in-house way of policymaking and implementation are embedded in a long history of powerful leaders and top-heavy policymaking institutions that have been resistant to change or to state it more bluntly, change that is not *controlled* by the executive. From an historical institutionalist perspective, Botswana demonstrates the influences that institutional legacies have on how ruling elites respond to crises or challenges. Hopefully this will change given the new circumstances. Time will tell.

Notes

1 Freedom House, Country and Territories Ratings and Statuses, 1973–2024, at Publication Archives | Freedom House.

2 The Ombudsmen is within the executive branch and is charged with investigating human rights abuses and other types of maladministration by government officials. One of the problems associated with the Ombudsman is its lack of resources. See United States Department of State (SOS), *Botswana 2022 Human Rights Practices Report*, Botswana—United States Department of State (accessed October 6, 2024).

3 Ndulamo Morima, "A Critique of Botswana's Trade Disputes Act," Master of Laws dissertation, North-west University, South Africa (2019), 1.

4 Nicola de Jager and David Sebudubudu. "Towards Understanding Botswana and South Africa's Ambivalence to Liberal Democracy." *Journal of Contemporary African Studies* 35(1) (2017): 15–33. 22

5 de Jager and Sebudubudu, "Towards."

6 Ndulamo Morima, "A Critique," 2.

7 Iana Taylor, "The Limits of the 'African Miracle': Academic Freedom in Botswana and the Deportation of Kenneth Good," *Journal of Contemporary African Studies* 24(1) (2006): 101–122. doi:10.1080/02589000500513804. See also Kenneth Good, "The Presidency of General Ian Khama: The Militarization of the Botswana 'Miracle'," *African Affairs*, 109(435) (2010): 315–324.

8 Good, "The Presidency," 318. Moreover, Khama liked to rule by decree, forbidding everything from the sale of alcohol at certain times to dress codes for civil servants, the purpose of these directives to bring Botswanans more in line. Good, "The Presidency," 320–322.

9 Republic of Botswana, *Intelligence and Security Service Bill* (Government Gazette Extraordinary, 2006).

10 SOS, *Botswana 2022*. According to this report, the conflict between the DISS and DCEC concerns the accusations made by the latter organization against the former over DISS efforts to illegally obtain files concerning corruption investigations into the DISS.

11 One of the more notorious cases was the murder of John Kalafatis on May 13, 2009. His murder was believed by the press to be an execution by the DISS. For more on this case, see Good, "The Presidency," 316–318. See also International Press Institute (IPI), Mission Report, *Press Freedom in Botswana 2022*, (February 2023), 5 at press-freedom-in-botswana-2022.pdf (ipi.media) (accessed January, 2024).

12 David L. Cingranelli, David L. Richards, and K. Chad Clay, *The CIRI Human Rights Project Dataverse.* (2021). Harvard Dataverse, V1, UNF:6:+N2W6SCqRsXxIn6+qCBSyg== [fileUNF]. Countries are scored "0" if an event happens frequently, is widespread and systematic; "1" if an event happens occasionally; and "2" if the event seldom occurs or is unreported. The data for 2022 have not come out yet.

13 Freedom House, "Perspectives: Heavy-Handed Pandemic Responses Could Fuel Unrest in Southern Africa," (May 11, 2020), at Heavy-Handed Pandemic Responses Could Fuel Unrest in Southern Africa | Freedom House, (accessed June 6, 2024).

14 Laws of Botswana ("Laws"), *Chapter 08:01: Penal Code*, art. 47(1), (Dublin, Ireland: Blackhall Publishing), at PENAL CODE (botswanalaws.com) (accessed July 7, 2024). Section 47(8) deems "public interest" to be what is "in the interests of defence, public safety, public order, public morality or public health." A similar provision in provided in Article 12(2) of the country's constitution. See Government of Botswana, *Constitution of Botswana*, at Microsoft Word - constitution - pdfMachine from Broadgun Software, http://pdfmachine.com, a great PDF writer utility! (gov.bw) (accessed July 7, 2024).

15 Letshiwiti B. B. Tutwane, "Government and Press Relations in Botswana: Down the Beaten African Track," *CS Canada, Cross-Cultural Communication* 10(5) (2014), at Government and Press Relations in Botswana: Down the Beaten African Track | Tutwane | Cross-Cultural Communication (cscanada.net) (accessed July 4, 2024).

16 Tutwane, "Government." See also Letshiwiti B. B, Tutwane, "The Myth of Press Freedom in Botswana: From Sir Seretse Khama to Ian Khama," *Journal of African Media Studies* 3(1) (2011): 43–55; doi:10.1386/jams.3.1.43_1.

17 IPI, *Press Freedom*, 14.

18 Laws, *Penal Code*, art. 50(1)(a).

19 Laws, *Penal Code*, arts. 51(b–c). Thus far Botswana's Constitutional Court has not ruled on the constitutionality of the sedition laws. SOS, *Botswana, 2022*.

20 Laws, *Penal Code*, art. 59.

21 IPI, *Press Freedom*, 8.

22 IPI, *Press Freedom*, 12. Also notable is the fact that state-run media is not subject to any standards and serves the purpose of being largely a mouthpiece for the government. Opposition parties obtain little airtime. IPI, *Press Freedom*, 13; see also MISA, *The State of Press Freedom in Southern Africa, 2022* (May 2023), at The State of Press Freedom in Southern Africa 2022 • Page 2 • Uwazi (misa.org), (accessed October 2, 2023).

23 Innocent Selatlhwa, Civil Society fights "flawed" constitutional amendment: Mmegi Online (April 22, 2024) (accessed April 26, 2024).

24 Keto Segwai, Constitutional amendment Bill out: Mmegi Online (March 15, 2024) (accessed April 26, 2024).

25 E.M. Immergut, "The Theoretical Core of the New Institutionalism," *Political Sociology* 25(2) (1998): 5–34, 20.
26 Katleen Thelen, "Historical Institutionalism in Historical Politics," *Annual Review of Political Science* 2(1) (1999): 369–404, 394.
27 For further discussion about the assumptions and literature of historical institutionalism, see Chapter 2 of this edited volume.
28 Emmanuel Quansah, *Introduction to Botswana Legal System* (Gaborone, Botswana: Pula Press, 2001).
29 Quansah, *Introduction*, 2.
30 Quansah, *Introduction*, 2.
31 Christian John Makgala, "The Relationship between Kenneth Koma and the Botswana Democratic Party, 1965–2003," *African Affairs* 104(415) (2005): 303–323, 304.
32 de Jager, and Sebudubudu. "Towards." Khama's succession to Chief of the Bangwato was by no means a done deal. His marriage to a white woman, Ruth Williams, and strong opposition from South Africa ended up costing Khama his hereditary position as Chief. Ronald Hyam, "The Political Consequences of Seretse Khama: Britain, the Bangwato and South Africa, 1948–1952." *The Historical Journal* (1986) 29(4): 921–947. https://search.ebscohost.com/login.aspx?direct=true&AuthType=ip,shib&db=edsjsr&AN=edsjsr.2639362&site=eds-live&scope=site. (accessed July 5, 2023).
33 Zibani Maundeni, "Succession to High Office: Tswana Culture And Modern Botswana Politics." In Zibani Maundeni (ed.) *40 Years of Democracy in Botswana*. 80–93. (Gaborone: Mmegi Publishing House, 2005), 82.
34 de Jager and Sebudubudu, "Towards," 19.
35 See NTLO YA DIKGOSI, at History.
36 Nimrod Raphaeli, Jacques Roumani and A.C. MacKeller, *Public Sector Management In Botswana: Lessons In Pragmatism (English)*. Staff working paper; no. SWP 709 (Washington, D.C.: World Bank Group, 1984), 14.
37 Raphaeli, Roumani and MacKeller, "Public Sector," 15.
38 de Jager and Sebudubudu, "Towards," 19.
39 de Jager and Sebudubudu, "Towards," 19.
40 The National Assembly now has a total of 69 seats, the 61 directly elected seats (now enlarged from 57) plus 8. These eight include "the President, the Speaker, and six Specially Elected Members of Parliament." Chris Brown, "Botswana Votes 2019: Two-Party Competition and the Khama Factor," *Journal of Southern African Studies* 46(4) (2020): 703–722, 703 at fn. 1.
41 Republic of Botswana, "National Development Bank: Country and People, 1991–1997," 3; see also Mpho Molomo, "Electoral Systems and Democracy in Botswana," *40 Years of Democracy*, 30.
42 Molomo, "Electoral," 31; see also Molomo, 'In Search of an Alternative Electoral System for Botswana', *Pula: Botswana Journal of African Studies*, 14(1) (2000): 109–121.
43 Molomo, "Electoral," 32.
44 The UDC is an opposition coalition with the Botswana National Front (BNF), Botswana Peoples' Party (BPP) and the Botswana Congress Party (BCP). Brown, "Botswana Votes," 703–704. Their challenges to the BDP's victory in 2019 were characterized as "immature" and a "smear campaign" by BDP spokesman, Kagelelo Kentse. Theo Mailakgotla Potlako Bogatsu, "Opposition Parties Plan Nationwide Protests against the IEC," *Botswana Guardian* (Mar. 1, 2024), at PressReader.com – Digital Newspaper & Magazine Subscriptions, (accessed July 4, 2024).
45 Brown, "Botswana Votes," 706.
46 Brown, "Botswana Votes," 712. The BNF eventually split into two groups, the BNF and the BCP.

47 Brown, "Botswana Votes," 714–716. This is not to suggest that the BDP is united and cohesive. Far from it. See Good, "The Presidency," and Brown, "Botswana Votes."

48 IPU Parline, "Botswana: National Assembly," at Election results | Botswana | IPU Parline: global data on national parliaments.

49 Constitution of Botswana, at Microsoft Word - constitution - pdfMachine from Broadgun Software, http://pdfmachine.com, a great PDF writer utility! (gov.bw).

50 Mogopodi Lekorwe and Onkemetse Tshosa, "The Organization of Elections and Institutional Reform," *40 Years of Democracy*, 56.

51 Badala Tachilisa Balule "Election Management Bodies in the Sadc Region — An Appraisal of the Independence of Botswana's Independent Electoral Commission," *South African Journal on Human Rights*, 24(1) (2008): 104–122, DOI: 10.1080/19962126.2008.11864947, 113.

52 Balule, "Election Management," 113.

53 Monageng Mogalakwe, "An Assessment of Botswana's Electoral Management Body to Deliver Fair Elections," *Journal of Contemporary African Studies* 33 (1) (2015): 105–120, 117–118. doi:10.1080/02589001.2015.1021210.

54 Statistics Botswana, "Vision 2016 and Millenium Development Indicators Report, 2014," at Vision 2016 Millenium development Goals indicators.pdf (statsbots.org.bw) (accessed July 7, 2024), 2. Moreover, a Vision Council was created to oversee implementation of these goals.

55 Statistics Botswana, vision 2036," at VISION 2036 | Statistics Botswana (statsbots.org.bw). The seven pillars of Vision 2016 were reduced to four: sustainable economic development, human social development, sustainable environment and governance, peace and security. See also Vision 2036 Presidential Task Force, *Vision 2036—Achieving Prosperity for All* (2016).

56 The dikgosi was the traditional governing system in Botswana and the bogosi, the chieftaincy, the latter of which was supportive of the BDP. The BDP's Constitution, "was founded on multiracialism and support for bogosi." The opposition, on the other hand, is generally anti-Bogosi. Mpho Molomo and Wilford Molefe, "Voters and Electoral Performance of Political Parties in Botswana," *40 Years of Democracy*, 102. In the Constitution, a section is provided which addresses the Ntlo ya Dikgosi. According to Part III of the Constitution, Sections 77–85, members to the Ntlo ya Dikgosi are chosen from various districts in the country, some through traditional means, others a Regional Electoral College, still others appointed by the president. Members have the authority to review legislation from the National Assembly that impacts the interests of their particular tribes (Section 85).

57 Data for total unemployment rate were obtained from the United Nations Development Programme (UNDP), *World Development Indicators* (various years); data for youth unemployment were obtained from the Central Intelligence Agency, *CIA World Factbook* (various years).

58 The GINI Coefficient, which measures inequality in a country, measures Botswana as a 53, indicating that income inequality in the country is high. A country that scores "1" is a country with absolute income inequality, a country that scores a "0" indicates perfect income equality. Data for the GINI Coefficient were obtained from the UNDP, *World Development Indicators* (various years).

59 "Botswana's New President: Who is Duma Boko and What Does He Stand For?" Your Botswana (Nov. 11, 2024) at Botswana's new president: Who is Duma Boko and what does he stand for? – YourBotswana; see also *The Conversation*, "Botswana's Election Shock: Analyst Reflects on Why Voters Kicked the Ruling Party Out After 58 Years," (Nov. 12, 2024), at Botswana's election shock: analyst reflects on why voters kicked the ruling party out after 58 years.

60 *The Botswana Gazette*, "Umbrella for Democratic Change (UDC) Manifesto Highlights," Umbrella for Democratic Change (UDC) Manifesto Highlights – Botswana Gazette.

61 *The Botswana Gazette*, "Govt to Probe Corruption Through Forensic Audit," at Govt To Probe Corruption Through Forensic Audit – Botswana Gazette.

62 Data for these variables were obtained from the OECD Social Institutions and Gender Index (various years).

63 On this latter measure, Botswana scores a "1" on a scale from 0 to 4, with higher numbers indicating greater equality. Data for these two variables were obtained by the Varieties of Democracy (V-Dem) Project (various years).

64 Tsaone Basimanbotlhe, "IEC Called on to Benchmark on Zim Women: Mmegi Online" (February 23, 2024) (accessed March 5, 2024).

15 Conclusions

Stacey M. Mitchell, Lem Lilian Atanga, and Miao-ling Lin Hasenkamp

Each chapter in this volume demonstrates that legalization is an extremely complex process that is certainly *not* unidirectional, nor is it an end goal that once achieved is finished once and for all. We can say that all the African States have made efforts toward the legalization of human rights prohibitions against torture, disappearances, and extrajudicial killings. Many governments have codified these prohibitions into their domestic statutes and have reported to the relevant treaty bodies. But clearly these are not the only measures of legalization. Instead, by looking beyond these more superficial measures to assess law as practice in these states, the contributors to this volume demonstrate that the openness and inclusiveness of the communities of practice involved in the lawmaking and implementation processes in a state provide a better way measuring the degree to which these laws become institutionally embedded. Realism, Institutionalism, Constructivism, Feminism, and Cosmopolitanism only tell a part of the story. How these human rights laws become embedded is more organic, shaped by the institutional experiences within each country which continuously inform the responses of political actors to their environment and the types of policymaking communities of practice that operate.

As a composite variable, our conceptualization of legalization as *congruence* allows the researcher to pinpoint which components of *congruence* are effectively working and which are not. This of course has policy implications for state leaders, and members of the international community, particularly as the collapse of one or more of these components in a state sends a red flag (or should) that rule of law in that state is on the decline (rapidly in cases like Mali and Niger).

We have shown that *congruence* varies rather dramatically between the more democratic states like South Africa and the more authoritarian ones like Zimbabwe with a host of states caught somewhere in the middle. States have also slipped backward in their progress. As Arfoui demonstrates in her chapter about Tunisia, what democratic progress was made after the Arab Spring is for now at least a thing of the past.

The ongoing crises that many African states endure, compounded by a lack of resource capacity, make the legalization process an uphill battle for

DOI: 10.4324/9781003471677-19

many. In terms of the five hypotheses tested in this volume, authors found evidence that indicates that greater international presence within a state does have a positive impact on *congruence* in that state, although with respect to peace missions, certain caveats are warranted. As the chapter by Hasenkamp and Mitchell demonstrates, interstate politics, national interests and a willingness to commit on the part of outside states tends to impair the progress of these missions.

For our hypotheses addressing economic and political stability, the results were more mixed. As the chapter by Mitchell, Nchotu, and Atanga showed, economic inequality in a state does not bode well for *congruence*, whereas a state's overall wealth was negatively connected to *congruence*. The chapters by Solo on Botswana, Gibson on Zimbabwe, and Hasenkamp on Mali indicate that regional and/or political stability and economic conditions do have a significant impact on the health of rule of law, such that the greater the *instability*, the weaker the rule of law.

An especially important facet of this study's primary argument is that how these exogenous or endogenous crises impact a state—its ruling elites, lawmakers, courts—is shaped by that state's institutional legacies. Botswana and the Botswana Democratic Party (BDP), Zimbabwe and the Zimbabwe African National Union-Patriotic Front, Cameroon and the Cameroon People's Democratic Movement are long-ruling hegemonic post-independence parties whose drive to stay in power continues to effectively limit the openness and fairness of the lawmaking and accountability processes. The fact that these governments have cracked down in recent years on freedoms of expression and dissent further demonstrates their unwillingness to share power. For Botswana, the slide toward rule by law rather than rule of law was not enough to save the BDP from experiencing a fate like that of the African National Congress (ANC) in South Africa, whose recent electoral losses took the ANC out of the majority for the first time in 30 years.[1] Now that the BDP has lost its majority, how it approaches the shift to UDC rule may be a real test for democracy in Botswana.

All the analyses contained in this volume contribute to a fuller understanding how exogenous and endogenous factors influence the risks for mass violence in a state, particularly when their relationship to rule of law is considered. Regional stability, economic crisis, and so forth severely weaken *congruence* in states that have institutional legacies of authoritarian rule and political violence. To ascertain why various crises have the impact they do on a state, the policymaking communities of practice within that state—their inclusiveness, how they operate, the types of background knowledge that influence decision-making choices—must be considered. Otherwise, policymaking will appear to occur in a vacuum, in which case predicting how and especially *when* mass violence erupts is a far more difficult task.

One area for future study is a closer examination of the use of discourse in and among the lawmaking communities of practice in a country.[2] Fuller himself emphasized the importance of communication as a cornerstone of the process of legalization.[3] How free and fair this dialogue can be, however, is influenced by a variety of factors. The political discourse surrounding the legalization process, the ways in which a government frames the actions of political opponents and other critics of its regime, is instructive. Leaders tend to rely heavily on the use of reference points to guide their arguments, including references to past episodes of group conflict, the value of democracy as an institution, colonial legacies, the ill effects of globalization, and/or the importance of maintaining political stability, among others. They do this for a variety of reasons. Leaders may be indicating their policy preferences, their willingness to compromise, or their desire to obfuscate or obstruct the legalization process.[4]

More broadly, this study has shown that *congruence* is not only a measurable concept but is one that can also be tested across cases. Future application of this model could include region-to-region comparisons. The possibilities for quantitative and qualitative analyses are many. As the authors indicate in Chapter 6 of this volume, the quantitative analysis of *congruence* in African states represents the first stage of a broader analysis of the types of phenomena that impair or promote *congruence* in countries around the world. Moreover, the composite nature of the dependent variable enables qualitative researchers to focus more specifically on which components of the process of rule of law in a state are in peril, as well as how each of the components impacts the other components.

The studies in this volume also raise many questions about societal engagement with the state. The chapter about Guinea by Onivogui, Gibson's chapter about Zimbabwe, and the discussion about Burundi in Chapter 6 indicate that less effective communities of practice may also be a result of societal anomie. Decades of misrule and corruption are themselves institutional legacies that influence policymaking and a society's willingness to opt out of the process altogether. In some cases, like Burundi's, there are other options below the state that meet the needs of a population. What impact do these peace communities and other similar groups have on system at the national level is a fruitful area for further research.

Notes

1 Government of South Africa, "Election Results 2024," at IEC election results home - Electoral Commission of South Africa (elections.org.za).

2 See Thomas Risse, Stephen C. Ropp, and Kathryn Sikkink, eds. The Power of Human Rights: International Norms and Domestic Change (Cambridge, UK: Cambridge Univ. Press, 1999); see also Adriana Estevez, "Human Rights in Contemporary Political Sociology: The Primacy of Social Subjects," *Human Rights Quarterly* 33(4) (November 2011): 1142–1162; and Fernando G. Nuñez-Mietz, "Legalization and the Legitimation of the Use of Force: Revisiting Kosovo," *International Organization* 72(3) (2018): 725–757.

3 Lon Fuller, *Morality of the Law*, Rev. ed. (New Haven, CT: Yale University Press, 1969), 186.

4 This argument is grounded in Political Discourse Theory, which focuses on the various ways in which language is used by politicians to signal their policy preferences and objectives. A large literature includes plenty of studies analyzing discourse, the application of discourse theory to specific examples, and/or both. Due to limitations on space, we list a few of these studies here. See, for example, Paul Chilton, *Analyzing Political Discourse: Theory and Practice* (London: Routledge, 2003); Daniel Ochieng Orwenjo, "Political Grandstanding and the Use of Proverbs in African Political Discourse," *Discourse & Society* 20 (2009): 123–146; and Filardo-Laura Llamas, "Legitimizing through Language: Political Discourse Worlds in Northern Ireland after the 1998 Agreement." *Peace and Conflict Studies* 15 (2008): 77–94.

Index

Pages in **bold** refer to tables.

Kolibri 360 GmbH
Ferdinand-Jühlke-Straße 7
99095 Erfurt, Deutschland
produktsicherheit@kolibri360.de